Praise for *MacArthur's Spies*

"It's a barn-burner of a story, a fight for love and glory, and Eisner's impeccable research and reporting bring it to life. Here's looking at you, Claire."
—*The Washington Post*

"Peter Eisner does a masterful job of telling the colorful, largely unknown story of an intrepid array of Americans in the Philippines, with a fabulous cast of characters that could have come straight from a Graham Greene novel."   —Lynne Olson, author of *Citizens of London* and *Last Hope Island*

"*MacArthur's Spies* reads like *Casablanca* set in the Pacific. With great historical detective work and narrative grace, Peter Eisner opens our eyes to the amazing story of Claire Phillips, a remarkable woman who, through her own cunning and considerable charm with the men in her life, manages to survive—a triumph of the human spirit."
—Thomas Maier, author of *Masters of Sex* and *When Lions Roar*

"Peter Eisner has done it again with this thrilling tale of deception, romance, and physical endurance set against the backdrop of World War II in the Pacific. Memorable characters, exotic locales, realistic dialogue, extraordinarily high stakes—this book has the ingredients of a great spy novel."   —Michael Dobbs, author of *Six Months in 1945* and *One Minute to Midnight*

"A well-researched, entertaining, and informative look at the resistance to the Japanese occupation."   —*Publishers Weekly*

PENGUIN BOOKS

MACARTHUR'S SPIES

Peter Eisner is a foreign correspondent and political editor who has worked at *The Washington Post, Newsday,* and the Associated Press. He is also the former managing director of the Center for Public Integrity. He is the author of five previous books, including *The Pope's Last Crusade, The Italian Letter,* and *The Freedom Line,* which won the Christopher Award. He lives in Bethesda, Maryland.

OTHER BOOKS BY PETER EISNER

Cuba Libre: A 500-Year Quest for Independence
(cowritten with Philip Brenner)

The Pope's Last Crusade

The Italian Letter
(cowritten with Knut Royce)

The Freedom Line

PENGUIN BOOKS
An imprint of Penguin Random House LLC
375 Hudson Street
New York, New York 10014
penguin.com

First published in the United States of America by Viking Penguin,
an imprint of Penguin Random House LLC, 2017
Published in Penguin Books 2018

ISBN 9780143128847 (paperback)

THE LIBRARY OF CONGRESS HAS CATALOGED THE
HARDCOVER EDITION AS FOLLOWS:
Names: Eisner, Peter, author. | Boone, John P.
Title: MacArthur's spies : the soldier, the singer, and the spymaster
who defied the Japanese in World War II / Peter Eisner.
Description: New York : Viking, 2017. | Includes bibliographical references and index. |
Identifiers: LCCN 2016056837 (print) | LCCN 2017013217 (ebook) |
ISBN 9780525429654 (hardcover) | ISBN 9780698407527 (ebook)
Subjects: LCSH: World War, 1939–1945—Secret service—United States. |
World War, 1939–1945—Secret service—Philippines. |
Philippines—History—Japanese occupation, 1942–1945. | Phillips, Claire,
1908–1960. | Parsons, Charles A. | Spies—Philippines—Biography. |
Spies—United States—Biography.
Classification: LCC D810.S7 (ebook) | LCC D810.S7 E396 2017 (print) |
DDC 940.54/8673—dc23
LC record available at https://lccn.loc.gov/2016056837

Printed in the United States of America
1 3 5 7 9 10 8 6 4 2

Set in WarnockPro
Designed by Francesca Belanger

MacArthur's Spies

■ ■ ■

The Soldier, the Singer, and the Spymaster
Who Defied the Japanese
in World War II

■ ■ ■

Peter Eisner

PENGUIN BOOKS

CONTENTS

PREFACE

JUST HOURS after the surprise assault on Pearl Harbor in December 1941, Japanese planes launched a second attack 5,300 miles away, bombing and strafing U.S. military airfields surrounding Manila in the Philippine Islands. The attack was less of a surprise but equally devastating. Though many more Americans died at Pearl Harbor, the consequences of the Japanese attack on the U.S. Commonwealth of the Philippines were at least as far-reaching.

The day of infamy was December 8, 1941, across the International Date Line: A single bombing run at Clark Air Base north of Manila wiped out half of the thirty-five B-17 bombers and seventy-five P-40 fighter planes stationed in the Philippines. Two days later Japanese attacks destroyed the U.S. naval base at Cavite. On successive days Japan swiftly wiped out U.S. defenses in the Philippines and then launched a full ground invasion of the 7,107-island archipelago. The United States had about thirty thousand soldiers and was training four times that many Filipinos to defend the islands, all too late.

Less than a month later, on January 2, 1942, Japanese troops marched into Manila unopposed by the U.S. forces commanded by General Douglas MacArthur, who had withdrawn to the Bataan peninsula and Corregidor Island. Tokyo saw conquest of the Philippines as essential to cutting off Allied supply lines and as a stepping-stone in its plan to control all of Asia. By the time they occupied Manila, the Japanese already had seized the U.S. island of Guam, had conquered British Hong Kong, and were moving toward control of Burma and the Dutch East Indies. Japanese leaders, said General MacArthur, knew that the Philippines was "the Key that unlocks the door to the Pacific."

Manila was a strategic port, a romantic American outpost, and a jewel of a city, dominated and transformed by the United States in the forty-three years since Admiral George Dewey had sailed to victory in Manila Bay during the Spanish-American War. Manila had become a commercial crossroads for the United States in the southwestern Pacific. At the outbreak of war in Europe, it also was a refuge for hundreds of people who otherwise might have perished in Europe under the Reich, including Spaniards who opposed Fascism and Jews from Germany.

Japan's quick conquest of Manila was an ominous sign for the future, but its expectations stalled in the Philippines. U.S. forces, mostly based in and around Manila, retreated to Bataan and fought the Japanese there for five months despite hunger verging on starvation, deadly diseases, and lack of reinforcements. U.S. commanders surrendered at Bataan in April 1942 (and at Corregidor a month later)—the largest surrender in U.S. history. The story of what followed—the Bataan death march—is chronicled as one of the cruelest episodes of the war. The victorious Japanese forced 75,000 already suffering U.S. and Filipino soldiers to march for days in the tropical heat to a POW camp north of Bataan. Hundreds of American soldiers and thousands of Filipinos died of hunger and disease or were hacked to death or shot in cold blood for falling down or begging for food and water.

Much less known is the heroic saga of resistance that ensued: Thousands of American and Filipino soldiers disobeyed orders to lay down arms and fled to the hills of Bataan. These stragglers formed flexible guerrilla battalions in Luzon, the largest and most populous of the Philippine Islands; they evaded capture for three years, harassed the Japanese, and prepared the way for General MacArthur's eventual return. How different it was from our perspective in the twenty-first century, when rebels stymie organized U.S. military forces in foreign wars and terrorists snipe and lay booby-trap bombs against them. In the Philippines the Americans were the rebels, planning raids and sabotage against a Japanese occupying army unable to stop them all.

I had written two other books about World War II when I started this story. One focused on Bob Grimes, a twenty-year-old American pilot shot down over occupied Belgium who was saved by a young people's brigade running an underground escape line through France into Spain. The other book was about Pope Pius XI (not to be confused with the more controversial Pope Pius XII) and an American Jesuit journalist, John La-Farge, whom the pope drafted in his little-told attempt to fight Hitler and Mussolini before the war. The life and times of these lesser-known historical figures told a larger story about war.

I had every reason to turn to the Philippines and the war in the Pacific this time. My father, Bernard Eisner, was a twenty-five-year-old officer on LST 463, part of the U.S. armada that fought throughout the South Pacific and then accompanied MacArthur back to the Philippines in late 1944. Like most members of the Greatest Generation, he hardly spoke about it. More broadly, the details of the Pacific war were less told than the many stories surrounding the fight against Hitler in Europe from the Battle of Britain to D-Day. Less known still was the battle for Manila, one of the bloodiest encounters of World War II. As I explored personal accounts to tell the larger story, a friend suggested that I read *Ghost Soldiers*, Hampton Sides's classic account of the mission in 1945 to rescue survivors of the Bataan death march. One chapter describes the men and women who provided life support to the Bataan survivors, American and Filipino civilians who smuggled medicine, food, clothing, and money to the Cabanatuan POW camp, about seventy miles north of Manila. "The most fascinating of all of Cabanatuan's clandestine enterprises," Sides writes, was "operated by a mysterious woman known to the prisoners only as 'High Pockets.'"

I set out to learn more about the mysterious High Pockets, nom de guerre of an American who came to call herself Claire Phillips. She had opened a popular nightclub in occupied Manila in 1942 so she could spy on Japanese officers, collect intelligence, and then send the information to American guerrillas in Bataan. It of course sounded like Casablanca East. Claire's nightclub was a gathering spot for officers, Japanese businessmen, visiting Nazis, top musicians, renowned actors, and artists. Virtually everything known about High Pockets up to now has come from Claire Phillips's own account in her book, *Manila Espionage*, published in 1947. On closer scrutiny I realized that most of the book was a fictionalized version of her life written by a Hollywood ghostwriter with the aim of making a movie. The story indeed became a film in 1951—*I Was an American Spy*, starring Ann Dvorak. It is a trite and obvious jingoistic romance made on a back lot, a bad imitation of Marlene Dietrich running after Gary Cooper in the film *Morocco*. The Japanese characters are drawn with racial stereotypes, complete with bad dialogue in fractured English; Claire herself is turned into a demure housewife thrust into war, bravely trying to keep her small nuclear family together single-handedly in a fight against evil. Claire as I found her was indeed brave and bold, but demure she was not.

Claire Phillips was famous for a while after the film's release; General MacArthur recommended her for the Presidential Medal of Freedom; she was embraced in Hollywood, danced with actors, was praised by Louella Parsons, was interviewed by Chet Huntley, became popular on the veterans' and women's club circuits, and even had her day on the program *This Is Your Life*. After she died in obscurity in 1960 at the age of fifty-two, biographies and eulogies emerged from time to time; the U.S. embassy in Manila honored her posthumously by naming the embassy conference room after her.

The problem was that Claire had embraced and adopted her own fictionalized story. There was a better story to be told, yet she remained that mysterious woman. Firsthand information was scant. Survivors could not be found. It took me several years after reading *Ghost Soldiers* to find new information that would as closely as possible tell the real story of High Pockets. Intelligence files, guerrilla operational reports, and military histories helped piece things together. Claire's ability to shift and obscure her personal background made the search difficult. She used multiple aliases and name changes. Finally I came upon an index card at the National Archives in College Park, Maryland, that indicated there should be information on a lawsuit Claire filed against the U.S. government after the war. Cross-referencing was difficult, because after the war Claire married a former prisoner of war in the Philippines, Robert Clavier, and she was using that name in the early 1950s. Thus, Claire's claim for restitution from the government for the money she spent feeding the guerrillas and prisoners of war was hidden under the unassuming title *Clavier v. United States*. That took me from the National Archives annex in College Park to the original National Archives building in Washington, DC.

Two sculptures by Robert Ingersoll Aitken—*Future* and *Past*—flank the entrance to the National Archives on Pennsylvania Avenue. Facing the building on the left to the northeast is *Future*, a woman dressed in classical garb, holding an open book on her lap. An inscription on the pedestal beneath her is from Shakespeare's *The Tempest*: WHAT IS PAST IS PROLOGUE.

At the right corner of the building is *Future*'s bearded male counterpart, *Past*, who holds a scroll in his right hand but whose left hand covers a closed book under the inscription: STUDY THE PAST.

Both images were appropriate. As I dove into the history of the role of Americans at war in the Philippines, I would have a unique picture of the little-known guerrilla war under Japanese occupation—the reverse of America's insurgency wars of the late twentieth and early twenty-first centuries. In the Philippines during World War II, the Americans were raiders in the hills, and the newly imposed government—propped up by an occupying army—sought to win hearts and minds but never managed to conquer the spirit of those who fought them. This was a central part of Claire's story.

Archivists could find no match for the court case, explaining that not every index entry that should be in the archives actually can be found. Then Robert Ellis, an archivist who specializes in federal judicial records, decided to do his own search. He asked me to wait in the ornately domed reading room of the revivalist building designed by John Russell Pope in 1931. Civilians are rarely able to go back to the archival shelves; one imagines the endless storage room in the final scene of *Raiders of the Lost Ark*. After a while Ellis returned wheeling an oversized cardboard box. Fortunately, he knew the arcane filing system in ways that a computerized index could not. Within the box were a number of fat court transcripts and a scuffed taupe file folder wrapped with a red ribbon. It appeared that the ribbon had not been undone since it was tied in a bow one day in 1957 when Claire Phillips was awarded $1,349.21 after a five-year proceeding, about $11,000 in 2017 dollars but a fraction of what she claimed she was owed. *Clavier v. US* was closed and its file placed in the National Archives by the U.S. Court of Claims. This federal court, originally established in 1855 to rule on the monetary claims of Native Americans, was abolished in 1982. The *Clavier v. US* folder contained depositions, court filings, and sworn courtroom testimony from Claire and the people she worked with in the underground. In some cases witnesses had never spoken publicly about their wartime experiences. It was a gold mine of information about the anti-Japanese underground and about how Claire and her allies supported both guerrillas in the mountains and prisoners of war who were starving and suffering in camps scattered around Luzon Island.

Another piece of evidence that had been tossed into the court file slipped out of the folder as I examined the container: a small leather date book that Claire had kept to make diary entries during the war and which she had not seen since making her last entry in 1944. The diary depicts in miniature the life and times of a woman who maneuvered her way through Japanese occupation in the Philippines, suffering through deadly disease, indignities, and imprisonment while concealing her efforts to spy on the Japanese. It is scribbled, sometimes crudely coded, not always decipherable, but has every sign of being genuine to the moment it was written. In all, the federal case file included about two thousand pages of transcripts and exhibits never before made public.

This discovery significantly changes the historical record about Claire Phillips and the people who worked with her. The present book, *MacArthur's Spies*, is the result. The exclusive material led to a reexamination and retelling of her story using these previously unpublished contemporaneous accounts. The Claire Phillips story is quite different from what has been told until now. Claire was indeed an American spy and provided comfort to guerrillas in the mountains and prisoners of war around Manila. Her diary and accompanying documents establish her connection to major Philippine leaders. Claire's guardian and protector during the war, Judge Mamerto Acuña Roxas, was the elder brother of Brigadier General Manuel Acuña Roxas, the most admired man in Philippine politics and a future president. The general was a former top aide to General Douglas MacArthur and a key opponent of the Japanese occupation.

My introduction to Claire and the search for her story led me to the larger Manila underground and the guerrilla network that she was involved with. Two players stood out: One was John Boone, a U.S. Army corporal who was separated from his men in Bataan and defied an order to surrender to the Japanese. The other protagonist was Charles "Chick" Parsons, a businessman in Manila and a U.S. Naval Reserve officer before the war. Parsons became MacArthur's greatest espionage asset in the

Philippines. The files I found at the National Archives provided new information about these men and the largely unsung, organized U.S. and Philippine opposition to the Japanese occupation.

Claire also was a victim of confining social mores and the double standard for women in the mid-twentieth century. And yes, she was willing to lie and deceive whenever it served her purposes. That quality made her a natural intelligence operative who knew how to use men when she could and when she needed to before, during, and after the war; undoubtedly she was able to carry some of her deepest secrets with her unresolved and untold for all time.

What emerges is the story of a valiant though not angelic American woman who brought unique skills in deception to the war, skills well suited to an underground fighter that helped her serve the war effort and survive. Her story also revives a little-known chapter of time when American guerrillas were the marauders in the hills. Moreover, in the course of researching the story of High Pockets, I learned about the role of the tens of thousands of Filipinos who fought and died alongside their American allies. More than 500,000 Filipinos died in World War II, most of them civilians; 100,000 of those deaths occurred during the one-month Battle of Manila, February 3 to March 3, 1945. I dedicate this book to them all.

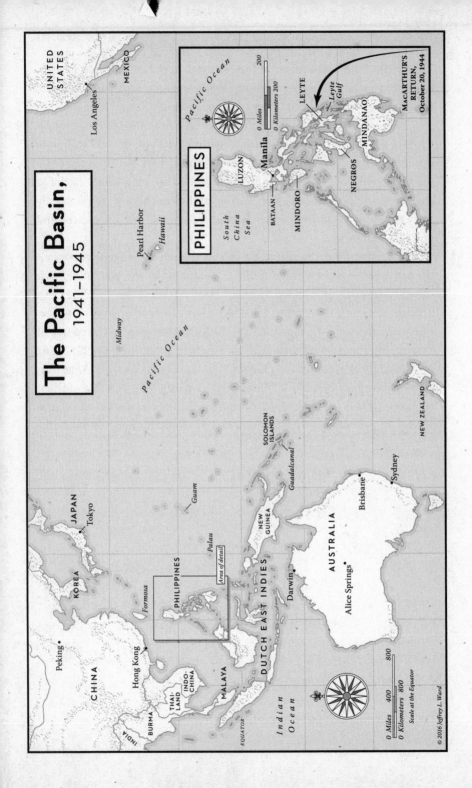

The Pacific Basin, 1941–1945

Pacific Ocean

UNITED STATES

MEXICO

Los Angeles

Pearl Harbor
Hawaii

Midway

Pacific Ocean

JAPAN
Tokyo

KOREA

Guam

CHINA

Peking

Hong Kong

Formosa

PHILIPPINES

Palau

Area of detail

NEW GUINEA

SOLOMON ISLANDS

Guadalcanal

INDIA

BURMA

THAI-LAND

INDO-CHINA

MALAYA

DUTCH EAST INDIES

EQUATOR

Indian Ocean

Darwin

AUSTRALIA

Alice Springs

Brisbane

Sydney

NEW ZEALAND

0 Miles   400   800
0 Kilometers   400   800
Scale at the Equator

© 2016 Jeffrey L. Ward

PHILIPPINES

Pacific Ocean

South China Sea

LUZON

Manila

BATAAN

MINDORO

MANILA

NEGROS

LEYTE

Leyte Gulf

MINDANAO

MacARTHUR'S RETURN,
October 20, 1944

0 Miles   200
0 Kilometers   200

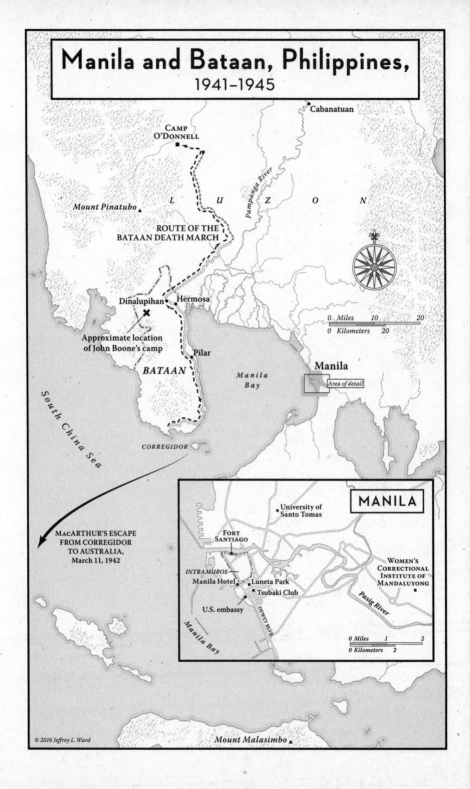

Manila and Bataan, Philippines,
1941–1945

Cabanatuan

CAMP
O'DONNELL

L U Z O N

Pampanga River

Mount Pinatubo

ROUTE OF THE
BATAAN DEATH MARCH

0 Miles   10   20
0 Kilometers   20

Dinalupihan   Hermosa

Approximate location
of John Boone's camp

Pilar

BATAAN

Manila
Bay

Manila

Area of detail

CORREGIDOR

South China Sea

MacARTHUR'S ESCAPE
FROM CORREGIDOR
TO AUSTRALIA,
March 11, 1942

MANILA

University of
Santo Tomas

FORT
SANTIAGO

INTRAMUROS
Manila Hotel   Luneta Park
Tsubaki Club

U.S. embassy

Manila Bay

DEWEY BLVD

WOMEN'S
CORRECTIONAL
INSTITUTE OF
MANDALUYONG

Pasig River

0 Miles   1   2
0 Kilometers   2

© 2016 Jeffrey L. Ward

Mount Malasimbo

PART ONE

. . .

The War

World on Fire

THE WOMAN THEY CALLED Madame Tsubaki sashayed onto the night-club floor after dark in a spotlight that cast her exotic silhouette against creamy drapes. She began to sing a tune from America, a song of love and longing:

I don't want to set the world on fire
I just want to start a flame in your heart

She searched the eyes of the men around her—officers of the Japanese occupation, businessmen, and the Filipinos who did their bidding. Many spoke enough English to understand, though her gaze and the husky sound of her voice served well enough.

I don't ever care to rise to power
I would rather be with you an hour

She could look around with satisfaction as she sang. Tsubaki Club was packed; they had turned people away. Everyone wanted to see the floor show at the Tsubaki—the name meant "camellia," a rare, delicate flower in Japan. The club was at a busy intersection across from the Luneta, a romantic downtown park where palms and acacia leaves rustled, not far from Manila Bay. Outside on San Juan Avenue nighttime and the gentle wind softened the tropical heat that had stifled the city during the day; streetlights cast shadows at the entrance of the two-story wooden house set back from the street.

At the start of the evening, Madame Tsubaki had welcomed each of the guests at the head of the long, winding staircase. As they climbed to the second floor, the slit in her long, elegant gown made an alluring line from her ankle to the lower part of one thigh, intoxicating as the experience of entering the club was intended to be.

For the things that one can buy
Are not worth a lover's sigh

She led them to one of the cocktail tables around the room or to rattan chairs on the periphery, where they could lounge and drink and relax and watch the show. When it was her turn to sing, they all were close enough to breathe her scent and admire the curves of her clinging dress. So she looked into their eyes and they all tended to fall in love.

In my heart I have but one desire
And that one is you, no other will do

Beautiful Filipina hostesses circulated in the room; each approached a table, bowing respectfully, as one must, and then waited to be asked to sit down. So sweetly they accepted offers of a drink. Yes, they could join them; the men smiled and the young women sat with them as if they were geishas ready to serve. A waiter would glide from table to table—beer, wine, whiskey, rum, gin, or some snacks. The men ordered, and the waiters bowed and returned. All for a fantasy, because whatever the women asked for, they drank only lemonade. The men received real drinks and paid a premium along with tips for their favorite hostesses; the women laughed and everyone smoked, a haze floating among them. All the while the band played with a Hawaiian lilt that sounded perfect in the Manila night.

Why not dream about an alluring singer and her song? It was a night for celebration—January 2, 1943, marked the first anniversary of the Japanese occupation and the ouster of the Americans. The puppet Philippine leader, Jorge B. Vargas, was exultant as he declared one year of "benevolent" rule by the Japanese: "The day is one of thanksgiving, especially for the residents of the City of Manila, because on that day they were enabled to resume a life of peace."

Why not be festive? The war was going well enough. The Japanese officers had a chance to relax and dream far from the front. Some led the original occupation force, and some were bureaucrats fortunate to have safe administrative jobs beyond the line of fire. Others had rotated in for a while.

None of them knew how long it would last, but for now they could brag of their victories this past year. If the Japanese soldiers blocked out the embarrassments—Doolittle's raid on Tokyo and the Battle of Midway— they could focus on the fact that Japan controlled a swath of Pacific terri- tory from Manchuria to Indochina and south to New Guinea. Early still in the war, a Japanese officer could take pleasure in such an evening in Manila, having ushered in a new Asian Empire of the Rising Sun: "Asia for the Asians." Madame Tsubaki smiled and shimmied just a bit as she sang:

> I've lost all ambition for worldly acclaim
> And with your admission that you'd feel the same
> I'll have reached the goal I'm dreaming of . . . believe me

While she sang, Madame Tsubaki could look around the room: A full house meant good money on the night—more than enough to pay the bills, perhaps enough alcohol to loosen the tongues of the homesick, love- sick men. Madame Tsubaki had trained the alluring young women to be ready to ask questions.

Darling, the dew-eyed women would ask their Japanese guests. Why must you leave so soon? Where are they sending you? Can I write to you? When will you come back to me?

Soon. I will come back soon, the officers would say, innocent as it was, speaking to a beautiful girl, even if they never came back: off to New Guinea, or to bomb the Americans from a carrier, or to a submarine pa- trol. And they would say, As soon as I fight the Americans and shoot down their planes and sink them in the sea, then I will come back.

Banzai! the men would shout, raising their glasses. Banzai! And Ma- dame Tsubaki and the young women would shout, Banzai! Banzai! with them and salute the defeat of the Americans. And Madame Tsubaki would keep singing, beseeching:

> . . . Believe me
> I don't want to set the world on fire
> I just want to start a flame in your heart

Midnight curfew approached and some of the men would want to take the lovely young girls with them and would offer them money. A few of the young women went along; it was good business and good money. A hostess could make tips, but if she went off with a customer, she could earn many times her salary at the club. Some of the women would just escort the young Japanese officers to a side couch for a bit of privacy. They could make extra tips that way and ask more questions. *How long will you be away? Where can I write to you?*

At the end of the evening, Madame Tsubaki said good night to the last of the guests. Women could be seen leaving arm in arm with their soldiers of the night. The Luneta and the Great Eastern Hotel were just a short walk away.

Madame Tsubaki retired to her dressing room, took off her gown, and wiped off her makeup. Some nights she had to fight men away from her own door. Most nights, though, she was quickly out the back door and down the steps in time to beat curfew, hoping to avoid a possible soldier with an attitude who might slap her for breaking the rules. She and everyone else under occupation knew that Japanese "benevolence" tended more to random stops on the street, a slap in the face for not bowing or not bowing deeply enough or making an unintelligible remark under one's breath. People preferred to avoid such encounters, but it could happen. Once in the street, Madame Tsubaki became Dorothy Fuentes—one of her many aliases. But if by chance she was stopped on the five-minute walk home, she could mention the name of an officer or bow and smile or hope that someone else on the street—some Japanese officer—might know that this was the gracious Filipina hostess who had entertained his fellow troops at Tsubaki Club.

It was three blocks home; only there could she relax quietly, hoping not to wake up her two-and-a-half-year-old adopted Filipina daughter, Dian. She might smoke a cigarette, have a real drink, and hope to fall asleep. The next morning she would go to the club after breakfast and gather reports from all the women. They collated the names of the men and their units and, if they were lucky, the destinations of their ships, their ports of call, and the times their ships were leaving port. A runner from the hills or one of the waiters could then hide the report in the fake sole of a shoe or in the lining of a shopping basket, then bring the latest intelligence to their American guerrilla contacts in the hills. Before long, Madame Tsubaki would prepare for the next performance that evening, hoping to set part of the world on fire.

Life Before the War
Manila, September 20, 1941

WHY HAD SHE come back to Manila? Claire never had a good answer. Her best friend, Louise DeMartini, awaited her at Pier 7 at the Port of Manila when the Swedish ship SS *Annie Johnson* edged into the harbor. The vessel nestled slowly into port guided by U.S. Navy vessels, weaving through the minefields that had been laid that summer. The tense passage was emblematic of the battle to come.

Claire came down the gangway carrying Dian, her eighteen-month-old foster baby. Louise, twenty-nine, an American from the West Coast who also lived in Manila, was shocked and said she didn't understand. Americans were leaving the Philippines if they could. The newspapers said that war with Japan would break out soon. What was Claire doing going in the opposite direction?

"That's newspaper talk," Claire said. "The Japanese threaten and bluff, but I don't think that they will ever fight us. They are not that crazy."

Claire gave only vague answers. "Call it restlessness, fate, wanderlust, or the whirligig of chance," she wrote much later. It might have been that it was easier for her to find work in Manila than back in the States, where her singing career had never taken off. Maybe she was running away from something, or running toward something. She never explained. Claire had many secrets and life had never been easy.

Claire sometimes would tell people that she had run off to the circus when she was around sixteen years old and worked with a snake charmer; others heard the story that she had signed on with the Baker Stock Company, a traveling vaudeville show organized by notorious showman and longtime mayor of Portland George L. Baker. She also said she toured the Northwest and learned to sing and dance, and she certainly switched and experimented with first and last names all the time. Whatever the real story, she was mostly a bit player and a chorus girl in the Baker shows that barnstormed the Northwest in the 1920s and 1930s.

She had been born Clara Mabel De La Taste on December 2, 1907, in Harvard City, Michigan, the second of three daughters of George and Mabel De La Taste. Early on, the family moved to Racine, Wisconsin, where her father was a barber. He was injured in a freak train accident while riding a passenger train north of Chicago in December 1909, just after Clara's second birthday. A loose rail tore through the floors of several train cars; two people were killed, and George and three others were injured. George and Mabel separated when Claire was about five years old, which would have been 1912. Mabel De La Taste moved Clara and her sisters, Eva and Georgina, to Boise, Idaho, after that and then in 1914 to Portland, Oregon, where she married Jesse Snyder, a marine engineer who worked in the Portland shipyards. Clara took the name of her new father and attended Portland city schools. Everything seemed straightforward up to that point. Clara Snyder was listed in the *Portland Oregonian* as being freshman president of the Girls' League at Franklin High School for the fall term of 1922. That would have carried a degree of commitment and school spirit and indicated that she was popular and had friends at the school. Yet the young girl quit high school and left home around the time of her sixteenth birthday.

Sometimes she was Clara Snyder, using the last name of her stepfather. Sometimes she used the family name of her birth father, De La Taste, often switching among the names Clara Maybelle (instead of Mabel), Maybelle Clara, and Claire De La Taste—sometimes writing her family name as three separate words, others times as Delataste. Claire said she never liked the name Clara—at some point she altered it to make it sound more Anglo.

Throughout her life Claire changed her name so many times that even the FBI and the courts couldn't keep up with her. She appeared to be concealing something. One constant: Claire always attracted many men, hauled them in for a while, and then cast them off. She was married at least three times in seven years, mostly to men much older.

She was still sixteen years old when she married Harmond W. Collier on September 5, 1924, in Vancouver, Washington, just across the Columbia River from Portland. His age is not known, but Collier legally could not have been younger than Claire was, and he was probably older. Claire was less than a year out of high school. She signed her name that day on the marriage certificate as Maybelle C. De La Taste.

Claire was still a teenager three years later when she married once again, this time in Salt Lake City, perhaps one of her stops on the vaudeville and carnival circuit. Her new husband was Edwin George Flinn. He was thirty years old and a World War I army veteran; she was nineteen. Their marriage certificate, issued on August 31, 1927, in Salt Lake City, Utah, gave her name as Clara Delataste and her marital status as divorced.

That second marriage could not have lasted long; Claire's third known husband was Joseph V. Enette, a thirty-seven-year-old African American tailor from Louisiana approaching twice her age. They were married in Seattle on December 12, 1929, just after Claire's twenty-second birthday; this time she signed as Clara M. De La Taste. That marriage lasted longer than the first two; she stayed with Joe Enette for a time. Joe and Clara Enette were living at 1017 Weller Street in Seattle, Washington, at the time of the 1930 census. The census form had a column for race, and that column listed both of them as "neg."—that is, Negro. Claire was not African American, but Washington was one of a number of states with miscegenation laws that made it illegal for people of different races to marry. Joe and Clara Enette would have been subject to arrest with a possible prison term and fine if Clara had declared herself as white. While census takers were not officers of the law, an official who reviewed the census-canvassing sheet could have taken action. In any case, Clara might not have had to present herself at the door when the census taker stopped by. Clara and Joe were listed in a 1933 mail directory as living in Everett, Washington. Biographical details during the mid-1930s are scant after that.

However, Claire appeared on the Seattle police blotter in May 1933, having been picked up for vagrancy and identified at the time as Dorothy Smith. She might still have been married to Joe Enette afterward, because when she left the States for Asia she was carrying a life insurance policy as Mabel C. Enette. County records in Washington, Utah, and Oregon show no record of Claire having legally divorced any of these men. A cynic might ask whether they survived their marriages to Claire. In the case of George Flinn and Joe Enette, both men lived long lives and remarried. After his marriage to Claire in 1924, no records about Harmond Collier can be found.

Maybelle Enette, née De La Taste, aka Snyder, Collier, and Flinn, alias Dorothy Smith, left the U.S. mainland for the first time en route to Hawaii at some point in the late 1930s. Documents show that she spent time in Honolulu, and she later said she had gotten work as a performer there. She also said she had traveled around the Pacific Rim, visiting Japan and Hong

Kong before arriving in the Philippines. There is no record of that. She was a passenger—listed as Maybelle Enette—in tourist class on the SS *President Pierce* of the U.S. government–run American President Line, which departed Honolulu on April 26, 1939, calling at Yokohama on May 6 and Hong Kong on May 11 before arriving on May 13, 1939, at Manila, where she disembarked. Some previous published accounts of Claire's travels have said that she arrived a year earlier on the same ship, and Claire herself said once publicly that she had come to Manila as early as 1937. But she also said she was not good at recalling details.

Once in the Philippines, she married for the fourth time, to Manuel L. Fuentes on August 15, 1939. Fuentes, forty-one, was a steward on the SS *Corregidor*, a Philippine interisland passenger ship, and a member of a prominent extended family. One cousin, Mercedes Fuentes, had married Mamerto Roxas, a well-known jurist in Manila and the older brother of General Manuel Roxas, the Philippine government liaison in the late 1930s to General Douglas MacArthur. Claire became friendly with the Roxas family, including Mamerto Roxas.

Claire and Manuel Fuentes owned a house on a pleasant street in the Mandaluyong neighborhood. They had servants, cooks, and helpers; middle-class life was good and not expensive in Manila, an elegant tropical city of 600,000. Claire and Manuel soon adopted a young girl, who had been born in early 1940. Claire told some people the baby, called Dian, was her own natural child or let them assume so, although it was not true. Many years later Claire admitted, finally, that she was unable to bear children. Other times she said Dian was a product of a relationship between Manuel Fuentes and one of their servants, who had died in childbirth. In any case, Claire was devoted to the child but said later that the marriage with Fuentes did not go well. Fuentes was frequently off at sea and Claire claimed he drank too much. She took Dian with her on a trip to the United States in February 1941. Claire said she had gone to Portland to visit her mother and stepfather. It was more likely that she was running away from her marriage. She had taken to referring to Manuel Fuentes as "Mr. Wrong."

Fuentes did not see it that way. He sailed to the United States in the fall of 1941 to chase down his wife. Either through miscommunication or because Claire was trying to avoid her husband, she and Manuel Fuentes crossed paths heading in opposite directions across the Pacific. By the time he arrived in San Francisco on October 2, 1941, Claire was already back in Manila.

War fever had been high for months in Manila; Japan had occupied a swath of territory in Manchuria and Mongolia during the 1930s and coastal portions of China more recently. The latest crisis developed after the Imperial Army took full control of French Indochina on July 24, 1941. President Franklin Delano Roosevelt responded by seizing Japanese assets in the United States; Britain and Holland followed suit at home and in their colonies, cutting off Japan from fuel, raw materials, and other crucial imports. Tokyo and Washington had now begun negotiating a settlement to avert war. The U.S. government had been recalling dependents and nonessential personnel from the Philippines all year. Reaction to the Japanese threat ranged from denial to paralysis, but the easygoing way of life in the tropical capital gave way to anxious conversations about what would happen if the diplomatic talks failed. The United States had sent hundreds of new recruits from the States to bolster the Philippines division of the U.S. Army, about 30,000 Americans and 120,000 Filipinos now under MacArthur's command. The general, who had been field marshal of the Philippines Commonwealth Army, was recalled by President Roosevelt to lead the newly created U.S. Army Forces in the Far East (USAFFE). Throughout the summer and fall, U.S. officers raced raw Filipino recruits through an intense course of basic training in parks and open fields; military preparations were hampered by years of lack of interest in Washington. Military planners had long concluded that the Philippines was too far away to establish a meaningful defense force. Recruits used ancient bolt-action rifles, or even wooden replicas, with promises of an eventual upgrade.

When they returned to Manila, Claire and Dian moved in for a while with Louise; Claire started looking for work instead of going back to the house she and Manuel Fuentes owned. Louise teased Claire for coming back but never explained why she herself had not gone back to the States. "We're birds of a feather," she told Claire. "Plenty of people keep telling me I should go home, but here I am."

It did not take Claire long to find a job working in a club, and she soon had enough money to rent an apartment. Manila was home to thousands of young American servicemen who plied the nightspots, drank, and fell for the easygoing ways of the women they saw. The city was a tropical paradise, a dream—beautiful, willing, exotic women in every direction, nightclubs of every description to fill every desire. What better place for an alluring chanteuse, especially when so many other women, her competitors, had taken ship and returned home? Claire started singing at private parties at the posh Manila Hotel, where General Douglas MacArthur lived and maintained his offices, though there is no mention of them ever having met. Claire found a steadier job at a popular local nightclub, the Alcazar, singing American standards most every night. One of those nights she was at the club when Manila held an air-raid drill. She kept singing all through the blackout.

Young enlisted men frequented the Alcazar; it was considered a less refined nightspot than the places that officers usually frequented, especially if they were married. On October 15, less than a month after her return to Manila from Oregon, Claire was singing one of her "nostalgic torch songs under a soft cascade of shifting pastel lights" when a good-looking, strapping young man emerged from the crowd, smitten by the sight of her. He was John Vincent Phillips, a twenty-three-year-old U.S. Army private just in from California and a member of the 31st Infantry or, as it was known by reputation, the "Thirsty First."

When her song was done, Phillips introduced himself and asked Claire to dance.

"The quiet type, I thought, watching his slow, graceful manner of dancing. I had never seen a more handsome man."

A relationship had kindled. During the day, Phillips and other soldiers were at their posts, training, gathering supplies, and patching together vintage equipment for a battle they were not ready for. At night Claire and Phil, as she called Phillips, took long strolls in the moonlight along Dewey Boulevard, a romantic promenade that hugged Manila Bay with the Pacific Ocean beyond, thousands of miles from home. Palm trees shimmered before the mansions of expatriates that lined the boulevard.

By November Claire and John Phillips were spending all their free time together. Within weeks, Claire later said, John Phillips proposed marriage, but she held him off. She said she was worried that she was much older—almost thirty-four—and he was more than ten years younger. She said that they should wait until they could make it back together to the States. Phillips wrote home to his mother, Vada May Phillips, in Wasco, California, in the San Joaquin valley, and told her about his beautiful new girlfriend. He did not tell his mother that he was getting married. Claire had avoided mentioning to Phillips that she was already married to Manuel Fuentes, not necessarily a problem in any case. Who knew when Fuentes would make it back to Manila?

It was easier to feel the ocean breeze and look at the glow of the mansions and the trees than to consider what was happening. One air-raid drill followed another, and newspapers began issuing civil-defense information in case of attack. All the while, people played along with civil defense but pushed away dark thoughts. What could really happen? How bad could it be? The Japanese would never go to war. And even if they did, they would never try to attack the Philippines.

Infamy Across the Pacific
Manila, December 8, 1941

WHEN THE NEWS BULLETIN came through after 3:00 a.m. Manila time on Monday, December 8, 1941, some people were still awake in Manila, partying from the night before. The attack took place across the International Date Line at 7:53 a.m. on December 7 in Hawaii, and at 1:23 p.m. on the East Coast of the United States.

"AIR RAID PEARL HARBOR—THIS IS NO DRILL."

Navy radiomen on station in Manila reported the Pearl Harbor attack to their commanding officers. At 5:00 a.m. Brigadier General Lewis H. Brereton of the U.S. Army Air Forces marched over to army headquarters to seek permission from General Douglas MacArthur, the commander of

U.S. forces, to bomb the Japanese-held island of Formosa (now Taiwan), just two hundred miles from the northernmost part of the Philippines. For reasons never explained, Brereton did not communicate directly with MacArthur, who was sequestered in his penthouse suite at the elegant Manila Hotel on Manila Bay. Some of those present said that MacArthur was paralyzed into inaction for several crucial hours; others said his aides blocked subordinates from even receiving the urgent plea. Others still said the lapse amounted to dereliction of duty and that, as with Admiral Husband Edward Kimmel at Pearl Harbor, MacArthur should have been sacked. For his part, MacArthur said in his memoirs that no one had suggested such a retaliatory attack, which he considered in any case would have been suicidal.

By 8:30 a.m., Japanese bombers had hit their first targets in the Philippines, in Davao on the southernmost major island, Mindanao. Planes then bombed and strafed airfields at Baguio in western Luzon (at the size of Virginia, the largest island in the Philippine archipelago, with Manila on its southwest coast) and at Aparri on its northern coast. MacArthur issued no orders until 10:15 a.m., when he authorized a series of reconnaissance flights over Formosa, obscured by morning fog. At 11:30 a.m., the planes, B-17 Flying Fortress bombers and P-40 Warhawk fighters, received orders to return to Clark Field, forty miles northwest of Manila. As they were refueling, high-flying Japanese bombers attacked Clark Field without American resistance, accompanied by dive-bombing Japanese Zeros that strafed the field at low altitude. Within minutes, almost half of all the U.S. bombers and fighter planes in the Philippines had been destroyed or disabled. The Japanese Imperial Army Air Force launched additional bruising assaults around Manila Bay for the next two days and devastated Philippine bases, including the U.S. naval facility at Cavite. With most airplanes gone and little prospect of reinforcements from the U.S. Navy, the Philippines was now wide open to invasion.

Monday morning, December 8, was misty and comparatively cool in Manila, but with the prospect of a typically hot day. The news spread quickly by radio. By 8:00 a.m. everyone on the street knew as they lined up for taxis and horse-drawn carts or walked to work. Claire's housekeeper and nanny, Lolita, woke her with the news.

"*Señora*, excuse me, please, but there is a war. What should I do?" When Claire paid no attention and rolled over to keep sleeping, Lolita repeated the words with more urgency.

"I speak the truth! There is a war!"

War came to the city in a slow, torturous haze. The residents of Manila picked up the news from news hawkers in the early morning and then huddled around radio sets to learn scant details about Pearl Harbor. Collectively they began the day only as they could—lining up for buses and streetcars, cabs and horse carts to work, dropping off children before going to the office or starting their chores for the day. It was the picture of order in the tropical business center. Men sauntered along the shaded galleries in their snazzy white suits and Panama hats; women in cream colors, pineapple-thread woven blouses, and stylish shoes went to work too. Slowly, though, the city changed in a day; easy steps were transformed into a maelstrom of activity. People went to the telephone to call friends and loved ones but could not get through; lines formed where they never had been before—at banks, pharmacies, and food stores; people saw the lines and joined them, seeking what everyone else appeared to seek: security with supplies, safety for their savings, a chance, too late, to prepare for what had now come. There were Manilans of the middle and upper classes with ties to America who sought money transfers to the States, but most of the lines were blocked. Many Filipinos with no such ties could only go about their business, drive their water buffalo carts to and from the port, do what they were told, or do nothing but watch the increasingly frantic scene.

Soon air-raid sirens sounded and rumors circulated for good reason: The attack on Pearl Harbor meant war. Manila was in the line of fire, yet some people did not comprehend. One Manila resident went out to buy some barrels of gasoline to supply his family while he still could. "What are you afraid of?" asked the British manager of a petroleum company, claiming there was no need to stock up on supplies.

"We are under blockade."

"Nonsense," the Briton replied. "There is nothing to worry about."

Life for the complacent people of Manila, an American city in denial, was about to change.

Repeated sirens broke the rhythm of the day. Though there were no bombs in Manila that day, the once calm, easy streets were chaotic. Amid the frenetic activity the blazing tropical heat of the day descended upon the city—tempers were short, and cars, people, and horse carriages careered about. People made runs on the banks throughout the day, standing in line and shielding themselves from the sun. Prices were much higher than the day before, shops imposed limits on each purchase, and they quickly were running out of food and medicine. Lolita managed to find a taxi for Claire, who raced about the city haphazardly in search of supplies. "When we reached the bank, it resembled a madhouse. After standing in line patiently for forty-five minutes, I abandoned the idea of being polite, and pushed my way through like everyone else." That night air-raid sirens sounded and Claire lay awake in the dark. She counted six separate warnings, but still no bombs fell on the city, at least. She was nervous and smoked continually. Sleep was out of the question.

Late that first day of war, John Phillips rushed over to Claire's apartment on a break from his job as a radio operator. He said that his 31st Infantry Regiment was moving inland from Manila to Fort William McKinley, a U.S. base on a plateau overlooking the city. There also were rumors they soon would be retreating to Bataan, and he wanted Claire to move along with them. Phillips gave Claire the keys to his blue coupé and said he would get back to her when he could.

For Claire, Bataan was the great unknown. The peninsula was a fifty-mile-long thumb-shaped appendage of coastal beaches, farms, and lush central mountains visible from the city in the western distance across Manila Bay. She could not know how long they would be in Bataan or what life would be like there.

After daybreak on Tuesday, December 9, Claire called her friend Louise DeMartini for advice. Tens of thousands of civilians were leaving Manila, but many people wanted to stay, convincing themselves that the war would be brief and the American Army would prevail. Louise said she was also nervous but was on the side of those who had decided to stay. "Oh, I don't think that there will be any need to go far from Manila," Louise said. "I heard on the radio that reinforcements are already on the way here."

On Wednesday, December 10, two days after the war began, Claire frantically went searching for Phillips when she heard that Fort McKinley had been bombed overnight. Sentinels outside the fort, five or six miles inland from downtown Manila, said that Phillips's Headquarters Company had already left for Bataan. As she pulled up to her apartment back in the city, Phillips was there waiting. He said he had gone AWOL to take Claire and Dian to Bataan with him and would rejoin his unit when they arrived. They filled the car with gas, packed some clothes, and took Dian and Lolita out to Phillips's car.

The road to Bataan hooked around Manila harbor and extended along the coast to the west of Luzon. Under normal conditions it was a couple of hours or a pleasant boat ride west across the bay. But the road was crowded and pocked with bomb craters, an eight-mile traffic jam at five to ten miles an hour snaking around the northern rim of Manila Bay. They shared the road with other members of the 31st Infantry, which had begun its company-by-company withdrawal from the city. The army had commandeered private cars, pickups, buses, and any other vehicle it could find. Nightfall came and they drove on, headlights darkened under the enforced blackout. Driving was frightening and dangerous.

At 1:00 a.m. they arrived at their destination, Pilar, a small barrio within a few miles of the new 31st Infantry camp. They found two decent rooms on the second floor of an inn just off the town square for two pesos (one dollar) per night. Phillips set off for his camp. Claire made sure Dian was comfortable and then lay down, exhausted. She slept for a few hours, the most since the Japanese attack three days earlier.

When Claire went for a walk the next morning, admirers trailed behind her. The locals were fascinated by the sight of a white woman in their little village in the hills. Adults and children followed her, gawked, and smiled. Others gathered around the water pump in the town square outside the rooming house, watching and waiting. When she didn't come outside, men climbed trees to catch a glimpse of her through the window. The village routine on those early days was punctuated by the sound of thunder when the sun went down, but it wasn't thunder: "Bombing far away . . . nearly every night."

The little store on the ground floor below their room sold warm Coca-Cola and gin, nothing more. They needed food. Claire caught a *carretela*—horse-and-buggy taxi—up the road to the closest market. What provisions she could find were expensive. Pilar and vicinity appeared to be safe despite the reverberation of bombs in the distance. Claire began compiling a diary during those days by scribbling notes with a nub of a pencil in a pocket date book, the kind given out by banks and insurance companies to their customers. The leather-bound 1941 date book, published by the Insular Life Assurance Company Limited, was embossed with an inscription in silver type: LIFE INSURANCE IS A PROOF OF DEVOTION. She complained to herself that she had brought along only three changes of clothing; after a while it made no difference. This was hardly a place for singing and dancing. She had no need for elegance in the hills. Before long, her dresses were threadbare; makeup and fashionable shoes were a distant memory of the city. Claire waited for Phillips, who had said he would visit as often as he could.

Invasion
Bataan Peninsula, December 12, 1941

GENERAL MACARTHUR KNEW the military situation was hopeless. Without reinforcements from the U.S. mainland, the Philippines was lost. Four days after the first attack, 2,500 Japanese troops landed at Legazpi on the southeastern tip of Luzon Island, about three hundred miles from Manila, the first wave of the assault on the Philippine archipelago. MacArthur rallied his forces as best he could, having long known that the Philippines was not adequately equipped for war. Japan's invasion force was as large as the American contingent, but better trained and with better access to reinforcements. MacArthur's commanders had been rushing to train up to 100,000 members of the Philippines citizens' army, but they had run out of time and could muster "little artillery, few tanks and only old Enfield rifles that had been discarded early in the First World War."

"Our air force in the Philippines contained many antiquated models," MacArthur recalled later, "and were hardly more than a token force with insufficient equipment, unfinished air fields and inadequate maintenance. The force was in process of integration, radar defenses were not yet operative, and the personnel was raw and inexperienced. They were hopelessly outnumbered and never had a chance of winning." For months MacArthur had been lobbying for an upgrade to antiquated Philippine air defenses, but Washington had not responded adequately.

Lieutenant General Masaharu Homma, the erudite English-speaking commander whose nickname was "the Poet," had been tasked with leading the Japanese invasion of the Philippines on a tight schedule. Securing Manila and the Philippines would give the Japanese forces a supply and transfer base for managing their Pacific conquests and would allow them to withdraw and leave behind a smaller occupation force. The Japanese High Command in Tokyo expected victory to be secured within fifty days. To meet the deadline, Homma intended to keep up pressure and overwhelm the U.S.-Philippine contingent. A main invasion force with eighty transports began landings at Lingayen Gulf, about 150 miles north of Manila, on December 21. General Homma came ashore himself on December 24, boasting that Japan was willing to lose ten million men to secure victory. "How many were the Americans prepared to lose?"

That same day, sixteen days after the Japanese attack, MacArthur initiated the long-standing U.S. defensive strategy against Japan known as War Plan Orange. He declared Manila an open city, meaning that he would withdraw military forces to avoid fighting in the capital. The intent was "to spare the metropolitan area from ravages of attack either by air or ground." Following the next step in War Plan Orange, he ordered the strategic retreat of U.S. troops and Philippine forces to the Bataan peninsula and to Corregidor Island, the impenetrable fortress that controlled access to Manila Bay. By then, troops had already moved several months' worth of supplies and ammunition to the hammer-shaped island citadel and to the town of Mariveles on the Bataan coast across the bay from Manila. The plan foresaw up to six months of defensive action on Bataan, during which time the United States was expected to mount a rescue operation, bringing in reinforcements and supplies to break the deadlock.

MacArthur, his wife, Jean, and their three-year-old son, Arthur, withdrew to Corregidor, where an estimated fourteen thousand soldiers set up operations and prepared shelter from attacks in the eight-hundred-foot-long tunnel built into the rock of Malinta Hill by the Army Corps of Engineers. The twenty-four-foot-wide tunnel had living space, work areas, a hospital, and headquarters offices for MacArthur, his family, and thousands of personnel.

The general spoke and acted in the heroic terms expected of him. He defied danger by establishing his headquarters boldly at the highest point on Corregidor, a symbol that although the United States was under attack, its command stood proud and defiant. He was the greatest of cheerleaders when he crossed the bay from Corregidor to Bataan on January 10, 1942, to spend a day walking among the troops. He later issued a letter to all commanders stating that while "the exact time of the arrival of reinforcements is unknown . . . help is on the way from the United States."

American troops on the ground banked on such persistent promises: Relief was on the way. There was never a chance. Washington had no intention of sending reinforcements to break through the Japanese blockade of the besieged U.S. forces. With the devastating attack on Pearl Harbor, all attention in the Pacific focused on how to regroup and protect Hawaii and the West Coast of the United States. The United States took no steps even to protect Guam or Wake Island, two U.S. outposts between Hawaii and the Philippines that could have served as relay points for rescue of the Philippines. Instead, both territories fell quickly to the Japanese. Officials in Washington kept to their strategy of dealing with "Europe first." Any reinforcements and the majority of engagement turned eastward toward Europe and combating Hitler's blitzkrieg. Manila was 7,400 miles from the U.S. mainland. It was just as distant from Washington's immediate plans for war.

MacArthur found out long afterward that a "top-level decision had long before been reached that the Atlantic war came first, no matter what the cost in the Far East. . . . Unhappily, I was not informed . . . and believed that a brave effort at relief was in the making."

The brave face was hard to maintain for long. After his January 10 visit to his troops, MacArthur received a threatening missive from General Homma: "You are well aware that you are doomed. The end is near. The question is how long you will be able to resist. You have already cut rations by half. I appreciate the fighting spirit of yourself and your troops who have been fighting with courage. However, in order to avoid needless bloodshed and to save the remnants of your divisions and your auxiliary troops, you are advised to surrender."

MacArthur did not respond. Japanese planes next dropped leaflets over Bataan, repeating some of the same language used by Homma:

The outcome of the present combat has been already decided and you are cornered to the doom. But, however, being unable to realize the present situation, blinded General MacArthur has stupidly refused our proposal and continues futile struggle at the cost of your precious lives.

Dear Filipino Soldiers!

There are [sic] still one way left for you. That is to give up all your weapons at once and surrender to the Japanese force before it is too late, then we shall fully protect you.

We repeat for the last!

Surrender at once and build your new Philippines for and by Filipinos.

MacArthur said the response to the Japanese message was unanimous: "Every foxhole on Bataan rocked with ridicule that night."

For weeks now, Homma had been applying pressure to dislodge MacArthur. In late December, he had sent in bombers to attack Corregidor and MacArthur narrowly escaped death. The planes "looked like silver pieces thrown against the sun. But their currency was death and their appearance a deceit." One bomb crushed the roof of his headquarters building and others, accompanied by strafing rounds, left the grounds pockmarked with craters. "Blue sky turned to dirty gray. . . . Machine guns chattered everywhere and ceaselessly. Then they left as shaking earth yielded under the pulverizing attack, and there rose a slow choking cover of dust and smoke and flame."

MacArthur withdrew to a new headquarters facility deep in the rock of the Malinta Tunnel. He held out for two more months until President Roosevelt ordered him to withdraw to safety in Australia and from there organize an American offensive in the Pacific. MacArthur wavered with the thought of resigning the army to take up a rifle himself and fight in the hills rather than obey the president. But the sixty-two-year-old general thought better and, though he delayed his departure, said he would follow orders. He would soon learn that some members of his fragmented forces did disobey orders to surrender and headed for the hills to fight.

Learning About War

Bataan, December 20, 1941

LIFE IN THE LITTLE mountain village of Pilar was Claire's introduction to war and hard days to come. The villagers asked Claire to teach their children because the local school had closed and the teacher was gone. She made a deal: She would teach English, and they would teach her Tagalog. The first day ten children came to school; by the third day attendance had more than tripled. Soon she had one hundred students.

War fever was increasing, but fighting had not yet come close to the village. Most mornings Claire and the nanny, Lolita, went out in search of stores that still had food to sell. Every night they heard rumbling explosions in the distance. Villagers were jittery, and by the weekend of December 20, they were digging air-raid shelters.

John Phillips showed up on December 22. According to Claire, he had taken the car down to Manila for supplies and come back with Christmas presents as a surprise, but the roads were bad and his car got a flat on the way back. It was late by the time he had commandeered a truck and delivered the presents and a bottle of rum. Phillips told Claire where to find the car about twenty miles south and then raced back to camp. He sent a message the next day that he was being punished with KP for a week and could not get away. Claire took a horse-cart taxi and then hitched a ride on an army truck, found the car, and had someone fix the tire. It was a bad day to be on any road in the open. As Claire drove back to Pilar on the main highway, Japanese planes swooped in; she stopped and leaped out of the car into a ditch, injuring her foot in the process. "I was hit in the toe with shrapnel," she said. By Christmas Day Claire's toe was infected and she could hardly walk. A doctor at the first-aid station treated the toe, removed the nail, and told her to stay in bed. She tried to obey the doctor's orders but she saw too many American soldiers coming along the road on their march north. "Every time they would stop by, I would give them some food."

For the rest of her life, Claire claimed that she had married John Phillips on Christmas Eve 1941 under the trees before a Catholic priest named Father Gonzales. The real story was less than romantic. According to her diary, she was still laid up in bed, and Phillips still would have been serving his punishment for going AWOL on his last visit. She did not mention Phillips in her diary on Christmas Eve or on Christmas Day. Instead, she wrote, they had no company for Christmas dinner. She received a message from Phillips on December 26 that he and his unit had moved on December 24 to the town of Hermosa, about twelve miles to the north.

Phillips was able to come down from Hermosa for a delayed Christmas dinner on December 28. "Cold chicken Xmas dinner," Claire wrote. Perhaps they made plans for the future after the war, but "Cry and laugh" was all she wrote about that visit. Phillips headed back to his camp the next morning. On December 30 Claire, Dian, and Lolita moved to Hermosa. Phillips had arranged a room for them at the home of Judge Fernando Rivera, two blocks from Phillips and his Headquarters Company. The soldiers spent their days training and waiting for orders and an expected Japanese invasion from northern Luzon. Claire set up housekeeping for Phillips, washed his clothes, and cooked dinner before he returned to camp at night. That lasted for about a week, the most prolonged period of time that Claire had been able to spend with her young beau.

Claire's decision to flee with Phillips's company to Bataan kept her closer to the center of battle than she could have imagined or wanted. The Japanese commander in the Philippines, General Homma, plowed across Luzon in pursuit of the retreating Americans, following his fifty-days-to-victory plan with no intention of slowing down. He directed his forces across the Pampanga River directly toward Hermosa, where Phillips was bivouacked and where he had taken Claire. Every time Claire, Dian, and the nursemaid moved northward and inland, the Japanese happened to be marching and bombing in the same direction. Softening up the American forces in retreat, General Homma ordered air strikes over the nearby town of Orani on New Year's Day. Many people in town, including Claire, were outdoors at 3:00 p.m. when the air-raid sirens wailed. A Japanese fighter swept over the village and bullets popped and raised dust in the town square. Claire was recruited to nurse the wounded at the local first-aid clinic, which was so crowded that medics took over another house to treat more people.

Phillips came over a few hours later and moved Claire, Dian, and

Lolita one last time to a house closer to his unit's new camp near Dinalu-pihan. That was not good enough; Claire saw fires and bomb craters; they could hear explosions as they drove along the highway. The next morning Phillips managed another brief visit amid the bombing and chaos. Claire helped doctors and nurses for the next two days, treating the sick and wounded.

On January 4, two days after the fact, word came that the Japanese Army now occupied Manila. She received one final message from Phillips on January 6 as the army moved farther north from Hermosa. Claire now realized that the Americans were in grave danger as they marched to the northern mountains of Bataan; the Japanese occupied territory on all sides. Now on her own, Claire gathered up the belongings and money Phillips had left behind and buried it all.

She probably did not admit the obvious to herself right away: If Phillips survived, and if she made it out of the hills herself, they might not find each other again. Claire did copy a famous sonnet by Elizabeth Barrett Browning into her little diary that night. She said that she and Phillips loved the sonnet and used it as a kind of code between them:

How do I love thee? Let me count the ways.
I love thee to the depth and breadth and height
My soul can reach, when feeling out of sight
For the ends of being and ideal grace.
I love thee to the level of every day's
Most quiet need, by sun and candle-light.
I love thee freely, as men strive for right.
I love thee purely, as they turn from praise.
I love thee with the passion put to use
In my old griefs, and with my childhood's faith.
I love thee with a love I seemed to lose
With my lost saints. I love thee with the breath,
Smiles, tears, of all my life; and, if God choose,
I shall but love thee better after death.

Unprepared for War

Manila, December 1941

THESE WERE the final days of the Manila that was. Forty years of American development had made Manila a powerhouse for banking and commerce. It was the Pearl of the Orient, a crossroads of cultures where American expatriates had come to settle at the outset of the twentieth century and mingled with the various ethnic groups of the islands. New Japanese immigrants had taken a prominent role in commerce and local politics, raising fears before the war of a fifth column of Japanese agents. The mix also included people of Chinese origin, Pacific islanders, and mestizos, the varied ethnic groups of the Philippines and descendants of Spanish settlers. In the late 1500s the Spanish colonial government had built a bastion around old Manila to protect the city from marauding pirates, with walls at some points forty feet thick and twenty-two feet high, and aptly called it Intramuros (Spanish for "within the walls"). The area just outside Intramuros had been a broad moat on three sides, now filled in for sports and recreation. The grounds just outside Intramuros had become a popular golf course; soldiers and children also played baseball there. Beyond Intramuros the port angled around the Pasig River, flowing into Manila Bay to the west. The Luneta—a sprawling downtown park— had been built just beyond the walled city, and to the south and all around was the central business district of Manila proper. For some reason, cars and trucks drove on the left side in the British fashion, sharing the roads with a jumble of transport: bright orange streetcars, horse-drawn buses, buggy taxis, and carts of commerce and industrial goods hauled by water buffaloes.

Manila was a divided society. Life was good for the small community of expatriate Americans. A 1940 government census listed 8,739 permanent American residents in Manila—a city of 623,000—not counting military families, temporary businesspeople, or diplomats and their families on assignment from the States. Americans and other foreigners did well in business and constituted an upper middle class. Americans benefited from the four decades of colonial rule since the United States had ousted Spain in 1898, one result of the Spanish-American War. Cuba and the

Philippines, a Spanish colony for more than three hundred years, were the spoils of U.S. victory. The Philippines became a commonwealth of the United States in 1935 as part of its planned transition to full independence by 1946.

The wealthiest residents, mostly Americans, lived in sumptuous mansions on Dewey Boulevard (named for Admiral George Dewey, the victor in the 1898 Battle of Manila Bay during the Spanish-American War). Hidden, though, beyond the mansions of the Americans were the working-class neighborhoods and shantytowns or the thatched-roof barges where the poor and voiceless of Manila lived in underdevelopment and squalor along canals around the city.

Education drew a new class of Filipinos to the city's universities, the University of the Philippines, founded in 1908, and the Pontifical and Royal University of Santo Tomas, founded in 1611 by the Spaniards, twenty-five years before Harvard, the oldest university in the United States. Expatriate Americans ran popular department stores and published dozens of newspapers. A new generation of young Americans had been drawn to the Philippines in the 1930s, attracted by romance, the wanderlust that Claire had felt, and an escape from the privations of the Great Depression.

A colonial existence was safe and comfortable for the Americans. Everyone knew but never spoke very much about the subservient relationship of Filipinos to Americans. Filipinos were second-class citizens in their own country. The relationship was demeaning and objectionable, recalls Joan Bennett Chapman, an American who was born in Manila. "Many people, it may sound very patronizing, but they had this disgusting phrase: The Americans were the big brothers and the Filipinos were the little brown brothers." And that was just the way the American colony thought it was supposed to be. "We will share the values of democracy and education with our little brothers and we will help them grow."

Joan Bennett Chapman's father was one of the most prominent expatriates in the Philippines. Roy C. Bennett, fifty-two, was editor and general manager of the *Manila Daily Bulletin*, the city's largest newspaper and one of the most influential English-language publications in the Pacific Rim. Almost daily Bennett blasted the Japanese military juggernaut and warned about what was to come. "There seems to be no road open to Japan except war," he editorialized on October 18, 1941. He called Japan's drive toward war a suicidal course, and he knew that any pretense by Japan of making peace with the United States was just that. "The Japanese government is a military organization, long has been under military domination, operating on a military program," he wrote. Argue and harangue though he did, Bennett could not awaken Washington to the dimensions of the impending catastrophe.

Bennett had lived in the islands for most of his life. Educated on the U.S. mainland, he had come back after college for good, because this was his home. He was enough of a friend of Douglas MacArthur that the general occasionally came to the Bennett house for dinner. Manila was home base for MacArthur as head of the colonial Philippine military in the 1930s, before President Roosevelt recalled him to active duty in 1941. Bennett's daughter, Joan, would quake when the general sat at the dinner table yet sometimes hid nearby so she could hear him speak. "My parents and MacArthur were in the same social circles," Joan recalled. "When I was maybe five or six, I was allowed to come down when there were parties. I was to carry a basket with candies around to people at the table and then disappear. But one night I saw this big man, MacArthur, who scared me. I heard him and watched him from behind the curtains and I wrapped myself up for protection."

Bennett predicted nothing but war and managed to anger Tokyo early on with his predictions that Japan and its "supermilitarism" would ultimately fail. "Japan is heading full speed downhill; with the accelerator stuck, heading for more war. The near certainty [is] that this further war making will be suicidal."

Bennett also said clearly that the Philippines was in the sights of the Japanese war machine. "Certainly we do not choose war—do not want it under any conditions," he wrote. But "if Japan is dead set on making war, the showdown might as well come now." He knew the consequences for the Philippines. "The natural wish of the Philippines is to see a way found to escape the necessity of war. But this should not mean the Philippine sentiment is in favor of peace at any price."

MacArthur knew that Bennett was right about Japanese intentions in the Philippines and had been lobbying the Roosevelt administration and Congress for years with minimal results. The United States "had begun an eleventh-hour struggle to build up enough force to repel an enemy," MacArthur wrote years later. "Too late, Washington had come to realize the danger. Men and munitions were finally being shipped to the Pacific, but the crucial question was, would they arrive in time and in sufficient strength?"

Bennett continued to publish and write pointed editorials throughout December 1941. General Homma stepped up the pace of invasion and bombed the unprotected capital on December 27. Japanese planes attacked at midday along the Manila waterfront, where several strikes destroyed piers and ships. Bombs also hit church buildings and schools in Intramuros, the walled city, on December 28. Cars burned and smoke billowed over the old city. About 40 civilians died and 150 were wounded. Bennett responded angrily with the power of his pen: He wrote that Japan was bound to lose and was "gambling with stakes that could mean their ultimate ruin." The words were prescient: "It is not understandable that the Japanese strategists could believe for one second that the United States, Britain and China will stop until the whole strength of the Pacific defense forces are brought into full action—and that means until the attacking enemy is crushed." From his new headquarters on Corregidor, MacArthur condemned the attacks on Manila as a violation of international law and said, "At the proper time I shall bespeak of due retaliatory measures." For the moment he could do little.

On January 2, 1942, Bennett managed a final four-page edition with a front-page banner: CITY AWAITS OCCUPATION. There was nothing left to be said. "Be calm," Bennett wrote as Japanese troops prepared to march triumphantly into Manila. "We know that it is much easier said than done when it comes to the business of being calm under stress, but there are those who demonstrate their ability to do just that."

Japanese military authorities and their agents in Manila had been monitoring the *Bulletin* for months and despised Roy C. Bennett's editorial position against the Rising Sun. There were three English-language dailies in the city, Bennett's *Bulletin*, the oldest in the city; the *Herald*, which also was anti-Axis and opposed Japanese warmongering; and the *Tribune*, which had been noncommittal but would quickly become the Japanese occupation mouthpiece. In contrast, so hated was the *Bulletin* that early in the campaign against the Americans, the Japanese commander ordered a special bombing run aimed at blowing up the *Bulletin* offices. The attack missed and wrecked adjoining buildings instead.

The Japanese occupation team, with General Homma as commander, moved to set up control. Tokyo chose Homma for this assignment in part for his knowledge of the West. He not only spoke English but even had served with the British Army in France in World War I. One immediate move was a clampdown on news media. On January 3, 1942, the Japanese arrested Roy C. Bennett, an obvious target and one of the first people seized by the new occupation army. They took him to Villamor Hall at the University of the Philippines for what they called "preliminary investigation," then tossed him into a twelve-by-fifteen-foot cage at Fort Santiago. The Spanish citadel was built on the Pasig River to protect Intramuros from invaders by sea in the sixteenth century. The fort was now the Japanese military's headquarters and its prison and torture chamber. Bennett's wife, Margaret, tried but failed for months to contact him or even confirm that he was alive. The Japanese Kempeitai—military police—had taken a page from the Gestapo method of *Nacht und Nebel*—night and fog; once seized, a prisoner would disappear behind the haze of a security state, into the bowels of a prison system in which torture was institutionalized and in many cases ended in death.

The Conversion of Santo Tomas

Manila, January 2, 1942

WITHIN HOURS of their arrival, Japanese occupation officials ordered that Americans and nationals of other countries at war with Germany and Japan report to the University of Santo Tomas, converted quickly and haphazardly into a civilian detention center. Meanwhile, they quickly set free 25,000 Japanese and Japanese Filipino residents who had been detained in the early days of the war. A month later President Roosevelt ordered the internment of more than 110,000 Japanese Americans in the United States.

Throughout the first days of occupation, the foreign nationals slowly did as they were told. Some walked to the gates of the university on their

own; some even rode in limousines, dropped off by servants and chauf-
feurs and carrying much more than the three days' worth of food and
clothing they had been told to bring with them. Squads of soldiers went
neighborhood by neighborhood to make sure the foreigners complied.
Filipinos and foreigners were taught to bow respectfully from the waist
before every Japanese soldier or official they encountered. Failure to comply could mean a slap in the face, a rifle butt in the stomach, or both.

Within a week or two, the Japanese herded more than three thousand
foreigners, mostly Americans, along with British subjects and others,
onto the campus not far from the center of town. If Claire had stayed in
Manila, she certainly would have been among them.

Other than the presence of Japanese guards and their bayonets, the
streets around the university almost appeared as if it were simply moving
day for a new school term. People could still come and go without a problem; Filipino servants came and went with supplies, and detainees went
out into the city in search of pillows and mattresses and cooking utensils.
Trucks loaded with detainees pulled up at the front gate every day, entire
families all at once, men and women segregated. People noticed soon that
the Japanese were exempting the elderly from reporting requirements,
though they sometimes came anyway to stay with their families.

Officials divided the fifty-acre university grounds into separate living
quarters for families, men, women, and children. Some lived in converted
classrooms in the modern four-story administration building; in the
courtyards and on the periphery people built open-walled lean-tos and
huts of rough-hewn wood and bamboo covered with palm leaves and
thatch. Soon the stately old university had become a muddy shantytown
for almost five thousand people.

For six months at least, occupation officials provided no food for the
detainees. With permission from Japanese authorities, the Red Cross sent
in as much food and supplies as it could. Some of the detainees arrived
with their own stores and shared with the less fortunate; others used what
money they had to trade and purchase food from the outside.

The authorities allowed the internees to designate their own leaders,
who would in turn liaise with occupation officials. They formed an internee executive committee that functioned much like a village council.

Before long, Santo Tomas was crammed and uncomfortable, but the detainees policed themselves, generally were not mistreated, and fared far better than Roy C. Bennett and the prisoners at Fort Santiago. An American banker, Fay Bailey, became one of the camp leaders and a liaison for the Red Cross to bring goods and services inside the gates. "The Japs were very lenient at first about letting supplies into camp for individuals and even in allowing personal contacts between Ins and Outs." Despite the crowding and the lack of food and medical supplies, the Japanese did not bother the prisoners as long as the prisoner-chosen internment authorities obeyed the rules. One exception came on February 11, 1942, little more than a month after the Japanese marched into town. Three men, Blakey Laycock, forty-three, an Australian engineer, and two British merchant marine sailors in their twenties, Thomas Fletcher and Henry Weeks, climbed over the fence and escaped. Japanese guards recaptured them and beat them up. The Japanese commandant, Hitoshi Tomayasu, seemed to accept the apology and a promise from American internee monitors that it would never happen again. Suddenly, though, he changed his mind, raging about the escape attempt, and ordered that the men be seized and punished to set an example. The three were taken away and executed by a firing squad on February 15. Tomayasu ordered that internee representatives witness the executions; they reported that at least one of the men was still alive when Filipino workers were forced to bury him and the others in a common grave. The execution achieved what the commandant had intended—he received no further word of escape attempts.

Some of the detainees eventually were released, however, for various reasons. Among them was Carl Mydans, a famed *Life* magazine photographer who had been reporting from Manila when war broke out. He and his wife, Shelley, were rounded up with the rest of the foreigners in January. Mydans was summoned to the commandant's office in June 1942. Colonel Tomayasu had been replaced by a civilian administrator, an ex-diplomat named R. Tsurumi. "The colonel has just had a report about you," Tsurumi said. "He says you are a famous photographer. He has seen your pictures of China in *Life*." He then proceeded to ask Mydans to photograph a military parade celebrating the Japanese victory in Bataan and Corregidor. Mydans refused on the ground that it would be treason; he was dismissed and did not suffer the consequences. More than two months later, Mydans and his wife were released, were given passage on the *Maya Maru*, a Japanese transport to Shanghai as part of a prisoner exchange, and then traveled onward to photograph the war in Europe and elsewhere in the Pacific.

Another internee got a furlough from Santo Tomas those early months of the occupation. Charles "Chick" Parsons was a longtime Manila resident well known as among the best polo players in the Philippines. Though he carried documents that showed he was a diplomat from Panama, Japanese soldiers detained Parsons more than once just because he looked like an American—which, in fact, he was.

Diplomatic Immunity
Manila, January 2, 1942

CHICK PARSONS WAS about to pull off one of the greatest scams of the Philippines war. His children were there to record the action. "It still runs before my eyes like a movie," said Chick's son Peter Parsons. Four years old at the time ("I was almost five"), he was swimming with friends in the pool of the family house on Dewey Boulevard on January 2, 1942, as he often did when a parade of Japanese soldiers marched past. "As the soldiers turned East down Santa Scholastica Street they raised their arms to us and shouted, '*Banzai!*' We raised our arms and *Banzai'd* them back." Japanese military police came around to the house a little while later looking for Peter's father. They ordered Chick, his wife, and their three children to put their things together and leave for Santo Tomas. Luckily, Parsons had anticipated this eventuality and had fashioned a crude sign that read CONSULADO DE PANAMA and tacked it to the front gate. He rummaged in his drawers for the paperwork and consular materials he had wangled from the consulate—the designation was official as far as the Philippine government was concerned, and Chick's status as consul had even been listed in the newspaper.

It was a stroke of luck. Countries with small staffs abroad sometimes designate foreign nationals as their diplomatic representatives. Parsons had been given the job temporarily until a Panamanian could be sent to represent the country. The Japanese assumed he was Panamanian, which he was not, and had no way of knowing who he really was. His designation as a diplomat gave Parsons time to come up with a better alternative than to sit out the war in Manila.

Fortunately, the Japanese sentries who came to the house that day did not understand when Michael, the oldest of his three sons, came running out of the house to protest, shouting in Spanish: "No pueden llevarnos a un campo cualquiera. Mi papá es un oficial de la marina." ("You can't take us to any old camp. My father is an officer in the navy.") It was true. The man claiming diplomatic status as a Panamanian was a U.S. Navy lieutenant assigned to the submarine service.

Parsons, forty-one, had lived in Manila for years. He was a handsome fellow, not tall, a robust fireplug of a man with piercing eyes and a broad, easy smile. He was born in Shelbyville, Tennessee, on April 22, 1900, but first came to Manila with an uncle in 1905 when he was five years old, and attended the Santa Potenciana School in Intramuros. He went back to the States, graduated from Chattanooga High School, then traveled once more to the Philippines in the early 1920s as a merchant marine seaman. Soon after returning, he was hired as stenographer to U.S. governor-General Leonard Wood, a famous former U.S. military officer who had climbed San Juan Hill in Cuba with his friend Theodore Roosevelt during the Spanish-American War. On frequent trips around the islands with Wood, Parsons made friends and contacts that would serve him well and learned the geography of the Philippines, as few others did. While living several years later in Zamboanga on Mindanao Island, he met and married Katrushka Jurika, known to everyone as Katsy. Her father, Stephen Jurika, was born in Austria-Hungary (which would later become Czechoslovakia); her mother, Blanche, was from California. Chick had a knack for language, spoke Spanish fluently, and quickly mastered the Philippine national language, Tagalog. Ironically, he was now the president of Manila's Luzon Stevedoring Company, a subsidiary of a Japanese mining concern. Everyone in the Philippines knew Chick for his exploits on the polo field. "To watch the sun-bronzed Chick at play, as if his entire soul were tied to the game, was to observe an American who had in every way fitted into our easy Philippine manner of living," said his friend Carlos P. Romulo, himself a prominent diplomat and statesman. "Chick was 'one of us' in Manila before the war." However, Chick had another dimension unknown to most people. He was not only a veteran officer in the U.S. Navy Reserve, attached to the submarine service since 1932; he was also a spy.

Parsons had been recalled to active duty on December 8, 1941, and quickly assigned to the district intelligence office at the Port of Manila. On New Year's Day 1942, the day before the Japanese marched into Manila, he deputized Katsy, who insisted on coming along on an odd mission. Along the way to the Port of Manila, looters roamed the street, unimpeded by the police. At the Manila Hotel, not far from the waterfront, people dressed in formal attire, clung to one another, and drank profusely as the band played on; throughout Manila people were staging last-minute holiday parties, something like dancing in the ballroom of the *Titanic* after the last life raft was gone.

Meanwhile, under Chick's command, a group of men moved with him from dock to dock and set fire to military warehouses to destroy weapons and other supplies that otherwise would fall into the hands of the enemy. At one final stop on the piers, Chick bade farewell to American servicemen who were sailing across the bay to Corregidor, where they would take refuge with General MacArthur. Parsons had decided not to leave with them. He and Katsy returned home and waited for the imminent arrival of the Japanese.

The next morning, squads of Japanese soldiers patrolled Dewey Boulevard to check houses one by one in search of U.S. officials and other Americans. They had no idea who Chick Parsons was, and he quickly informed them he was a diplomat from Panama, which had not sided with the Americans or the Axis powers. Therefore, Parsons said, as neutrals he and his family should be left alone. Within an hour, consular officials appeared from the Japanese embassy, "hissing like radiators" and asking to see the honorable credentials of the honorable consul from Panama. Everything appeared to be in order, Chick's name was actually on record at Malacañang Palace (the office of the Philippine president) as consul for Panama, and the officials withdrew, with many bows.

For the next three months Parsons used his diplomatic status to conduct covert activities and gather information about the locations of Japanese installations and bases, along with all the intelligence he could scoop up. Fearless, suntanned, and disguised as a peasant, Chick could just blend in if he had to. He traveled into the hills of Bataan and saw signs of American and Filipino soldiers evading capture, willing and still able to fight. If Japanese patrols stopped him along the way, he showed Philippine documents, spoke Tagalog and Spanish, blended in, and gave no hint that he was an American, much less a spy.

Nurse and Midwife
Mount Malasimbo, Bataan, January 1942

CLAIRE LIVED AMONG desperate people these days, trapped and isolated in the jungle, left without food or the drugs to combat disease in their little settlement on the slopes of a volcano. When the doctors and nurses went away to treat the war victims, villagers turned to Claire, who had no medical training, as their nurse. Suddenly she was treating wounds, caring for children, and delivering babies. For the first time in her life, she was serving others; this became the new reality. Here the growing problem of sanitation became more dangerous than the threat of war. Children and adults fell to diseases of the jungle, contaminated water, swarms of mosquitoes, rat bites, high fevers. Little Dian soon developed diarrhea and dysentery. Even in the shade of the jungle canopy, the heat was wilting; it was ninety degrees every day. Unable to escape the smell of open sewage, flies, and insects, people fell victim to malaria, cholera, and diseases they could not identify. Stores of quinine to fight off malaria were gone; people began to use herbs and home remedies that did not work well enough.

Claire, Dian, and Lolita moved more than once among settlements of people who had fled the larger towns of Bataan, hiding in the foothills and mountains inland. Not everyone was willing to shelter a light-skinned woman; Japanese planes were dropping leaflets calling on the Filipinos to fight the Americans alongside them. Harboring an American from the city was dangerous. During the day Claire sometimes lay down in the sun to tan her skin in hopes she would be less conspicuous. After a week or two, Claire met Carlos Sobreviñas, a well-to-do *haciendero* who was willing to risk taking in an American woman—there was no danger for Dian or for Lolita, as both of them had black hair and dark complexions.

Carling, as Sobreviñas was called, had brought workers to set up several dozen huts for his wife, infant child, brothers, and extended family up in the hills to avoid the fighting below. Carling was "a tall, wavy-haired man of about twenty-five years, very good-looking . . . clean, neat and spoke excellent English." The Sobreviñas family welcomed them, but life was increasingly difficult; rains pelted them, bombs in the distance kept them awake; despite the heat and misery during the day, it grew cold overnight. Cooler nights did not drive away the insects. Without mosquito netting and unable to light fires, which might draw the attention of the Japanese, Claire tended to Dian and then put on extra clothing at night, covering her arms and legs to avoid mosquitoes and other vermin.

Food was scarce. At first Carling could send his men back to the family hacienda in the dark and move stores of sugarcane, blankets, and whatever they could find up to their mountain hideout. Japanese soldiers now camped in the sugarcane fields of the hacienda. It was dangerous to leave the hills. Many days they had only a small ration of rice, some edible leaves, maybe bananas; meat was hard to find. People took to catching and boiling frogs and mixing them with the rice for dinner. Water supplies were often contaminated. By February 1 malaria swept the Sobreviñas village. Without a doctor, they could hardly identify what other diseases were hitting them—diphtheria, typhoid, beriberi, a lethal cocktail of tropical diseases. Claire counted fifteen deaths that month; many people were dangerously ill, at least one person in almost each of the thirty huts around them. The deaths were awful and agonizing—fevers, vomiting, convulsions, most horrible when she watched children waste away and die. Yet five babies had been born in the village over the same period. Claire helped with the deliveries and struggled to keep the infants alive when she was healthy enough to be on her feet. She, Dian, and Lolita also had bouts of dysentery from bad water and contaminated food.

Filipino travelers who managed to make it back from Manila said things were tough along the route. The Japanese had installed a new government in Manila and occupied every small town between the city and the upper reaches of Bataan. "A Japanese flag [flew] on every hut," not out of support for the Japanese but on demand and out of prudence. Rumors said that the Japanese soldiers were on the lookout for villages in the interior jungles that they had not yet taken. Eventually a Japanese patrol might find the hidden Sobreviñas settlement in the hills above Dinalupihan.

. . .

Rumors spread quickly via messengers who traveled village to village, carrying food and the latest news on the war. One day one of these messengers brought Claire an offer of hope. Father Eduardo Cabanguis, the parish priest of Maite, a barrio outside Dinalupihan, sent word that he had met an American soldier among several others who were hiding from the Japanese not far away. Was Claire interested in meeting them? Father Cabanguis did not give Claire the names of the Americans, but she had hopes that John Phillips might be one of them, or at least that the Americans might offer hope that Phillips was alive and well. She sent a messenger back to say that she was definitely interested.

Boone's Guerrillas
Bataan, February 1942

JOHN BOONE, a twenty-nine-year-old American corporal, had lost contact with his army unit in the early weeks of the Japanese invasion and was one of the first men in Bataan to start organizing a guerrilla army. He had been able to evade the Japanese so far through guile and instinct, and now that he was gathering enough men in central Bataan, he was more cautious than ever. In the process of establishing his insurgency, he received word from Father Cabanguis "that there was an American woman loose and moving around up there." Boone was rightly suspicious: Who was this priest and could he be trusted?

Boone had obvious reason to worry about security. He could not know who might have been recruited or bribed by Japanese intelligence operatives on the lookout for Americans. Boone knew from everything he saw that he was operating in a friendly sea, but it took only one turncoat to cause trouble. An American guerrilla leader would bring a premium from the Japanese. Boone had plenty of security concerns. Aside from the Japanese, he had to worry about a homegrown Filipino communist army, the Hukbalahap—the Army of the Common People, known as the Huks for short. Boone was competing with the Huks for recruits, and they were not particularly friendly to American and Filipino rival guerrillas.

After checking the priest out, Boone came to meet him, partly to find out about the American woman and partly because he had been told that Cabanguis had an excellent radio receiver that would give him news about the wider war. "It was pretty obvious to me that this particular padre was a dyed-in-the-wool pro-American. So I established contact with him and I went in there every night for, I don't know how long, a couple or three weeks, to listen to the news." They agreed that the priest would make arrangements for Claire's meeting with Boone.

Claire set out for Maite after dark on the evening of February 20, dressed in men's clothing and accompanied by a team of six guides. The crescent moon was waxing into the first quarter; the weather was not too humid and even a bit cool before dawn in the hills this time of year. A little moonlight would not hurt in the dark of night, but a full moon would have cast shadows that would have revealed them as they scrambled toward town.

It was a five-mile hike; for safety they trekked across fields, jungle paths, rice paddies, and streams, skirted the main highway, and only crossed the road, always on the lookout for Japanese patrols, when they approached the town of Dinalupihan. By the time they reached Cabanguis's church in Maite around midnight, Claire's feet were blistered and her muscles were sore. There was some relief at least in finding cigarettes and matches, although the prices were high—one peso per cigarette and thirteen cents for a penny box of matches.

Cabanguis provided the latest news from Manila and on the war, though it was not good. American forces were in retreat and men were dying. Claire told him she had seen a big fire close by during the trek in from the hills. Yes, the priest said, the Japanese sometimes burned their dead, and there were many of them. He said there were many American casualties as well. The fighting was ever closer and it was inevitable that the Japanese soldiers would occupy the town. The priest gave no details of the upcoming meeting with Boone other than the location, which required another walk to the outskirts of Dinalupihan, several hours away. He suggested that Claire rest and lay low for the night.

At daybreak Claire and her helpers walked from the parish into the

Maite valley. The rendezvous point was a high plateau that would provide secure entry from all sides. Boone, traveling with a bodyguard, also had walked through the night. His route also crossed the main road from Dinalupihan to Zambales; as in Claire's case, the highway was certain to be patrolled by considerable Japanese military traffic. Boone reached the meeting site and waited. The sheltered piece of high ground was hidden by banana trees, part of a plantation on the west side of the valley.

Boone emerged from the tree cover when Claire approached. She saw a slender young man, emaciated, really, appearing older than his age, looking back at her "with friendly twinkling, grey eyes, and a neat Vandyke beard." Boone extended a hand. "Are you really an American, or am I seeing things again?" he asked.

"Yes, I'm an American," Claire said. She said she had expected to find Boone traveling with two other soldiers. No, he said, they were Maromis and Henderson and remained back in camp. "What about Phillips?" she asked. "He is my husband." She had been hearing rumors that he was captured, even dead. Did Boone know Phillips? Claire said that Phillips was a sergeant. Boone laughed to himself. Sure, he knew who John Phillips was, "a buck-ass private, a private in the Thirty-First Infantry, stationed in the same *cuartel* that I was in in the walled city of Manila." She realized immediately that Boone would not bring her any closer to finding John Phillips.

Yes, Boone said, he had heard of her husband, but not since the war. Boone said he would try to find out. It would not be easy. He did not get into the specifics of his interest in having a woman working on his side. This meeting was more general—among other things, for Claire it meant enjoying contact with a fellow American; for Boone it was about the pleasure of meeting an American *woman*. Boone had been a theatrical producer in the United States before enlisting in the army in 1940. That was common ground—Claire was a performer.

When war broke out, Boone was a corporal in the 31st Infantry. Phillips was a private in the regiment's Headquarters Company; Boone was assigned to Dog Company, a heavy weapons group in the walled city of Intramuros. Dog Company was sent to hold positions in tall buildings in Manila, prepared to shoot when the Japanese attacked. When Phillips and other elements of his regiment moved to Bataan, Boone's unit moved out to the Luneta, the downtown commons also known as Rizal Park, named for José Rizal, the Philippine national hero who fought Spanish colonialism. When General MacArthur decided to pull back from Manila, Boone's Dog Company provided security. "It seems to me we moved to Corregidor on Christmas Eve," Boone said. After MacArthur was secured at Corregidor, Boone's company commandeered whatever boats they could find and sailed across from the island fortress to Bataan at Mariveles.

Boone recalled: "The first battalion moved across to Mariveles, north, to the extreme (southern) end of the Bataan Peninsula, where we were dug in . . . a bit north of that—in the Dinalupihan area. And we dug in there, my battalion, with elements of scout outfits, as I recall, on my right and left; I think, the 45th and 57th Philippine Scouts were on our right and left."

The company's next mission was to hold back a Japanese invasion force moving in from the north. A Filipino regiment was sent in to augment the size of the defense force significantly, but reality made the prospects very tenuous: The Filipinos had little if any training and were not battle ready. "We had to go out in front not more than a thousand yards and dig that regiment in and show them how to put their guns in position." The battlefield training was just about complete when the Japanese launched an attack from the north. It was January 6, Boone's birthday, around the same time that Claire had last seen John Phillips. Boone showed a flash of emotion and anger as he later recalled what happened. "A military farce is what it was. The Japanese attacked us with this artillery and intense small arms fire and we, in other words, made a very poor showing. I recall that my Baker Company, out of my battalion was hurt badly."

They were decimated, and Boone and the company scattered. He and two other men cut off to the hills. "I was already an evader of capture and was already up in the high ground in the peninsula of Bataan." He had no intention of surrendering.

John Boone's plight after the strategic U.S. retreat was repeated hundreds of times among the soldiers pinned down in Bataan. U.S.-Filipino operations thwarted Homma's forward progress, but by March the situation was dire. Suffering from bare-bones food rations, the U.S. forces began to starve, surviving on small supplies of rationed water and protein, a few hundred calories a day. When they ate and drank, they risked amoebic dysentery; they contracted every possible tropical infection, insect bites, jaundice, and beriberi and were attacked by rats and lice. When Japanese patrols passed by, they scrambled to hide low in the underbrush; sometimes a weighty snake slithered over one of them and he had to remain still, suppressing fear and the instinct to scream or to run. Boone, among those cut off from the main ranks of his battalion, fled into the hills to join up with other ragtag units that still wanted to fight. Eventually, he realized that he and the men around him were willing and able to mount an organized guerrilla opposition to the Japanese.

Boone sympathized with Claire about her husband, and for the rest of the war he referred to her as "Mrs. Phillips," one of the few people who did so. Claire and John Boone agreed to meet again soon. They left the banana field in opposite directions, Boone looking to enlist more guerrilla fighters, Claire still in search of John Phillips. She headed back to the Sobreviñas encampment that evening, the same overnight hike in reverse, five miles in the backwoods and between fields and houses, and then to a sentry line close to the main road. Just as Claire and the men approached the sentry line, a Japanese truck came rolling along the highway and spotted them. She and the others ran back to a collection of empty huts on the close side of the hill, ducked into the front door of one hut, and then ran out the back. Japanese soldiers thought they had them trapped and surrounded; they tossed a firebrand onto the roof of the hut and watched. "They thought they had burned us in the hut," Claire recalled, "but we stayed in the thicket in the back and we just stayed there until the Japanese drove the truck away." When it was quiet, they crossed the road and climbed the rest of the way back into their safe haven in the hills.

A few days later Claire and Boone sent notes back and forth through Filipino messengers; on February 27 they met again. This time Claire's guides were Aeta tribesmen. She had not met members of the Luzon ethnic group before. Sometimes called *negritos* ("little black men" in Spanish), adult Aeta men averaged no more than about four feet eight inches (1.45 meters) tall. Aeta were sometimes referred to as pygmies and had lived and hunted in the Luzon mountains for ages. They were renowned as mountain guides, a skill especially useful to the guerrillas. The Aeta knew every path through the mountains, even when they had to hack and reopen the way through jungle brush themselves. It had been hard to find guides willing to lead a tall white woman on such a dangerous trek. That was even more the case after a Japanese patrol almost caught an advance team of Aeta who were on their way to pick her up for her second visit with Boone. Nevertheless, a few of the Aeta relented and kept their promise to lead her across the hills. When the time came to leave, she turned around and one of the Aeta was standing behind her smiling, shouldering a bow and arrow and wearing only a G-string. Claire was startled. The man looked up and reached out for a handshake. Carling Sobreviñas, her host in the mountain camp, had come along to introduce her to the Aeta tribesmen; he nudged her to smile in return and shake hands.

There were no run-ins with Japanese on the second crossing. But as they walked, they flanked a deserted battlefield and Claire saw dead soldiers and horses splayed about; in the distance she saw smoke and thought it was a Japanese funeral fire. On this visit Boone laid out his plan. He was committed to fighting a guerrilla war for the duration, no matter how long it would take. He was now a guerrilla officer in a widespread organization of Americans and Filipinos. His mission was to organize in this section of Bataan, gather forces and supplies. It would have to be a highly mobile force capable of harassment raids and sabotage. What Boone needed was a Manila connection. If Claire was willing to help, she could be that connection. "We could make a deal," he said. If Claire "was interested in going to the city of Manila, if she was willing to carry out some sort of military intelligence mission for me, that I might be able to help her get there."

The Chances of Survival

Bataan, March 1942

CLAIRE REALIZED she was just one more among the many desperate denizens of the hills of Bataan. Every day she treated the sick people around her, nursed their babies and children as best she could, and cried along with them as they all confronted death. Despite her precautions,

Claire figured it was a matter of time and chance before she and Dian succumbed to some sickness or other. Added to that danger, they faced deteriorating food supplies and the precarious shelter of their jungle village. All the while the war was coming closer. Cannon fire was keeping them awake at night. Life in the hills meant more sickness and increasing danger as the Japanese marched on. In short, Claire had every reason to want to get back to Manila.

Emilio V. Reyes, the ex-mayor of Dinalupihan, the nearest town, helped Claire weigh her options. He received word that Japanese convoys were moving into the vicinity, which meant soldiers might stumble upon their settlement. At the same time, some families were taking the chance to move down the hill, back to Dinalupihan, on word that people would not be punished when they came back to town. If Carling and the rest of his family made that decision, as an American Claire could not go along with them and would be stuck on her own.

If she went back to Manila, she might be able to hide from the Japanese. She also figured that she would have a better chance of tracking down John Phillips if she was in the city. However, Emilio Reyes and Carling warned that sneaking back to Manila was still too dangerous. Carling himself had made the trip and so had his friend Reyes. People still were able to go back and forth to Manila, carefully, as long as they did not appear to be white Americans.

More people in the hillside settlement were dying of malaria. Claire was not surprised when she came down with malaria symptoms herself and was laid up for several weeks. She mostly stayed in bed, with just enough energy to drink a bit of water. At night as she lay there, she listened to thunder and explosions in the distance, played solitaire, and read the Bible, the only book left to read.

For the time being, thoughts of life and fear of death overwhelmed any thought of escape. The Sobreviñases' youngest child, Ronny, was running a high fever. Carling hurried to Manila on March 9 in frantic search of a doctor and some medicine. It was too late. Ronny died four days later; Carling had not returned and almost did not make it back at all. Along the way Japanese guards opened fire with machine guns on the road and he narrowly avoided being hit. He arrived at the camp on March 19 to find his wife and family already in full mourning. Claire participated in the four-day period of mourning, staying up all night to offer prayers and songs in remembrance. Nine days after the death, as was the custom, the Sobreviñases observed a night of ritual feasting.

Ronny's death was frightening, especially when Claire considered Dian's fragile health. The child had been sick frequently and was not getting enough nourishment. A two-year-old's reserves and resistance to disease and hunger were limited. Carling warned again that Claire had poor chances of making it to Manila and that Dian would suffer the consequences. From what he could see, Japanese sentries would be sure to catch them and there would be no way to explain why an American, woman or man, had been in the fighting zone.

If all that was true, there was only one obvious alternative. As an American she herself couldn't go, but maybe Dian and her nurse could make it, since they both had Asian features. Three days later, on March 25, sadly but with resolve, Claire sent Dian to Manila accompanied by now-pregnant Lolita and several guides. She gave Lolita a letter of introduction to Judge Roxas, who would remember that this was the child she and Manuel Fuentes, his wife's cousin, had adopted. Claire gave Roxas stark details about life to the north and the suffering of the people of Bataan. She also asked his opinion of the danger she might face in trying to reach Manila herself. She enumerated the problems of staying in the mountains. The hunger and pestilence in the village were overwhelming. "We all have head lice and fleas. . . . There are rats, also snakes." Snakes and rats, when caught, were becoming the only possible protein to blend with rice (when they had it), tropical leaves, and snails.

"She told me that the living conditions in the place where she was in Bataan were extremely difficult due to the lack of food and the prevalence of malaria," Roxas later said. "To save the life of her child, she had decided to make the sacrifice of separating from her, and she asked me to take care of her in my house."

After several days Claire got word back from Carling's workers that the child and the nursemaid had made it safely and that Judge Roxas, as kind and welcoming as expected, had taken them in. He wrote back that Dian and Lolita were doing fine. It was unlikely they would have problems with Japanese authorities, mostly because they appeared to be Filipinas and were not traveling or even leaving the house. The judge knew and understood that Claire missed Dian and expressed deep concern about Claire's life in Bataan, but he agreed with Carling and warned her not to come, at least not right away. He even checked with Filipino friends inside the newly established government to see if he was being overly cautious.

His talks with his Filipino government contacts confirmed his concerns. "I agreed with the opinion of my friends that it would be very dangerous for [Claire] if the Japanese would come to know that she was an American who went to Bataan with the army, and that it was also dangerous for me if the Japanese happened to know that I was showing interest on behalf of an American."

Occupation authorities, he warned, "required official passes to go in and out of Manila, especially from persons of the white race."

Claire remained with the kind and welcoming Sobreviñas family in the little village above Dinalupihan. They confronted the daily uncertainty of finding food while doing what they could to remain healthy. Sometimes bands of long-tailed macaques robbed their meager food stores at night. People started to trap and eat them, overcoming a traditional fear that capturing monkeys for food was bad luck. One American soldier hiding in the jungle mentioned having beaten a tree monkey to the ground, but said that when the primate looked up at him, he could not handle killing it. Occasionally there was string beef for purchase or meat from water buffaloes—the docile animals that served as beasts of burden throughout Luzon.

On March 31 Claire was jogged awake when rats crawled into her hut; she wrote in her diary that she "kicked the rats off covers all night" and wrapped herself tightly in the covers, hoping the rats and the mosquitoes would not bite.

More Than a Dozen Tremors

Bataan, April 1942

THE EARTH ITSELF began to shake, the great equalizer beneath every one of them. A strong earthquake rolled across the Philippines after midnight; the magnitude was 7.3, capable of major damage, but its center was beneath the sea about two hundred miles south of Bataan, off Mindoro. Some of the starving soldiers on Bataan thought it might be divine intervention to prevent the surrender to come. "Was God going to rescue us in the final hour?" Felipe Buencamino III, a Filipino soldier, wondered as he prepared for the formal surrender the next day. "My heart beat fast. . . . I was sure something would happen . . . to turn the tide of defeat . . . but nothing did . . . and I waited and waited till I fell asleep."

A dozen tremors followed, but divine intervention was not in store. The quake and aftershocks registered strongly in Manila, causing some damage but less than expected. Claire was jogged awake in her hut in Bataan, as were the internees at Santo Tomas; boulders swayed, water supplies sloshed, earthen huts and concrete buildings cracked. The quake, strong as it was, shook deep below the sea and damage was slight.

More rats than ever had been turned out from every hiding place. Poisonous vipers and crushing pythons were dislodged when the earth shook. The Aeta pygmy people hunted the snakes set out by the temblor and had no qualms about eating them. All mammals, reptiles, and insects were edible if they could be caught. Claire saw at least one nine-foot python that had been hacked before it could attack. Besides pythons, there were cobras and other poisonous snakes to worry about; given the negligible chance of finding antivenom, an attack would be fatal.

Death stalked the mountains. Sickness overtook the fear of war. Claire's diary became a list of tending to the dead. "Five more deaths by malaria," she wrote. "Twenty now." A few days later the total number of deaths from malaria had crept up to twenty-five. Increasingly, the days in hiding were spent washing and burying the dead. Now and then, Claire was able to nurse one or two people back to health, but not often. Claire felt that hope was abandoning them. She counted thirty deaths on

March 28 and worried whether she would survive. "One son and one daughter [got] fever[s] today. Guess I'm next."

Of twenty huts in their hideout, all but three had been abandoned by early April; "all others moved down hill to get away from fever up here," she wrote in her diary. Anyone who did not leave was either too sick to stand or was caring for those people. "In the three huts we are thirty, and all but eight are down with fever. That keeps us eight very busy. I have six under my care now." A few days after the earthquake, Claire awoke in the middle of the night to what she thought was guns blasting "so loud we must shout to be heard." There was no sleep at all on the night of April 14. The next day someone said that the infernal noise was an explosion at a Japanese ammunition dump. Suddenly there was no more fighting. The Americans in Bataan had been ordered to surrender. As they pulled back, the combined U.S. and Filipino forces were trying to burn and destroy anything that might be useful to the Japanese. The villagers on the hill, those who were upright, considered moving now with word of the American defeat. "We're in a tight spot, but can move," Claire wrote. "Pray we come through safe."

The Death March
Bataan, April 9, 1942

I don't think his story has been told back in the United States and I think it ought to be.

—LIEUTENANT BEN S. BROWN, A FIGHTER PILOT,
RECALLING CAPTAIN WILLIAM E. DYESS AND THE DEATH MARCH

THE TEMBLOR was nothing compared with the exhaustion, after weeks of depleted rations, felt by the troops, already decimated by disease and starvation. The morning after the earthquake, Major General Edward P. King, the commander of forces on Bataan, knew that he had only one alternative. After informing his commanders and ordering that all weapons be dismantled, military gear destroyed, he sent a message across Japanese lines with his "ignominious decision" to surrender.

The decision came after months in which the U.S. forces had withstood seemingly insurmountable odds. The U.S. and Filipino forces held their own for a time with the fervor of men ready to keep fighting until reinforcements arrived. Despite their uneven training, the combined forces scored a significant victory when Japanese invaders attempted to outflank entrenched American positions in the so-called Battle of the Points along the western coast of Bataan. Of an estimated two thousand Japanese troops on hand when the series of battles began on January 22, only forty-three survived when it was over on February 8.

The valiant defense had been a major source of concern for General Homma, who had been expected by his superiors in Tokyo to secure final victory by now. His troops also were war weary and suffering from tropical diseases but could expect better supply lines and the arrival of fresh fighters when they needed them. The American victory in the Battle of the Points came with the recognition on both sides that MacArthur's forces, increasingly exhausted and facing dwindling food supplies, could not survive indefinitely.

On February 7 MacArthur sent a message to Washington that included dire warnings. At best, only half of his original force was in fighting shape; the other men had been wounded in battle or were sick or starving. "Their spirit is good, but they are capable now of nothing but fighting in place on a fixed position. All our supplies are scant and the command has been on half rations for the past month." With no supplies or reinforcements in sight, he wrote, "you must be prepared at any time to figure on the complete destruction of this command."

A series of messages between Washington and MacArthur's Corregidor fortress led to Roosevelt's order on February 22 that MacArthur withdraw to Australia so that he could reorganize an offensive war against Japan. MacArthur delayed until March 11. As he left Corregidor for Mindanao on a patrol boat with his wife, Jean, their son, Arthur, and aides, MacArthur looked back at the troops he was leaving behind at Corregidor. "On the dock I could see the men staring at me. . . . My eyes roamed that warped and twisted face of scorched rock. Great gaps and forbidding crevices still belched their tongues of flame. The desperate scene showed only a black mass of destruction."

From Mindanao, MacArthur and family survived a perilous B-17 flight to northern Australia, evading Japanese planes whose pilots could not have known their valuable target. A month earlier Japan had begun punishing bombing runs on the naval port and Allied air base at Darwin in the lightly defended and sparsely settled Northern Territory of Australia. MacArthur and company landed at Batchelor Airfield, forty miles south of Darwin, and switched from the B-17 to another transport plane. Ten minutes after MacArthur left the airfield on that plane for a flight toward Alice Springs, Japanese planes blasted the tarmac where he had stood. MacArthur and family then transferred to a narrow gauge railway for Adelaide. Reporters were waiting for him en route at Terowie Station, about 135 miles north of Adelaide, where he issued his famous pledge. He told reporters that President Roosevelt had ordered him to regroup and plan an offensive against the Japanese. "A primary objective," he said, "is the relief of the Philippines. I came through and I shall return."

MacArthur encountered panic in Australia, where leaders and the populace were traumatized by fears of a full-scale Japanese invasion. He rejected an Australian defensive strategy of effectively circling the wagons and ceding a vast swath of northern and western Australia to eventual conquest. Instead, he promoted an offensive into the heart of Japanese-held territory at historic speed, into New Guinea and beyond—"to make the fight for Australia beyond its own borders. If successful, this would save Australia from invasion and give me an opportunity to pass from defense to offense, to seize the initiative, move forward, and attack." MacArthur's passionate arguments reversed Australian defeatism into "almost fanatical zeal" to succeed. Long before notions of victory, however, tragedy lay ahead in the Philippines.

On Bataan, three weeks after MacArthur's flight, General King determined that now only 15 percent of his original 120,000-member combined U.S. and Filipino force was in fighting shape. On April 9 he surrendered before Colonel Motoo Nakayama, senior operations officer for the Japanese Fourteenth Army, with a simple request. He begged that his troops be treated well. "We are not barbarians," Nakayama replied.

General Homma and the Japanese command did not anticipate the number of American prisoners they now saw emerging from the hills to surrender. Homma had prepared for about 25,000 prisoners, who were to be transported about sixty-five miles north to Camp O'Donnell, a former

Philippine Army training facility near the town of Capas. Trucks and trains were not sufficient for three times that many POWs; food and health facilities were not available in sufficient quantity. The Japanese had not realized the fragile condition of most of the American and Filipino troops. Homma was a moderate in Japanese military circles, a democrat by nature, a cultured man who had traveled widely in the United States. His intention of treating the American prisoners with kindness and restraint sounded sincere. Speaking impeccable English, he told one of the prisoners who emerged from the jungle, Colonel James V. Collier, "Your worries are over. Japan treats her prisoners well. You may even see my country in cherry-blossom time. And that is a beautiful sight."

Whether because of the overwhelming numbers or his inability to control his subordinates, the treatment of the POWs was grotesquely different. The Japanese began to corral their American prisoners the same day of the surrender in stages up along Bataan's eastern road. Portions of the road were in firing range of Corregidor, where ten thousand Americans were under siege and were not part of the surrender. Japanese artillery fired from the beach and drew return fire from Corregidor that left some of the prisoners in the line of fire. A number were killed or injured. Within hours of surrender on April 9, the Americans were prodded onto the road at the start of a trek that became known as the Bataan death march. Mostly starving and thirsty prisoners were forced to march north for hours in the wilting sun.

"It would have been an ordeal for well men," said Captain William E. Dyess, who marched and survived. "Added to the strength-sapping heat and blinding dust were the cruelties devised by the Jap guards. Considering our condition, I often wonder how we made it. We had had no food in days. Chronic exhaustion seemed to have possessed us. Many were sick. I know men who never could remember arriving at Orani. They were like Zombies, the walking dead of the Caribbean."

The march northward was a horror show of inhumanity. Sadistic Japanese guards brutalized and slaughtered the Americans and Filipinos at will. When the POWs tried to stop at streams or begged for a drop of water, some were just forced back in line; others were bayoneted on the spot. Japanese guards looted money, rings, watches, and other artifacts from the prisoners. When one Japanese soldier found a man with a lighter marked "Made in Japan," he lopped off the man's arm with a sword. One guard decapitated an army captain for the crime of carrying Japanese yen in his pocket.

Day and night they were forced onward.

"I wondered whether the Jap buzzard squad was following us as it had," Dyess recalled. "A flash and the crack of a shot answered my question. The executioners were on the job to kill or wound mortally every prisoner who fell out of the marching line. All through the night, there were occasional shots. I didn't count them. I couldn't."

Many factors explained the Japanese treatment of the Americans. Some of the Japanese soldiers were sadists, no doubt. However, the Japanese foot soldiers were educated to view the Americans with disdain because they were less honorable and less duty bound than were subjects of Imperial Japan. They were told that their American adversaries might often be taller than they were, but they also were weaker in moral character and less likely to put up a strong fight. Propaganda also said that the U.S. military command would deal fiercely with insubordination—as if the Japanese themselves would not behave in the same manner. Half-baked analysis of the American fighting spirit filtered out throughout the intelligence community; the word was: *They may be strong in numbers, but Japanese fighters are superior.*

"When the battle becomes fierce," a Japanese command document said, "the [American] officers and enlisted men dislike being moved up to the front lines; and again due to the prolonged war, they are homesick, bored, etc. Afraid of being punished severely, there are many who show a front superficially, although they are dissatisfied."

There were other cultural factors. For the Japanese, surrender was the lowest of disgraces, and American prisoners were unworthy of sympathy. In terms of field training, the Japanese were used to longer marches without readily available trucks and jeeps for transport. On surrender, General King suggested that the Japanese transfer his men with American vehicles. His advice was disregarded, and there probably were not enough operable vehicles to do the job quickly in any case.

Survivors began stumbling into Camp O'Donnell mostly by foot, sometimes by train, a few days after surrender. Waves of soldiers kept coming for several weeks until they were crammed into the fifty-acre camp. Hundreds of Americans and thousands of Filipino prisoners had died along the march route from mistreatment, hunger, disease, and outright murder, and thousands more died at Camp O'Donnell before it was ordered closed at the end of 1942. Many of the surviving Filipino prisoners were furloughed in early July and allowed to return to their families. Thousands of Americans were moved to Cabanatuan, about forty-five miles east of Camp O'Donnell. It took months before news of the atrocities reached MacArthur and officials in Washington.

Escape and Evasion
The Mountains Above Bataan, May 1942

IN THOSE EARLY DAYS of the Japanese occupation, John Boone could only hope to gather enough troops and ammunition to fight a guerrilla war. However, after starting with several dozen men and eight World War I bolt-action Springfield rifles, his luck changed. An old Filipino stumbled into his camp one day, a man too old to fight but bringing tantalizing news. "I know where there are guns," he said. "Many guns and much ammunition."

With the old Filipino as his guide, John Boone organized his first major insurgency mission, accomplished with surprising results even before his guerrilla army was fully constituted. He took advantage of the chaos after surrender and gathered up more volunteers, a corps of Filipino civilians willing to retrieve surrendered American weapons before the Japanese had a chance to seize them. Under Boone's command, teams of three dozen Filipinos hiked down to sea level just south of the main coastal highway that Claire had once used to drive to Pilar. "We knew we would find weapons there," Boone said. "But we were amazed to find . . . great quantities of medical supplies." It was almost a field hospital supply of ointments and antiseptics and bandages, but also drugs, including large amounts of quinine tablets. This was lifesaving medicine.

Along with the hospital supplies, they hauled in automatic weapons and crates of ammunition. The men ported everything up to Boone's base camp quickly and stealthily, knowing the Japanese could come at any moment. The hoard of drugs included sulfa drugs that would combat dysentery and other diseases, as well as injuries. Digging further, they came upon the quinine—the only reliable treatment against malaria. "Five grain

American quinine tablets," Boone said, still recalling his amazement years later. "I can remember it now. There were thousand-pill bottles" in quart-sized jugs. The contraband also included "surgical instruments and bandages and antiseptics and so forth."

The medical supplies lasted for months. After that, he realized there was one other ready way to obtain medicine and food. Claire could take on a wider role than she or Boone had originally envisioned. Boone had one more meeting with Claire while she was in the hills. He needed a base for gathering and sending intelligence reports, but he also needed critical supplies in the jungle. Claire was ready and willing to help.

Word circulated about Boone's guerrilla army, now equipped well enough to defend itself. Boone, meanwhile, was on the lookout for others who could join the fight. "I was very guerrilla conscious, because I knew that there was already an American guerrilla commander sent out behind enemy lines months before the surrender." He was referring to the already legendary exploits of Lieutenant Colonel Claude A. Thorp, who had been pre-positioned in the mountains by order of General MacArthur before the surrender of Bataan. There were Filipinos who wanted to fight and American stragglers who had not surrendered, men who were disoriented, wounded, or shell-shocked. Some of the soldiers had tried to cross the three-mile channel between Bataan and Corregidor Island; they would have been sitting ducks for Japanese spotters. Others thought they might be able to escape by island-hopping across the Philippines to Australia. A few did make the 1,500-mile trip from Mindanao in the southern Philippines to Darwin, mostly open ocean waters controlled by Japan. Some never intended to surrender—disobeying the direct order of General King to surrender amounted to desertion. Moreover, once disobeying the order, a soldier captured by the Japanese would be considered not a prisoner of war but a fugitive who could be killed on the spot.

Just after surrender, there was the case of Brigadier General William E. Brougher, commander of the Eleventh Division, who called his men together for a farewell speech as they surrendered their arms, awaiting imprisonment. Japanese troops burst into the clearing where the Americans and Filipinos had been assembled and began mowing them down with rifle and machine-gun fire. A few, such as Lieutenant Colonel Arthur

"Maxie" Noble, managed to escape into the jungle, seething with hatred and dropping any possible thought of surrender. He worked with guerrilla commanders in the hills for more than a year before being captured and tortured by the Japanese. By the end of the war he was presumed dead, but his remains were never found.

Stories such as that of Brougher's surrender contributed to the decision to head for the hills. Since Boone was one of the earliest to organize, he was able to guide and help stragglers who showed up in his camp. Two army officers, Major Frank Riley Loyd, who had come to the Philippines with his family from Texas, and Lieutenant Edwin Price Ramsey, a cavalry officer from rural Illinois, crossed paths with Boone early on, eventually worked with him, and made contact with Claire.

Before the war Frank Loyd, forty-four, had been provost marshal at Fort McKinley, just south of Manila, a job that usually involves leading a military police contingent. As the probability of war increased, General MacArthur assigned Loyd to be chief instructor of the lightly trained, poorly equipped Philippine Constabulary. It was a challenge to whip the force into fighting shape and with scant resources to outfit them as a factor to combat a Japanese invasion. Loyd lost contact with his Fourth Philippine Constabulary Regiment during fierce fighting a few days before surrender. He survived with the help of Filipinos in the hills, foraged for berries, and roasted giant lizards and monkeys before he practically crawled into Boone's camp, disabled for months by amoebic dysentery and malaria.

Lieutenant Ramsey, twenty-five, was one of hundreds of men clinging for survival on the side of a hill in sight of the coastal road north from Mariveles. Japanese Zeros strafed their position; bombs exploded around them. "Some fled for the jungle, while those of us closest to the bluff had no choice but to dive over the edge. It was terrifying; dozens of us hung there, grasping at vines and shrubs, flattened against the cliff face as plane after plane roared in, bombing and strafing. The concussions were endless, convulsing the ground, blasting our ears, and raining down on us debris of equipment and flesh." The cavalry platoon leader stumbled upon John Boone at Mount Malasimbo.

Boone was able to help both men. Frank Loyd was thinking about escape to Australia, but Boone advised against it. He sent Loyd with guides to join other guerrilla commandos at a nearby camp. He sent Ramsey to recover at a sugar plantation within two days' march of Boone's jungle headquarters. Ramsey eventually took a command position in the regional guerrilla army and promoted Boone to field commander. Boone's job was to organize a full-scale guerrilla army, thousands of other stragglers like him and Filipino soldiers, to resist the Japanese occupation. He was now circulating around Bataan, moving clandestinely at night, evading capture and looking for help. That was where Claire might figure into his planning. Once they were organized, the goal was to gather intelligence, to spy on, infiltrate, and harass the Japanese occupiers in any way possible.

Hidden in Plain Sight

Manila, April 18, 1942

SPEAKING SPANISH and flashing his diplomatic credentials, Chick Parsons had been able to roam around Manila most of early 1942. However, on April 18, 1942, ten days after the surrender of Bataan, the situation changed drastically. The Japanese occupation army reacted furiously upon word that Lieutenant Colonel Jimmy Doolittle had led a surprise U.S. bombing run on Tokyo. Doolittle's attack with sixteen U.S. Army Air Forces B-25B bombers was billed as a retaliatory strike for Pearl Harbor. The planes hit military targets and caused some damage, but bombs also hit six schools and a military hospital. Fifty people died and four hundred were wounded, including civilians. Americans back home and in Manila— news came across on the grapevine—cheered Doolittle as a hero exacting vengeance. Unsubstantiated rumors circulated in Japan, though, that the American raid had caused hundreds of civilian deaths. The Kempeitai staged an indiscriminate roundup of non-Asians around Manila, slapped Caucasians in the face when they encountered them on the street, arrested some and beat and tortured or threw them into dungeons. Despite his Panamanian diplomatic credentials, Parsons was imprisoned at Fort Santiago—the citadel where newspaper editor Roy C. Bennett still was being held incommunicado. Fort Santiago had quickly become the feared location for the Japanese occupiers to torture and break prisoners. Parsons did not give details about his treatment at Fort Santiago. He confessed nothing, and the Japanese never explained why he had been detained; they had no evidence other than his status as a businessman and Panamanian diplomat. After some days he was released to Santo Tomas and then to a Manila hospital on medical leave. Though he said nothing specific, he was treated for a kidney ailment, often associated with water-boarding, a frequent Japanese torture tactic. Water-boarding had been used for centuries, but the practice first came to wide U.S. public attention during the Spanish-American War; American soldiers in the Philippines often used the technique on prisoners.

When he was arrested, Parsons told his wife to destroy the documents and reports he had been compiling in the weeks since occupation. Katsy decided not to do it. "My mom apparently thought the items too important to destroy," Peter Parsons said. "Aside from the fact that we were being observed indoors and outdoors by our four [Japanese] sentries." Finally Parsons was free to go home one last time; the Japanese occupation authorities announced that diplomats could expect to be repatriated to their home countries. When he came home, Katsy had a surprise. In the weeks of Chick's absence, she and her mother had gathered Chick's intelligence reports and added even more material: messages "from his far-flung guerrilla contacts," names and identification of several hundred prisoners of war, and various propaganda documents that might help the war effort.

"Where is it?" Parsons asked his wife.

"It's all here," Katsy said proudly.

"Where?"

"In the little suitcase, under the baby's diapers."

"Good God!"

Hiding the documents in one-year-old Patrick's diaper bag was a fine tactic, assuming that their luggage was never searched.

Meanwhile, on June 4 Chick received word from the Japanese consul general that tacitly reaffirmed his diplomatic status: He and the family would be allowed to leave Manila on a Japanese ship, the *Ural Maru*. He eventually learned that the voyage was part of an exchange of diplomats and civilians with the United States arranged by neutral nations.

Chick Parsons's final evening in Manila gave a hint at his strange, charmed life. As president of Luzon Stevedoring Company, he was actually running a Japanese firm, the Nihon Kogyo Kabushiki Kaisha. The subsidiary had been given an English name under U.S. commercial laws requiring that local companies be majority U.S.-owned. In effect, Parsons was the president of a Japanese company. His nationality was well known to Japanese residents of Manila, and someone easily could have turned him in. Instead, his friend Pete Yamanuchi, a photographer, stopped by on the evening of June 7 for a warm send-off that included a case of beer. Yamanuchi, like Parsons, had been called to active duty—as a Japanese naval officer. The two friends from enemy nations drank and talked into the night and then bade each other luck and farewell.

The following morning Chick and Katsy rode to the Port of Manila with their children, prepared for the first leg of the trip to China and onward to safety. The voyage was overshadowed by the fear that the secret documents might be discovered. At the pier, officials told all the passengers to line up with their luggage and prepare for a search. Parsons was prepared. He had brought along a little fishing pole attached to a piece of string. He gave the pole, along with the diaper case, to his middle son, Peter, who now had turned five. He told him to use the little suitcase as a seat and to go and try to catch some fish over the side of the dock. But whatever you do, his father said, *Do not let go of the bag!*

The boy dutifully listened to his father, walked to the side of the dock, and dangled his feet over the water, clutching the diaper bag. "I never even let go when a Jap soldier came over, put me on his lap and started giving me candy," Peter recalled as an adult more than half a century later. "I was supposed to be fishing but my line only had a piece of bread at its end, no hook. The guard thought this was hilarious." The soldier kept laughing and began asking the boy questions in Japanese. He laughed even more when this boy with European features answered him in Japanese—Peter had picked up the language from guards at the Manila house during those months of the occupation. "I still remember the fish that came up to nibble at my line and the Jap soldier laughing at me."

Meanwhile, a stern Japanese customs official looked over the Parsonses' larger suitcase and asked Chick why he had declared two pieces of luggage when he was only carrying the one. Parsons said he had been confused—he had counted the small briefcase in his hand that contained their travel papers and passports as a second item. The man moved on to the next family, and the Japanese soldiers led Peter back to his parents, patting him on the head while he held on to the incriminating diaper bag in all earnestness. The boy could not have comprehended the moment. Discovery of the documents inside most likely would have meant torture and death for Parsons and detention or worse for the rest of the family. Instead, they were ushered through, boarded the *Ural Maru,* and set sail for Takao, Formosa. From then on, they were officially designated a diplomatic family, honored with all immunity. Two days later they traveled by plane from Formosa to Shanghai. There Chick Parsons, the honorable Panamanian consul to the Philippines, was interviewed on Japanese-controlled news media. Yes, he said, he had just come from Manila. The Japanese are doing a fine job in Manila, he said. "He said he was impressed by the strength of the Japanese military and by the efficiency of their occupation of Manila."

They boarded the exchange ship *Conte Verde* in Shanghai and reached the neutral Indian Ocean Port of Lourenço Marques in Portuguese East Africa on July 22; there the Swedish exchange ship *Gripsholm* awaited them, ready to transfer Japanese passengers bound for Tokyo in the other side of the prisoner and detainee trade. Parsons, his family, and more than 1,400 other Americans then sailed for the Western Hemisphere. The *Gripsholm* arrived on August 10 in Rio de Janeiro, where Brazilians cheered the passengers. Newspapers were already reporting that U.S. officials feared the Japanese had planted spies among the passengers. The ship continued northward, hugging the Atlantic shore up the East Coast of the United States to New York, where it arrived on August 25, 1942. Until that moment Parsons had been listed officially on navy rolls as missing in action. He had managed to slip through the Japanese intelligence net by just walking out through the front door and taking his entire family and intelligence documents along with him.

Lieutenant Charles Parsons, U.S. Naval Reserve, stood proudly on deck when the *Gripsholm* entered port, with the Statue of Liberty before him, now ready to fight World War II. Moments later he was under arrest. FBI agents came on board at dockside and took him into custody. Nothing personal, the agents said. The attorney general of the United States, Francis Biddle, had ordered the detention of hundreds of those on board, and Parsons was just one of them. "Every precaution must be taken in time of war to prevent enemy agents slipping across our borders. We have already had experience with them and we know them to be well trained and clever."

As Parsons did a slow burn, the agents looked at the specifics and asked him why exactly the Japanese had released him. He told the truth, that they had accepted his status as the consul general of Panama, a neutral country. The agents also may have had access to the interview Parsons had given while still technically a Japanese prisoner in Shanghai. Could he even prove he was who he said he was? The FBI suspected him of being an enemy spy. While the State Department and Naval Intelligence sorted it out, Parsons and family were held in detention. Parsons fumed. When it was over, he told the FBI investigators "they were nearly as bad as the Kempeitai."

Back from Bataan

Bataan, June 2, 1942

THE TIME HAD finally come to get out of the hills. Claire spoke with Carling once more, and this time he agreed. With the American Army defeated, it would be somewhat easier to move around. If Claire had the energy after weeks suffering from malaria, they could now try to get her to Manila. She was ready, but it had taken months to organize the trip.

Ever since her meetings with Boone, Claire had been ready and eager to take him up on his offer. If she had a plan about how to become a spy, she told no one. However, Claire was bold and unconventional, and she never took the easy road. She had been scraping a life together ever since she quit high school. She had no experience dealing with the Japanese, but she had the will to fight and had developed hatred for the Japanese these last months in Bataan. This much was evident: She would have to establish herself in Manila and avoid detention; most of her friends were already locked up at Santo Tomas. If she could do that, she would have to make contacts and earn money. Only then could she figure out a plan to help the war effort by supplying Boone. She also wanted to pick up the trail of John Phillips. If he was still alive, he would be a prisoner somewhere, but she had no idea how to find him. There was much planning to be done; once in Manila, she would have to approach the Japanese and somehow earn their trust. Then she would need a way to establish contact with Boone from Manila, probably with help from Carling Sobreviñas. A young Filipino, Damian, who had been serving as her guide and helper, might be the perfect conduit. It would require an official transit pass, and locals usually had no trouble coming by foot if necessary or via public transportation, including the trains that traveled north from Manila to Baguio and beyond. Increasingly, Carling was sneaking back and forth to Manila when he had to, but always at night to minimize the chance of coming across Japanese sentries who demanded paperwork. Apparently, even he did not have a pass yet.

The steaming spring of 1942 advanced toward the hottest days of the year. Claire was besieged by rats and bugs, covered by lice and fleas; she would have leaped out of this hellish existence, but for more than a month she was too weak to even get out of bed. She was hardly able to move or even write in her diary from April 18 to late May.

The fever broke by early June, and though she was still feeling shaky, Claire finally had to try to get down to Manila. Carling understood better how to manage schedules for crossing Japanese control points on the road back to the city. One advantage was that with the cessation of fighting, the Japanese occupation authorities had cut back on wartime blackout and martial law provisions. There had been a dawn-to-dusk curfew since January, but as of May 18 they had heard that the curfew was only from midnight to daybreak, and officials also said they would suspend the requirement for passes to travel from one province to another. That should make it easier for Claire on the road from Bataan, but as a European-looking woman, she would still be suspect if found traveling into Manila.

Carling had worked out a relatively safe plan with Boone, who had a stake in getting Claire to Manila. They had tried for weeks to find someone who would prepare fake documents or some other travel papers for Claire. "I've tried my best to get a pass for you," he had said. "But everyone is afraid to help an American. All of my friends said that sooner or later you will be caught and sent to Santo Tomás." Finally Carling found someone who could forge a document with a fake name and authorization.

Nevertheless, the best thing was to avoid getting caught. The forged travel pass identified Claire as a Filipina authorized to be on the road. She would leave all other papers with Carling, who would bury them back at the settlement for the time being. John Boone came down for one final meeting with Claire to offer any last-minute help and advice. Claire would find a way to start gathering information about the Japanese. They agreed that Damian eventually would come down to Manila and keep Boone informed.

Claire set out with Carling on Tuesday, June 2. The first five miles or so followed dark paths out of the mountains and beyond Dinalupihan, eventually south along more hidden trails. After several hours they came to a road and Claire piled onto a truck with Carling and twenty other people. The truck was loaded with sacks of charcoal and other supplies as it bounced along the rutted roads of Bataan carrying about twenty very uncomfortable people to Manila. The air felt heavy and hot after the long march from the mountains. The rainy season was starting; perhaps the rain would not come tonight.

She may have drifted asleep and then nodded alert again. The recurrent malaria attack had left her shivering in the humidity and the heat with fever that wasted her energy and made it impossible to think clearly.

Jostled by the other passengers and bumps that shifted the sacks of charcoal, she was covered by soot. To all appearances Claire was just a sick peasant among many, but if a suspicious Japanese soldier took a closer look—and Carling hoped one would not—there was something suspicious about this particular peasant. She was taller than most of those around her. That might lead to discovery of the fake travel pass. Male or female, despite the suntan, the rough clothing, the soot, and the scraggly hair, she did not have the features of a Filipina.

Carling had planned it so Claire would arrive in Manila well before the midnight curfew. If the Japanese found out that one of the people on the truck was far from a peasant, she could be killed on the spot. Just transporting an enemy alien was punishable by death.

Coming down from the hills represented a new beginning for Claire as much as a dangerous foray directly into the Pacific war. Claire would be more than a bit player, more than a person who shuffled from place to place, job to job, man to man. A high school dropout who worked as a circus performer, dancer, and nightclub singer half her life now had decided to join the guerrilla underground that was challenging the Japanese occupation of the Philippines. How could an American woman from Portland, Oregon, survive in war-torn Manila?

She asked herself that question every day. The only answer was that she had survived so far. In six months she had grown hardened to suffering and war, angered by the death she had seen, and prepared to do what she could to challenge the Japanese. She had one advantage—she knew how to adapt and deceive. The way to spy on the Japanese was to carry on as she always had. No one really knew who she was. She kept it that way.

They rode to the outskirts of Manila by evening and to Dewey Boulevard along Manila Bay shortly after. Although she felt ill, Claire was ready to celebrate. They stopped at the Luneta Hotel café to collect the steak dinner promised by their friend Emilio Reyes, the deposed mayor of Dinalupihan, who had bet jokingly that they wouldn't make it. "A clever ruse," Sobreviñas bragged, "I smuggled her to Manila right under the very noses of the Japanese." The celebration went beyond curfew and Claire slept that night at the hotel, by far the best accommodations she had experienced in six months. For some reason the curfew extended to noon the following day, June 3. Claire rested and bathed and was ready when the streets were open again. She made her way to Judge Roxas's house on Batanga Street in the midafternoon. Despite misgivings about the danger of hiding a fugitive American, the judge and his family welcomed Claire warmly; they could see that she was exhausted from her months in the mountains. She took heart, though her reunion with little Dian did not go well. The two-year-old did not recognize Claire after two months of separation. Claire collapsed in utter exhaustion and stayed in bed for some time.

"It was necessary for my family doctor to take care of her for a certain period," Roxas recalled. The doctor said that the malaria had left her anemic and that she had a case of scurvy; he prescribed vitamins and iron to restore her blood counts. There were other problems, including a persistent eye infection that blurred her vision and frightened her. He referred her to an eye specialist; her eyes were covered with sores and abscesses that had to be cleaned; she said her vision was never good after that. Meanwhile, the possibility of chronic relapses of malaria was always lurking, and she was susceptible to colds and spent days in bed.

Claire did not intend to lie still for long. She wrote in her diary that she was feeling like "the girl in *Rebecca*," the 1940 Hitchcock film about a young woman who suddenly finds herself having the run of an opulent mansion. The only difference, Claire said, was that "this is a rich relation's home, not mine." Twenty-five people and eight servants were living at the Roxas home. She was well taken care of and could complain only that she was "eating like a pig" because "everything tastes so good."

The rich relations she was referring to, of course, were the cousins of Manuel Fuentes, her husband, who had been caught out of the Philippines on an American ship when the war started. If alive, he was probably doing something for the war effort. No one knew and it did not seem to trouble Claire. She had already told Boone that she was married to John Phillips, and Boone had taken to calling her Claire Phillips. By the time she arrived in Manila, she had taken Phillips's name as her own. Even after the war, Phillips's name would be a lasting memorial to him and his comrades, prisoners or those who had died in the Japanese invasion. But few if any in Manila would hear her use that name.

PART TWO

. . .

Occupation

A Brave New World

Manila, June 1942

As CLAIRE LOOKED out on Manila, nothing was immediately different. Few buildings had been bombed in the city proper during the Japanese takeover. Streetcars ambled along the main avenues, fashionably dressed people walked the streets, commerce was brisk. People, cars, trucks, and carts crushed together in the open markets and on the streets; shoppers jostled and elbowed looking for sugar and rice, meat and fish, and buckets and soap powder. It was the city it had always been. But a closer look showed stark changes. Japanese soldiers wearing white pith helmets and bearing rifles patrolled the streets. Japanese plainclothesmen, recognizable as cops, eyed people with suspicion as they passed by. Japanese officers expected civilians to make way, bow deeply, or risk the consequences. People with European features could expect a sneer and extra scrutiny, including random ID checks. Protest was futile and dangerous. Manila would now follow the rules of the Empire of Japan.

The military occupiers had moved quickly to declare a new regime with new rules. They urged compliance and understanding, arguing that Japan had freed the country "from the oppressive domination of the U.S.A., letting you establish the Philippines for the Filipinos as a member of the Co-prosperity Sphere in the Greater East Asia." This was "Asia for the Asians."

In the early days of the occupation, residents of Manila remained off the street, disbelieving those words of friendship. Most people never bought into the rhetoric. They were shoved and slapped and pushed and cajoled from the outset. So they hid their cars when rumors proved true that Japanese soldiers were commandeering vehicles at will and prayed that their houses would not be confiscated as well. Despite every token effort and every claim the Japanese made in favor of the great friendship their two countries enjoyed, the Filipinos quickly learned to hate the Japanese and the life imposed upon them.

The occupation authorities were well prepared to challenge and punish misguided pro-American holdouts. They created a neighborhood watch system that divided Manila into a grid in which designated district and neighborhood leaders were responsible for the good behavior of those in their territory. It was a system ripe for snitching and false accusations. Regulations for the neighborhood watch went in both directions; residents were expected to "be on guard against activities of bandit or bandits or suspicious character or characters and to report the same immediately to the constabulary officers, the leader of a neighborhood association or other competent authorities." Meanwhile, a neighborhood leader was expected to "prevail upon residents within the area or areas under his jurisdiction not to commit illegal or unlawful acts . . . and to hold himself or herself responsible with regard thereto." Within the regulations was a warning: Residents were expected to inform on others; if they did not, the consequences could be dire. The call for questioning at Fort Santiago was tantamount to an invitation to a torture session and possible death.

Rumors of torture replaced actual testimony, although many people lucky enough to survive Fort Santiago feared even admitting to having been there in the first place. "The last thing we are told before leaving that bastille is that we must keep our mouths shut about what we have seen, heard or experienced during our incarceration," said one survivor. "And if we violate those orders it means re-arrest. . . . Do not ask me to tell you about the beatings and the torturers for my blood turns cold whenever I think of them."

Japanese officials combined organization and rhetoric with enforcement. Resistance was to be expected: The Americans had been running the islands as their most important Asian outpost since the Spanish-American War. The Japanese commandeered radio and the newspapers and hammered at the notion that their arrival amounted to liberation from the Americans, that benevolent plan to return Asia to the Asians. Those who did not accept that, they warned, would suffer the consequences as traitors. Foreign radio broadcasts were banned and foreign newspapers could not be imported; for that matter all broadcasts in English were prohibited by decree—this was to be temporarily suspended while Filipinos got used to speaking Japanese, the language of their Asian brothers and benefactors. People took to lowering their voices and listening to the news in the dark at very low volume—in the Manila heat, the windows were always open and radios might be overheard on the street.

When declarations of friendship and voluntary compliance weren't enough, they stepped up the repression. Intelligence agents discovered a clandestine printing operation run by two well-known men, José and Eduardo Fajardo, brothers who responded to the Japanese call to celebrate Emperor Hirohito's birthday on April 29 by distributing leaflets that urged a boycott. The Kempeitai announced on June 25 that the Fajardos and six other men had been executed. It was the start of a comprehensive intelligence campaign in Manila to search for anti-Japanese activities. The military police fanned out to compare the typeface of the leaflets with the characteristics of every printing press throughout the city. After halting the Fajardo operation, they went progressively further. Soon they were requiring every typewriter in the country to be brought in for registration. The goal was to create a detailed file for each, including owner, make, model, and serial number, along with a sample printed page using every key on the machine. They intended to do the same thing with mimeographs and printing presses. While it was a meticulous, ultimately impossible task, the attempt would make potential perpetrators think twice about taking the risk. The message: You will be caught.

Next officials extended the ban on Western radio broadcasts. Soon they were requiring everyone in the country to bring their radios to police headquarters, where they were to be altered so that only authorized stations could be received. In practice many people did comply, but some brought in one radio and then hid spares that still could receive open broadcasts. Shortwave radios hidden under floorboards continued to haul in stations broadcasting war news to U.S. forces at sea and to anyone else who could listen. Despite the dangers, people defied Japanese authorities and risked imprisonment and death to distribute newsletters that compiled information from the illegal shortwave receivers. Thus, despite Japanese propaganda, Filipinos had a good idea about the progress of the war at home and on both the Pacific and European fronts. Japan was losing the war of information.

It was lucky that Claire had a few days to recover at Judge Roxas's house so she could begin to understand the basic guidelines of occupation. The judge was an important person to know, but he was in a precarious position. He was the older brother of General Manuel Roxas, the Philippine government liaison to General MacArthur before the war. The general, a former speaker of the Philippine House of Representatives and finance secretary under President Manuel L. Quezon, had traveled south to Mindanao after December 8, planning to start a guerrilla insurgency there. Japanese forces had captured and imprisoned him; rumors circulated that he had been executed. The Roxases were influential and had friends who were major power players in Manila's business community. Among them was Juan Elizalde, the wealthy owner of a major brewery and distillery who secretly sought ways to oppose the Japanese occupation. He was also friends with Chick Parsons, who had sailed out of Manila Bay four days after Claire had managed to sneak back into the city. Parsons had already touched base with Elizalde and others about organizing underground operations.

Judge Roxas played the role of supporting the occupation and the puppet government. He was friends with many who had signed on with the Japanese; collaboration was controversial and dangerous, but some of the collaborators were secretly pro-American and waiting for an opportunity to subvert Japanese rule. Pragmatically Filipinos, whether under the Japanese or under the Americans before them, needed rational governance. They needed leaders dedicated to public welfare and responsible for maintaining services, utilities, and food supplies and keeping transportation operating as well as possible.

In the tightly knit, family-oriented life of Manila, everyone in the neighborhood would likely know that Claire was the wife of Manuel Fuentes and thereby the judge's cousin by marriage. Her presence would not raise suspicion that the judge was harboring a fugitive. Yet since she did not appear to be Asian, it still made sense for the judge to establish some rules to avoid attracting the attention of Japanese authorities.

The judge laid down a series of "suggestions," including one that she was "not to leave the house except when absolutely necessary in view of the danger to herself and to us." Should Claire go outside, she was to limit the time on the street and she had to remain close to home. Non-Asians would be noticeable and an attractive woman would stick out even more. Look no Japanese soldier in the eye and bow carefully and deeply to every soldier she saw, Roxas warned. Japanese guards slapped people in the face or beat them when they failed to bow. And once that happened, who knew what might follow? People had been left lying in the street; some had died.

However, Judge Roxas knew well enough that Claire rarely followed the rules, and he was not surprised to see her start causing trouble almost as soon as she got out of bed. Claire apparently decided that the best way to start her career as a spy was to find out if she could make friends with the enemy. One day the judge was distressed to see that Claire had gone out and was not listening to him. "I saw her in a refreshment parlor with two Japanese officers."

The judge had no idea what to make of this and told his wife, Mercedes, with some alarm as soon as he got home. Mercedes was neither concerned nor surprised. Claire had told Roxas's wife forthrightly that she was preparing to work with the underground and that she wanted to spy on the Japanese. "It must have been because of this that I saw her in the company of Japanese officers."

Friendly or not with the Japanese, Roxas needed a plan that would keep Claire and the family safe. As Filipinos the Roxases were subject to unannounced visits by Japanese authorities, especially if Claire was seen coming and going. She could not remain at the house without regularizing her status; she was a danger to herself but a greater danger to the judge and his family, especially since the name "Roxas" sent up warning flags. The judge figured that the best alternative sometimes was the most straightforward option. He explained his plan to Claire, who was not accustomed to doing anything the simple way. Roxas said that the idea was just to acknowledge who she was—an American woman in Manila—but that as the wife of Manuel Fuentes, she was also a citizen of the Philippines, presented no danger, and should not be detained. "We agreed that I was to write a letter to the chief of the military police telling him that although [she] was an American, having been born in America, legally she was a Filipino being legitimately married to a Filipino and that her parents were Italians."

Japanese military police headquarters responded quickly, perhaps because of Judge Roxas's prominence. Send her in, said Lieutenant Colonel Seichi Ohta, the chief of the Kempeitai, the elite Japanese military police force. She was to appear at Ohta's office at Fort Santiago headquarters on the morning of Wednesday, June 10. Roxas sent along one of his assistants and gave Claire another piece of advice: Do not speak unless spoken to. Let the Japanese officers do most of the talking.

A trip to Fort Santiago was fear producing, yet the relaxed atmosphere surprised Claire that morning. Far from menacing, a uniformed guard stationed at the front gate looked up from a first-grade reading book when they arrived, ready to practice his English. He ushered Claire and the assistant quickly through the gate to Ohta's office. Ohta asked Claire to confirm what the judge had written:

> Her husband Manuel Fuentes was casually in the United States having gone there to fetch her a little before the outbreak of the war, without knowing that she had already taken a ship bound for the Philippines . . . that she had come to my house from a province in Northern Luzon where she evacuated when war was declared, and that being an American, I thought it proper to inform the Military Police of the fact of her stay in my house and that I was asking for instruction as to what to be done.

She promised that everything the judge had written was true. Ohta was satisfied and said Claire "could continue living in [Roxas's] house, and that she should refrain from performing any act showing hostility to the Japanese Armed Forces." The entire visit to Fort Santiago had taken no more than half an hour, and Claire was back with Roxas more quickly than expected.

Now that she was legal and healthy, the time had come to prepare to meet her commitment to John Boone. Claire had several priorities: One was to earn enough money to support herself and to keep Dian, now two and a half, healthy and safe. Next was to set up a regular information and supply run to Boone. She also desperately wanted to find John Phillips, who remained close to her heart.

Claire was adding to the list of aliases that always seemed to keep her ahead of detection by old suitors and free from unwanted scrutiny. Her official documentation with Japanese authorities specified that she was the wife of a Philippine national, Manuel Fuentes. She kept the name "Fuentes" and decided that her first names (Clara, her birth name; Claire, her stage name; and Maybelle, her middle name) would not do. She decided to change names again, apparently for purposes of confusing authorities. She took up a name that she had used on the street back when she was arrested in Seattle. She would now call herself Dorothy Fuentes.

Becoming Madame Tsubaki

Manila, August 1942

AFTER A FEW WEEKS of rest and recovery prescribed by her doctor, along with doses of quinine, vitamins, and good food, Claire launched herself fully into the new world of occupied Manila. At first she took on the role of volunteer nurse, an extension of what she had been doing in the mountains of Bataan.

Judge Roxas's sister and sister-in-law invited her to join them at a training course at the Red Cross. She also got a quick lesson in sewing nurse uniforms. "I borrowed their patterns and promptly turned myself out two uniforms. The three of us reported for duty on the following Monday." By the end of July, she was a part-time volunteer assigned to twenty patients on a ward at the Remedios Hospital. She used contacts whenever she could to seek information about her lost lover, John Phillips, but no one had heard of him.

The Japanese condoned volunteer work of this sort, so Claire was abiding by Judge Roxas's admonition that she stay out of trouble. However, she kept up with the nursing only long enough to plot a more dangerous course. Judge Roxas was not surprised when, despite the explicit warning from Lieutenant Colonel Ohta of the Kempeitai against anti-Japanese activity, Claire finally admitted that she had other work in mind. She told the judge that she was reaching out to others who wanted to fight clandestinely against the occupation. She "continued with her underground activities, joining a group of Filipinos, who were devoted principally to sending money and foodstuffs to the American prisoners who were in an internment camp in one of the provinces in Central Luzon."

She also felt she was overstaying her welcome and knew that he could not approve of what she was doing. Her underground operations might cause him trouble. In Japanese eyes, the judge had vouched for Claire's loyalty, and he might be held responsible for anything she might do.

After about ten weeks living at Judge Roxas's house, Claire, along with Dian and their new Chinese nursemaid, Ah Ho, moved back to the Dakota Apartments, where they had lived before war broke out. Out on her own, Claire needed money to meet expenses and then to set up a way to send support to Boone. She went back to what she knew best—singing and dancing. She got a job for twenty-five dollars a week plus tips at Ana Fey's, a nightclub in the Ermita section of Manila close to the bay and not far from Intramuros and Luneta Park. Ana Fey's was popular among Japanese soldiers and people with money. It was one of dozens of clubs in Manila before and during the Japanese occupation. The importance of such clubs to the Philippine economy grew exponentially during occupation, when jobs were scarce and the prices of food, medicine, clothing, and other products were spiking. Singers and orchestras performed while the hostesses circulated and sat with single men—now mostly Japanese soldiers or Japanese businessmen visiting town. The women would flirt and coax the men to buy beer, wine, and whiskey while ordering drinks for the women. The girls pretended to be drinking wine and champagne but drank cheap nonalcoholic beverages instead to run up the bar tab of the men they were with. At the end of the night, the women kept a portion of the drink tab, along with tips for whatever service they might provide.

Unemployment was high after the Japanese invasion; the women working in the clubs did not brag about the nature of their jobs; the bars were a perfect setting for prostitution, which offered much more income than bar tabs and tips. Women and some gay and transvestite men who had lost their jobs when war broke out or could no longer go to their schools and universities opted instead to work at one of the clubs, often earning more in a week than they could earn before the war in a month. There were well-known hotels that catered to such action within walking distance. A woman who was a child in Manila during the occupation said that there was no doubt that nightclubs in Manila were not just gathering places for innocent chat and socializing. Women could turn tricks with the Japanese soldiers and make good money. "Make no mistake," said the woman, adding that she was speaking from personal experience, "no matter what they said or didn't say, that was the only reason that the clubs were so popular."

Ana Fey's was one of the early hot spots in Manila under the Japanese occupation. Part of the reason undoubtedly was her liaison with a man named Horiuchi, a correspondent for the Tokyo newspaper *Asahi Shimbun*. Claire also noted that Ana Fey was able to function normally even though she was Jewish, one of the odd characteristics of occupation in the Pacific. She carried a German passport, and that meant freedom even if she looked like an American or spoke English. A number of Americanized or American-educated German Jews in the Philippines managed to remain free; the Japanese alliance with Nazi Germany was strong, but the Japanese did not bother to treat Jewish Germans differently from other Germans, even when hard-line Nazi diplomats complained. Claire described Ana Fey as "a tiny, doll-like little person with platinum blond hair and baby blue eyes." Claire fell quickly into the routine of singing and was happy to be making some money. One night in late September, Ana Fey asked her to serve as a hostess between songs, to sit with and entertain certain high rollers; problems soon developed. Claire said that a Japanese officer had slapped her after she refused to bring ice for his drink and summoned a waiter instead. Claire slapped him back; striking a Japanese officer was dangerous and possibly lethal. Other officers held the officer back and he calmed down a bit. After negotiations, Claire was going to have to pay. She was forced to submit to a beating in a back room so the Japanese officer could make up for the insult and embarrassment. Rather than trying to intercede, Claire's boss stood guard at the door while she was kicked and beaten. Ana Fey then told Claire to cover up her bruises and return to the club floor. She stumbled through the rest of the night, but she had been beaten badly enough that, even with her bruises covered by makeup, she couldn't return to the club for several days.

Claire's time at Ana Fey's amounted to a long lesson on how to deal with Japanese officers. The beating was bad, but it could have been worse. She had heard that a hostess at another club had thrown beer in a Japanese officer's face and he had killed her on the spot. Other stories about atrocities had been circulating that frightened and angered Claire. She had seen a man brought in with a hernia caused by a kick from a Japanese soldier. She heard of another patient hospitalized after a soldier batted him in the head with a saber sheath.

Claire knew her own nature and it was hard for her to take an insult, whatever the consequences. Claire blamed Ana Fey for not standing up for her, though probably unfairly. Ana Fey likely could not have done anything to help her even if she tried and might also have been beaten in return. The Japanese were going to win any argument.

When she complained to her friends at the club, they suggested she go out on her own and open a competing nightclub. If she kept her temper, she could be her own boss, and even challenge the supremacy of Ana Fey's and other hot spots. The friends, Felicidad Corcuera and Judith Geronimo, encouraged her and said they would come along to the new club. Claire liked the idea.

She approached several people who could loan her some money; Chan, a sympathetic, trustworthy Chinese restaurant owner on Mabini Street not far from Ana Fey's, came through. He agreed to lend her money for rent and renovations and suggested she choose a second-floor space once used as a restaurant and dancing school nearby at the corner of San Luis and Mabini streets, a few blocks from Dewey Boulevard, where she and John Phillips had strolled and looked out at Manila Bay. As collateral Claire gave Chan two rings and two hundred dollars in U.S. bills—useless during the occupation—and promised to repay him in pesos. Judith and Felicidad—Fely for short—were popular headliners at Ana Fey's and would be a great draw at the new club. Fely, twenty-two, was a star attraction. She had studied business and accounting at the University of Manila before the war, but she now specialized in Japanese folk songs. She even chipped in a little money on her own to help Claire set things up. Other hostesses also came along, including Fahny, a Filipina with African features whose father was American and had been detained at Santo Tomas. These were important relationships. Claire trusted the women and knew that they were pro-American. Judith Geronimo recommended her brother Mamerto, eighteen, who came along as a bartender. Mamerto was acquainted with important businessmen in town, such as Juan Elizalde, the popular polo player and businessman who had begun running a secret insurgency to undermine the Japanese occupation. He also knew Chick Parsons.

Within three months of her return to the city, Claire had connections to people who would soon be playing an important role in intelligence gathering for General MacArthur. They were committed to fighting and subverting the Japanese occupation on behalf of the United States; the question was how one could best fight the Japanese inside Manila. Judge Roxas was trying to maintain proper relations with the Japanese occupation and with the Philippine leaders chosen for the government, including his old friend José Laurel, now interior minister. Claire and the others were preparing to defy the occupation.

As Claire got ready to open her nightclub, the best thing was to have an amicable break with Judge Roxas. She decided to do it aboveboard, something uncharacteristic for her—she formally asked the judge's permission. Claire told the judge that she had "decided to open a nightclub with the end, according to her, of getting more contact with Japanese officials who much frequented the nightclubs and also for the purpose of earning more money to enable her to continue sending help to the American prisoners. And she asked me for permission to leave my house." He feared the consequences, but the judge acquiesced. He could certainly understand the desire to fight the Japanese.

Claire's nightclub was in a wooden building in a prime location across the street from Luneta Park, set back behind a gate; downstairs were a furniture store and an illicit gambling parlor. Claire had the second floor, an open space with a sweeping, broad stairway leading up to the entrance. A workman came in to paint the walls a cream color; she brought in an electrician to install accent lighting and a spotlight, and she set up a stylish entrance, a main room with cocktail tables, and room for dancing and a stage for a show and small house band. Claire and Fely hung off-white and pastel curtains. She saved money by renting furniture. "I lined the walls with comfortable low-slung rattan settees and occasional portable armchairs. In front of the settees, low cocktail tables provided space for drinks and ashtrays. The whole effect was that of a luxurious lounge, rather than of a restaurant or cocktail bar." Claire asked advice from one of her more ardent admirers at Ana Fey's—Mr. Hochima—a Japanese man who was in the mining business. She told him she wanted it to be a high-class operation that would attract well-heeled civilians and Japanese officers. The businessman suggested a distinctive Japanese name—Tsubaki Club. *Tsubaki* meant camellia, a vibrant flower much loved in Japan. The word evoked a lush air of exclusivity. Hochima also suggested that they set up a side area for privacy—the kind of privacy that would bring more tips for hostesses and revenue for Claire's business.

Claire decided that Tsubaki Club would not prepare food; it would

serve beer and liquor along with hors d'oeuvres and snacks such as peanuts, crackers, and eggs, along with cheese and corned beef, when available. If guests wanted something more, Chan was ready to send over
orders from his Chinese restaurant. The liquor was no problem at all. Juan
Elizalde, as owner of the biggest distillery in town, already was secretly
organizing to operate against the Japanese. When Juan found out what
Claire planned to do, he made things easy. He provided a constant supply
so that Claire "was able to get large quantities at practically no price at all;
he found out what I was doing, and he said we were all working together
and it didn't make any difference." Besides the alcohol, Claire said Juan
Elizalde also gave her some start-up funding.

She did not forget that she would be competing with other such clubs,
including Ana Fey's, and looked for an edge. While Ana Fey had a piano
player who accompanied the singers, Fely put together a quartet that specialized in traditional Hawaiian music as well as standards. Fahny brought
in her sisters, Anna and Lily, as hostesses, and Claire hired five waiters,
including an attractive young man named David, who danced as he served
drinks and participated in the floor shows.

When the preparations were done, Claire advertised the opening of
the club in the *Manila Tribune*, still publishing mostly in English with an
occasional article in Japanese. The paper had become a propaganda sheet,
widely read by people around town, including Japanese officers and businessmen. Opening night was Saturday, October 17.

Opening Night
Manila, October 17, 1942

"COME ONE, COME ALL," read the advertisement in the *Manila Tribune*.
"Under New Management. Tsubaki Club." And they did come, standing
room only. Japanese officers, businessmen, and the Filipinos who worked
with them crowded into the nightclub a few blocks from the Port of Manila. Claire had a commanding spot at the top of the regal staircase. She
was dressed in a leggy, "clinging, halter-necked white evening gown."
High society and top Japanese occupation officials appeared, just as Claire
had hoped, opting for something new on the night scene. Mr. Hochima—

Claire's admirer and consultant on naming the nightclub—came along with some mining friends. Also attending was a Japanese conductor and composer, Mr. Ichikawa, who became a regular because he had fallen for the lovely Fely, the twenty-two-year-old with the creamy complexion and intoxicating smile who could coo in Japanese as well as in English and Tagalog.

Claire was able to attract for the opening Colonel Jiro Saito, the head of the Japanese propaganda office, who lent official endorsement and acceptance of Tsubaki Club by the Japanese administration. That brought in luminaries of the arts and politics who regularly toured the Philippines and other occupied territories as part of the effort to promote Japanese culture. The Tokyo film star Seizaburô Kawazu attended, among other visiting celebrities. Colonel Saito brought with him other officers, including several army doctors, along with George Terada, a Japanese American businessman who was in good standing with the occupiers. Claire said Juan Elizalde also came to the opening. The Japanese assumed he was interested in business and nothing more. When anyone asked, "Who is responsible? Whose club is this?" one could nod toward the woman in the long dress and say: "Madame Tsubaki." It became her latest alias.

The Hawaiian combo played, smoke wafted to the rafters, and soldiers gathered at tables and settees, surrounded by Madame Tsubaki's comely hostesses. When everything seemed right, the floor show began. The music turned to rhythmic drums and a chant with origins in the mountains of Luzon. A few of the hostesses—now wearing traditional robes, barefoot, and carrying woven reed baskets—danced in unison, ready to sow the seeds of the folkloric Filipino rice-planting dance.

> *Kay págkasawíng-pálad*
> *Ng iníanák sa hírap,*
> *Ang bísig kung di íunát,*
> *Di kumíta ng pílak.*

The syncopated rhythm, the drums, the coordinated movements, the smiles of the young dancers, the fine threads of their garments did not betray the meaning of the sad folk song of people oppressed and broken under the sun. The song was about "hands becoming tired from working in the mud . . . then harvesting and husking," they sang, "shaking the trays, throwing the imaginary grains in the air, and blowing away the chaff."

> It is a misfortune
> To be born poor,
> If one doesn't work
> One doesn't earn . . .

The dancers raised their baskets to the sky and to each side, forward and back, thrusting downward as if to sow the rice plants.

> Bent from morn till set of sun,
> Cannot stand and cannot sit,
> Cannot rest for a little bit.

Moving a bit faster now to a quickened drum, they twirled as their baskets came close to the ground. The women set the baskets on the floor and let out rhythmic whoops as they spread the rice plants. And they repeated the motions, now "harvesting and husking, shaking the trays, throwing the imaginary grains in the air, and blowing away the chaff."

> Come friends and let us homeward take our way,
> Now we rest until the dawn is gray,
> Sleep, welcome sleep we need to keep us strong
> Morning brings another workday long.

Finally they lifted their baskets to the sky, gazed forward and upward to a new dawn, then circled again and left the stage.

The Japanese officers applauded warmly. Whatever they took from the dance, the traditional message played to the Japanese sense of the new Asia against the American oppressors. In actuality, the song was about oppression, and the Japanese were now the oppressors.

Next a spotlight illuminated the image of a goddess: Fahny, "strikingly costumed in gold brassiere and panties, with a trailing purple, taffeta skirt." She wore a headdress copied from a pointed, pagoda-like costume that Hedy Lamarr had worn in a movie that had come out in 1939, *Lady of the Tropics.* She posed as a motionless statue on a black pedestal. David, the singing waiter, came to the stage, muscular, lean, wearing loose trousers, strips of gold cloth at his waist, and a turban. He placed an incense burner at her feet. "The scent of the incense brought the ebony statue to life, and as the tempo increased, dusky worshippers sprang from the shadows and joined the mad dance. As the performance continued with weird steps and contortions, I noted that our visitors were open-mouthed and attentive."

David then stripped to a G-string and danced once more, gyrating and carrying a flaming torch in each hand. "Our orchestra accompanied his unpredictable leaps and bounds, more or less, with 'Rhapsody in Blue.'"

One more performance: the Igorot wedding dance, a ritual celebration of the Luzon mountains. The evening was a great success; receipts were high and Claire saw she had a hit that could challenge and replace Ana Fey's as Manila's go-to nightclub. The opening could not exceed the Manila curfew. "When midnight arrived there was no doubt about the success of Tsubaki Club. All the varied parts of my little machine were running smoothly, and compliments showered down on me from the delighted patrons. Our achievement was reflected in my full cash box and the unfeigned gaiety of each member of my staff."

Opening night was an immediate success on several fronts, both overt and covert. Importantly, newspapers reported the overnight triumph of Tsubaki Club. Meanwhile, the hostesses had gathered bits of information right away—ships in port, departures of Japanese squadrons, names of officers and crew—everything they could find. Only four months after coming down from Bataan, Claire had begun to solidify her position in occupied Manila as a trusted member of society. Word of mouth quickly made Tsubaki Club the latest hot nightspot in town. Japanese businessmen and men on international trade missions from Germany and other Axis partners began to visit. Tsubaki Club was also the place to go for visiting Japanese movie stars and performers. The world-renowned xylophone virtuoso Yoichi Hiraoka stopped by when his tour came to Manila. Japan had celebrated Hiraoka's return to Japan when he decided to leave New York after at least a decade of performing there.

Two months after opening, Claire was making enough money to cover expenses in Manila and was almost ready to send supplies to Boone in

Bataan, along with intelligence reports. She put together a new floor show for the holidays with decorations and a Christmas tree. Her Japanese patrons did not celebrate Christmas but crowded the place and did not even know to complain when Claire and the staff sang "God Bless the Philippines" to the tune of Irving Berlin's "God Bless America."

After the successful performance, Claire tallied receipts and saw she had a surplus. The next morning she jotted off a quick message to John Boone: "Our New Show a Sellout, You can count on Regular Backing. Standing by for orders and assignments." She gave the message and some money to Damian and sent him off to the hills.

People sometimes sailed across Manila Bay from the south shore around Corregidor, though Japanese patrol boats might stop fishing boats and others on the water. Claire's messengers probably took trucks and trains as far as Dinalupihan and then stealthily slipped off the road into the mountains. Either way, it took half a day to travel the sixty or seventy miles up to Bataan and a few hours more to reach Boone's camp. Damian showed the way to one of Claire's earliest helpers, Bonifacio Reyes, nick-named Pacio, who sometimes hid papers in the hollowed-out soles of his shoes. Waiters from the club also made the trip. Soon Boone started sending his Filipina girlfriend, Filomena Guerrero, though she often took a boat across Manila Bay for part of the trip.

Boone sometimes sent his second in command, a Filipino, Major Santiago Sunsheen, to Manila to meet with Claire. Boone was impressed with the quality of intelligence he received and was thankful for the supplies Claire was sending. He soon developed messenger routes and sent Claire's reports to his fellow guerrilla leaders—Edwin Ramsey, Frank Loyd, and a team of American holdouts on Mount Pinatubo.

Claire found out quickly that most of the people she had known before the war were in prison camps if they were soldiers or were detained at the University of Santo Tomas if they were civilians from hostile nations—France, Britain, and other Allied countries. Claire's friend Louise DeMartini was one of the civilian detainees. It might take some time to arrange shipments to Boone in the hills, but Claire began sending supplies to Louise within days. She had some money of her own and borrowed two hundred dollars in pesos from Judge Roxas for that purpose.

If the Japanese had any interest in providing food to the Santo Tomas internees, they had no infrastructure to do so. The food that internees had brought with them in January soon ran out. The Japanese officers in charge allowed friends and relatives on the outside to bring parcels of food to the gates surrounding the Santo Tomas compound. Louise was surprised and delighted when Claire's first care package showed up, but she could not understand how Claire had managed all this time to be on one side of the fence while she and almost every other American friend were locked up.

Outsiders sometimes were allowed inside the gates on the proviso that they not speak to detainees. Slowly, however, the outside world got a clear view of daily life in Santo Tomas. The place was very overcrowded, with as many as four thousand people within. The crowding made it unbearable and conditions during the rainy season were worse. The smells of human waste were unbearable, even though the internee executive committee had organized sanitation squads. Food was sparse. Flies and mosquitoes plagued them all, spreading malaria and the kinds of maladies Claire had suffered in Bataan.

A well-to-do resident of Manila, Marcial Lichauco, was monitoring the plight of the detainees. Thirty-nine years old and married to an American, he was an attorney and a graduate of Harvard College and Harvard Law School. A proud Filipino nationalist, he also was a friend of Judge Roxas and others in Claire's circle. Lichauco kept a diary and became one of the great chroniclers of the Japanese occupation. He said the detainee executive committee at Santo Tomas had turned exterminating insects into a game for the camp children. "Mosquitoes are troublesome only after darkness sets in and the internees can protect themselves against them with mosquito nets, but the flies are a nuisance all day long. The committee in charge of keeping the premises clean recently offered a prize to the boy or girl who could kill the greatest number of flies in one week. A boy, twelve years old, won the contest by swatting approximately 14,700 flies."

Claire vowed not to miss any opportunity to deliver food and clothing to the detention camp. Usually on Sundays and often more than once a week, she lined up with dozens of other people outside Santo Tomas. As required, she carried her ID card showing she was a Philippine citizen. A Japanese guard was stationed at the gate alongside American trustees wearing armbands who were designated to receive and deliver the packages. Claire usually hid messages to Louise in the packages. These were words of support and updates on her efforts to find a way to get Louise released from detention, either with false identification as an Italian national or on a forged medical pass. Bob Humphries, a fellow detainee who later married Louise, said Claire's parcels were a godsend. "The food was crucial. We received packages of food, packages weekly, containing fresh vegetables, meats, fruits, occasionally there were vitamin tablets, medicine in the packages. The food we needed very badly at the time, and we shared it with others who were sharing space at the table where we were eating."

Though direct contact was generally taboo, sometimes, through bribery or laxity, visitors could get close enough to the detainees to speak with them or even visit. One of Claire's new Japanese acquaintances introduced her to an officer in the Kempeitai named Masamoto, who worked at Santo Tomas. She tried to keep Masamoto at arm's length—he was willing to help but he expected payback for his declarations of eternal love. He arranged a hearing for both Louise and a mutual friend, Mona, a pretty, red-haired twenty-year-old who was half Filipina and half American. There were no grounds for Louise's release—she was American and healthy (sick and elderly inmates were sometimes released). Masamoto told Louise that he was willing to make "a trade-off," letting her go in exchange for certain "services rendered," but she wasn't willing to do it. At that point it was too late to manufacture false identification for her, so she was stuck on the inside.

Mona, however, did get out of Santo Tomas based on her mixed parentage. She also had someone vouching for her on the outside, a well-to-do Japanese American businessman named George. Authorities also required a loyalty oath, but Mona went further than Claire had. Mona happily renounced her American citizenship and, when Claire criticized her, defended herself on pragmatic grounds for siding with the enemy. "At least, I'll be living. George has the best of everything. You can't imagine what the food was like at Santo Tomas."

If she couldn't spring Louise from detention, Claire vowed she would never miss a chance to send in food and supplies. She bribed guards so she could deliver a birthday cake and sent in enough food every week so that

Louise and her boyfriend, Bob, could share with others. In the course of gathering supplies for Louise, Claire heard horror stories about thousands of American and Filipino prisoners in Manila and at POW camps far from the city suffering disease, torture, and neglect. Claire met like-minded people determined to save lives at any cost.

Night and Fog

Fort Santiago, Manila, August 1942

LUCKILY, JAPAN'S IMPORTED Nazi tactic of holding political prisoners incommunicado had failed in the case of Roy C. Bennett. After a number of months, Bennett's family received word that the imprisoned anti-Japanese editor was alive. An American survivor of Fort Santiago was able to deliver the news to Santo Tomas that Bennett was still imprisoned there, holding on, defiant, though weak and hungry.

Not long after the surrender of Bataan, Japanese patrols had detained the survivor with two other Americans, all claiming to be civilians. Japanese military police intended to interrogate them and then—assuming their stories checked out—send them to Santo Tomas. On the ride from Bataan to Manila, one of the men, Lieutenant Edgar D. Whitcomb, a navigator in the Army Air Forces, had been successful so far in convincing his Japanese captors that he was a civilian mining engineer named Robert Johnson. As he was driven, supposedly to civilian detention, he rehearsed his story. He would say he was the son of Fred Johnson, superintendent of Lepanto Mines. The real Fred Johnson, an actual mining engineer, had escaped Manila for the States when the Pan Am Clipper was still flying the Pacific route. Whitcomb hoped he could make the story stick. As the car carrying Whitcomb and his two fellow officers entered the city, they drove along Dewey Boulevard and saw bone-thin figures of POWs repairing bomb-damaged bridges or performing menial jobs. Instead of turning away from the coast as it should have, the car took them past Intramuros and through an archway to Fort Santiago.

The privileged treatment ended. Whitcomb and the others followed their captors to a courtyard, toward an iron fence that enclosed a row of barred cells with men crammed inside. Whitcomb was roughly separated from the other two men and shoved into one of the cages.

A dozen sickly, almost-naked men stared emptily and said nothing. When Whitcomb spoke, one of the prisoners pointed to a sign on the wall:

> YOU MUST NOT TALK WITH ONE ANOTHER OR SPEAK YOUR MIND TO OTHERS WITHOUT PERMISSION.
>
> MAKE IT YOUR PRINCIPLE TO DEAL OBEDIENTLY AND FAITHFULLY. POLICEMEN WATCHING YOU.

The caged prisoners were to sit on the floor between 7:00 a.m. and 7:00 p.m. and then to remain lying down from 7:00 p.m. to the following morning. Whitcomb sat close to the thinnest, most cadaverous of them all. The man's bearded face and sickly frame made him look almost translucent, one arm was withered and paralyzed, and he wore only a pair of shredded underwear.

The man came close to Whitcomb's ear.

"It's alright to whisper," he said. "But don't let them catch you. Don't tell anything to anyone in here. You don't know who the informants are."

The scraggly man, who spoke in an erudite tone, was Roy C. Bennett, barely surviving, it seemed, fifty-two years old but appearing much older. He had been taken to Fort Santiago after confinement for about three months at a holding center set up in Villamor Hall at the University of the Philippines. All the while he had been crowded in with a dozen men or more, usually in cages like this one. Among the other prisoners were Chinese and a few other Americans and Europeans, among them anti-Fascist Frenchmen and Spaniards. One person Bennett had recognized was Robert McCulloch Dick, the seventy-year-old publisher of the *Philippines Free Press*. On pain of further beatings and other punishment, the prisoners learned to cower before the brutal realities of imprisonment. The cages had no furniture nor beds, only two holes in the cement floor; one served as a toilet, and the other had a pipe and a trickle of water to drink and wash with. The prisoners could bathe once a week in theory, but Bennett said he had sometimes gone two weeks without a bath; prisoners were not allowed to shave, brush their teeth, or use toilet paper. They tried to trim their nails by rubbing them against stone or pieces of glass. Of course, the Japanese interrogators who summoned them from time to time said both

Bennett and Dick could easily end their time in prison by simply agreeing to see the light. All they had to do was accept the new regime. Why not serve as journalists in the new Philippines, informing the world of the great, just society their Japanese brethren had created? Bennett and Dick steadfastly refused and were beaten for it.

When Whitcomb came to Fort Santiago in mid-August, Bennett had been there for several months. The beatings and torture at the hands of the Kempeitai had been frequent at first, but lately he had been left alone, though as Bennett warned Whitcomb, one could never be certain. It was possible that some of the Japanese finally had relented, realizing he would not break; perhaps they were impressed: "He was crippled, this old man, and they could torture him, they couldn't break him." Bennett told Whitcomb who he was, who he had been. He was the former editor of the *Manila Bulletin*, separated from his wife and daughters these months. He figured that they were somewhere in Manila but couldn't say where. Bennett's wife had determined that he was held at Fort Santiago and had tried to send him food and some basic supplies. The guards at Fort Santiago had refused to deliver anything. Bennett knew nothing of that, and the lack of information about the family was maddening. He gave Whitcomb his own key to maintaining sanity and survival: *Be prepared. They may come for you tomorrow and never again. Now, or in two weeks, or two months, or never. You will never know.*

Bennett appeared delighted to have Whitcomb to talk to. He was a sophisticated man; yet the severe treatment had converted him into a submissive, bowing prisoner of war under the Japanese boot. You must bow, you must not look directly at the soldiers, and you must answer roll call, learning the numbers in Japanese, he told Whitcomb. Whitcomb was dragged away. He was also beaten and questioned, but he held on to his assumed identity. Then the Japanese gave up. Not found guilty of anything other than being Americans, Robert Johnson, mining engineer, and his two partners were transferred to the civilian detention camp at Santo Tomas. At Santo Tomas they would be able to provide word to Bennett's wife and children that they had seen Roy and he was still alive.

The Kempeitai

Manila, October 1942

THE SCREAMS of prisoners echoed through the arched dungeons of Fort Santiago. One of those who survived, Jose M. Lichauco, described how torturers tied him to ropes and chains dangling from the ceiling. Lichauco, a cousin of Judge Roxas's friend Marcial Lichauco, was "beaten with a rubber hose, clubs, wire and wet rope [and then] was ordered to scrub latrines with bare hands." Japanese guards also tied him down and forced water into his mouth and lungs—water-boarding—a tactic that brought its victims close to the point of drowning.

Colonel Akira Nagahama, the new commander of the Kempeitai in the Philippines, knew well what was happening. His office was meters away from the dungeons. Nagahama had come to Manila from Taipei in October to replace Colonel Seichi Ohta. The Kempeitai (Japanese for Military Police Corps) was the equivalent of the Gestapo. In fact, Adolf Hitler and SS chief Heinrich Himmler sent a key Gestapo officer, Colonel Josef Meisinger, to Tokyo to serve as liaison with the Kempeitai.

The Kempeitai functioned parallel to and often separately from the regular Japanese Army. It had been formed in the 1880s as a select corps within the military in direct service to the emperor. With the rise of militarism in Japan in the 1930s, entrants were volunteers chosen from among experienced members of the military. The diverse training included advanced military courses—horsemanship, armed and unarmed combat, and strategy—but also specialized training in propaganda, espionage, counterespionage, and basic policing. As the war years approached, training programs had proliferated and the Kempeitai had also functioned as secret police within Japan to root out opposition to government policy. The Kempeitai's importance in Japanese society had grown when Major General Hideki Tojo was appointed commander of the corps in Manchuria and promoted to the Tokyo area in 1935. Now that Tojo was the prime minister of the war government, the Kempeitai had a preeminent role. Kempeitai officers had a wide range of authority: They could police the conduct of soldiers and could regulate the comportment of and punish members of the regular Japanese officer corps, even those who outranked them. Civilians and military personnel at home in Japan feared the Kempeitai, and they soon would become just as terrifying in Manila.

Beyond the walls of Fort Santiago, Nagahama appeared to be an urbane, deliberative man who believed that conquest of the Philippines and the broadening Japanese empire had to be sensitive and pragmatic. He took the position that the Japanese occupation had to adapt to reality, accommodate the new members of the Japanese empire, put forward a friendly, forgiving face. Early on he spoke of leniency and persuasion instead of brutality. He quoted a Chinese proverb for penal reform as his method for dealing with criminals: "Arrest seven times, reform them, release seven times."

Not everyone within his organization agreed with the policy of a gentle hand. Nagahama himself did not operate on the street very often, nor did the prisoners at Fort Santiago usually see him. He relied on his subordinates to carry out their duties while he directed affairs from his office at Fort Santiago. Discipline often eroded in proportion to the distance Kempeitai officers strayed from the occupation offices at Fort Santiago.

It is questionable whether even Nagahama himself believed what he said publicly. By the time of Nagahama's arrival in Manila, rumors circulated widely about torture, rape, and murder at the hands of Kempeitai officers, and there was no sign that things had changed. Mention of the name "Nagahama" and "Fort Santiago" was enough to halt conversations and bring a chill.

Colonel Dionisio Banting Jr. survived as a witness and victim. Banting, a Filipino guerrilla officer in the mountains of Luzon, was held for almost five months. He admitted that he was a guerrilla, but that did not save him from torture. He was beaten, starved, left hanging in his cell, submitted to water-boarding, and forced to squat the rest of his time in a squalid cell. He had seen Nagahama in the hallways when being led around the building. The cries of the tortured could be heard. Nagahama "must have heard screams of people being beaten."

From Nagahama's point of view, he himself was a victim of excessive zeal by other officers and bureaucratic problems beyond his control. He did not have a large Kempeitai contingent in the Philippines, about five hundred men for the entire country, about a third of them in Manila. Another was that he desperately needed to show Tokyo that resistance to the occupation had been eliminated. No one else had been able to accomplish that. The Kempeitai commander insisted that gentle persuasion had its place. He knew, for example, that face slapping had become a major topic of conversation in occupied Manila. Slapping was commonplace for the Japanese; not so for the Filipinos nor for the Americans. A random slap in the face was a sign of subjugation and powerlessness. Nagahama said he wanted his men to be sensitized to the fact. "To govern alien nationalities, it is absolutely essential to know something of their national traits and idiosyncrasies. . . . Slapping a Filipino on the face [is] an unbearable insult. . . . It is often more effective to appeal to his sense of duty rather than to try using a third degree method to get truth out of a Filipino." That sounded logical, but Nagahama seemed to be unable or unwilling to stop face slapping or more brutal techniques practiced by his subordinates.

There were others in the Japanese occupation force who sought to play up cooperation with the Filipinos, now "liberated" from American rule. Military propagandists played the incessant "Asia for the Asians" card—Japan had liberated the Philippines from colonial rule, went the argument, and now as brother Asians the Japanese would protect Philippine sovereignty. Only a minority, however, bought that line.

The Japanese occupiers produced films and books to promote and glorify the goals of the empire. One film debuted in December 1942 to commemorate the first anniversary of the war. The film, *Glory of the Orient*, argued that the American president, Franklin Delano Roosevelt, was a warmonger who had challenged the peaceful aspirations of the Japanese people. A narrator intoned: "We endured in the Hope that Our Government might retrieve the situation in peace, but our adversaries showing not the least spirit of conciliation, have unduly delayed a settlement; and, in the meantime they have intensified the economic and political pressure to compel hereby Our Empire to submission."

Marcial Lichauco attended a showing of the film. "The last few scenes were offensive," he said. "While the commentator kept up a running statement to the effect that the present war had been initiated by Roosevelt, a large American flag lying on a piece of muddy ground appeared on the screen. Over this flag marched hundreds of Japanese soldiers. Little by little, it shriveled until, finally, the Stars and Stripes completely disappeared in the mud over which the men were tramping."

If the Kempeitai propaganda department thought they were winning over converts, Lichauco said, the film was greeted "in complete silence. . . . The Propaganda Bureau may be working hard but they are just wasting a lot of film."

The propaganda department kept churning out material, always focused on the glory of the Asian "race." A few months later the bureau published *The Flowering of Racial Spirit*, extolling the glories of victory over the Americans in the form of a diary by a soldier. Clearly, the author said, the Japanese, though physically smaller than the repugnant Americans, were superior in every way. "Only one Japanese soldier guards 200 or 300 American soldiers. In some cases, only one soldier leads as many as five hundred American surrenderors. The height of the Japanese soldier reaches only up to the shoulders of the American soldiers. . . . These American soldiers are citizens of the haughty country which in the past attempted to heap outrageous insults upon our fatherland. Observing these crowds of a tremendous number of surrenderors, I felt as if they were foul water flowing down from the sewerage of a country that has been formed upon impure foundations and have thus lost their racial pride."

In the Japanese telling of it, the Americans themselves even perceived the superiority of the advancing army of the Rising Sun: "When we entered into the town of Mariveles, a group of fifteen or sixteen officers came to our quarters. They were Americans and there were a colonel and a lieutenant colonel among them. And that colonel requested us to teach him the Japanese language. We wondered what words he wanted to learn and found out that he wanted to learn words in Japanese for 'Give me water,' and 'Give me food.' I felt a desire to spit at him seeing such a shameless attitude."

Propaganda notwithstanding, military police units, plainclothes Kempeitai officers, and their informants circulated around Manila and other cities gathering information on resistance and opponents of the occupation. They were very willing to use brutality and murder to extract information.

Nagahama was under new orders to eliminate all such opposition, which Tokyo considered an embarrassment. Prime Minister Hideki Tojo dangled the possibility to the Philippines government under Jorge B. Vargas—propped up but not always loyal—that success in efforts to quell opponents would lead to Philippine independence for the first time in history.

Tojo declared, "Substantial progress is being made in the degree of cooperation rendered to the Japanese Empire by the people of the Philippines as well as in the restoration of internal peace and security." But more needed to be done. "On condition that future tangible evidences of cooperation are actively demonstrated, it is contemplated to put into effect the statement previously on the question of Philippine independence in the shortest possible time."

No promise of independence could fool the Filipinos—the Japanese would remain in control. The Philippines would never be free as long as Filipinos were subjects of the Japanese empire.

The Japanese forced the Filipinos and all others subject to the Rising Sun to honor Emperor Hirohito's birthday on April 29 with all due reverence. Along with more pledges of friendship and solidarity, Japan sent in a special commemorative newspaper along with a rare photograph of the emperor. An accompanying caption warned that readers must not wrap food inside the newspaper photograph of the emperor or desecrate the picture in any way. Many Filipinos, who might have had another idea or two of what to do with the picture of Hirohito, decided to burn it in effigy and eliminate the problem.

Japanese military intelligence was only beginning to understand the depth of resistance and recognize that it extended beyond urban opponents. The American and Filipino soldiers who had evaded the surrender were now forming troublesome guerrilla bands on every major island in the country. Nagahama applied pressure on his agents. He might have spoken of leniency with a velvet glove, but the plan, at least for the American guerrillas, was to kill them all.

Killing General Roxas
Mindanao, June 1942

GENERAL MANUEL ROXAS had the distinction of having been twice declared dead. For a long while Filipinos thought that Roxas, one of the country's most admired leaders, had been either executed or killed in combat. His brother, Judge Roxas—Claire's friend, relative by marriage, and guarantor before the Japanese—and the rest of the family were in mourning. However, it was not true; the general had been taken captive early in the Japanese invasion. The military occupiers had been engaged in a debate about exactly whom among the Philippine leadership they could trust. The answer was probably very few, but they also knew that Roxas and other popular Filipino leaders were pragmatic and could be useful in maintaining a semblance of pan-Asian solidarity and friendship. For that reason Colonel Nobuhiko Jimbo was deeply concerned on June 22, 1942, when he received a directive at his outpost in Mindanao from General Homma's office in Manila: "This is to order you to execute Manuel A. Roxas secretly and immediately. As soon as the execution is completed, a written report should be made."

Colonel Jimbo was appalled. He considered himself a good soldier and loyal subject of the emperor. However, he was convinced that executing General Roxas, one of the most respected Philippine officials in the country, would backfire. He thought that killing Roxas would also establish him as a martyr to the cause of rebellion. In any case, Jimbo also liked Roxas and was willing to do everything possible to protect him.

Despite the possible consequences—Jimbo's own imprisonment or death—he brought his objection to his commanding officer, Major General Torao Ikuta. Roxas, he argued, would be an important figure in future relations between Japan and the Philippines. "We can't carry out a wise occupation policy by oppression only," he told Ikuta. "Roxas is loved by the Filipinos."

"I know," Ikuta said. He also admired Roxas and agreed completely with Jimbo. Then, he added, kill him anyway. It was an order. "You have to do it."

Jimbo saluted, turned on his heel, and gathered up Roxas and another condemned man, Teofisto Guingona Sr., the governor-general of Mindanao. He assembled a three-car convoy, one vehicle in front, one in the rear. Jimbo and the two condemned men rode in the center car toward a designated execution grounds five miles away. Jimbo wore a khaki uniform with shorts and regulation Japanese riding boots. Roxas was also in khaki; Guingona wore a white suit.

Guingona began to whimper and cry. "Please help me!" he told Jimbo. "I am an administrator, not a soldier! I'll cooperate with the Japanese army. Help me!"

Jimbo said nothing, and Roxas was impassive for a while before turning to the Mindanao politician and saying: "Don't cry. Don't worry. What a beautiful day! Look! Sampaguita blossoms at the foot of Mount Alpo. Did you ever see them more lovely?" Roxas's attitude in the face of impending death pushed Jimbo over the edge.

"There will be no execution," he told the soldiers accompanying him when they arrived at the planned execution site. "Take these two prisoners to the Piso farm by boat. They may be useful later."

Back in Manila, Jimbo's commanders assumed that he had carried out the execution and that General Roxas was dead. Jimbo was not surprised when he was summoned to occupation headquarters in Manila several days later. He expected to be hanged. His only course of action was to reason directly with General Homma and describe the value Roxas could hold for the Japanese occupation government. Arriving at military headquarters, he presented himself to the general's chief staff officer.

"I respectfully request permission to speak to General Homma," he said.

The staff officer refused. "He is very busy, you know." Homma was in the process of upbraiding his entire staff for having issued the order in his name to execute Roxas. How could it have happened? Who had ordered this? Why did the staff think General Homma would want Roxas dead? Roxas was beloved by his people; Roxas was a man of honor and a pragmatic one. "Roxas could have been useful to us." Jimbo's own sense of relief must have been close to what Roxas and Guingona, the Mindanao governor-general, had felt when he stopped their execution. Jimbo would not die, and neither would Roxas.

Roxas was not dead, Jimbo told Homma's chief of staff. "I have him alive on the Piso farm near Davao." When Jimbo returned to Mindanao, he found that Roxas had been rearrested by others and was being interrogated and tortured. He rescued the general a second time and made sure Roxas was safe until he could be brought back to Manila. Roxas soon agreed to enter the puppet government and, after his rescue by Jimbo, walked the walk of a man who saluted the Rising Sun. Privately he hated the flag and the military behind it. That was likely no surprise to the Japanese. No matter, as long as he could be kept in line.

Banzai!

Manila, November 1942

WHERE ELSE WOULD a Japanese Army Air Force pilot relax and celebrate his time off? Tsubaki Club was perfect. Claire welcomed them all and gave personal attention to the high-profile guests among them. Claire took one officer to his seat on this night, Friday, November 20, 1942. She had been thinking that evening about the home front, about her family back in Portland, and planned to write a letter after work. (The Philippine post office remained open during the occupation, though with universal censorship and numerous delays; Claire could also try to send mail through the Red Cross or much later in the war with her couriers to Bataan and then on to Australia.) For the moment she had to focus on the business at hand. The pilot she had just shepherded to a table was important enough for special treatment. Out of respect and for the sake of business, Madame Tsubaki herself had to entertain and sit with him. Drinks and more drinks, tips for the hostesses, and then the floor show. Claire sang one of her standards; some nights it was the Ink Spots, or perhaps "Some of These Days," a popular tune back in the States. "My rendition did not equal that of the inimitable Sophie Tucker," she said, "but it served its purpose." Ironically, the Japanese officers loved the American standards. Mamerto's drinks, plus more rapid-fire entertainment, had the desired effect.

Soon enough the pilot had drunk too much and began to brag in broken English about how many American planes he had shot down. The Americans didn't have a chance. As the night went on, more and more Americans were going to die, accompanied by more and more cheers.

"Banzai!" Claire and the officer drank to his success. Dozens of Americans.

"Banzai!" the pilot shouted and raised his glass. Claire toasted and took another drink. Hundreds of Americans.

All the officers raised a glass to that.

And here's to killing many more Americans in the future. "Banzai!" Claire raised her glass once more. "Had to drink to the death of more and smile," she confided to her diary that night. "Not easy." Oftentimes during such displays by the Japanese, she would excuse herself for a moment, walk away to the toilets, throw up, and then return, smiling once more. Perhaps she kept her food down this evening. As curfew approached, she raced home "to send letter to mother and family. May take 3 or 4 months to reach her."

Mamerto, David, and the others who worked for Claire watched with amazement how she and Fely sweet-talked the Japanese officers. She knew it. The "employees think I'm crazy. Don't understand when I drink to downfall of England and America with finger crossed. Hard to do but must do." While she toasted with the pilot, she gathered tidbits about him, his plane, and his unit that could add up to intelligence on the Japanese war machine. Dutifully she sent messages with her couriers up to the guerrillas in the hills.

Claire said that she and the hostesses went about getting information methodically. She and Fely took the lead: "If they were army men, we led them on to tell about troop movements, and the conditions of roads and bridges. If naval officers, we lured them into talking about their ships. We pumped many newly arrived businessmen about the locations and nature of their establishments. Boone, for one, was certain that much of the new Japanese materiel was now being manufactured in Manila."

When they weren't serving lunch to American prisoners on work detail, the club hostesses had begun teaching dancing to Japanese soldiers. The Japanese command had decreed that dancing was not proper for the war effort—but far from the front the soldiers did it anyway. Claire would watch the men rehearse their steps—they were probably more interested in being close to the women than in dancing themselves. At the same time she could gaze beyond the ballroom to the windows, where one saw the contrast with the life they were living. Prisoners frequently marched by to and from maintenance tasks around town. The contrast was madness.

If Japanese officers might otherwise feel guilty for dancing in violation of orders, Fely was the one hostess most likely to persuade them to break ranks. Fely's main job at the club was as a singer in the floor show; when she sang Japanese folk songs in her sweet soprano, Japanese officers swooned. After the floor show, she circulated in the room, hauling in an average of ten or twenty dollars a week, a decent sum on top of the few pesos a week that Claire paid her and the 50 percent commission for every drink the officers bought her. Sometimes they asked her out; sometimes Fely posed for photographs with her admirers. She did what she had to do to maintain her allure. If there was anything more to tell, she was not telling.

Fely had been able to speak some Japanese before the occupation, but she started taking language classes to improve her comprehension. A number of language schools had opened up and Japanese was now mandatory in grade schools. The officers appreciated her ability to exchange pleasantries with them in their own tongue as she circulated around the room, but they did not know how fluent she was actually becoming. She could now listen in quietly and sweetly, pretending she did not understand when officers spoke about the war among themselves, all the while listening for useful scraps of information.

The pressure of operating underground while consorting with the Japanese amounted to a difficult dance even for Claire, who was used to maintaining various versions of the truth about her life. She juggled letters and shipments to her friends at Santo Tomas, intelligence gathering, scrounging for increasingly hard-to-come-by provisions. People had been decapitated on the spot for lesser crimes by the same men she was consorting with. She heard constant horror stories of people being humiliated and slapped on the street, beaten to a pulp with whips, and of one case where a woman at another club was forced to drink boiling water.

Sometimes drunken or surly men slapped women for no reason, just because they could. That was the least of the problem. They bragged, they pawed, and when they went further, Claire tried to say she had a husband out there somewhere whom she was looking for. But she wasn't sure how long she could stomach the Japanese bravado about the war, about beating the Americans on land and sea, the toasts and the banzais she had to sit through and join.

As food became scarce, as Japanese officers rotated in and out, there were hard times at the club; business was not always even. Gathering supplies was increasingly time-consuming, and Claire ran up against the rationing system for rice and alcohol. She had trouble getting enough beer. Sometimes there wasn't any, or maybe the officials were making it too difficult to get. Juan Elizalde and his brother, Manuel, could help with that by way of their legitimate, aboveboard liquor business. Juan Elizalde was capable of giving Claire beer and alcohol on credit, or not charging her anything at all. Behind the scenes Juan had made arrangements on intelligence procedures with his old friend from the Manila Polo Club, Chick Parsons; Parsons by now was back in America, but he was going to find some way of sneaking back into the country to fight the Japanese.

In the mornings Fely and Claire compiled and copied the conversations they had gathered and did a rendering of the previous evening's receipts; Fely kept the books and could provide Claire with updates whenever she wanted on how much business they had done and how much money they had on hand. They also had a payroll book, a book of disbursements, and a book that tracked how many drinks of lemon water the hostesses received so they could be paid their 50 percent share of each drink. On average 90 percent of the evening business was conducted in cash but up to 10 percent of the receipts were in scrip or chits to be covered and paid later. They had little recourse when soldiers left town without paying up. They could try gently appealing to the men most dazzled by the show, especially to the ones who were pledging them their undying love and devotion. That might work—maybe one officer would remind another to settle the tab before shipping out. It was equally possible that asking for money would lead to a loss of face and a fight. The probable outcomes were the nonpayer ignoring the request or, just as likely, stopping by to give Claire another slap in the face. It didn't happen so much to the alluring Fely, but Claire in the light of day was an Anglo, and she was slapped too often. She didn't want to lose money, but she would be weighing the indignity of being slapped one more time against having a scofflaw officer leave Manila without paying.

Organized Resistance

Brisbane, Australia, December 1942

WHILE CHICK PARSONS was still on the high seas en route back to the United States, a surprising, even suspicious radio message arrived at General MacArthur's USAFFE headquarters in Brisbane, Australia. For the first time since his flight from the Philippines, the general had proof that Americans and Filipinos were forming guerrilla bands to fight the Japanese.

The message was addressed to MacArthur himself from Lieutenant Colonel Guillermo Nakar, who had been a battalion commander of the Philippines Army 14th Infantry. He was transmitting from a clandestine wireless set somewhere in Luzon.

"Detachments of Fil-American forces—we have not surrendered—are actively raiding towns [in central Luzon]." Nakar reported he was distributing a newsletter in Manila and other cities to counter Japanese propaganda and to encourage Filipinos for the fight ahead. "Your victorious return is the nightly subject of prayers in every Filipino home."

MacArthur was elated by the contact with Nakar. "Short as it was, it lifted the curtain of silence and uncertainty, and disclosed the start of a human drama with few parallels in military history," MacArthur said. "I knew that the remnants of my soldiers were not abandoning the fight while they lived and had the means." MacArthur opened a message exchange with Nakar, who provided a status report on Japanese troop movements and the information available so far about the condition of prisoners of war. However, on August 7, less than a month later, Nakar sent an ominous message: "Intelligence report reveals that enemy has detected the existence of our radio station, possibly by geometric process, and detailed a large force to look for us." Nakar's transmitter went silent. The Japanese military police had caught him.

For three months MacArthur received no further clandestine transmissions. Then, in November, a new round of radio transmissions came in. This time it was Major Macario Peralta, another Philippine Army officer, reporting from the island of Panay. Peralta had massed an eight-thousand-man guerrilla force in the Visayan Islands against only eight hundred Japanese troops. He said that he was in need of supplies that could be air-dropped or brought in via submarine. MacArthur answered swiftly and enthusiastically but warned Peralta about taking offensive action.

"Primary mission," he told Peralta, "is to maintain your organization and to secure maximum amount of information. Guerrilla activities should be postponed until ordered from here. Premature action of this kind will only bring heavy retaliation upon innocent people."

The contact with Peralta was followed by a series of messages from Mindanao and Luzon via the southern island, with reports showing that U.S. and Filipino soldiers operating clandestinely said they were gathering information and hankering to fight. They awaited MacArthur's command.

▪ ▪ ▪

MacArthur saw that organizing and supporting the guerrillas would be important for the morale of those he had left behind in the Philippines and that their success could pave the way for his eventual return. The goal would be in part "to arouse the militant loyalty of a whole people by forming resolute armed centers of resistance around which they could rally [and] to establish a vast network of agents numbering into the thousands to provide precise, accurate and detailed information on major enemy moves and installations."

The United States already was reversing the tide of the war. After Japan had blasted across the Pacific during the first six months of 1942 with early victories in the Philippines, Guam, and Wake Island, the imperial armed forces had completed the conquest of Burma, Borneo, and the Dutch East Indies. But then, after Jimmy Doolittle's morale-boosting attack on Tokyo in April, the United States had held off Japan in May in the Battle of the Coral Sea off New Guinea and then scored a decisive victory by stunning Japanese forces at the Midway Islands, a fifteen-mile-circumference atoll thirteen hundred miles northwest of Pearl Harbor. MacArthur understood the importance of Midway. "This decisive victory restored the balance in naval power in the Pacific, and removed the threat to Hawaii and the West Coast of the United States." As autumn arrived, Britain had begun an offensive in Burma, and the United States was holding off the Japanese at Guadalcanal in the Solomon Islands.

Instead of merely holding defense lines, it was time to challenge Japan to the south. MacArthur devised a plan to leapfrog across New Guinea, a strategy that would surprise, confound, and outflank Japanese forces. MacArthur's streamlined offense had one unwavering goal en route to total victory: liberation of the Philippines as soon as possible. Throughout the war MacArthur brushed aside criticism that he was dedicating so much time and equipment to that mission. General George Marshall, the army chief of staff, advised MacArthur at one point later in the Pacific campaign "not to allow our personal feeling and Philippine political considerations to override our great objective, which is early conclusion of the war with Japan." However, MacArthur disagreed with what Marshall was implying and said that his interest in the Philippines was strategic, not emotional. "I felt that if I could secure the Philippines, it would enable us to clamp an air and naval blockade on the flow of all supplies from the south to Japan, and thus, by paralyzing her industries, force her to early capitulation."

Colonel Charles Willoughby, MacArthur's intelligence chief, said the guerrilla movement in the Philippines had the potential to bog down Japanese operations, "to force upon the Japanese the commitment of large numbers of troops for occupation duty, but, like the inexorable flow of the tides and the winds, it could not be stopped." There were two immediate questions: How could MacArthur determine whether the radio transmissions were bona fide contacts or ploys by Japanese counterintelligence agents? Even if they were real, what course of action could the U.S. command take?

The general had the answer on his desk: an analytical report signed by Chick Parsons, who had also turned in his smuggled intelligence documents and had begun lobbying to get back to the Philippines within days of his arrival in the United States.

Once released from FBI detention, Parsons had raced to Washington, DC, for a luncheon reception at the Shoreham Hotel, the headquarters of Manuel Quezon, the Philippine president in exile. (Quezon had taken refuge at Corregidor with General MacArthur in December 1941 and later made his way to Washington.) Lunch quickly turned into a debriefing session for officials and U.S. intelligence officers starved for firsthand information about family, friends, and details of the occupation. Members of the Quezon war cabinet included Joaquín M. Elizalde, a brother of Juan Elizalde, who was involved with Claire and her underground comrades. Parsons told Quezon and the luncheon guests that the occupation was harsh, but the residents of Manila were resilient and defiant.

On balance, Parsons reported, life goes on. Details about the Bataan death march and the large-scale atrocities had been known in Manila at least by some people while he was still there, but he apparently said nothing at this debriefing, at least not for public consumption.

"Quezon was thrilled to learn that his radio addresses are heard in the Philippines," one of those present reported. "Parsons says the Japanese did not seize radios—only took antennae—so the Filipinos have installed new antennae buried in the ground."

Parsons had one main message for Quezon: He wanted to serve the U.S. war effort in the Philippines any way he could. After the luncheon he took a few days of personal time to get his family settled, arranging a house for them in Biltmore, North Carolina. Next he paid a quick visit to his parents in Tennessee, then drove back north and reported for duty in the intelligence branch of the Office of Naval Operations. For the next three months he lobbied for a return to the Pacific. Throughout the summer and into the fall Parsons, now promoted to the rank of lieutenant commander, remained insistent that there was work to be done in the Philippines. He wanted to fight. He wrote a detailed report on his travels and observations in Manila and beyond during the first six months of the Japanese occupation. He was certain that he could help organize a united guerrilla front. Washington military analysts had trouble believing that Americans in the hills beyond Manila could amount to a significant factor in the war.

By now MacArthur had read Parsons's report and he had his answer. There was no way to sort out the information without a skilled Philippines hand on the ground. MacArthur had known Parsons for years, as long as he himself had been in the Philippines. He knew that Parsons was fearless and that he had wide knowledge of the islands.

The general fired off a terse message to the Navy Department:

SEND PARSONS IMMEDIATELY

(signed) MacArthur

Parsons reported for duty at MacArthur's headquarters in Brisbane on January 18, 1943, ready to take up the battle for the Philippines.

MacArthur gave him marching orders: Assess the guerrilla operations and enforce a unified command structure managed from U.S. headquarters. He had two basic questions: How significant is the guerrilla operation in the Philippines, and how can we support it? Parsons had sensed that the raw capacity was in place, but structure, leadership, and support were required. There was only one way to get the answers MacArthur needed. The goal was "to ascertain the extent of the guerrilla movement in the Philippines—its leadership, armament and personnel; to introduce into the islands and Intelligence organization; to set up coast-watcher and radio stations for the purpose of forwarding word of Japanese movements to the proper Task Force commander; to carry supplies to the unsurrendered soldiers and generally to encourage the people of the Philippines in making intelligent and effective resistance to the enemy."

Though some officers scoffed that Parsons was too old, he was assigned to the Allied Intelligence Bureau and received several weeks of intensive commando training. One month after reaching Australia, he was now ready to go. MacArthur issued one final order: He demanded that all intelligence from the guerrillas be delivered directly to him.

On February 18, 1943, Chick Parsons boarded the USS *Tambor*, commanded by Lieutenant Commander Steven H. Armbruster. The submarine sailed out of Fremantle, the U.S. Navy base on Australia's western coast just south of Perth. The *Tambor* was one of several workhorse submarines assigned to a unique supply and espionage mission and destined for the southern Philippine island of Mindanao. Little more than half a year after Parsons had left the Philippines as a Panamanian diplomat, he was returning to fight the occupation.

The first shipment of equipment was relatively small. The *Tambor* carried fifty thousand rounds of .30 caliber (7.62 mm) ammunition and twenty thousand rounds of .45 caliber (11.4 mm) pistol ammunition. Parsons was carrying ten thousand dollars in Philippine pesos to distribute as needed. The greater purpose was to establish contact and analyze what needed to be done on the ground.

"The trip, according to Chick's mental log, was fairly uneventful. A few torpedoes loosed against careless Japanese shipping. A few depth charges received in return. All very routine."

Against all advice, Parsons had not gone to extreme lengths to disguise himself for his eventual infiltration of the islands. As he had done before, he would pass himself off as a peasant, hiding behind his knowledge of Tagalog and Spanish even though he didn't look like he was Filipino. He had told his superiors at U.S. headquarters in Brisbane that he didn't need to fool the Japanese into thinking he was a native. "I don't intend to run into 'em. I'm not going in as a commando. I'm going in as a spy." He did carry one item that was not often discussed or commented about—a couple of cyanide tablets to use if he ever was captured. He didn't intend to run into the enemy, but if he did, he didn't intend to live long enough to be tortured by them.

The *Tambor* surfaced late in the afternoon of March 4, 1943, off Tukuran on the south-central coast of Mindanao. Parsons and three others boarded a rubber dinghy and headed for shore. "When our beach patrol saw him, they fired at him," recalled Roberto de Jesus, a Filipino guerrilla on Mindanao. Parsons shouted *"amigo, amigo."* The firing stopped and Parsons and his three comrades waded ashore. To his surprise, the guerrillas on hand already had commandeered some boats and were ready to move. They were able to transfer the supplies from the submarine to shore, and Parsons said he could expect to message Australia and ask for a pickup in several weeks. It was the start of dozens of submarine supply missions and several forays by Parsons himself into the heart of the Japanese-occupied islands. Parsons delivered the supplies to Wendell Fertig, who had declared himself a guerrilla general. That would not do—this was now a U.S. military operation organized and sanctioned by General MacArthur. "There are no generals in the Philippines guerrilla army." Fertig was now commissioned as a full colonel in the guerrilla army, commanding the insurgent forces on Mindanao. With broad authority from MacArthur and making clear that was so, Parsons proceeded to make contact with other guerrilla commanders. His assignment was to assess the capabilities of the forces available and then to analyze the need for supplies, logical support, and training. His instinct and brash sense of purpose would range far beyond that.

The organized guerrilla war in the Philippines had begun.

Steve the Greek

Manila, November 1942

CLAIRE HAD COME back to Manila with three goals—staying alive, supporting the guerrillas, and finding John Phillips, not necessarily in that order. She already had seen suffering and death in the mountains and faced the possibility, even likelihood, that she might die. In the city she was not letting soldiers push her around, even if they tried to kill her. She seemed to be developing a sense of fearlessness born of her willingness to challenge and confront authority. Now she saw more suffering and more people who needed help.

American men, dazed, thin, wearing prison garb, had become the slaves of occupied Manila. Anytime a work crew marched by, Claire ran to the highest window in the highest building to look at their faces, to search for John Phillips, for any familiar face, and for clues to what she could possibly do. They would pass by—she recognized none of them but she felt somehow she knew all of them. The sight of them marching to their workstations was wrenching.

Every morning, just after dawn, they would march under the eyes of rifle-toting guards from the Park Avenue School in Pasay, from jails around Manila, hundreds of prisoners, a ragged, defeated army of hungry men. A pitiful sight, men tied together by rope, under guard, marching along with the look of those who were humiliated and had little hope. Yet many were the hardier survivors of the death march in Bataan during April. During the day they shifted around the city to repair bridges and roads, to replace runways at army air bases, to do anything a prisoner could do at the whim of the Japanese Army.

While about four thousand POWs were held at Cabanatuan to the north, there were about two thousand others in and around Manila. Some were under interrogation at Fort Santiago; several hundred of them were at Old Bilibid Prison close to downtown—and some of those men were ill and had been brought to the prison hospital. And Claire heard there were about seven hundred Americans living in squalid conditions at the Park Avenue School in the Pasay district, four or five miles from the club. Most of the able-bodied prisoners in Manila were pressed into work details, essentially as slaves. Some of them would be seen in small groups working on the street, others waiting for rare opportunities to find a little gasoline at gas stations, fuel being always reserved for official purposes, and then driving around other prisoners under Japanese guard. At night she would see them come from the opposite direction, heading back to prison, where they had no comfort and little rest.

It was dangerous to talk to the prisoners—many of the Japanese soldiers guarding them were apt to be violent when Filipinos on the street expressed sympathy for the Americans. In one case three Filipina women tried to hand over the groceries they were carrying when they saw a prisoners' detail working on a bridge. A guard ordered them to stop and began to slap them, screaming, "Don't you know that Americans are your enemies? Americans are bad people." He continued the tirade as the prisoners watched, unable to intercede. Some "were in tears but there was nothing they could do about it." All that Claire could do was search the faces from the window. Then she met Steve the Greek.

Stephen Handras was actually a Philippine national who, with an American father and a Filipina mother, was not subject to detention. He was an affable fellow who had figured out a way to game the system. Steve ran an open-air soda shop on Nebraska Street, the Acacia, named for the acacia tree that cast a cool shadow on the sweltering street, a few blocks from Tsubaki Club. Claire hadn't known much about anyone else working to help them. But ever since those days in the mountains, when villagers had looked to her for help, she wanted to aid the sick and wounded wherever they were. Many people in Manila also were drawn naturally to fill the need. Claire had started out looking for John Phillips; then she had come back to Manila to support the guerrillas in the hills. Now she saw that there was more to be done.

Steve the Greek was as disturbed as Claire was as he watched the POWs trudge by every day. He had the gumption to try to challenge the system, even if it was by doing what he always did: offering a cool drink on a hot day. He watched carefully—these Japanese guards didn't want trouble; they were supposed to keep the soldiers well enough to do their work. If he could find a way to make the soldiers happy, maybe he could break through the system. He offered free drinks but was beaten back more than once when he tried to approach the POWs. Finally he tried tossing little packages of cigarettes, a bit of food, some clothing small enough for the men to pick up and carry.

Sometimes the guards stopped him. But not always. "American prisoners who were driving Jap trucks used to stop in front of Acacia Soda Fountain, operated by me, and picked up bundles of clothes and food stuff which I was collecting for them. If the boys were unable to stop because of their being guarded, they would drop me notes, and I used to pile supplies for them under the acacia tree which were carried away as soon as they had the opportunity. Twice I was slapped by Jap sentries for doing this."

Twice slapped, but not every time. Not all guards were the same. One morning a group of Americans came marching along.

"There were several civilians among the watching crowd, waiting for an opportunity to help the prisoners. My chance came when I saw one prisoner [fall] down exhausted at the very corner of San Luis and Nebraska Streets. I ran towards him with a bottle of soft drinks mixed with a few drops of whiskey, purposely prepared for the occasion, and I offered it. He was able to recover and continued the march."

No one slapped Steve this time. After the Japanese guards allowed this to happen, Steve tried it again. The next time some prisoners came along in a truck and stopped in front of the soda stand. The guards did not seem to mind. Steve had broken through, whether because the guards got better work out of the prisoners or because some of the guards were more lenient than others. He learned that the Japanese occupation force was not a monolith. Prison guards and detention camp guards were not all the same. These were not frontline soldiers fighting the Americans. Most were thrilled that they were not at the front, and many were more interested in avoiding trouble and having an easy time than in kicking and beating the people around them. Even the children at Santo Tomas could see this. The guards were sometimes friendly; they seemed to love children and they innately respected old people. Steve and other Filipinos were learning about how to deal with the Japanese.

Steve the Greek lived upstairs from his soda stand under the acacia tree. One day he was sitting at the window. "I saw a truck with six American prisoners slowing down near my door. I shouted to the boys: 'come closer, I will throw you something.' I looked around my room and grabbed two cartons each containing 25 packs of cigarettes and a few cans of food stuff, but when I returned to the window I noticed the boys were already standing at my doorstep accompanied by a Japanese officer, who had a saber at his side, knocking at my door."

"You are the Greek?" the officer asked.

"Yes," Steve replied. Steve was frightened, but the POWs motioned to him that everything was okay. The officer pushed his way into the room and the six prisoners entered after him. Steve had hoped for such an opening. The Japanese officer said he had a Russian girlfriend who lived nearby; he wanted Steve to take charge, as long as the prisoners promised not to run away and Steve took responsibility for the consequences. It was a deal. The officer ran off to do whatever he could do in an hour. The prisoners relaxed in the apartment, and Steve gave them food and cigarettes to take with them. The officer came back as planned, thanked Steve, and left with the men.

Steve alerted others in the neighborhood that he had managed to set up his shop as an odd sort of safe haven for POWs. Claire put together a care package with some of the clothing John Phillips had left behind. Five or six times the Japanese officer brought the men back for visits. Each time, Steve was ready to give them supplies. Years later he could still remember some of their names: Gene Whitaker, Jack Ferguson, Picket, and Herbert.

Claire and Steve the Greek became friends and decided to seek out other sympathetic Japanese guards. They got another chance when an American POW driving a truck with about a dozen POWs on board stopped at the gas station across from Tsubaki Club on Mabini Street. Steve approached the Japanese soldier guarding the men, bowed, and asked if he and the prisoners would like to have some lunch. He said yes and Claire brought over some food. The next day Steve was able to persuade the guards to come have lunch at Tsubaki Club with the prisoners. The club was closed to customers during the day.

Emboldened by their experience, Claire and Steve went out separately to Luneta Park. Steve was selling snacks and cigarettes; Claire was walking with Dian, since experience had shown that lonely young Japanese soldiers liked seeing children. She walked close to one group of POWs, crossed the street, and approached some guards. The guards warmed up when they saw Dian. Claire bowed, looked toward Steve, and addressed one of the Japanese soldiers: "Could I buy cigarettes for the Americans?"

"Yes," he said.

Claire wanted to proceed deliberately and assumed nothing. She bought the cigarettes from Steve and started to hand them to the guard, who she assumed would in turn give them to the prisoners. But the guard was relaxed about it and indicated that she could do it herself. So she approached the nearest American POW with some cigarettes and matches.

She had written a little note ahead of time and stuffed it into a matchbox. It read: "You can trust the man that sells cigarettes here because I know him."

That simple act established a long-standing supply and lunch operation, thanks to that guard who had been kind enough to allow her to give cigarettes to the men—she came to know him as Yamada. He treated the prisoners with respect. She recalled later, "I almost insulted him once by asking if I could give him some money to spend. I found out then I didn't have to bribe him." If she wanted to give money to the POWs, he said to do it openly. "Anything you want to do, do it in front of Yamada. You don't have to do it behind his back."

Yamada began to bring men regularly to the club; Claire fed them all, including Yamada and the soldiers with him. He only took money when it was to deliver the funds to prisoners who couldn't get out. One case Claire remembered involved William Bruce, a mechanic who had broken his arm and lost some teeth when a tire rim fell off a truck he was repairing and hit him in the face. Claire said she put together a package with a splint, surgical tape, and antiseptics, then gave it all to Yamada for Bruce. Yamada brought Bruce to the club one afternoon a few weeks later and Bruce thanked her for helping treat him.

Claire then faced the tricky business of feeding the men, Yamada, and the guards under him, while at the same time trying to keep Yamada at a distance. As Madame Tsubaki, she found that men were always looking for special privileges and attention she was not willing to provide. He wanted to spend time with her during off-hours and she gently pushed him away. Finally she had to give in by at least agreeing to go to the movies with him. She tried to keep the relationship friendly but limited. Still, though, people saw her in the company of a Japanese soldier. That was a potential problem.

Through Steve, Claire began to meet others who already were helping the POWs. One new contact was Nancy Belle Norton, an American woman who dared to carry supplies directly to the POWs. Norton, a frail-looking, seventy-year-old retired schoolteacher, had been in Manila for twenty years. She appeared to be immune to Japanese rules. Out of respect for older people, the Japanese had decided she was too old to go to Santo Tomas. Mrs. Norton was allowed to travel freely around the city; she gathered clothing and food and marched right in to deliver the supplies. Her daily rounds included visiting Bilibid Prison, where the Japanese warden approved her visits.

Bilibid had been a civilian prison before the war but now also was housing POWs who needed hospital care. The warden was a doctor named Nogi. Mrs. Norton visited Nogi and asked if she could provide help to the hospitalized men. "Unlike some of the other arrogant Japanese commanders, he was most helpful and gave me permission. I was told, however, that I must not speak to any of the boys, and they must not speak to me, or permission would be withdrawn and I would be punished."

Working with Nancy Belle Norton, Claire was able to assemble a list of prisoners in Manila and determine which needed the most help, and what kind of help. She noted which prisoners she had been in touch with and what kind of help had been or might be provided. The list was also useful intelligence to send out to Boone and onward to his superiors. The list would not only be confirmation for family back home that the men were alive; it could also be used as a logistical aid when eventually the United States could plan a rescue on MacArthur's promised return to the Philippines.

Claire began to send supplies regularly to Mrs. Norton, all the while working with Steve and helping Louise and friends at Santo Tomas. She learned that many people around Manila were interested in doing exactly the same thing, gathering supplies for prisoners and finding a variety of routes to deliver the material on a regular basis. Contact with Steve the Greek and Mrs. Norton in turn brought a meeting for Claire with a woman who would become her friend and rival, trusted ally and antagonist. Her name was Peggy Utinsky, an American nurse who also wanted to do whatever possible to help the prisoners.

Peggy's Orders
Manila, 1942

As THE THREAT of war had grown in the summer and fall of 1941, Peggy Utinsky, a registered nurse, had defied her husband's insistence that she leave the Philippines along with other women and children being sent back to the United States.

"Orders were orders," Jack Utinsky had told his wife, but she was not buying that argument. "I told him that I had not disobeyed an order, that nobody had told me to go home, that they had just told me to get on the boat, that they didn't tell me to stay there."

Jack was a reserve U.S. Army captain and a civil engineer with the army. He had now been called to active status and was to report for duty in Bataan. Peggy and Jack had come to the Port of Manila to act out a familiar scene in those last weeks of 1941 before the war. Taxis and private cars, horse carts and trucks had jammed the docks. Hundreds of women and children had stood forlorn on the deck of the SS *Washington*, bidding tearful farewell to their husbands and fathers. The *Washington*, a luxury liner of the United States Lines with a capacity of about one thousand passengers, bound for California, was one of the last ships carrying Americans out of a possible battle zone in the South China Sea. President Roosevelt had ordered American dependents to leave the Philippines months earlier. Many top U.S. military brass in Manila had come out for the send-off, including Major General Jonathan M. Wainwright (second in command under General MacArthur), who was dispatching his family back to the States.

Despite Peggy's protests, they had packed up their furniture, gathered her clothing, and moved out of their apartment; Jack had booked her a one-way ticket. But Peggy kept complaining. She reckoned that orders did not apply to her. And what was she going back to? On her return to the States earlier in the year for the first time in more than a decade, she had not felt at home.

Margaret Doolin Utinsky, forty-one, had been born in St. Louis on August 28, 1900. Her first husband, John Martin Rowley, died in 1919 after three years of marriage. They had a son, Charles Grant Rowley. Peggy became a registered nurse in 1922 but decided not to make the easy choice of getting a job somewhere in the Midwest. She wanted instead to try something exotic; she and her nine-year-old son sailed for Manila in 1929. Peggy liked what she saw and decided to pursue a nursing career in the Philippines. Jack and Peggy were married in Manila in 1934.

After vacationing for a few months in the United States in 1941, Peggy could see no good reason for staying away. Charles now was in his twenties and lived on his own in the United States. She came back to Manila, certain that nurses would be in demand should war break out. Jack kept insisting that the departure order was mandatory. However, she countered that since she was not in the army, she had no orders to obey. Peggy did not stop arguing.

Now, on the dock, Jack was trying to comfort her, but she was having none of it.

It was for her own safety, he said. "It won't be long. We'll make short work of the Japs if they do come. You'll be back before you know it."

"Before you know it?" she asked. "I won't be one of those thousands of women back in the States who have to sit and wonder every minute what is happening here in the islands. What can I do over there? Here at least I could help if anything happened."

They continued to bicker as the minutes ticked away until bells sounded and a steward circulated calling out the dread words: "All ashore!" There was one last kiss and embrace, and then Jack took the gangway, went to a car, and drove away. Peggy, "all dressed for traveling and plastered with orchids," watched him leave.

When the bell and announcement sounded once more, Peggy took the chance she had been waiting for. General Wainwright, who had lingered long on board, "was the last one to leave the ship, at least he thought he was. When General Wainwright walked down the gangplank, I walked right close behind him. I knew that I was so close behind him that no sergeant or MP would ever dare stop me. So he turned to the left, walked to the other end of the pier where General Willoughby [Charles A. Willoughby, MacArthur's chief of intelligence, then a colonel, later promoted to major general] and many other men were, and, of course, there were a lot of Spanish and Filipino people there and they were all waving 'Goodbye' to their friends."

Peggy had planned ahead. Jack had paid five pesos to a porter to load her luggage onto the ship; Peggy had slipped ten pesos more to the porter to hold it back onshore.

"The boat backed out, turned, went through breakwater. My heart ached for the men standing on the pier, taking a last look at their wives through field glasses." Jack Utinsky had already left for town. He boiled over when she caught up with him at the hotel where they had been living since moving out of their apartment.

"My husband was just coming out of the hotel, he had checked out, and the trucks were there ready to take the men all back to Bataan." He hustled her back into the hotel and yelled "loud and long."

"It was an order," he said.

She replied once more that she was not subject to military orders.

"Stay in the hotel," he snapped. Nothing was going to happen, he told her, but stay inside. "He would be back in a few weeks. . . . Nothing was going to happen. . . . There wasn't going to be any war right in Manila."

He stared at her as he boarded a truck for the trip north.

Jack did yell loud enough to put the fear of God in her—at least for an hour or so. "And then I went out and rented an apartment."

It became increasingly obvious every day to Peggy that war was indeed coming and Manila might not be spared. She began saving up food and supplies just in case. By the time of the Pearl Harbor attack, Peggy was working a full nursing shift at Remedios Hospital. She hardly even had time off when Jack got a pass and came in from Bataan for a few days after Christmas. She said they spent little time together. After bombing raids the hospital staff was working around the clock. In the end, Jack made sure to tell her she was right to have stayed in Manila. "I came back here thinking I'd have to pull you out of a ditch. Instead of that, I found you scurrying around, pulling other people out. I'd like you to know, darling, I'm very proud of you."

A few days later the Japanese occupation of Manila was imminent. Peggy took advantage of an offer by the commissaries at all U.S. military bases to empty out their warehouses, first come, first served. She hired taxis and carts and took everything she could, then piled supplies floor to ceiling in her small apartment. Starting January 2, the day the Japanese marched in, she kept the lights off and pretended the apartment was empty. She avoided going out in daylight for more than two months, then finally ventured outside.

The primary order of business was to avoid detention as an American. Like Claire, she had arranged a fake identity card and an alias to avoid being dragged off to Santo Tomas. She was now Rosena Utinsky, the spinster daughter of a family from Lithuania, a Baltic state under Nazi occupation and therefore considered to be on the side of the Axis. With forged Japanese signatures and a passable travel document, Peggy could circulate freely. She returned to Remedios Hospital and began assisting doctors in their normal duties. After the U.S. surrender at Bataan and Corregidor, the Red Cross petitioned Japanese authorities to provide help to prisoners of war who had survived the Bataan death march (not called that at the time, at least not within earshot of the Japanese). Officials approved the request—as long as only Filipino prisoners were treated. This was in line with the Japanese view of the occupation: Japan was the Philippines' benevolent savior, and Filipinos and Japanese should be considered Asian allies. Only the Americans were the enemy.

One of the doctors Peggy had been working with, Ramón Atienza, received permission to set up a small Red Cross facility at Camp O'Donnell to treat Filipino patients with the proviso that he and his staff were not to have any contact with the American POWs. Though they were isolated in a separate section of the camp, Atienza managed to establish contact with Colonel James W. Duckworth, the physician caring for American POWs at the camp, and with Captain Frank L. Tiffany, the camp chaplain.

In early June, around the same time that Claire was sneaking into Manila, Atienza summoned Peggy to work with the Red Cross mission at Camp O'Donnell. Peggy's role was confirmation that her tough decision to remain in the Philippines had been well founded. "After this trip through filth and nightmare, when everything seemed to be festering death, I knew that I could not stop until I had given every ounce of my strength to help the men who still lived."

With help from Atienza, Peggy was able to smuggle food, medicine, clothing, and small amounts of money into the camp on ambulances returning empty after having transported sick Filipinos to his clinic just outside the gate. It was a dangerous enterprise.

Peggy knew she looked enough like an American to be the focus of suspicion on the train rides from Manila up toward Camp O'Donnell, especially as she began bringing more and more gear on every trip and had to depend on porters and conductors to get all of the sacks of supplies on and off the trains. When Japanese guards stopped her, she smiled and showed them her travel permit and her Red Cross ID and armband. That usually worked, but it was only a matter of time before she would be questioned more carefully.

One day she was just unloading her latest package of supplies when a Japanese soldier ran up to her, yelling and pointing. "American! American!"

Doctor Atienza raced up in alarm and protested, "No, no, not American, Lithuanian. That is like German—friends to you."

This Japanese soldier stopped yelling, but he did not appear to be convinced that Peggy was either Lithuanian or German. Atienza pointed to

Peggy's uniform and said, "*Kankoshi, kankoshi*," one of the only words they had learned in Japanese: nurse.

If that was the case, the Japanese soldier said, how do you say *kankoshi* in German?

"That stumped me. The only German word I had ever heard was *Deutsch* [which means German]. But it was a start, so I might as well use it. 'You say *nursie, Deutsche nursie*,' I told him, and the Japanese turned away satisfied."

Back in Manila, Peggy asked a German friend about the word for nurse—*Krankenschwester*, or just *Schwester* [sister]. It was a good idea to commit it to memory for future reference, in case the next Japanese soldier she met knew enough English to realize how silly "*Deutsche nursie*" sounded. Something similar had happened to Claire at the nightclub. She now carried false papers that gave her Italian citizenship. Since she was presenting herself as half Filipina and half Italian, a Japanese officer said he had been stationed for a while in Italy. "Can you sing 'O Sole Mio' for me?" he asked. "*Sì, sì-sì, sì-sì-sì*," she responded, belting out the song and a bunch of gobbledygook sounds whose lines always started or ended with words that sounded like *sole mio* and *amore*, whatever that might mean.

With increased volume and despite the ability to fool Japanese soldiers a few times, Peggy had the reasonable fear that she would eventually be found out as an American. Meanwhile, the work of filling sacks of goods and transporting them with the Red Cross was getting busy enough that she needed help and more supplies. By the time Claire and Peggy met in the fall of 1942, Peggy was gathering a loosely knit crew of Filipinos and foreigners willing to gather donations and ship supplies to prisoners in Manila and up north to the Cabanatuan prisoner of war camp. Her work was to aid the men who had survived the Bataan death march but were now dying by the hundreds every week. Before the war, Claire and Peggy had lived within blocks of one another; soon they would be working together.

The Prisoners of Japan
Camp O'Donnell, Capas, Philippines, 1942

THE JAPANESE MILITARY viewed surrender as a shameful act and believed that prisoners, especially American prisoners, had disgraced their country and themselves. Accordingly, they treated the Americans as lesser beings, and their survival was a minor topic worth little consideration. The Tokyo High Command often sent the lowest of the low to be prison camp guards and commanders—disabled soldiers, men unfit to fight and destined to remain far from the prestigious front lines of battle. For some of them their only glory was the systematic, sadistic torture of the American POWs. Camp O'Donnell, about sixty miles north of Manila, had been the terminus of the Bataan death march in April 1942. O'Donnell had been designed as a Philippine Army outpost for ten thousand men, but construction had not been completed. About fifty thousand Filipinos and nine thousand Americans were forced into cramped, inadequate facilities under the camp's tyrannical Japanese commander, Captain Yoshio Tsuneyoshi, who greeted the POWs with a long rant, berating them as cowards and common criminals, not prisoners of war.

> It is regrettable that we were unable to kill each of you on the battlefield. It is only through our generosity that you are alive at all. We do not consider you to be prisoners of war. You are members of an inferior race, and we will treat you as we see fit. Whether you live or die is of no concern to us.

Filth, hunger, and depravity followed. Some men were shot outright; many more died of neglect. The Filipino and American POWs died at an appalling rate; as many as sixteen hundred Americans and possibly ten thousand Filipino prisoners died in the first six weeks. The survivors could hardly describe the horror they had suffered—every form of jungle disease, black flies, green flies, parasites, typhoid, malaria, and tropical plagues that had no name.

On June 1, after about two months, General Homma himself removed the camp commander and reported him to Tokyo for incompetence. It was none too soon for the prisoners, who called Tsuneyoshi "little Hitler," among other things. "He was one of the ugliest mortals I have ever seen," one of them said. "He breathed the very essence of hate."

The replacement, a higher-ranking officer known as Colonel Ito, set out to improve conditions, at least somewhat. In an effort to alleviate the overcrowding and disease, Japanese authorities began to furlough sick and dying Filipino prisoners and transfer surviving Americans to a different facility. Release of the Filipinos was billed as a goodwill gesture; few people took it that way, but they raced to the rescue. Family members had been allowed to register and travel to the camp by train in baggage cars so they could fetch their loved ones. The prisoners often collapsed in their arms when they arrived for the trip home. Some were so sick and malnourished that the strain of the transfer back home killed them on the return train trip before they could reach Manila.

The scene at the station in Manila was heartrending. The Filipinos saw through Japanese claims and realized that the furlough of the prisoners was hardly a humanitarian act. Rather, it was a pragmatic decision to avoid their dying while still in custody, which would have turned public opinion against the Japanese. Nursed back to health, most of the former prisoners were defiant and wanted to find a way to keep fighting. "If given the opportunity," said Marcial Lichauco, "they would like to get another crack at the enemy."

The Japanese then drove most of the remaining Americans by truck in small groups to a new location about forty-five miles to the east. They named it Cabanatuan; the camp was close to the Pampanga River, about four miles from the center of Cabanatuan City, the capital of Nueva Ecija Province, and about one hundred miles north of Manila. The transfer to Cabanatuan, which was divided into three living areas, was somewhat better for the remaining Americans, but they were still sick, starving, and in need of help. Some of the able-bodied Americans were being shifted to prisons and detention centers in Manila to serve as the laborers, servants, and drivers whom Claire, Steve the Greek, Peggy, and their allies saw performing menial and clerical and hard-labor tasks in the city. They lived in thatched and palm-leaf-roofed barracks in one quarter of the camp, isolated by barbed wire and rifle-toting guards in wooden towers.

At first the Cabanatuan camp was hardly better than Camp O'Donnell. Cruelty and deprivation reigned. More than seven hundred men died in July, the first month they were there; five months later the prisoners were amazed to record a milestone: One day, December 15, 1942, had been death free. That was far from the norm. By the end of the war, almost a third of the nine thousand men who had passed through Cabanatuan had died there or at other camps.

The prisoners themselves took steps to organize and improve conditions; they built latrines, and their officers lobbied for better hygiene and better food, though their requests were rarely granted by the Japanese officers in charge, not as sadistic as the hated Captain Tsuneyoshi but often capable of neglect and great cruelty. POW doctors staffed an infirmary, others established a commissary, and others organized maintenance and sanitation. The Japanese officers also soon did allow limited contact with outside food vendors—mostly because they could not supply enough food to keep the Americans alive. The Japanese authorities did make a show of following or at least paying lip service to the Geneva conventions governing treatment of prisoners. POWs were allowed to have Red Cross contact and occasional food supplies, along with the right to send and receive messages home—in practice food was often stolen or rifled before the POWs received it, and their messages were deeply censored and unevenly transmitted. Observing the conventions when convenient, the Japanese even paid the POWs wages—between five and forty pesos a month, depending on rank—as payment for doing work at the camp, though it was often backbreaking and bruising under the tropical sun—and not voluntary. Local Filipino merchants delivered supplies to the small camp commissary, where the prisoners could buy food and other basics. This quickly became part of an elaborate black market system. A man who worked at the commissary, Horacio Manaloto, quickly made contact with outside relief workers who wanted to help the prisoners.

The Underground
Manila, November 1942

THANKS TO STEVE the Greek and Mrs. Norton, the retired teacher, Claire came to visit Peggy at her apartment, which was just a few blocks up Mabini Street from Tsubaki Club. They realized they had much in common—both Americans with assumed names, they were both already sending support to the POWs. They also were looking for lost soldiers, Jack Utinsky and John Phillips, who both might be prisoners at Cabanatuan.

Peggy introduced Claire to her committee of like-minded Filipinos and foreigners—all of them had seen the prisoners marching by and wanted to do what they could to help. They began to solicit funds and donations, each operating under a code name, sometimes together, sometimes apart, trusted allies with a goal of helping the POWs. The key members were a forty-four-year-old Irish priest, Father John Lalor, who hid supplies and passed along messages at his nearby parish church; Ramón Amusategui, a well-to-do Spanish Basque businessman, and his Filipina wife, Lorenza, organizers and fund-raisers; and Naomi Flores, who was in charge of actually making contact with the POWs at the new American camp at Cabanatuan.

Naomi and Peggy had met in May 1942. Naomi was working at the American-owned beauty salon where Peggy went to have her hair done. The owner, Charles, had been sent to detention at Santo Tomas. They chatted generally one day about working on a clothing drive for prisoners in Camp O'Donnell. Gathering supplies for men in the prison camp was not necessarily considered seditious. Peggy told Naomi she had already safely taken duffel bags of clothes and shoes by train up to Capas, the town nearest O'Donnell, and delivered them directly to Dr. Atienza. Naomi told Peggy she had also been gathering clothes with friends at the YWCA. "If you are working the same way, well, let's get together and collect clothes," Peggy said. Naomi soon moved into Peggy's apartment.

Now that they had a larger group, it was logical to start using code names to compartmentalize their activities. A captured message could not reveal the source—a POW would not know the real name of his outside contact. If anyone in the underground was arrested, no one person would have the full picture of their operations. Meanwhile, few people knew that Claire was also supporting the guerrillas.

The code names were amateurish, but they apparently worked. Peggy became "Miss U," hardly an undecipherable choice, and that became the name of their group. More often the others referred to her as "the old lady" or "auntie," which she probably did not like; Naomi became "Looter" because her principal occupation was to smuggle goods from Manila to Bataan. Ramón was "Spark Plug," because he was the most able and the smartest—he made the operation roll smoothly; his wife, Lorenza, was "Screwball," because she appeared in public to be mentally unbalanced. She was far from it, but people were afraid to approach her. When questioned by the Japanese police, and it happened at least once, she said, "they didn't bother me, they thought I was crazy." Claire had been doing a good job with multiple aliases without help. She now added an additional name—she would be known in underground circles as "High Pockets." Claire said it was because she was known to stuff messages down her blouse into her brassiere.

Breaking Through to the POWs
Cabanatuan, June 1942

IN MID-JUNE, Naomi made her first trip with Peggy up to the train station at Capas, north from Bataan, and onward by horse-drawn cart with clothing, medicine, and money for the prisoners at Camp O'Donnell. It worked well, and this was still aboveboard and legal under the aegis of the Red Cross. A diminutive Filipina with an easy smile, Naomi had an easier time passing through Japanese checkpoints on the way to deliver supplies to the prisoners. However, when the Americans were separated and sent to Cabanatuan, the women lost regular contact with them. Naomi's job would be to reestablish the supply line. It proved to be difficult.

Naomi's first attempt in November 1942 was little more than reconnaissance. She visited a nearby barrio on the road to the new POW camp and came back with a helpful survey of the scene but no contact with the POWs. She went back again in early December. This time Naomi decided to blend in with the locals. She dressed in peasant garb, unlikely to provoke suspicion. With the other women joining her, she began to sell fruits and vegetables from a makeshift stand on the road, close to the camp's rice paddies. The first day she had no luck in reaching out to any of the Americans; the camp appeared to be impenetrable. Then finally, a few days later, she spotted prisoners a couple of hundred feet from the road, bent over, tending rice and gathering straw for the carabao water buffalo in the camp.

The POWs hated pulling the farming shift; even if the compound was suffocating with flies and mosquitoes and stinking sewage, most of them were too weak and tired to want to move; even when they got a small increase in food and water, it still was not worth working in the hot sun all day.

That morning, guards were not allowing the prisoners to come close enough to buy food at the stands. Nevertheless, when no guard was close by, Naomi called out to the closest prisoner. All she could see was a person wearing a hat hunched over at a distance. The man looked up and shielded his eyes. She shouted that she had been working with Captain Tiffany and Colonel Duckworth at Camp O'Donnell and now wanted to set up a new transportation system for Cabanatuan. Tiffany, the camp chaplain, and Duckworth, the doctor, could vouch for her. "Call me Looter." The prisoner must have been surprised to hear a woman call to him in English. He acknowledged that he understood.

That was the opening.

When the men and their guards went back inside the camp gates for lunch, Naomi wrote a note with more information to say that Tiffany and Duckworth knew how the operation had worked at O'Donnell and wanted to start it up again here. She also asked for information about Peggy's husband, Jack Utinsky. After lunch the POWs came back on the water buffalo carts; the Japanese guards were more lenient and let the Americans approach the fruit stands for a break. "They were allowed to come near us to buy bananas and peanuts." Naomi pretended to take money but really slipped the bills back to the same man she had seen in the morning. He was Lieutenant Colonel Edward Mack. She handed over some fruit with a message concealed underneath. Mack then returned to tending the rice field.

The following day Lieutenant Colonel Mack had a message for her, which he left dangling from a piece of straw. "After they left the field, I went there and dug out this little note in the grass." It was confirmation from Tiffany and Duckworth that they were ready to start receiving supplies. Mack also sent along confirmation that Jack Utinsky had been a prisoner of war there. He had no further information yet.

Soon the supply line of food, medicine, and clothing was back in operation. Naomi had some clothing and medicine on hand in Capas and went back to the field to deliver a first shipment. The prisoners were able to hide small quantities under sacks of rice and straw, along with the fruit they "purchased" from the local stands.

"After that, we got together a few clothes and medicines and I went back to Cabanatuan to make more contacts." Naomi then returned to Manila to report that they could resume shipments.

When she returned as planned some days later, all the men on the prison detail had been briefed ahead of time and were ready for a young woman at the fruit stands who might be slipping messages and free food to them. Again this time they were allowed to approach the fruit stands, where Naomi and others ostensibly were selling their bananas and peanuts.

The other women at the stands were now in on the deal. They also stuffed notes and medicine in between packages and banana leaves. Naomi did not see Mack this time, but a man walked up to her and said his name was Price. "I handed it to him by selling bananas, by covering it with the money that I was exchanging, pretending that he bought the bananas and bought it with his money."

This time Naomi received a note in return, a letter directly from Lieutenant Colonel Mack. When she read it, the only proper thing to do was to deliver the message directly to Peggy as soon as possible.

Condolences
Manila, March 1943

NAOMI RETURNED straight to Peggy's apartment on Mabini Street, carrying the message from Lieutenant Colonel Mack. He had made his inquiries about Jack Utinsky and this was his report:

I am deeply sorry that I have to tell you what I found out. Your husband died here on August 6, 1942. He is buried here in the prison graveyard. I know how you have tried in every way to get word about him. I am sure that this is the true story. You will be told that he died of tuberculosis. That is not true. The men say that he actually died of starvation. A little more food and medicine, which they would not give him here, might have saved him.

Peggy said she was too numb to cry. "In one way, it was a relief to know the truth. . . . With every atrocity story, with every hideous thing I saw, I wondered, 'Is that happening to Jack? Is he being tortured? Is he ill? Is he starving? Where is he? Where? Where?' Now at least I could remember him without fear."

Not long after that, Claire also had her answer. On a subsequent visit, Naomi asked the POWs about John Phillips. It took longer to find his name, but finally another message came through, again from Mack and from Colonel Jack Schwartz, one of the camp POW physicians. Naomi left the message with Peggy, who in turn went to see Claire on March 13, 1943. Like the message to Peggy, the letter was an expression of sadness and condolence with the confirmation that John Phillips had died of malaria at Cabanatuan on July 27, 1942. Claire tried to hold out hope it was wrong. But she knew this time it was true. She got drunk that night, then dropped into bed.

Claire and Peggy both had known that this was a possible outcome; the grief and final confrontation of the truth were overwhelming. Peggy had heard nothing about her husband's whereabouts since the day he left town for that one last visit at Christmas in 1941. Claire had been tormented for weeks by rumors and unconfirmed sightings and was frantically searching for news of John Phillips. She had sent notes to all of the prisons. She had obsessively searched the sad faces of the Americans trudging by in work details or crammed onto the backs of trucks. "Pray to God I can see him," she had written. "If I don't see [him] soon I'll go crazy. Think of him every day. Can't get him off my mind." Every few days some piece of news had gotten her hopes up. In February even one of her Japanese would-be paramours, a colonel, had agreed to take a look at official death lists and had said Phillips's name was not there. One day someone had said he had been spotted driving a truck; a day later, no, "he's at the Ayala Bridge." After that, one of the POWs on truck detail who came into the club occasionally had said that he had seen a guy who he thought was John Phillips. This man had been taken out of the city but was supposed to be coming back in two weeks. A few days after that, on February 21, Claire had come across Joe Rizzo, the sergeant who had been in charge of John Phillips's platoon. Rizzo was an internee at Fort McKinley, frequently on work details in and around Luneta Park. Rizzo was sorry to say that he had heard that Phillips had died. Claire had not wanted to listen. Instead she had written love letters to Phil, as she called him, and forwarded them to every prison she heard of; she had asked every contact she could make to pass the word on. *Where is Phil?*

One afternoon a few days after Peggy delivered the letter about Phillips, Ramón Amusategui stopped over to express his condolences. Claire was still in shock and still did not want to believe that Phillips was dead. Ramón suggested that she ask for confirmation from Father Heinz Buttenbruck, a German parish priest who was allowed to come and go at Cabanatuan to minister to the prisoners. Ramón said that the priest was trustworthy and apparently got along with the Japanese because of his German nationality. "There is no need to worry about him. He's a real Christian and no Nazi."

The priest told Claire he would make inquiries the next time he traveled to the camp. She wanted to take advantage of Buttenbruck's trip north and asked if she could send messages and money to the POWs. The priest said he was always searched by the Japanese guards and could not take the risk. However, he had been able to bring clothing and supplies. Perhaps if she brought a shopping bag of supplies and hid the note carefully it would get through.

"I thanked Father Buttenbruck and hurried back to town where I bought shoes, pants, socks, a shirt, toothbrush and paste, quinine, aspirin and a few cans of food." She packed the gear in a bag as instructed and returned to the priest. Buttenbruck said he would do his best to find John Phillips.

"Thank you, Father. I don't know how to express my gratitude."

"There is no need for that. We are all doing our best and God will repay us in His way. Good-bye and God bless you."

It took weeks for Buttenbruck to make the trip and get back to Claire. He returned on April 24 with a list of men who had died on July 27, 1942, nine months earlier. It included John Phillips and listed the service number on his dog tags. The final digits were "13"; she and Phillips had joked about the luck of having a serial number ending that way. She wrote in her diary that night: "Phil Darling, Father Buttenbruck arrived, said you died July 27. I know it's not true. I know you wouldn't leave me. I'll always wait for you. I love you more than I even thought possible to love anyone."

Claire suffered Phillips's death all over again and drank herself into a stupor. "Fely and the others carried on for me, explaining that Madame was suffering with a miserable headache. They couldn't say heartache."

In her diary she confessed to feeling on the verge of madness and despair, to nights of drinking too much and probably entertaining too much. Now convinced that Phillips was dead, she thought about killing herself. She was Madame Tsubaki at the club, the elegant, exotic songstress in the shimmering dark. But during the day, on the street, she was a subjugated woman in an occupied country. Bitterly she thought about how guards pushed her aside as they sauntered by, slapping and beating people as they went. Without hope, what did she have to live for? "Wish I could join him then, but I'm a coward."

A note from Captain Frank Tiffany, the chaplain POW at Cabanatuan, finally pulled her out of the funk. He expressed sympathy but he had one other message. The men needed her. He asked her "not to forget the ones that are left." She said that Tiffany's appeal brought her back to the world. Claire had teased herself with talk of death, with drunkenness, and with a nervous breakdown, but she also seemed to know that writing those things to herself in her secret diary was an escape valve. She was hard on herself, but she kept distance and perspective from the words of death and despair. A few weeks after closeting herself away, Claire went back to the club with new resolve. Phil had come to represent all of the men who had fought and been captured or died. He became a symbol of the fight to help the survivors. That was the role she could play in the war.

She did keep drinking; she knew what she was doing and kept doing it. But the act of jotting it in her diary at the end of the day showed that she was fighting the urge and finding balance within herself. The days were all about hauling in supplies. The nights were about running the club, singing, shimmying on the stage, and sitting with the top officers. Plus, Japanese officers would come in sometimes, open a tab, and not pay. Claire was drowning in chits, and how was she supposed to demand payment? If the goal was to keep the club running, what was more important, keeping up profits or gathering information? So she kept up with the daily motions, counting receipts, watching prices going up, feeding Dian, gathering information, and making ends meet. Cloth was increasingly hard to come by, as was new clothing. So they took down the drapes at the club and went to work. The performers needed new costumes at the club; and the men in the POW camps also needed clothes. Some afternoons, Dian's nurse would come downstairs, and the hostesses would arrive early and they all would stitch shirts and shorts for the prisoners. One day Claire found some more clothing that Phillips had left behind. She packed it all up and gave it to the POWs. When the prisoner work details were allowed to stop by, she gave them the best food she could—man by man, she was trying to keep hope alive.

Peggy's Collapse
Manila, April 1943

AT FOUR O'CLOCK one morning, the lights were dim on Mabini Street and all of Manila under curfew; no one was supposed to be there. A rather dowdy woman in her forties was reeling along the street, coming from some nightspot or someone's home, extremely drunk and in danger of being arrested by Philippine constables or, even worse, by Japanese military police.

It was Peggy or, if she could remember that much, Rosena Utinsky, the Lithuanian nurse, according to her forged identification papers. That was how Ramón and Lorenza found her, stumbling, quarrelsome, highly inebriated. It was not the first time; Lorenza and Ramón were angry and very worried. "Ramón did his utmost toward convincing her of the risk of talking too much and of drinking almost every night, sometimes into a stupor—unfortunately without results."

Claire had pulled herself out of mourning; Peggy had not. Both of them were drinking, but Claire admitted it. Peggy did not. Who could say why? Peggy, feeling the pressure and possibly because she was holding back the grief of losing her husband, was not admitting her problem. The danger of being noticed and picked up was too great. That was not all.

It was true, Peggy had founded the organization and it was named Miss U—the supply operation to Cabanatuan was the embodiment of Peggy Utinsky. But no more.

Perhaps she had cracked under the pressure; the reason did not matter. Peggy had become argumentative and dangerous and was breaking her own rules. Early on, Peggy had been adamant and vigilant on matters of operational security. They were to avoid any suspicious activities, to be careful about whom they spoke to or spoke about. The more people they spoke to, the greater the chance that there was an infiltrator among them. Now Peggy was the one to worry about.

One of their most important contacts, Horacio Manaloto, a Filipino civilian, had visited recently. The Japanese thought he was a businessman plying his trade by selling things to the prison commissary and had given him a permit to come and go on supply runs from the Cabanatuan POW camp. Secretly he was working with the Manila underground to smuggle money and supplies on his truck into Cabanatuan. However, Peggy had been abusive to him when he came to town, so he had started dealing only with Ramón. The problems were growing. Not only was Peggy rude and bossy, but she also was talking to people outside the group and bragging about her exploits. Ramón, Lorenza, and the others needed complete secrecy. All too obviously, if Peggy or any of them attracted unwanted attention, Japanese authorities might investigate, capture, and kill them. Claire was very cautious about her contacts and never spoke to anyone until she could confirm who they were.

Claire spoke with the others about their problems with Peggy. "She did start and do a good job, and I tried to stick with her," Claire said, but she saw the clashes. "There is no love lost on my part. . . . None of the gang and Miss U got along too well." But she didn't abandon Peggy and tried to maintain the friendship.

Theoretically, Claire was in the more dangerous situation, spending time with Japanese officers every evening, yet she was discreet and so managed to avoid any suspicion. Not so, Peggy. "Unfortunately," Lorenza said, "Mrs. Utinsky, the so-called head of our group, was very fond of talking and arguing, thereby creating an atmosphere of tension in the group."

Naomi also noticed the change in Peggy's behavior and quietly began to make plans to get away. She had brought a longtime friend, Evangeline Neibert, into the group to help her carry shipments to Cabanatuan. Eventually Naomi would leave Manila and move closer to the POW camp so she could manage shipments and supplies at Cabanatuan; Evangeline would take over the deliveries from the city to the camp. Peggy, however, had berated Evangeline more than once, leaving her crying and thinking about quitting entirely. Peggy also had been crude and abusive with Naomi and had even drunkenly threatened the Filipino helpers that she would turn them in to the Japanese. Whether it was a reaction to Jack's death or a sign of the pressure they all were operating under, even one mad tirade was too much. Whatever its cause, Peggy's behavior could be lethal to them all. As early as April 1943, Ramón "without her knowledge . . . took over her place as head of the group."

Ramón did this without embarrassing Peggy, slowly taking on a larger role. Ramón and Lorenza were concerned that if Peggy realized what was happening, she would follow through on her drunken outbursts and turn people in. Operations to pack supplies for the north slowly shifted from Peggy's apartment to the Malate parish church, where Father Lalor and the other priests coordinated and stocked supplies until shipment. The group avoided gathering at Peggy's apartment when possible.

Naomi, however, was living in Peggy's apartment, and it was hard to move out without a reason—no one wanted to set off Peggy and make things worse. The opportunity finally came, although the circumstances were almost a disaster. A friend had begged Naomi to help hide two American stragglers trying to evade capture. They were young soldiers who had escaped Bataan, traveling ever since then in the shadows, liable to be caught at any moment. Naomi took them in but needed help and advice on what to do with them.

"Their names were Tommy and . . . Tommy Larson and Barney. I don't know his last name," Naomi said. The men said they had been on Corregidor and in Bataan when the surrender came but managed to evade the Japanese and the death march. Hungry and ragged, they had been hiding for months. Claire did what she could and gave them food and something to drink. This was dangerous enough, because the Japanese military police had been systematically conducting house-to-house searches. The club was tacitly endorsed by the Japanese officials who came to drink and see the show every night. Madame Tsubaki was not under suspicion. Nevertheless, it would have been foolish to hide Tommy and Barney at the club with Japanese officers on the other side of the wall.

Naomi turned to Peggy. She said that since Charles, the American owner of Naomi's beauty parlor, had been detained and his business was shuttered and abandoned, it would be a safe hiding place for a while.

Eventually, perhaps, the boys could make their way up to the hills to join the guerrillas.

"In the meantime," Peggy said later, "we would at least be able to feed them and no one ever entered the deserted shop."

Naomi took Peggy's suggestion, set up cots, and sneaked Barney and Tommy over to the beauty shop. A woman who lived across the street saw the men through a window and reported suspicious activity at the closed shop to the police. Japanese troops raided the beauty parlor, shot and wounded both Americans, then took them away. Now the Kempeitai were looking for Naomi. Peggy told Naomi they had to take the offensive. If Naomi ran, the Japanese would take it as an admission of guilt and it could lead to a larger investigation of all of them. "Go to them," she said. "Ask what they wanted, tell them [you] had hired the boys—whom [you] took for mestizos—to guard the shop."

Brave though frightened, and for good reason, Naomi went to Fort Santiago the next morning to say she had heard that Kempeitai officers were looking for her. The police interrogators asked their questions and made her repeat the story many times.

"I didn't have anything to do with those boys," she said each time she was asked. "I didn't know they were Americans."

The man in charge, Captain Tossino, slapped and punched her when he didn't like her answer to one question: How many times had she gone to the shop after the men began working for her? "A couple of times," she said. Tossino did not understand the translation of "a couple" or did not like the vague answer.

Tossino asked repeatedly: *Who were these men? Did you know they were soldiers?*

She repeated once more: "I didn't have anything to do with those boys. . . . I didn't know they were Americans."

Finally, in mock frustration, she told them to get it over with. "They kept on hammering that I was telling a lie." If they didn't believe her, she said, they should just kill her.

"Go ahead and shoot me. . . . Go ahead and shoot me and get it over with."

Her show of anger and frustration brought an end to the interrogation. They believed her. Tossino thanked her for coming and let her go.

All the while, Peggy was waiting for news at the apartment. The day passed slowly, dusk approached, and there was no news. If the police did not believe Naomi's story, everyone could be arrested; they all might be killed. Finally, at around 7:00 p.m., Naomi walked in. She had been slapped around but was not actually injured, or at least didn't mention it. The main thing was that she was free and they were safe. The ruse had worked. Naomi took a long breath and told Peggy what had happened.

They slept well that night. Everything was fine until the next morning, when there was a knock at the door. A pair of Japanese military policemen walked in; one of them had been questioning Naomi the day before. They were cordial and had some questions for Peggy—that is, for Rosena, the Lithuanian nurse with a supposed non-American-sounding first name.

All very casually and friendly as the women served tea, the Kempeitai officers chatted about nothing in particular. One of the men opened an atlas that was on the table and pointed to Asia and Europe. "This is for Japan—this is for Germany," he said. "That is the way it will be after the war. Where will you live then?" he asked Peggy. "In Manila, I think. Lithuania will probably be destroyed." The men bowed and left, apparently satisfied that Rosena Utinsky, as her forged papers indicated, was Lithuanian and supported the Japanese cause. Two weeks later Claire heard that Barney and Tommy were still alive and were being moved out of Manila, presumably to Cabanatuan or another camp. There was no further word of their whereabouts.

Dangerous as it had been, the visit from the Kempeitai gave Naomi the excuse she needed to leave Peggy's apartment. She obtained a permit to move out of Manila after informing the authorities that she had to take care of her aunt, Miss Bell, who lived just outside Cabanatuan City. Naomi then persuaded Evangeline Neibert to stay on as the main transport person from Manila to Cabanatuan, but working directly with Ramón. From then on, Naomi rarely traveled to Manila and when she did, she made other lodging arrangements.

Messages at Dawn

Cabanatuan, May 1943

WHENEVER A DELIVERY was ready to be smuggled into Cabanatuan, Naomi emerged after dawn from the home of Miss Bell—not really her aunt, as she had told authorities—on the main road, where she was renting a room. At that time of day the temperature was still tolerable, not yet steaming, with the rainy season a few months off. At Cabanatuan, POW work details were mustering to ride the oxcarts through the gates and over to the fields.

Naomi pretended she had just gotten up. She wandered outside the house, close to the main road. She lived a couple of hundred feet from the rice fields where the Americans would soon begin their farming chores. When the oxcarts had passed and the men had come out to the fields, Naomi knew that Fred Threatt, the prisoner in charge of the cart detail, would be able to see her. They would park the oxcarts at the bridge along the road, in sight of the fields, and from there Naomi and Mr. Threatt could see each other.

To the Japanese she was just a young woman stretching in the morning out in front of her house. Any man, Japanese guard or American prisoner, would appreciate the sight of a lovely girl standing by the road. She would run her fingers through her thick black hair once, twice, three times. And what of it? Then she would casually go back in the house.

That simple gesture was her signal to Mr. Threatt—code-named Mango. Threatt, forty-seven, was a World War I veteran from Louisiana who had settled in the Philippines with his wife before the war. He had enlisted in the navy in December 1941, but the POWs still considered him a civilian and always referred to him as "Mr. Threatt." He looked out toward Naomi in the distance: Three strokes of the hair meant three packs of medicine and supplies buried under the tree. Later in the day Mr. Threatt always stopped on the bridge heading back to the camp so he and the other cart drivers could water their animals and get a drink of their own. The guards allowed prisoners to hop off the carts to buy fruits and vegetables. The guards would not be paying particular attention. Another slow, warm day. What danger could there be? The POWs made a show of pretending to pay for rice cakes, bananas, and small calamansi lemons. Naomi had repacked the supplies sent up from Manila in smaller quantities (easier to hide), along with letters and money stuffed into sliced banana peels and leaves. The men at the stand appeared to be paying for fruits and nuts but were really handing over notes and requests for more supplies. Meanwhile, Mr. Threatt hopped down below the bridge and retrieved whatever packages Naomi had left for him, then hid them on his carabao cart under the sacks of rice and straw being hauled in. So went the days, the same routine once, even twice a week. So far they hadn't been caught.

Just in case, if the Japanese wanted to make sure the women were really selling fruit, they could ask Naomi to show them her money. She always had enough crumpled Japanese occupation notes—the Filipinos and Americans called it Mickey Mouse money—on hand to show them.

Threatt used a careful tracking system when he delivered the supplies to Mack and to Tiffany and then onward to the prison hospital or to individual prisoners. A soldier's name might be checked off on the Manila note to Tiffany and might have an extra notation: "with onions." This guy was to receive money. The system was simple enough in both directions that the operatives knew who was expected to get what and that there would be confirmations flowing back to Manila. Signaling Threatt was by no means easy, though, nor without danger. Naomi's rented room by the road was the terminus of a sixty-mile smuggling route from Manila to Cabanatuan. All along the way, everything needed to appear innocent, simple, and homespun. Naomi and her friend Evangeline carried travel passes, and they had to make sure their movements seemed irregular and haphazard. If they crossed paths with Japanese guards, they had to appear calm as they slowly and humbly bowed to them, making sure to avert their eyes.

They would take as much as they could carry—a large sack and half a dozen woven paper shopping bags. Evangeline or Ramón himself would hire a horse cart at dawn to take them to the train station in Manila. One or two of the bags were different from the others, and they carried concealed money and notes in those bags; Evangeline always kept these closest to her on the train. Before packing the bags, Ramón and Lorenza censored and reviewed every piece of paper and looked at the overall appearance of the packages. They made sure that no language in the letters could refer to an identifiable person—code names only.

The entire supply operation, though, depended on Naomi and her ability to communicate with the prisoners. She and her friend Evangeline were in constant danger. Claire downplayed her own role compared with the daring of the Filipina women. "I don't know of any other girl that would have done the dangerous work that you . . . did. I am sure there is no American girl who would have done the dangerous work you two girls did. I am really proud that I know you."

Naomi and Evangeline learned to pack so that messages and money would be easy to miss. "It was concealed by mongo [mung] beans or black-eyed beans or candy. By putting the candy on top of the big bags," they ensured that if the Japanese soldiers "stick their hands in, they will find out that it is just candy or mongo beans in there."

Buried deep within were small shipments of food, medicine, tools, and letters to and from the POWs. Threatt also had to maintain a casual, low profile. When the amounts became greater, Horacio Manaloto, the authorized merchant supplying the prison commissary, used the same method for his truck but carried greater volumes than the women could handle on their own. Manaloto could ship far more than what the women could bring up on the train, more than Threatt could carry on his oxcart—sacks of rice, tomatoes, baskets of potatoes, and black-eyed beans. A few times Manaloto even corralled shipments of water buffalo purchased by the Manila underground, then herded to town by local Filipinos. The Japanese officers actually allowed the delivery of the animals for slaughter. The Americans could pool some money to make it look like a legitimate purchase. Many of the Japanese guards were more than happy to accept bribes along with a portion of the slaughtered beef. The water buffalo could be a high-protein food source: Hundreds of pounds of meat definitely could make a difference. However, divided among thousands of prisoners, the shipments never added up to enough protein for a prolonged period of time—no more than a few ounces each for thousands of men for a week or two. They were always hungry.

Members of the network were always alert to potential dangers, possible infiltrators, or anything suspicious and out of the ordinary. Whenever they suspected a problem, they would interrupt shipments for a while. Naomi would send a message to hold back and supplies would back up. Lorenza and Ramón saw it as part of the problem of doing business. "This work brought us into contact with humanity in the raw," Lorenza said, "often times leaving us in a bitter state."

Fan Dance
Tsubaki Club, Manila, December 1942

ONE NIGHT a Japanese submarine commander came into the club and fell for Claire, her long legs, and her American torch songs. The commander was prominent enough to warrant special attention from Madame Tsubaki herself. He said that he had traveled in the United States and Claire reminded him of one experience he would never forget. When he got to San Francisco, he had seen Sally Rand perform her world-famous fan dance. Could Claire do the fan dance? If she could, the commander said he would hold over a night in port and bring in other officers with him to see the show. Claire figured that an extra night meant her hostesses could work more information out of the men. Of course, Claire said, she was happy to do it.

Sally Rand was a burlesque performer who had started in silent films directed by Cecil B. DeMille in the 1920s; she popularized her glimmering fan dance at the 1934 Chicago World's Fair and on that success opened a burlesque house in San Francisco in 1936. Sally's show used shadow and backlighting, along with the oversized feathers, to make it appear that she was pirouetting naked across the stage to a romantic piano accompaniment. It was an illusion—all the while Sally wore a skintight body stocking. No matter for the Japanese commander, who probably did not know the technicalities. He and his friends wanted to see some flesh.

Claire really had not ever paid much attention to Sally Rand, but she got the idea—it was a matter of skin and fantasy. The following day she and the other women sewed together substitutes for feather plumes, one for each hand, from pieces of fabric and designed skintight cream-colored clothing. Mamerto split bamboo stalks to serve as a frame for the feathers. In the dim light of the club, it would do. The idea was to lift one plume and to spin just as she lowered the other plume, then move one plume to the right and cover up with the left, then reverse and back again. At showtime Claire suited up. When the house band's pianist began playing, Claire started swirling. "The commander and his forty guests almost lost their eyesight . . . straining their orbs to determine whether I was really nude behind the fans . . . as they hoped, or wearing tights . . . as they feared."

The dance worked well: The men loved it and the hostesses and the drinking kept them late into the night. Along with it came the same old billing and cooing repartee by Claire and the hostesses—"I love you, don't leave me"—and in return for the special performance the commander and his crew held over as promised.

When the night was over, the hostesses had circulated and gathered the information they could: names of officers and details that slipped out about their travels, including word that at least some of the men would be heading to the Solomon Islands next. Before dawn, Claire already was preparing an intelligence report on the submariners and sent it with a courier up to Boone as quickly as she could. Claire might have held out hope that the men watching her Sally Rand dance eventually would be the targets of Allied bombers or depth charges launched by ships; the United States didn't have real-time capacity to do that. She assumed all along that the intelligence she was sending might be of real-time help to MacArthur and company in Australia. It was not; neither Boone nor anyone else on Luzon had a working transmitter yet. It would take at least a day before he would get Claire's report. In practice, information from Claire or Elizalde or General Roxas or any of Chick Parsons's other friends in Manila was not actionable in terms of targeting specific ships leaving port after their commanders had taken time off in Manila. Communications were too slow and too unreliable for that. However, the intelligence was always worthwhile in completing the map of where Japanese forces were traveling and when. Over the course of time, Claire's reports on troop concentrations, the locations of patrols, and the anticounterinsurgency movement fed the overall intelligence picture of the Japanese occupation. Boone did not discourage her from sending messages as quickly as she could.

Despite the rush of gathering information and supplies, Claire had low points. A Russian man named Alex came into the club and asked if she wanted to escape the Philippines. A friend had a sailboat large enough to take them away, probably to Australia. Others had tried it. It was tempting, especially after a night of smiling and conning her customers. When her mood sank and she was being slapped around and drinking to the praise of the Japanese Army, and when she worried about Dian, she entertained the thought. However, Alex did not return to the club—either he had managed to leave or he had been caught in the attempt. One could never know.

She took the work day by day. Claire jotted in her diary that she still needed to control the drinking sometimes, though drinking to forget was what she wanted to do. She warned herself to cut back and tried to keep it controlled and hidden within the confines of the club. She was proud that she never lost the respect of the people working for her.

Claire had put up a good challenge to Ana Fey's up the street. Business was good, although it tailed off sometimes with the competition. While Japanese officers paid well and left liberal tips, they had other alternatives for nightlife, more than just Tsubaki Club and Ana Fey's. Casa Mañana was nearby and also catered to Japanese officers. There were dozens more, notably a few hot spots close to downtown: Flamingo, *La Famille*, the Stork, and *Tambourin*. The clubs were not large, and the entertainment scene was popular.

The floor show at Tsubaki Club was always a draw. An advertisement in the *Manila Tribune* on December 17, 1942, promised a surprise party for Christmas Eve. "Everybody is welcome," said the advertisement, "Fely Singing Nippongo Songs," "Josephine Baker and Company in Surprise Numbers," probably referring to Fahny's exotic dance and musical number with David. Though no one knew it at the time, Josephine Baker, the great American expatriate singer and dancer, was performing her risqué show in occupied Paris, spying all the while on German and Italian officers for the French Resistance.

Fely's Japanese folk songs were warming and nostalgic for the men far from their homes in Japan, and Claire's suggestive gown and her torch songs brought many admirers. However, there was a secret life surrounding Tsubaki Club that Claire did not mention. Of course the young women, many of them teenagers, were out to charm the Japanese officers and the civilians who came to spend their money at the club. Sometimes a night of charms could become something more.

Everyone knew there were brothels for men who were interested strictly in sexual encounters. Claire had said from the outset that Tsubaki Club—"sophisticated" and "high class"—was not *that* kind of place. Her protests were hard to believe. Even if Tsubaki Club wasn't that kind of place, it was an easy stepping-off point. Tsubaki Club and the other nightclubs did not prohibit women from taking the trade outside. Perfectly adequate hotels were close by. Some of the dancers and courtesans circulating in the night catered to specialized business.

Among them was Walterina Markova, an exotic dancer and singer who enjoyed performing at Tsubaki Club. She was a popular singer and dancer, slim and attractive, in her twenties. When the young officers approached her, she was willing to step out. Sometimes that was a good thing; sometimes it was not—once they touched Walterina the right way, they would realize that Walterina was a boy. He was a transvestite performer and, when it got that far, was happy to turn tricks. "That was where I performed for Japanese customers. They didn't know that I was a gay. And some of my gay friends were working there as receptionists. Five of us were working there but only me doing the floor show." One night, Walterina said, the club didn't have many customers, and he went out for a walk with a few other cross-dressing friends, wearing evening gowns and strolling through Luneta Park.

Four Japanese officers approached them, struck up a conversation, and invited them to their hotel, the Luneta, a block or two from Tsubaki Club. "We went to our separate rooms and the Japanese were kissing, kissing, kissing." Then the man Walterina was with started moving his hands south and soon realized what was happening. Sometimes, Walterina said, the officers didn't mind at all. In this case the officer was angry. "'You're a boy!' He got mad. He was furious." The Japanese rounded up Walterina and his friends and dragged them off. Walterina said he and his friends were held captive for a month, raped, brutalized, and tortured for days until they could escape. Claire never mentioned the incident or whether she tried to intervene to help Walterina and his friends.

Relief for the Greater Need
Manila, December 1942

CLAIRE'S EMPLOYEES at Tsubaki Club had become fervent participants in the supply, rescue, and intelligence operation. One of the waiters, Totoy, came in one day with a wrenching story. The sickly, emaciated American prisoners at the old Park Avenue School in the Manila suburb of Pasay were dying at a frightening rate. Totoy's aunt, Clara Yuma, and her family lived close to the school and watched in horror as the men marched by every day to and from their work details.

Totoy took Claire for a visit. "Those poor men are dying like flies," Clara Yuma told her. "I've seen the awful food they are given, and a pig would not touch it. . . . It is a miracle that these men could live on that swill." Their main job was to repair the runway at Nichols Field, damaged by bombing runs as MacArthur's air units tried to fight off the Japanese occupation. Nichols was about four miles from the Park Avenue School. It was a long walk followed by grueling work in the heat, and the men were starving. The women put together a plan. Clara would set up a stand outside her house where they would sell rice cakes, bananas, and other fruits. Claire would provide the money and supplies. When they were ready, they sent a blind message into the school with a trusted Filipino mechanic named Pedro for whoever among the prisoners might be in charge. A note came out from one of the officers inside, known only as Captain Muir. Muir told them that he would distribute any money Claire could send in and asked that she supply some money directly to him to replace a pair of broken eyeglasses. The women sent in 150 pesos, 50 for the glasses and the rest to be distributed. Muir sent back a receipt for 120 pesos—the Japanese had taken a cut of the money. It was the price they had to pay. Claire returned to the club very excited that night and showed the letter and receipt from Muir to Mamerto, her bartender.

Eventually they were able to bribe the Japanese guards posted outside the school with money and gifts as they marched by with the Americans every day. "The soldiers would be allowed to stop at the stand, pretending, of course, to buy food, we would have bags with food and money inside, and that kept up for well over a year." More than once, though, a mean-spirited guard forced the stand to close. One day one of the guards walked over and slammed Clara Yuma in the face with his rifle butt. She recovered, and after a few days they reopened the stand.

Any POW supply operation that involved secret communications and bribery came with serious risks, but in the end Claire and Clara Yuma were able to provide relief and lessen the suffering of the POWs at Park Avenue. Before Claire had come to visit, the prisoners "had nothing. They were eating with their fingers." The women sent in eating utensils and plates and shoes, because many of the men had been left with worn boots or no shoes at all. Under the circumstances, Claire and her allies were ready to take almost any risk to help escapees and evaders of imprisonment.

Still, they had to be on the lookout for con artists and traps. Claire was burned more than once. A young American soldier identified only as "Beans" was sent over to meet her one day. Beans was one of the occasional army stragglers who would show up in the city, moving frequently as they managed to elude capture. Claire said he was a charmer, tall, handsome, and twenty-two years old, making her think of her lost lover, John Phillips. She even gave money to Beans, along with two of Phillips's suits.

A couple of days later Beans stopped by, wearing one of the suits and asking for more money. He had gone out gambling and lost all she had given him. Claire threw him out. She resolved to be more careful after that. In this case Beans was a money-grubber, nothing worse. However, one day the Kempeitai might try to test her loyalties by sending in someone like that. "It made me think and think hard, of the very thin ice on which we were all skating, and I resolved to be much more careful in my future dealings with strangers."

Love Letters and Lives
Cabanatuan, June 1943

CLAIRE, PEGGY, and the Manila underground could measure their success in lives saved. The relief operation was definitely having an effect in Cabanatuan. In the months after the death march, dozens of men died every day in a fetid, overcrowded camp hospital from dysentery, malaria,

and other jungle diseases or just exhaustion from the lack of food. Now at
the three sections of the Cabanatuan prisoner complex more food was
available and fewer men were dying. Colonel Arthur Lee Shreve Jr., a
forty-six-year-old POW officer, was keeping track of life and death in the
camp and could document the change. Shreve kept statistics on everything; making lists, cataloging life, and writing a diary kept him sane. He
had been called to active duty from his home in Baltimore and arrived in
the Philippines only weeks before the start of the war.

Shreve recorded 149 deaths at Cabanatuan in December 1942, which
actually was a grim improvement, and he was the one to announce that
December 15 had been the first day without a fatality among the prisoners. On February 6, 1943, he sounded even hopeful. "The additional food
is having its effect, both that supplied by the Japanese and from the Red
Cross. Everyone is gaining weight and our death rate is falling steadily, 72
last month and less than 10 so far this month." Shreve and other officers
had a separate and slightly better living situation than enlisted men in
the camp, and he was mostly too isolated from them to know the difference between Red Cross shipments and the supplies sent in by Peggy,
Claire, Ramón, Naomi, and their coconspirators. The International Red
Cross did manage to get rations into Cabanatuan several times, but hunger still ruled.

Despite the improvement in food, there were severe problems. Shreve
said that men under forced labor were rebuilding a nearby airstrip but
sometimes were barely able to move. On February 15 the American POW
officer in charge of the airport work detail appealed to Colonel Shreve for
help in interceding with the Japanese. "The men were faint from lack of
food doing so much hard work."

Many officers hardly knew anything about the Manila supply operation. Shreve vaguely had information that some "Spanish girls" were helping out. Even in Manila operational security was maintained. Claire had
her side operations and so did Ramón and the others.

Some prisoners knew more than others—Captain Tiffany and Lieutenant Colonel Mack were part of the operation. Others also were in
touch with the women in Manila through morale-boosting letters. Claire
was writing to at least half a dozen men, who told her the letters were as
important as food and medicine and some of whom proposed marriage
sight unseen. Love letters, they called them, morale boosting mixed with

flirtation in every envelope, combined with money in various denominations so the prisoners could bribe guards and send out for food and medicine. The Japanese prison had allowed the creation of the commissary, but food costs were just as high there, and soaring. Claire and the others were giving as much free food and credit to the prisoners as they could afford. Many of the men rejected charity and sent trinkets and jewelry back with Naomi for sale in Manila. Claire said she was happy to sell the trinkets, but was not interested in taking money from the prisoners. "Between you, me and the lamp post," she wrote one of the POWs, "I don't want or ever expect to get one-tenth of this money back."

Claire's flirtatious, lighthearted letters were uplifting for men who were starved for more than food. Where the Japanese saw scraggly prisoners trudging along muddy camp roads, the men had created a city of culture and light. They named Cabanatuan's main gathering area Times Square. The main camp road was Broadway, and it intersected along the way with Fifth Avenue. Many had died and some were still dying, but the men of Cabanatuan willed themselves to live. And Claire was one of the stars of their surreal fantasy.

The prisoners of Cabanatuan could dream beyond the barbed wire; they established reading and study groups, scrounged a library and a film projector to watch old American movies, staged periodic song-and-dance revues, and even performed Shakespeare. Enterprising men used hand tools to fashion musical instruments from wire and scraps of metal and wood, then gave regular jazz performances to packed audiences. They organized lectures, card games, and religious services, filched seeds to plant their own victory gardens, and bartered contraband for food with willing guards.

And now, in the spring of 1943, a woman who called herself High Pockets was sending in money and letters and supplies and helping the men dream. Around the same time, one of the POW officers, Major Dwight E. Gard of the U.S. Army Air Corps, was noticing a difference in the health and mood of the men around him. At first, shipments and letters had mentioned Miss U—Peggy was their benefactor. The change was evident. In the course of the spring, Gard and Captain Tiffany saw that someone new was communicating with them and was supplying the food, medicine, and money to the camp. It was about the same time that they had told Peggy that Jack Utinsky was dead. Gard said later that High Pockets was taking over. "It was all High Pockets. . . . The change was in about February of '43, as I recall; it was only about a month that I heard about Miss U at all, then I didn't hear no more about it at all."

In a long note to one of the POWs, Lieutenant Colonel Frederick Yeager, Claire teased him and was alluring about her name and her appearance. "My code name is High Pockets," she wrote. "I am one of the main people in the group to deliver and collect mail for the several Prison Camps. Also sometimes I have to carry other material that it would not be healthy for me to be caught with. . . . I put them down the front of my dress. . . . Also I am very tall and my pockets are very high. I am five feet six inches, 35 years old, a widow, dark and not bad looking. But . . . hey, this is not a proposal. I'm getting ahead of myself." When Yeager wrote to her about his living conditions, she turned that into a teasing comment too. "So you meant the Bahays [huts] were 18 foot square not the man. I was wondering what kind of men were there."

When Claire learned that Gard was from Portland, she wrote to him too and went out of her way to help and comfort him. Gard said the letter "was a greeting and a hope for my health, and she enclosed, the first time that I ever received a note from her, it was either a five or ten peso note was enclosed with it." Often the men would not even speak to one another about the letters. "The people who were receiving notes were a little nervous because there was always a possibility there might be a traitor who would tip off the Japanese for personal gain. So it was kept somewhat hush hush."

Claire's letters had a major impact on morale. Gard wrote back and thanked her. He didn't need the money to buy food, he told her, because he was healthy enough compared to others around him. He said that Captain Tiffany, one of Naomi's main contacts at the camp, was focusing on those who needed the most help.

Gard knew that Captain Tiffany, the camp chaplain, was already in touch. High Pockets had asked for a list of men who were hungry and sick and who had a particular need for help. She sent in duck eggs, a crucial source of protein. She was also providing other nutrients and medicines; Tiffany told Gard the supplies included citrus juices—Claire, Peggy, and the others were boiling down calamansi lemons into concentrate for juice,

Roy C. Bennett, the editor of the *Manila Daily Bulletin*, wrote anti-Japanese editorials during the buildup to World War II. He was arrested and tortured at Fort Santiago, then finally transferred in 1943 to spend the rest of the war with his family at the University of Santo Tomas internment camp.

In January 1942, the 400-year-old University of Santo Tomas in Manila was converted into a detention camp for more than three thousand Americans and nationals of countries at war with Japan. It was liberated in February 1945.

Some internees lived in university buildings and others built grass-hut shanties in courtyards and open spaces.

Internees in Manila used communal bathing facilities during the Japanese occupation.

Claire Phillips and her adopted five-year-old daughter, Dian, in March 1945, reunited after the U.S. liberation of the Philippines. Peggy Utinsky, her friend in the Manila underground, had cared for the child while Claire was imprisoned by the Japanese for more than eight months.

Peggy Utinsky, a registered nurse, had defied her husband's insistence that she leave the Philippines before the war and stayed in Manila to treat wounded and ill American prisoners. She joined forces with Claire Phillips and others to smuggle food, medicine, and supplies to POWs. Her husband, Jack, died at Cabanatuan POW camp in 1942.

Lieutenant Charles "Chick" Parsons, a U.S. Naval Reserve officer and spy, traveled secretly throughout occupied Philippines, bringing supplies and organizing guerrilla operations.

Parsons, who spoke Tagalog and Spanish, masqueraded as Panamanian consul-general in Manila in the first months of the Japanese invasion. He and his family left the Philippines on a detainee exchange ship in June 1942.

General MacArthur summoned Parsons to Australia in 1943. Parsons returned to Japanese-occupied Philippines on a series of submarine supply and espionage missions.

Major John P. Boone and Filomena (Mellie) Guerrero Boone, circa 1945. They were married in the hills of Bataan in 1943. Mellie carried messages and supplies between Claire Phillips and the Bataan guerrillas.

Marcial Lichauco, an American-educated attorney and diplomat, chronicled the Japanese occupation in letters he called, "Dear Mother Putnam," written to his host mother from his time in the United States. His wife, Jesse, a Cuban-born American, worked with him to provide aid and shelter to people in need in Manila during the war.

Claire's Tsubaki Club opened on October 17, 1942, catering to Japanese officers and boasting the best floor show in town.

Colonel Akira Nagahama was the head of the Japanese military police, the Kempeitai, in the Philippines from 1942 to 1945. While he publicly advocated gentle persuasion with prisoners, the Kempeitai were feared for their torture and interrogation techniques.

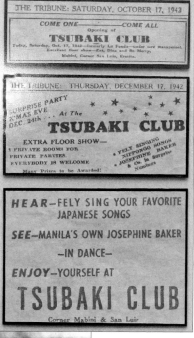

Filipino children outside a government building in Manila during the Japanese occupation. The notice lists occupation regulations, including a requirement that residents salute Japanese soldiers and obey their orders.

A POW and his victory garden at Cabanatuan. Thousands of American prisoners of war were held at the camp north of Manila. Many died of disease and malnutrition; others survived with food and medicines sent in by the Manila underground.

Fely Corcuera, the most popular performer at Claire's Tsubaki Club, was often wooed by Japanese officers. An officer known only as Arita, the captain of an aircraft carrier, had fallen hard for Fely and often gave her gifts. Claire said, "Anyone could see that he was mad about Fely."

Brigadier General Manuel Acuña Roxas had been a liaison to General Douglas MacArthur before the war. Released from Japanese custody, he served in the Philippines occupation government but secretly worked with U.S. and Filipino guerrillas. He was president of the Philippines from 1946 until his death in 1948.

and sent in fruit and candy. Gard said Tiffany "had been charged by High Pockets to pick out the very sick prisoners and distribute the money and other materials she sent in to the very ill prisoners, which he did, and very conscientiously, I might add."

Gard, thirty-four, was lucky compared with the thousands of men who did the forced march to Camp O'Donnell after the fall of Bataan in April. He surrendered in May 1942 with the fall of Corregidor and was sent to Bilibid Prison in Manila for six days before he and other men were packed into a boxcar and taken to Capas Station, the closest to the new Cabanatuan POW camp. From the station they marched eleven miles one day to Camp No. 2 and then five miles more two days later to Camp No. 1. He was in reasonably good health when he got there and complained little as he saw the grave illnesses of others.

In some sense and to some degree, the worst of the horror was over once the Filipinos had been furloughed from Camp O'Donnell in June 1942 and thousands of Americans were taken to Cabanatuan. However, many more died; prisoners still were suffering from neglect, still mired in filth, subject to disease and a daily dose of cruelty.

The camp commander also issued a projected food plan for the prisoners. Gard kept a diary in which he listed the daily amounts: about 270 grams (less than ten ounces) of uncooked rice, 100 grams (about three ounces) of greens from a sweet potato, and the same amount of corn for men who were on work detail, 20 grams (less than an ounce) of fish and 15 grams (half an ounce) of vegetable oil. This was a starvation diet and some of the food was rancid. Colonel Shreve, Gard's fellow officer, said that to add insult to injury, "there is so much that is spoiled or full of maggots that we cannot eat that we average less than fifty grams (less than two ounces) per ration." By 1943 the Japanese officials overseeing Cabanatuan were looking the other way or accepted bribes so that extra food, medicine, and supplies, meager though they still were, made up the difference.

While Gard and the other POWs starved, they conjured up gourmet menus of meals they imagined cooking and savoring, instead of the scant, bland diets they suffered through. Gard made a list of meats that should be on hand at a fine restaurant: ("beef tenderloin, (bake and fry), T. Bone—Porterhouse—(Fry), Top Sirloin") and also produced recipes, including one contributed by a fellow officer, Major Marshall Hill Hurt Jr.: "Cheese Casserole, Layer of stale, broken bread in casserole—layer of grated cheese—build up in layers until full. Beat eggs in milk, salt, pepper, butter. Pour mixture over layers of bread and cheese. Leave in refrigerator overnight then bake. Ingredients can vary." Gard added a sobering postscript at the end of Hurt's recipe: "The major died before the end of the war—he would never be able to enjoy the recipe himself."

Gard also kept lists of clothing in an imagined closet: uniforms, shoes, and hats, where they were purchased, and how much they cost. Making up a wardrobe was as surreal as inventing a gourmet meal: The men were almost naked. They wore shredded shorts or G-strings, which they kept on until they fell off, and only some were lucky enough to have shoes. Claire, Peggy, and their allies were able to send in some shoes, but not enough.

Gard was delighted with his correspondence with High Pockets, especially when she wrote she was from Portland. "I told her that when we got back [to Portland]," he said, "I would take her to Jack and Jill's," a popular Portland tavern and nightclub.

Gard's diary also had a more utilitarian function: He kept a phonetic list of useful words in Japanese that might help him avoid a beating or worse:

wakarimasen—I do not understand
yasume—at ease (as you were)
bango—count off

While the prisoners tried out such Japanese words and phrases with the guards, they also gave them nicknames for how they appeared and acted: Donald Duck, Laughing Boy, Web Foot, Little Speedo, and Beetle Brain.

Of all the lists Gard recorded in his diary, his box score of the POWs of Bataan was the most meticulous: Of 22,000 Americans at the start of the war, he listed 1,650 Americans dead at Camp O'Donnell in the six months of its operation, 2,600 at Cabanatuan through the end of the war, and thousands of others at other prisons and for other reasons. In total, he estimated that 8,355 men had died, 38 percent of the original number. The exact number was hard to calculate. Along with that, he wrote down the addresses of the men he knew, either to contact them after the war or to memorialize them if they hadn't made it home.

Japan had a total of 132,134 Allied prisoners in the Philippines, Japan, and more than a dozen other occupied countries in the Pacific, of whom 35,756, or 27.1 percent, died. The death rate of American POWs alone was much higher, more than 33 percent. By comparison, 235,473 Allied prisoners were held by Germany and Italy in Europe; 9,348, or 4 percent, of them died.

Life and Death Foretold

John Boone's Camp, Bataan, February 1943

"I'M A PSYCHIC," said George Williams, a Filipino officer with John Boone. Williams was fairly certain that the Japanese were about to attack their camp. "I know things." Lieutenant Colonel Edwin Ramsey looked hard at Williams, who had mixed British and Spanish heritage. "I know, for example, that I will not survive the war." Williams said the guerrillas would be hit hard and soon.

The prediction about an attack was not difficult to make. Boone and Ramsey were now the constant target of Kempeitai patrols operating based on intelligence reports from advance teams and turncoats and interrogations of villagers in the mountains.

Boone was now on Japanese military intelligence search lists as a leading guerrilla chief, and Ramsey, who spent weeks at a time in the camp with Boone, was regional commander of ten thousand men. At this point Boone and the other guerrillas focused on organizing and training their recruits and gathering material, gearing up to undermine the Japanese occupation any way possible. All of them were making contact with intelligence operatives in Manila and other cities. They also were sending Filipino infiltrators to work inside the occupation government in any capacity they could. Ramsey had been making one of his periodic visits to strategize with Boone and was now ready to move on.

"As I was preparing to start north," Ramsey said later, "two prisoners [most likely Filipino collaborators with the Japanese] from Boone's camp escaped. An alarm went up, and as the two darted past the outpost, shots were fired. One of the prisoners was hit several times and killed, but the other got away."

The escape put the guerrilla camp on alert.

Boone had been promoted to brevet captain of the irregular corps and was now answering to Ramsey, the American straggler he had helped by sending him to recover at a sugar plantation soon after the American surrender. By the end of 1942, Ramsey, wiry thin and with a pencil-line mustache, had recovered from the months of illness and starvation and made a return trip to meet with Boone in the mountainous region above Dinalupihan, where Boone had met with Claire. Boone immediately recognized the chain of command and welcomed Ramsey. "He greeted me with the same brash grin I'd remembered from our meeting in April" (the previous year). Boone was confident of his role in the growing organization and told Ramsey he could see only one problem—not a logistical issue. He had fallen in love with his messenger, Filomena (Mellie for short). Mellie, twenty, had been spying on the Japanese garrison in Dinalupihan, pretending to be working on their behalf, sewing and cooking for them. Claire said, "Mellie gathered considerable information about troop movements and ammunition dumps, and then slipped off to the hills." Then Mellie started shuttling messages and supplies from Claire to Boone's camp. Now Boone and Mellie had fallen in love and wanted to get married but did not have a priest and could not go find one or risk bringing an outsider into camp. Problem solved. "I'm the senior officer in this area," Ramsey said. "I'll do it." There in the jungle hideaway, the guerrillas built a bower and a reception area out of bamboo and palm fronds. Ramsey officiated at the wedding on February 19, 1943.

The guerrillas gave speeches in English, Spanish, Tagalog, and local Luzon dialects; they partied, but some of the men remained on station all night keeping guard. Bad enough they were dealing with the escape of a prisoner. On top of that, Williams was playing Cassandra, predicting doom. Ramsey, nevertheless, was confident that the headquarters was well hidden and adequately protected. Williams, going on with his predictions, had told him they were safe for a few more days. "Good, then maybe I'll get a decent night's sleep," Ramsey said. Boone and Mellie also bedded down for the night.

From the small, ragtag group he had gathered around the time he met Claire, Boone's force had grown into the thousands. "It wound up that I, by some luck, was able to control my own province and develop them from the original guerrilla band," Boone said, "to a military table of organization, a square division." Boone's guerrillas now comprised four 400-man regiments and 400 more in his headquarters unit—a 2,000-member guerrilla army that was still growing. There was a smattering of Americans among them, but most were Filipinos, young and old.

Boone and the other guerrilla leaders operated underground; they organized against the Japanese, infiltrated occupation offices wherever possible, and gathered information and intelligence. Eventually, MacArthur's orders were made known: Avoid overt attacks on Japanese troops—supply lines would not support major offensive action, and killing Japanese soldiers would bring retaliation against Filipino civilians. When Boone did authorize a mission, it was usually an act of sabotage carried out without leaving a trace that could cause civilian reprisals. "Nobody gets hurt, the men make a little money, and they get to harass the Japs, which is good for morale. Everybody wins—except the Japs."

Boone had his sector wired and well organized—so much so that he was able to counteract a new effort by the Japanese, who had set up a Filipino constabulary force to combat the guerrillas. He placed men inside the Japanese-controlled constabulary police force, accomplishing a number of goals. The double agents would be fed and housed by the Japanese, though they were steadfastly loyal to the American side. Slowly Boone went beyond the constabulary to infiltrate broad sectors of the occupation infrastructure. "They were guys who had administrative ability and more value there than being in the high ground. . . . At one time there . . . we controlled all of the key men in the municipal governments and the provincial government were [also] our people." It would have been impossible to feed and support a two-thousand-member army in the field. Those who had not infiltrated the Japanese ranks trained in the jungle but lived at home with their families. The guerrilla enclave was their rolling headquarters, a tight-knit mobile group operating deep in the jungle hills west of Dinalupihan.

His men had done such a good job of infiltrating the occupation government that they even were able to place agents at Kempeitai headquarters itself in Manila. A contemporary aphorism described it well: "The guerrilla must move amongst the people as the fish swims in the sea." These were the words of Mao Zedong, who by this time had already been leading a peasant insurrection in China for more than a decade. The guerrillas of the Philippines had been successful in winning hearts and minds. The Japanese knew this was so, and that was why they fought so hard to eradicate them.

Things were quiet for a few days after the wedding, as George Williams, the seer, had predicted. Boone had scheduled a much larger ceremony than his makeshift wedding three days later—a jungle induction ceremony for five hundred new recruits. It was Washington's Birthday, February 22, 1943, a date to remember. It had not been a wise thing to do. Nagahama's Kempeitai agents and informants had been providing information about both Boone and Ramsey; one report said that Nagahama even had in his office a printed wanted poster with a line drawing of Ramsey, offering a reward for his capture of $100,000.

Sometime after midnight they were all jolted awake by the screams of a boy in the camp, yelling, "Japanese! Japanese!" The camp mobilized; Boone ran to a hill to survey the countryside. All appeared quiet. After a while they settled down again.

The attack began before dawn. "There was a sudden cacophony of rifle and machine-gun fire," Ramsey said. "In a moment mortar rounds were chugging into the camp, heaving up huts and blasting palm trees from their roots." Boone and Ramsey, Mellie, and George Williams all managed to escape into the jungle as an outer ring of guerrillas held off the attack. Boone's forces regrouped at a prearranged site higher in the mountains, and the commanders were able to assess their position. There was no report on casualties, but the bulk of the resistance fighters had been able to disperse to their villages, disappearing back into their cover identities, where they could not be targeted as part of the resistance. Ramsey stayed on for a while with Boone—they both kept moving and eventually split up. The Japanese assault was not a killing blow, but it had disrupted operations. Nagahama's forces did interrupt guerrilla operations in the region for a time and had captured supplies; they could not track down Boone or Ramsey. Nothing in the camp gave evidence that Claire or anyone else in Manila was the source of their baseline support. Boone said he "was isolated and cut off from all contacts for anywhere up to two months. And the first person who re-established the Manila contact after that was my wife, and she did bring back an average shipment of supplies and money from Claire Phillips."

After that initial trip from their new mountain hideout, still close to Dinalupihan and to the west, Mellie made weekly treks to Manila for much of the year to replenish supplies and exchange messages with Claire. Claire was able to send food, wine, office supplies, and medicines, along with occasional pieces of clothing. The guerrillas needed quinine, often in short supply, and they needed antiseptics, aspirin, and bandages. Boone shared Claire's shipments with other guerrilla units whenever there was enough. Some of the food came from aboveboard purchases. Claire filed an application with Manila authorities claiming falsely that the club was a restaurant serving food, which entitled her to additional rations of staples like rice and sugar; those supplies could also go to the hills.

Neither Boone nor Claire had originally conceived of a massive supply operation. It would not have been feasible with thousands of troops to support, far more men than they could equip and feed. Claire's base in Manila was intended mostly for intelligence, although she sent key supplies as often as possible. She then was able to put other relief workers in touch with Boone so there would be more sources more frequently. While food for that many people was procured locally, more and more supplies of medicines and specialized items came from Manila. She continued providing care packages to Louise at Santo Tomas and began sending food and supplies north to Carling and the Sobreviñas family once in a while. Carling, in turn, also sent food to Boone when he could. The cost of living in Manila was high, but prices in Bataan were much worse. The price of cigarettes was a good indicator. Everyone was smoking. When Claire came out of the hills in June, she said, she could buy a pack of cigarettes for one peso. Now, in November, the price had gone up to four pesos or more. Price inflation had an impact, and the extra cash from earnings at the nightclub would help. Prices of the basics—cigarettes, bread, flour, and eggs—were way up. Claire was trying to send in tomatoes when available. They were triple the prewar price—three cents each—and they were only about the size of golf balls. Quality was not to be expected, but sometimes the bread she bought at gouging prices had bugs in it and had to be thrown away. Boone also needed administrative supplies for the jungle hideout. Claire also was out shopping for paper, carbon paper, and paper clips. Intelligence information was sometimes easier to come by than extra food and supplies.

While Mellie was making her trips, their longtime helper Pacio also continued to travel back and forth between Claire and Boone. One of Boone's most difficult requests was for a radio transmitter. It was a difficult and dangerous task. "Pacio told me that this was to be sent up into the hills, piece by piece, using different carriers and over a period of time to avoid detection."

The carriers might come up with an excuse for carrying fruit, eggs, shoes, even medicine into Bataan, but the Kempeitai would certainly kill anyone caught with radio parts. Claire's carriers faithfully managed to ship the gear piece by piece to Boone's camp, where it was reassembled. Claire had tried, but the parts were either too old or too low-powered to be of any use. Essentially, Boone said, it was "radio junk, an amateur radio transmitter, which never did operate." He continued to send Claire's intelligence reports to Ramsey by messenger.

Mellie's supply runs were convoluted and dangerous. If it was safe, Mellie and whoever was traveling with her on the trip could take a bus part of the way—especially when they were empty-handed inbound to Manila—a trip that took three or four hours on routes not usually subject to roadblocks. The long way was mostly hiking, twelve hours out of the mountains to Hermosa; if the weather was good, she usually could take a boat into Manila across Manila Bay. She was carrying enough supplies gathered by Claire that she needed helpers—usually her four sisters helped at either end of the boat trip. Careful, dressed unobtrusively as peasants carrying loads of supplies, five women were most likely to avoid suspicion. Together they would carry supplies in baskets, bring along other runners when necessary, and load and unload the supplies on the boats that carried them across the bay. The whole trip usually ended up taking a full day. It was arduous and always nerve-racking, but they survived.

The flow of intelligence was central. Every night Claire would compare notes with Fely and the other women. Thanks to their liaisons with Japanese officers, the material she sent up to Boone provided information on potential battles to come—that is, where men were being sent elsewhere in the Pacific and when, along with the names of unit and company commanders. She was also sending up newspapers and, when she could, copies of Ramón Amusategui's newsletter based on stateside reports from a clandestine radio receiver.

When it was safe after the February raid, Ramsey moved farther north. Boone sent messengers to Ramsey with Claire's intelligence reports. A few months after the February raid, Ramsey remembered George Williams, who had predicted the attack and had said that he himself would not survive. Boone sent one message to Ramsey that included the news that Williams had made another correct prediction, though his last. "'By the way, George Williams went into Dinalupihan this morning for supplies, walked into an ambush, and was killed.' George had been right; he had not survived the war."

Tojo's Parade
Manila, May 5, 1943

SOMETHING BIG WAS happening on the morning of Wednesday, May 5, 1943. Claire awoke to a virtual lockdown throughout the city. "Police everywhere," she wrote in her diary. "Guards on every street in town." The Japanese Rising Sun flag was flying on most houses. At noon teachers canceled classes, handed out the little white flags emblazoned with a red circle, and had their students line up on the sidewalk along Taft Avenue. What was it? people asked. It must be someone very important; it had to be a Japanese official. In fact it was none other than Japanese prime minister Hideki Tojo, who had come to the Philippines on his first overseas trip since the beginning of the war.

The prime minister's unannounced visit demonstrated the importance of the Philippines in Japan's scheme to create a new Asian empire. He brought with him a new enticement as part of Tokyo's propaganda campaign to demonstrate noble intentions: Japan was about to offer Filipinos the elusive prize that the Americans had not given them in forty years—independence.

Tojo had said before the Imperial Diet in January 1943 that he planned to push ahead on the question of independence because Filipinos deserved it. "Substantial progress is being made in the degree of cooperation rendered to the Japanese Empire by the people of the Philippines as well as in the restoration of internal peace and security." He presented a time-table for independence later in the year and told the Filipinos designated to run the government that his aim was no less than "to bring about the complete capitulation of the United States, Britain and the Netherlands" (all colonial powers in Asia) and "the establishment . . . of a new order based upon moral principles, an order in which each and every race will enjoy a place in the sun."

Tojo, meanwhile, knew something about public relations. He met with Filipino soldiers who declared their loyalty and readiness to fight and die for Japan. He spoke with schoolchildren and mingled with factory workers and men on the docks. The Japanese-controlled *Manila Tribune* gushed that Tojo, fifty-nine years old, tireless, and showing the stamina of a much younger man, had "won the hearts" of the people.

That claim was far from true. He represented a system that had made people miserable, physically sick, sad, and morally corrupt. Filipinos on the street were subject to petty indignities; people were slapped or beaten for no apparent reason; everyone had a friend or relative who had been imprisoned, even tortured. A happy, easygoing city had become regimented and highly controlled by Japanese soldiers and police at every street corner. People now scrounged for food, and petty theft was commonplace. Manilans eyed one another with suspicion: Who was a collaborator? Who was spying on whom?

Expressions of support for Tojo and for the Japanese in general were staged and performed under duress. While Filipinos were pressed into the pro-Japanese constabulary and some of them rose in the ranks, most people in Manila reviled Tojo and what he stood for. "The pro-American sentiment prevailing among the great majority of our people here in Luzon" was obvious, wrote Marcial Lichauco, friend to the Roxas family and the Philippine upper crust. Moreover, he said the Filipinos in the southern islands were even more opposed to the Japanese. In the south, he said, "Filipinos who are seen fraternizing with Japanese officials seldom live long enough to reap the fruits of their friendship with their new masters."

Thursday, the day after Tojo's arrival, was a holiday. The Japanese occupation government staged a massive parade in honor of the prime minister. Attendance was mandatory for every adult male in the city. Children again had the day off. Government workers and leaders of neighborhood committees took attendance.

Tojo marched out front wearing the field uniform of a general, weighed down with medals, strutting confidently in his gleaming knee-high leather boots. He smiled and raised his right hand as he marched to acknowledge the throng of 400,000 (as estimated by the *Manila Tribune*). Aides and other high military officials trailed dutifully a step behind him. Tojo approached the podium escorted by José Laurel, the interior minister. Next he was greeted by Jorge B. Vargas, the top-ranking Filipino leader under Japanese rule, while Laurel stood to one side of the podium and exhorted the crowd to welcome Tojo, shouting out: "Banzai!" People "cheered him spontaneously," the newspaper reported. Actually, the response was tepid.

The gathering, Tojo said, was a "huge thanksgiving assembly held in the midst of this great war." Japan, he said, had "completely routed the enemy" and "they will never again be able to contaminate Oriental soil."

Some people might have bought the notion, but not many. News from the outside world was limited in print and on the official airwaves. Although tens of thousands of people had turned in their shortwave radios for Japanese "adjustment," brave souls still risked death to listen to the news. While Tojo declared a rout and that he would crush the Allies, it was true neither in the Pacific nor with his Nazi allies in Europe and the Middle East. The purloined stateside news headlines reported that same day that General MacArthur's forces were pounding positions in New Guinea in a continued assault on the Japanese and that the Allies had driven German forces out of Bizerte and Tunis in North Africa. The news filtered through to the city, and Tojo's drumbeat of victory was recognized as hollow rhetoric. That Saturday night, May 8, the internees at the University of Santo Tomas heard more good news about Nazi Germany's loss in Tunisia and staged a celebration of their own; their Japanese guards probably would have protested had they known the reason for the revelry. The feeling on the street was that the Americans sooner or later would be on their way.

The internees at Santo Tomas were in the mood for celebration. On April 21, two weeks before Tojo's arrival, Roy C. Bennett had been released from the cage at Fort Santiago. After a stay at a hospital, where he recovered from the months of beatings and starvation, he was reunited with his wife and daughters. It was a joyous reunion, even under the circumstances. His daughter Joan, now going on nine years old, knew that her father had been in a place called Fort Santiago but did not know what that meant. All she knew was that the family was together again. She followed her father everywhere whenever she could at the camp; she knew he was often meeting with members of the executive committee and gathering the latest news on the underground news mill that somehow always filtered into the camp. Roy C. Bennett was well known to the internees as the bold newspaper editor who had spoken out against the Japanese before the war. For his part, Bennett was amazed that he had survived. Despite the deprivations of Fort Santiago, the worst part had been the lack of information about his family. "I lived under bestial conditions, with no chance to shave or bathe, and more important, without word concerning the welfare of my family. . . . I do not understand how we who went through those experiences managed to last."

On special occasions friends of the people trapped in Santo Tomas were allowed to send in extra food. For holidays there still were enough supplies in Manila for a party. People brought ice cream, turkey, roast pork, cakes, and fruit. Claire waited with the rest of them and sent in whatever she could, along with hidden notes whenever she dared, with words of encouragement.

Despite all the celebration, occupation authorities provoked concern and anxiety when they announced they would be moving a portion of the detainees at Santo Tomas to a new facility at Los Baños, about forty miles from Manila. An advance group of male detainees already were detailed there to start building barracks. At the same time, hundreds of elderly Americans and others—including people who had been furloughed from Santo Tomas for medical reasons—were notified they had to rereport and would be among those sent to the new facility. For the first time in a year, Claire missed her Sunday visit to bring food, money, and gifts to Louise at the detention center, assuming that Louise had already moved. However, she found out Louise was still at the camp, although her boyfriend, Bob Humphries, had been sent to Los Baños. Claire resumed her shipments right away. About eight hundred internees were sent to the new detention facility, mostly single or unattached American and British men.

▪ ▪ ▪

Tojo was back in Tokyo by the weekend. While his remarks in Manila were upbeat and triumphal, American monitors picked up an interesting subtext. On his return, Radio Tokyo reported that Japanese forces were still fighting in the Philippines, a year after the American surrender. Japanese troops were "carrying on . . . military operations . . . in the establishment of peace and order, while overcoming all manners of hardships and inconveniences on land, sea, lakes and swamps on countless islands where traffic is difficult and in labryinthe [sic] water areas." Translation for U.S. intelligence and planners at General MacArthur's headquarters: The guerrillas were successfully harassing the Japanese occupation forces.

Japanese occupation authorities knew—even sometimes admitted— that their "Asia for the Asians" program was a failure. About three weeks before Tojo's visit, Japanese and Filipino officials mingled on the reviewing stand during another parade, this time on April 11, 1943, to celebrate the one-year anniversary of the fall of Bataan. A simpering Filipino official, trying to play to a Japanese counterpart next to him, said: "I think there is little doubt now that the great majority of our people are pro-Japanese. I should say that ninety per cent of them at least understand Japan's true objectives in fighting for the unification of Great East Asia."

The Japanese official dismissed the comment and mocked the quisling's attempt to ingratiate himself. "You are mistaken—I am afraid that forty-five percent of the population continues to be pro-American, five percent are pro-Japanese while the remaining fifty percent are comedians."

On June 4 officials followed up on Tojo's promise by ostensibly turning the process of controlling opposition to the Japanese occupation over to the Filipinos. They created a national pacification committee intended to build support and influence in the provinces. The *Manila Tribune* was publishing stories about the capture of guerrillas, both Filipinos and American military escapees. All the while the pacification committee had the mandate to coordinate efforts to find the guerrillas and to discourage support for them. The head of the committee was a logical choice: José Laurel, a respected prewar politician with a law degree from Yale who also had been a justice of the Supreme Court of the Philippines. Laurel, the interior minister, had rationalized his decision to join the government, as many others had, on grounds he would be able to protect and defend the interests of Filipinos better than were he outside the government or dead for declining to participate. His role and his loyalties were difficult to interpret, but the Japanese occupiers trusted him.

On the morning of Saturday, June 5, the day after his designation as chair of the pacification committee, Laurel headed off with some friends to the Wack Wack Golf Club, north of the Pasig River, a popular spot created by an American businessman in 1930. The name "Wack Wack" could have seemed to Americans to refer to the sound of repeatedly hitting a golf ball, probably not the slang organized-crime meaning of executing someone. *Wakwak* in Philippine mythology referred to a mythological vampire-like bird that was said to carry humans away to their death. All connotations were apt. Laurel was standing at the seventh hole waiting for his turn at the tee when an unknown attacker shot him three times. Laurel crumpled to the ground. His friends managed to find a car and raced him to Philippine General Hospital. He had lost much blood by the time he arrived, but a six-man medical team, including the chief military surgeon for the Japanese occupiers, managed to save him.

The Japanese facade of "pan-Asianism" and independence had suffered a grave insult. Tojo sent wishes for a swift recovery and Laurel did survive. Within weeks he had an extra job under the occupation—he was assigned to the commission that would draw up a new constitution for a newly independent Philippines. Despite extensive interrogations, the Kempeitai military police did not find Laurel's attacker. However, they arrested suspected collaborators and threatened and warned others about their behavior in the following months.

Japanese intelligence operatives reported in August 1943 that their efforts had met with some success. After Nagahama's appeal "for closer cooperation and for the abandonment of any feeling of antagonism and resistance," more than seven hundred Filipino fighters had surrendered to Japanese forces. Using confidential sources and interrogation, Japanese military intelligence officers mapped out links from MacArthur to the guerrillas and to their underground supporters in Manila.

Tokyo had already ordered a change in command at Manila occupation headquarters, in part a reaction to the ongoing opposition throughout the Philippines. General Masaharu Homma, who had led the invasion and conquest of the islands, was marginalized for failing to make quick work of defeating the Americans on Bataan and had been forced into retirement. He was replaced by General Shizuichi Tanaka and then in May 1943, just after Tojo's visit, by Lieutenant General Shigenori Kuroda. Kuroda in turn ordered Colonel Nagahama and the Kempeitai to increase pressure on Filipino resistance and on the American guerrillas hiding in the mountains. That was no easy task. While Nagahama continued to advocate the velvet-glove approach, at least in public, Kuroda ordered that he pursue a new crackdown on the guerrillas. Following orders, Nagahama announced on the radio and in the newspapers that Americans or other insurgents who turned themselves in would be guaranteed their safety and treated fairly. But after a deadline they would be shot on sight. Nagahama had only a few takers.

Parsons on the Move
Manila, March–July, 1943

CHICK PARSONS'S WANDERINGS during his first trip back to the Philippines between March 4 and July 8, 1943, became a matter of folklore and speculation that could never be resolved. He was spotted around Manila several times, but the dates were contradictory. Claire noted in her diary entry of July 3, 1943, that he had arrived and that she had to make special efforts to get material to him, but he was apparently back in Mindanao by then waiting for his submarine ride back to Australia. Claire's bartender, Mamerto Geronimo, said that he had seen Chick disguised as a peasant walking along the waterfront not far from where his mother-in-law, Blanche Jurika, was staying at the convent of the Sisters of the Immaculate Conception in Intramuros.

John Rocha, a five-year-old boy, was walking hand in hand with his father in the Malate neighborhood of Manila one afternoon when a priest rode up on a bicycle. Without stopping, the priest looked at father and son, smiled, and dropped a package containing American magazines and candy. "That was Chick Parsons," Rocha recalled his father saying. "Do not mention that you saw him."

One of the most intriguing sightings involved General Roxas, who had been brought to Manila and was under house arrest while authorities sorted out what to do with him. One day Roxas's Japanese protector, Colonel Jimbo, was at the house when a priest arrived. The priest greeted those present and then took confession from the general, in private of course. "The visitor was attired in missionary's clothes," Jimbo said years afterward. "Several years later I came to know that the visitor was Chick Parsons."

The fake priest could have spoken fluent Spanish and Tagalog, possibly avoiding speaking English at all. Though Chick did not have Asian features, he was only around five foot six, so he would not have been as suspicious as a tall American might have been. Chick Parsons was brazen enough that he might have actually come to see Roxas more than once—taking advantage of priestly prerogatives. Those who knew him could imagine seeing him smile calmly, then exchange pleasantries with the Japanese guards and officers as he came and went.

The conundrum about all the sightings was that Parsons was definitely on Mindanao for much of June and was on the southern island in early July waiting for his submarine ride back to Australia. It is not clear that he could have traveled clandestinely so far, so quickly. It was more than six hundred miles from the submarine staging point to Manila. "We all know that Chick was a fast mover all over the islands; and he was very resourceful," said Peter Parsons. However, he said he could not determine with certainty when and in which year—1943 or 1944—his father made it to Manila.

In any case, in 1943 Parsons was not yet the subject of a manhunt—Japanese intelligence did not know that the man who had once been in their custody and detained at Santo Tomas was now General MacArthur's chief aid in organizing and supplying guerrillas around the country and the flourishing intelligence network in Manila. One Japanese intelligence report did mention the name "Parsons" but claimed that this was the nom de guerre of one of the American guerrilla commanders, Captain Ralph Praeger, who was operating in Kalinga Province in northern Luzon.

Parsons was not only eluding detection by Japanese military intelligence but also operating off the grid part of the time after he arrived in Mindanao by submarine in March 1943. He spent some time during June meeting and staying with Senator José Ozamiz, a friend of Juan Elizalde who, in turn, was in touch with Claire and Ramón. MacArthur had expected Parsons to avoid engagement with the Japanese and to stay away from secret communications with Manila, let alone personally going there. Parsons's son, Peter, analyzing his father's mid-1943 mission to occupied Philippines, was almost certain that his father had been in Manila for at least a week. Chick wrote a report from the military command in Mindanao dated June 1, 1943, focusing on guerrilla progress around the islands. Chick's whereabouts were not traceable for about two weeks after that, which was characteristic of a man who was willing to buck authority and operate on the front lines. He filed a report on his mission so far to MacArthur and then went off the grid. "I think that Parsons wrote the report (possibly even postdated it) and hightailed it . . . to Manila," Peter Parsons said of his father. After the war, Peter Parsons was certain he had overheard his father admitting that he disguised himself as a priest, but he had no evidence that it was true.

"He was likely in that city for a week to ten days." Then he returned to Mindanao by the same means, in reverse, probably with a guerrilla courier.

"We have no documents to work on to determine the deeper purposes of Parsons's penetration into Manila," Peter Parsons said. "Nor do we know if he was able to see General [Vicente] Lim [a Philippine brigadier general and underground operative] and tell him that General MacArthur had not granted him permission to board a submarine. I am supposing here but with pretty strong conviction that Parsons's main purpose was to contact [General] Roxas and set in motion the process of extracting him from the Philippines. [Roxas did not leave the country.] It is fascinating to me that Jimbo himself focuses on this crucial event as central to the whole resistance movement. He proved himself to be a shrewd observer."

Meanwhile, Claire wrote in her diary on June 30 that a man named Sam Wilson had arrived, and she said a few days later that Wilson was traveling with Parsons. "Will be very busy for four days" gathering "all news," she wrote. On July 3 she wrote that Wilson and Parsons had arrived and that she "must get all to them." The notations were cryptic as they had been since Claire had started keeping the diary in December 1942. Now she had begun using a crude, jibberish code with misspelled words and added syllables. The annotations were brief, but contained a significant amount of information. They confirmed that Claire was an integral part of the underground operation that Parsons had established in Manila with all the players they both knew—including Juan Elizalde, who supplied her with alcohol so she could keep entertaining Japanese officers and gathering information; Ramón, who had almost daily meetings with Judge Roxas; and through that connection, General Roxas.

On the record Chick Parsons gave no indication to his superiors at U.S. command headquarters in Australia of having gone to Manila on that trip in June 1943 or having engaged in attacks or knowing anything about attempted assassinations. Doing that could have been a court-martial-level offense. MacArthur had directed that the guerrillas and insurgents focus on pure intelligence and organization. If an organized guerrilla force had dared to launch blatant attacks, Filipino fighters knew that "their wives and children would suffer" reprisals and MacArthur would be in no position to help.

Whether or not he was physically present in Manila, Parsons was definitely in touch with the underground. Ramón Amusategui was in touch with Juan Elizalde, and that was a potential link to reports from Claire. Through his Manila contacts Parsons knew that the Japanese were stripping the Philippines of resources—automobile parts, scrap metal, agricultural equipment, melted-down nickel and copper coins for bullets and weaponry. Japan was also rumored to be planning to move American POWs from the Philippines to work camps in Japan and elsewhere in Asia, desperately seeking new ways to feed the war machine.

With Parsons's successful trip to the Philippines, MacArthur and his intelligence staff now had a reliable communications link from Manila via Mindanao couriers. The guerrillas with Parsons's help set up radio and coast-watcher stations at Davao, the largest city on Mindanao, and at Panaon, a small island between Leyte and Mindanao. This meant the underground had a relay network to headquarters in Brisbane. One way or another, Claire's information was getting through. The immediate reports arriving at Pacific headquarters were a compilation of intelligence gathered from various sources including her dispatches. If Claire had not provided the intelligence reports herself, they certainly sounded like whoever had written them knew about Tsubaki Club, Claire, Fely, and their colleagues.

On June 30, the same day Claire was gathering information to send to Parsons, a dispatch went out directly to MacArthur: "Filipinos employed to serve and entertain guests in night clubs. Manila Avenue Hotels also frequented by Nips." A dispatch the following day went along the same lines: "Hotel and club employees are Filipinos recommended by Jap civilians. It looks better if agents know a few common words and tunes. Some agents report that Filipinos required to bow when passing sentries and addressing Japs." Then there was one more point: "As to whether high-ranking Japs susceptible to women, that depends on kind of woman. For example, it is rumored that former beauty carnival queen Paquita de los Reyes was for some months the common law wife of a Jap officer."

Meanwhile, U.S. intelligence reports from the street gave an idea of how American operatives might be able to circulate.

White men are common in Manila streets but in suburbs and country roads they are rare and would attract immediate attention. Currency in Manila nearly all Jap Military notes. Flashing a twenty peso old Philippine bill would excite attention probably cause investigation. In Manila, doctors may use cars and travel after curfew which is between twelve midnight and six a.m. Curfew not very strictly enforced. Patrols consist of Jap plainclothes men in addition to uniformed groups and neighborhood patrol.

Whether or not Parsons skirted MacArthur's warning about offensive action, the order had already hit home with commanders on the ground. After almost six months in the Philippines in 1943, Parsons reported to MacArthur that the people of the Philippines were aching to fight. Filipinos were "completely fed up with the Japanese, bitterly disillusioned, acutely aware that in place of a pleasant democratic way of life they had gained only misery, hunger, and poverty, both spiritual and physical."

Who Is She?
Mount Pinatubo, Bataan, Spring 1943

AT HIS HIDEOUT in the mountains about sixty miles northwest of Manila, Doyle Decker received the latest weekly shipment of news, newspapers, and intelligence reports from High Pockets. Who was this High Pockets? Nobody exactly knew, other than assuming that High Pockets was a woman, which was enough to have him daydreaming at his post on the slopes of Mount Pinatubo.

Every week High Pockets sent the men in the mountains the Japanese-controlled newspaper, the *Manila Tribune*, but also a summary of U.S. radio broadcasts from San Francisco, compiled by Ramón Amusategui and distributed whenever possible. Decker and his allies received the news summary, as did John Boone and other guerrillas. Decker had met Boone early on when they all were attempting to set up their guerrilla operations. Decker, twenty-seven, had been an army private in the 515th Coast Artillery and was now with an outpost of the 155th Provisional Guerrilla Battalion. He had not seen Boone since the days after the surrender and knew nothing about Ramón or High Pockets or anyone else in Manila. All for the better.

High Pockets had become a folk hero among POWs and guerrillas. The Filipino messengers who brought supplies to Decker's camp told him they knew virtually nothing about her. They knew that she was a guerrilla leader in Manila, that she had messengers who dodged Japanese military police, and that she sent the weekly packets of information despite the danger of discovery. High Pockets was brave. "I think she is called High Pockets because she is tall," said his Filipino friend and guerrilla liaison, known only as George, after arriving with the latest shipment. "She is rumored to be half American and half Filipino."

The lack of information was a good thing. So far internal security was working well. If any of these messengers were captured and tortured, they might confess that High Pockets was their contact in Manila. But the most they could say about her was that High Pockets was a tall Filipina; such a description would never lead to Dorothy Fuentes, Madame Tsubaki, the chanteuse/bar owner who was serving drinks to many of the same Japanese agents who were searching for guerrillas and their supporters in Manila. The downside of Claire's anonymity was that Decker might have been one of the last people to spot her boyfriend, John Phillips, before he was captured. A man named Phillips had wandered into Decker's camp in May 1942, saying he had been lost for a month since the surrender at Bataan. Decker and the other escaped American soldiers brought Phillips along as they evaded Japanese patrols and sought a safe place to stay. Phillips stayed with the men for a few days, but was weak and sometimes had trouble keeping up with them. The men eventually did find safety in the mountains and split up into other groups; Decker had no more information about Phillips.

Each of the categories of information forwarded by High Pockets had its usefulness. The intelligence reports responded to requests to map the precise location of Japanese military installations and storage facilities, as well as gather details about POWs and detention camps. The news summary came from radio transmissions by KGEI, the powerful shortwave transmitter that was the only independent source of news available. KGEI broadcast directly to the Philippines and carried information about MacArthur's progress of the war, along with patriotic messages from exiled President Manuel Quezon. The *Manila Tribune* even had value. Decker and his friends discounted the *Tribune's* propagandistic dispatches: The U.S. Navy was reeling; the Japanese were scoring glorious victories in the Pacific; and the Nazis were taking new ground in Europe. George the messenger said that everyone understood. "If you read the paper and it says something can't happen, it has already occurred. If it declares a great victory for the Japanese, they have lost the battle. If the Americans have been driven off an island, it means they have captured the island." Moreover, the Americans were interested in seeing where the Japanese were claiming their major victories: on islands progressively closer to the Philippines. They could deduce from such reports that MacArthur was fighting his way back to Luzon.

Climbing the Wall
Manila, Spring 1943

CLAIRE MIGHT HAVE bragged that the work was easy—just supply her with alcohol for enough Japanese officers to get tongues wagging, and then the men would be willing to divulge military secrets to the closest beautiful woman. It was not so easy. The price of being High Pockets was high. Claire had to remind herself that the pressure and the fakery surrounding her life were for the purpose of producing these intelligence reports, of doing anything possible to fight the war and to save lives. Otherwise, she felt she might go insane. The daily routine, the clandestine work right alongside the Japanese, and the duplicity of celebrating Japanese victories were unrelenting. She trusted no one completely, not even Peggy, the only other American woman she saw frequently.

One night she had trouble with a sergeant whom the hostesses had nicknamed Tarzan after he actually climbed up the side of the building, barged drunk into her dressing room on the second floor, and stripped off his clothes. Claire managed to get out of it. Another time he threw a beer bottle and demanded that she give in to him or he would send her to Fort Santiago. If he sobered up the next morning and still wanted to do that, Claire would have to run. He did sober up and did not act on his threat.

Claire still had a succession of Japanese men chasing her, usually more than one man at a time. One officer, Colonel Komina, had made what he considered a formal oath of love to her. The colonel said he could not work, eat, or sleep out of longing for Claire. "Have colonel where I want him," she wrote in her diary. "Madly in love with me . . . I know he'll do anything I ask him now." Claire said she actually liked Komina, but did not betray in her diary or her memoir how far their relationship had gone. It sounded like they were lovers and Claire was mining him for information. They had been walking together in the Luneta one day when Komina had said he would be shipping out soon. Claire started to cry and Komina thought it was at the news of his impending departure. However, she wrote in her diary that she was thinking about John Phillips. She was relieved when Komina finally left town.

Claire's connections with the Japanese officers continued to be a balancing act and were likely to intensify. Boone had begun asking more detailed questions about intelligence matters. She needed to entice men to keep coming to the club but did not want to entice these men so much that they would force her into a sexual affair.

One intelligence request, she said, anticipated the impending arrival of a damaged Japanese aircraft carrier at Manila harbor. Claire recalled: "I was told when to expect it, find out where it would be repaired, how long the reconditioning would take, and send if possible, the exact date and hour of its departure, plus its destination."

With the club's proximity to the port and its reputation among the troops, the carrier's captain and crew did come to Tsubaki Club when they came ashore. Claire said the captain's name was Arita; both she and Fely developed a warm relationship with him. "Anyone could see that he was mad about Fely," Claire said. "He brought her many gifts, and was at the club every night to hear her sing." Arita took Fely one day to the Metropolitan Theater across the Luneta, inland from the bay. In a photograph taken that day, they made a striking couple: Arita in uniform, head tilted slightly with a slight smile; Fely, a bit shorter, was lovely, with black curled hair brushed back and falling at her shoulders, long earrings, and pearl-like beads over a shawl or tunic. However, her intense gaze toward the camera was impassive, revealing nothing.

Arita was not the typical officer on shore leave—he drank only soft drinks and the innocent lemonades usually served to the hostesses. Claire remembered him as "a really fine chap. He told us of his home and family in Japan; how he would be glad when the war was over, so he could join them. He hated war, and was quite an anomaly for the commander of a fighting craft."

After repairs were complete, Claire staged a farewell party for Arita and the crew. "I even cried real tears when he left, as I knew I was sending him to his doom," Claire said. "Yes, I cried real tears when he left, but war is war. As he and his staff departed by the big front door, my runner left by the back door." She hoped the message would help target him for attack—Arita was sailing from Manila to Singapore and on to Rabaul in New Guinea.

Consorting with an occupying soldier was unacceptable to the majority of Filipinos, who hated the Japanese presence. It was also dangerous—people had been killed for siding with the enemy. Women had taken up with Japanese officers, lived in fancy hotels, and were reviled for it. Claire had also seen that her old friend Mona was living with her Japanese boyfriend, a civilian close to the occupation army. Claire wanted nothing of it, but she had to play the part. Despite her caution, she had to keep up her charade, and she and Fely were known and seen to be spending time with Japanese officers. Claire was sometimes shunned on the street. How could anyone know what she was really doing? Sometimes she fretted and thought about closing the nightclub. She was drinking, she was smoking, she was tense all the while, and she had the pressure of caring for Dian, now three years old. She would walk in the park with Dian sometimes, knowing the Japanese soldiers would usually smile and treat them kindly. Other times the only refuge was a stolen moment to scribble a few lines in her little date book. "Fear for my sanity, really. My book is a comfort. Can let my hair down to it and it alone."

The Japanese officers came and went. One colonel who loved her shipped off and she heard a few months later that he might have been killed. She hoped it had something to do with the information about him and his unit that she had been sending up to the hills. On a personal level she could not help caring about some of the men she spoke to at the club. Nevertheless, she was taking down the name of every Japanese officer she could find. She was fighting a war.

Claire knew that Fely and the other hostesses at Tsubaki Club had the same trouble she did as they gathered information. They deceived the Japanese as they served them, laughed at their jokes, toasted straight-faced to their victories over the Americans. Later in the night the Japanese would get drunk, using their hands and whips and scabbards at times to show their superiority. Filipinos young and old were subject to petty brutalities without recourse, even when they bowed and averted their eyes. It was obvious that Japanese officers were not honoring Colonel Nagahama's entreaty not to slap people. It was a constant indignity and sometimes worse. "I don't know how long I can take this face slapping. Twice tonight." Someone also had hit her with a rubber hose. "Leg better today. But still swollen. God how I hate them."

Claire converted her anger and hatred into a compulsion to stay busy all the time, gathering supplies and writing reports during the day, operating the club and gathering bits of information at night. The goal was to send more support than ever before, even when prices were going up and beer was sometimes hard to buy. Without beer and other alcohol, business and receipts dropped. She decided to tackle high expenses by giving up her apartment at the Dakota. It would also help avoid the excess contact with military police caused by having to race home every night before midnight curfew.

"The Japanese curfew was a nuisance and some nights I had not been able to reach home. It only took a friendly carpenter a couple of weeks to convert some of the smaller rooms into a four room apartment, in the rear of the club." That also meant that Dian would be with her more of the day, cared for by her nanny, Ah Ho, the Chinese woman who had taken over when Lolita went home pregnant with her own child. The new quarters included an extra space with a bunk in case any American stragglers had to be hidden from sight.

Everyone in Manila was economizing these days. Grocery stores were running out of staples like sugar, flour, beef, and even fruits and vegetables. Rationing was supposed to provide bare necessities, but people were forced to turn more and more to black marketeers who gouged them and became rich. Claire, now living at the club, cut back on her budget even more, avoiding expensive food and diversions such as movies and books and eating out. "Only bare necessities now," she wrote in her diary. "Everything stay[s] high. Hard to make both ends meet."

Paranoia

Manila, July 1943

ONE MORNING in July, Peggy called Claire, in a panic for no obvious reason. She said she needed to clean house; there was incriminating evidence all around her apartment and she had to do something about it. She was coming right over to the club. Peggy was tightly strung—even calling and saying this on the phone was a danger. Phones were routinely tapped. Claire could do without someone else's panic attacks or Peggy breaking security and showing up at the club to dump a pile of papers and messages in Claire's lap. What if she was stopped on the street?

Tsubaki Club was the best and the worst hiding place. Claire said that Japanese officers sometimes wandered into her room—she never said why these men were in her room. They loitered about talking to her, not exactly searching but laying hands on everything. Madame Tsubaki seemed to be immune; but beneath the surface, she was scared too. Peggy's papers added to the cache of material she already had—the lists of prisoners in Manila and at Cabanatuan, unexplained papers destined for Boone, and Claire's little date-book diary. That was not all. "I was terribly worried as I had a contraband radio concealed in my dressing table. They sat right by the table and admired all the lipstick and other things but never thought to look under all the fancy trimming."

Claire imagined that the military police, some of them her evening visitors, had plainclothes operatives and snitches all around. She never saw them. Until this day the danger had been only theoretical—Claire had not seen any signs of actual trouble. However, later that same day the phone rang. Claire answered and no one was there. Her stomach turned.

She could not know whether it was a coincidence, whether Peggy had set off an alarm, or whether Peggy herself had turned snitch. She could do nothing, say nothing, only write in her diary that night that the hostesses saw that something was wrong. "The girls think I'm nuts." Nothing happened.

Worse still, as if Peggy had had a premonition or advance warning, the Kempeitai staged a sudden lockdown. Claire had just swept the apartment clean, removed any incriminating papers from plain sight. Soldiers did come to the club, but the search produced nothing. "We were not allowed to leave that area of four square blocks for one solid day, 24 hours" while they searched.

Over the next month, Claire sped up her activities to make as much money and gather as much information as possible. But money was tight for everyone, business was unsteady, and prices were ever higher. She did what she could to support Boone and Louise—who was still at Santo Tomas, although many people had been shipped off to Los Baños—to send supplies to the prisoners at the Park Avenue School, and to ship whatever she could to Cabanatuan. The POW network in the north was still working with Evangeline Neibert, coordinated either by Peggy or, more and more frequently, by Ramón Amusategui. One day Carling Sobreviñas, Claire's friend and protector in the hills of Bataan, came to the club with documents he had hidden for her: her passport, insurance certificates, and other papers that had been buried in the hills. Claire hid them again and was always hiding her little date book with notes about the passage of days.

Fear, suspicion, and terror had become the ever-present reality on the streets of Manila. Beatings, torture, and death became commonplace, so much so that people just stepped around dead bodies they encountered on the street. Newspapers avoided the subject of the random killings. A silent war left bodies sometimes floating overnight on the Pasig River: collaborators executed by the guerrillas or guerrilla sympathizers killed by the Japanese. People did not always know. One of the more prominent and brazenly killed victims was seen by many as a collaborator with the Japanese—Alejandro Roces Jr., manager of the *Manila Tribune* and the son of its owner. Roces had originally been an ally of the now-exiled president, Manuel Quezon. Quezon had given him the ceremonial title of captain in the city police force, although he was no policeman. He stayed on in the force under Japanese control and now was said to be leading the investigation into the assassination attempt of José Laurel. A young man on a bicycle approached Roces's car just after the newspaperman had dismissed his bodyguard for a few moments as they approached his father's house. The young man "whipped out a .45 caliber pistol and fired point blank at Roces and his wife. Then he calmly got onto his bicycle and pedaled off."

Alejandro Roces Sr. heard the shots and came running. His son and daughter-in-law lay dead on the ground. News spread around the city, but the newspaper, which had been avoiding stories of violence that put the occupation in a bad light, neglected to tell the real story of the killing on its pages the next morning. The *Tribune* printed a picture of the younger Roces, reporting that he had died of a heart attack. The lesson taught by unseen hands was clear to collaborators, and it gave Claire something else to worry about. She knew that some freelance assassin might target her as a courtesan serving the Japanese. When one colonel left town, another officer was romancing her and causing trouble. She did what she had to do.

It was a sad month. Claire observed July 27 as the anniversary of John Phillips's death. She commemorated the day by working harder, quietly packing supplies and food for the POWs at Cabanatuan. She said she had gathered fifty pairs of shoes for Cabanatuan and about two hundred pesos' worth of medicines, including quinine, sulfa drugs, and emetine, used to treat the amoebic dysentery that was rampant at Cabanatuan and the other camps. She dedicated her time to the memory of John Phillips, "a quiet day gathering money, clothes etc for your remaining friends. That's the best I could do to commemorate your memory." Mixed with that were recriminations—perhaps if she had been faster to start her club and to get her relief operation working, she thought, torturing herself, she could have done something to save Phillips. "My only regret is: that I did not know how to do it a year ago. It might have saved you. But I know you're waiting for me. And as soon as my duty is finished here, I'll join you. So please wait for me."

"We're in the Movies!"

Manila, August 16, 1943

AFTER MORE THAN a year in detention, the POWs at the Park Avenue School in the suburb of Pasay were living with appalling conditions, filth, a bare minimum of hygiene, and near-starvation diets. By now they were used to wearing fetid rags and G-strings and rough-hewn wooden shoes if they could even lash them to their feet. So on Monday, August 16, a typically steamy morning, they had reason to be suspicious, even worried when their guards herded them into a central courtyard. They stood before a mountain of clothing and equipment, a stockpile of new gear. The guards motioned them forward: It was for them.

One of them, Ted Lockard, said they all were baffled. What was happening? Was the war over? Where were they going? "They gave us new everything . . . trousers, belts, shirts, helmets, and guns." They moved carefully to the rifles and could see quickly that the weapons had neither bolts nor bullets. It was all a show.

While they were gearing up, something strange was also happening in downtown Manila. All the week of August 16, workers were erecting scaffolding and platforms on central streets and along the approach to Jones Bridge that led across the Pasig River toward Taft Avenue and city hall. Soon—judging by the gear, it was evident—the Japanese were making a movie.

The occupation propaganda department had decided to make the best picture of the war, a well-filmed motion picture that would tug at the emotions of the Filipinos and would illustrate the Japanese reason for going to war and attacking the Americans. They brought in Yutaka Abe, a forty-three-year-old Japanese filmmaker who had trained as an actor and director in the early days of Hollywood. Abe was now making propaganda films for the government. He was teamed with Gerardo de Leon, thirty, already well known in Manila film circles as an actor and director.

The melodramatic plot portrayed the life of a young man forced to leave his family to fight for the Americans. He finds, though, that the Americans are heartless lugs and the Japanese are bringing a new world order to the Philippines. In the end he comes to his senses and realizes that the Japanese are his true friends. Two Filipino American actors, Bert Leroy and Frankie Gordon, were drafted, probably compelled to take starring roles. Early in the film, benevolent Japanese liberators arrive to free Manila from the clutches of the craven Americans. The POWs were to re-create the American retreat from Manila and later the American defeat in Bataan. This was why the Japanese needed Ted Lockard and his POW friends.

Word spread quickly. Claire and her friends converged on the avenues surrounding Jones Bridge when they saw that cameras and scaffolding were being set up. The size of the crowd grew in anticipation. Finally a convoy approached, incongruous and otherworldly. Lockard and his friends were just as surprised as the people on the street were. "They took us into the city, and we drove down the streets in these big trucks past big movie cameras." They wore clean new uniforms and shiny helmets. But with a closer look, one could see the men were thinner than soldiers should be. The crowd cheered and nervous Japanese guards shoved bystanders.

As the cameras rolled, Lockard and his fellow prisoners, resplendent in new uniforms for the first time in almost two years, were amazed by the spontaneous reaction on the street. "You know the funny thing was, word about the filming had spread among the Filipinos, and they came out and just bombarded all our trucks with fruit and food. I think it was just a sign of the Filipinos' hope."

Claire also brought food and gifts; she got as close as she could. The crowd was so large that she could avoid the attention of Japanese soldiers and managed to call out to the Americans. She spoke to as many as she could; they must have been doubly amazed to see an American woman with a hometown accent among the people on the street. She was not alone. Some people were able to throw money up to the men, who were excited and exchanging jokes and cheers.

"We're in the movies now!" one of the prisoners yelled from a truck.

The incongruity between the Americans portrayed as fleeing Manila in shame and the cheering of the crowd was an obvious irony that would be edited out of the final footage. The presence of so many people was unnerving to the overwhelmed, outnumbered guards watching the prisoners. A few Japanese soldiers on the periphery of the crowd rounded up some Filipina women who they thought were too boisterous and dragged them off to Fort Santiago.

After the filming at Jones Bridge was over, the filmmakers, directors Abe and Leon, needed to show one more scene with the Americans, this time in a jungle clearing that would represent the American disaster on Bataan, minus the barbaric treatment during the death march. For this scene they decided to use the prisoners at Cabanatuan. Weldon Hamilton said he and his fellow POWs were as confused as the men had been in Manila. "We had no idea what they wanted, they gathered us and sent us out with a bunch of food. We drove into the mountains to this open, hilly area. . . . Then we had to walk over this hill in a line, throw our weapons in a huge pile and act like we were surrendering. We were treated really nicely that day."

When it was all over, the men got a ride back to their respective prison camps and were ordered to deposit the gear they had been given in a big pile. Lockard said the men responded with an act of defiance. They dumped the useless guns and helmets as ordered but kept the clothing, leaving instead a pile of their fetid, ragged clothes from before. "For a few days, the guards gave us a hard time for keeping the uniforms, but all of a sudden they just quit."

After the daytime activity was done, Claire returned to the club, where the rhythm was as demanding as ever. Foreign civilians sometimes mingled with the Japanese officers; so did traveling Japanese businessmen and others, including the film crew of the Toho Motion Picture Company, which was working on the final touches. They announced the title was to be *Dawn of Freedom*. Claire seemed to beat the competition as she hoped—Tsubaki Club was the go-to place for Japanese officers. It would not be a surprise if one of the officers invited Claire out to see the movie. Attendance was compulsory anyway—it would be fatal to refuse.

The work toll mounted and Claire drove herself on. She was taking care of Dian, working with Fely to manage the club accounts, and worrying that the Kempeitai eventually would realize who they were and arrest them all. At best, she was sleeping five hours a night, lying awake as she imagined where the military police were circulating that night, which suspects they were hunting down, who among them might provide dangerous information, and what would be the outcome. Claire did not always back off on the drinking. Sometimes a guest at the club pushed a real drink toward her and insisted she drink it instead of the cheaper, safer option of lemonade with a spot of crème de menthe to make it seem like an alcoholic beverage. "Even to Madame Tsubaki, a Jap wish was a command," Claire said. The officers wanted to party. The strong-willed woman behind the mask was reaching her limit.

Giving Thanks
Tsubaki Club, Manila, September 29, 1943

FOR WEEKS, Claire had tried not to pay attention to the growing pain in her stomach. It was getting worse. She had been watching what she was eating and was following a bland diet; that meant rice and water and little else. Milk would have been soothing; eggs, meat, and other proteins would have helped but they were hard to find. She wrote it off to nerves— the pressures on her were taking a toll.

One Wednesday afternoon the club was not open yet as Claire and some of the staff were preparing for the evening. Suddenly Claire collapsed and nearly passed out, writhing in pain. Fely stayed with her and sent one of the helpers to fetch Peggy, who found her in agony in her bed, screaming and running a high temperature. They called in a doctor, who confirmed Peggy's suspicion. Claire had a perforated ulcer—a life-threatening rupture in the wall of her intestine. She needed emergency surgery.

Wartime realities made the prospects grim. A surgeon was available, but transportation to the hospital was not. Private cars and taxis were not on the street. Peggy tried to commandeer the ambulance at Remedios Hospital, where she still worked, but the gas tank was bone dry. Gasoline was severely rationed and even emergency vehicles sometimes could not find any at all. The hospital had been using alcohol from the storeroom to run the ambulance but had run out of that as well. Peggy thought quickly and remembered that their friend, Mrs. Kummer, had a permit to be on the road with a driver and often was able to get a ration of gasoline to keep the car rolling. Mrs. Kummer said she could take Claire. The driver came and they carried Claire to the car. Doctors Hospital was closest, about four blocks from the club. By the time they got her in, Claire's temperature was dangerously high and her vital signs were unsteady. Her personal doctor contacted a surgeon, who quickly went to work. Claire could be nonchalant after the fact. "Doctor Guerrero called in one of the best local surgeons, who operated without delay, removing a perforated ulcer and about six inches of intestines. I dimly remember when I came back to this world Doctor Guerrero joked, 'Too bad, you haven't got the guts you used to have.'"

The danger should have been over. Just in case, Claire's friends kept a vigil. Peggy stayed as much as she could and monitored Claire's progress; as she watched nurses come and go, she did some of the nursing herself. "At the end of the fourth day, the doctor said that I didn't have to give the intravenous feeding every four hours, so that permitted me to go home after midnight and then come back early in the morning."

At some point in the ordeal, when Claire knew she was seriously ill, she managed to give final instructions to Peggy. If I don't make it, if something should happen, she told Peggy, make sure that my mother is notified in Portland; and take care of Dian. It was no surprise that Fely had called Peggy for help. Peggy and Claire were friends and allies. They had worked together, grieved together, shared time together, and often looked out for each other. But although both were assertive women and big drinkers, they had their differences. The women became trusted friends, but there was also a certain rivalry.

Peggy was only seven years older, but she appeared much older than that. Claire was an effusive presence and an attractive woman who drew men's attention. Peggy could have been jealous. Both women would write to the men in prison, but Claire's missives came across as lonely-heart love letters. The men, suffering and deprived, sometimes felt they were reading the words of an angel who gave them hope and the will to survive. Claire was the only one receiving multiple offers of marriage, sight unseen.

After some days Claire was still recuperating at the hospital and the danger seemed to have passed. Her doctors were ready to start her slowly on solid food. Then Claire started to notice she was having trouble speaking and opening her mouth. Her fever spiked and Peggy came running from her nursing chores at Remedios Hospital. Whether from a dirty needle or an unsterilized instrument, Claire had developed lockjaw—tetanus. No one had stocks of antitetanus toxoid. Doctors began to scour the city.

Once before, while in Bataan the previous year, Claire had thought she might die, sick as she was from malaria. Now she was rarely lucid enough to consider the possibility: The doctors did not expect her to survive.

Her fever went up again, she ranged in and out of consciousness, she could not speak beyond a mumble, and a new complication developed. "When I started to cough, I almost strangled, and the doctors administered oxygen." She had contracted bronchial pneumonia. "By the fourth day, I was suffering convulsions, and only semi-conscious." She awoke occasionally to see Peggy and sometimes Ramón visiting at her bedside. She said Father Lalor also had come once to pray for her health. She was rarely coherent. Finally Doctor Guerrero managed to find a substantial stock of antitetanus serum and decided the case was so far advanced that he had to administer an unusually high dose, which could either kill her or shock her system into responding. "On the following day, after I had received the third shot, my jaws started to unlock and my temperature dropped to 103 degrees. My good friend, Ramón, managed to find some sulfa tablets which were pulverized and given to me in powdered form."

Her friends worked together to make sure Claire was getting the best care—they argued years afterward about who had paid Claire's hospital bill. Claire thought she had paid for herself. Lorenza thought she and Ramón had paid. Peggy also took credit. That was never sorted out. Claire recovered slowly. Doctors who had feared the worst said she had beaten tough odds; it was a matter of luck and perseverance. As Claire regained consciousness and visitors came and went, she was startled by the presence one day of an unexpected familiar face. It was Yamada, the Japanese guard who had allowed prisoners to come with him for lunch at the club. Smiling, he gave her a basket of flowers to wish her well.

Ramón got in touch with Judge Roxas, who recalled later, "He told me that the person who was sick in the hospital was a certain lady by the name of Dorothy."

"I don't know anybody by that name," Roxas said.

"You do know her," Ramón said. "It is the code name we use in the underground."

The judge realized it was Claire. Ramón said she had been very ill but was improving.

When Claire opened her eyes, she saw the judge. She was recovering by now and could move her jaw and speak, though weakly. For reasons of

caution and safety, they had not seen each other for months, but the judge had known all along what Claire was doing in the underground. He was steering clear of direct involvement, though his brother, the general, was getting deeply involved through channels in touch with Ramón, Juan Elizalde, and, by extension, Claire and the guerrillas in the hills. He worried still about the consequences of their all being caught in the conspiracy. Now Judge Roxas was worried about Claire's health and stamina. He urged her to stop and told her she had done enough already, but Claire said she had no intention of stopping. The club would continue. Gathering supplies and intelligence was important for the war effort and she took solace from the help she was giving the prisoners of Cabanatuan. The judge argued the danger of being caught was greater than ever, especially now. The Japanese were on the offensive against the guerrillas.

Claire respected the judge but her answer was an emphatic "no." "She told me that she felt very happy doing that work . . . in compliance as her duty as an American."

For now, Fely was doing fine at the club and Dian was well. But even from her hospital bed Claire told Ramón she wanted to get back to work.

Ramón agreed the work needed to go on. The POWs at Cabanatuan needed food. The rations were low. Despite the regular shipments of food from Manaloto, and although the men were still allowed to come out to the fields and pretend to buy fruit and vegetables hidden with money and messages from Naomi and Evangeline, their caloric intake had been low lately. The men needed protein. He was working on a new plan to send in more water buffalo.

As Ramón got into details, Fely arrived.

"Well, I had better see you later," Ramón said.

"No. Fely understands all about the work we are doing. . . . I may need her."

The plan was the same as always. They had a good price for the water buffalo, but they needed more money to bribe the Japanese guards. "There are several different people who are going to contribute and I wonder if you could," Ramón said.

Claire said he could count on her. If she was still in the hospital when he was ready, Fely would be the contact. "You go to Fely, and whatever she has, why she will give it to you."

Turning to Fely, she added, "You give whatever you have to Ramón."

By the time she was ready to get back to work, Ramón was moving ahead with the plan—through her contacts Claire was able to help raise about twenty thousand pesos.

Claire stayed in the hospital from September 30 to November 13. "I was able to go home in time for Thanksgiving and I was thankful for my miraculous recovery." She had lost thirty-five pounds. She resumed her coded notations in her diary with a shorthand summation of what she could remember. Those days, she "saw and felt death."

Arrest and Ransom
Manila, October 1943

AS PEGGY WAS checking in at the hospital one morning, she heard "the tramp of heavy feet in the corridor coming toward the ward where I was. I stiffened up. They were at the door, eight of them, fully armed, bayonets fixed."

"You will come."

They said nothing more and led Peggy away to Fort Santiago. "The Japanese soldiers took me into a large sunny room on the second floor. Through its open, screened side, I could see the lovely patio, the soft lawn, the flowers . . . the prison itself with its stone cells, many of them out over the water. In the days of the Spaniards, the floor had openings through which the bodies of luckless captives could be dropped into the river with scarcely a sound."

It turned out that the Kempeitai had remained suspicious after coming to check up on Naomi at Peggy's apartment back in April. For the next two weeks, Peggy endured endless interviews and interrogations, sometimes brutal, sometimes not, all focusing on whether she was Lithuanian, as she had claimed on her official documents under the Japanese occupation authority, or whether she was an American, as her captors suspected.

One interrogator asked about her father.

"He died when I was a little girl."

What was her mother's name?

Peggy thought quickly and made one up.

If she was Lithuanian, why did she not speak Lithuanian?

"My aunt had taken me to live with her in Canada when I was very small. We always spoke English because my aunt was English."

"We know you American," the inquisitor said. "We put you into Santo Tomás."

The Japanese could not break her story, even when they showed her documents from the Red Cross and from an American company in which she identified herself as an American. Peggy said she had faked her answers on those documents because she figured the Americans would not have employed her if they knew she was from a country friendly with Nazi Germany. The stalemate went on. The Japanese wanted to prove in the court of public opinion that they had real evidence, rather than making it appear they were randomly punishing the innocent.

Prisoners at Fort Santiago were routinely tortured. As Roy C. Bennett had told Edgar Whitcomb, part of the torture was not knowing whether and when the torturers would come—in an hour, in a month, or never. Peggy suffered that emotional torture and said she had been beaten mercilessly. After several weeks the Japanese inquisitors told her without explanation that she was being released. They demanded, however, that she sign a document declaring that her treatment had been courteous and that she would be friendly to the Japanese. She willingly signed in return for freedom.

Within hours of Peggy's arrest, Ramón Amusategui had begun secret negotiations for her release. He knew that her Lithuanian papers were in order and that claims to the contrary could not be proved. If the Kempeitai had more serious allegations, they all would be in jail already.

He was, therefore, on safe enough ground to contact people he knew inside the occupation government and to arrange a five-thousand-peso bribe to get her out. He might have done the same for someone else, but there was a certain urgency in this case. Ramón and Lorenza worried that Peggy could be manipulated and, threatened with torture, might reveal the larger operation and put everyone—including Claire and Ramón—in lethal danger. Ramón had been able to use enough leverage that whatever torture had been applied was quickly halted.

On release, Peggy took a cab to her apartment, bathed and changed her clothes, then went to Lorenza's father, Gerardo Vásquez, a physician. Terrorized, she begged Vásquez to hospitalize her, hoping this would keep her from being arrested once more. By coincidence, Peggy had been putting off an operation to remove a benign uterine cyst. Lorenza's father confirmed this but agreed with Ramón. Peggy was unbalanced and at times hysterical. She did have the operation, but Lorenza's father found someone else to perform it. "We kept close watch on her movements while in the hospital, and kept away from her once out of it," Lorenza said. "This [was] because we did not want the Japs to have proof of our relations with her in case of a second arrest. Ramón was the only one visiting her when back in her house to help her in whatever way he could, also to keep track of her movements."

Peggy's arrest was a sign that Kempeitai agents were stepping up their search for dissident activity. Another problem had now developed, this time a communications breach that threatened the future of the entire relief operation to Cabanatuan. Some of the prisoners at Cabanatuan were sending messages back and forth through the underground mail system with their family members and friends at Santo Tomas. The main contact at Santo Tomas was Bert Ritchie, who had been a U.S. Navy intelligence officer during World War I. He told Ramón and Lorenza that five American women in the camp "were overheard squealing to the Japanese commandant about us, about our underground activities." Bert warned everyone to lay low for a while.

As a result, "we just kept piling up all these letters and money" for Cabanatuan until Ritchie finally gave the okay. Now Ramón and Lorenza decided to censor every piece of mail in both directions. "When we started censoring, many of these women were mentioning our names. They were writing to their loved ones in camp, and they would say thanks to Ramón Amusategui, or his wife . . . or whoever happened to be their contact. . . . If the Japs got that they would catch us."

"You'll Have to Kill Me First"
Malacañang Palace, Manila, October 1943

COLONEL AKIRA NAGAHAMA'S staff car sped past the iron gates of Malacañang, the presidential palace, and circled around the drive, where a flagpole flew the Philippine flag—blue, red, white, and a shining yellow sun—which had replaced the occupation flag of the red Rising Sun. The change symbolized the so-called independence of the Second Philippine Republic, conceded by Japan on October 20, 1943.

He vaulted up the stairs and barged into the office of the newly designated president of occupied Philippines, José Laurel.

"I demand the arrest of [General] Roxas," Nagahama said, nearly snarling as he spoke with neither preamble nor handshake. He threw a sheaf of intelligence documents onto the president's desk. "I have waited for a long time and at last I have the evidence. I demand that you turn Mr. Roxas over to me, and if it is the last thing I will do in this country I will kill him with my own hands."

Laurel knew well Nagahama's propensity for rage but also knew what they both understood: The colonel could not overstep his powers. The national flag fluttered outside the window, symbolizing the transfer of sovereignty to the Philippines. The Japanese government was making a show of Philippine independence, and Nagahama would have to abide by it. The president did not bother to examine the papers thrown before him. He looked up mildly from his desk and spoke confidently.

"You can go and get Roxas, but you'll have to kill me first."

All the while, General Roxas's office was only a few doors away. Yet Laurel deftly used the power of his office, the fiction of independence, and the strength of his image as a pro-Japanese leader to protect his friend. Nagahama was powerless.

"If you insist on arresting Roxas, you must get orders from the High Command," Laurel said. "You are a mere subordinate and I refuse to deal with you. I deal only with the diplomatic representatives of your country. You cannot arrest Roxas without orders from the High Command."

With that, Nagahama stormed out of the office past Laurel's son, José Laurel III, who then entered and stood before his father. Father and son smiled. Nagahama had offered no specifics, but the Kempeitai chief was correct about Roxas and his true loyalties. Nagahama had never believed in or accepted General Manuel Roxas's conversion as a friend of Japan. One soldier knew another: The man who had been liaison to General MacArthur simply would not change his stripes. However, the Japanese High Command ruled otherwise, believing Roxas was more valuable alive than dead. When Roxas was saved from execution and returned to Manila, his potential propaganda value on behalf of the puppet government was judged highly important. If General Roxas could be won over "to our side," intelligence officers reported, "Roxas's influence [would be] far greater than we had originally imagined."

From the outset Nagahama suspected Roxas had connections with the underground and sent out his men to prove he was right. Meanwhile, President Laurel named Roxas to a vital post, chief of the Government Rice Procurement Authority. Control of the rice supplies and pricing was power politics in Manila. Roxas and Laurel secretly blocked Japanese access to the rice stores controlled by the agency—they wanted to project that the largest possible supply of the staple food would be available to the civilian population at the lowest possible price. They managed the system successfully. But when the Japanese occupiers were forced to use their own procurement methods outside of the Laurel government, short supply and high demand drove the prices up for everyone.

Roxas had indeed maintained important contacts in the underground movement in Manila and was passing information along through a daring intermediary, Ramona Snyder, who in turn provided the information to Ed Ramsey, Boone's commander in the hills of Luzon. Ramsey had fallen in love with the young woman. "Diminutive, round-faced, with a frank, cheerful personality, she was absolutely fearless—indeed she seemed to enjoy danger as something of a quaint diversion." Starting in September 1943, Ramona was sneaking up to spend time with Ramsey and passing along all possible information from General Roxas, the guerrillas' best possible contact at Malacañang.

Informers had told the Kempeitai that someone within the Laurel administration was passing information to the pro-American underground and that Laurel probably knew. Ironically, President Laurel had faced harsh criticism from pro-American Filipinos for agreeing to be a pawn of the Japanese. By protecting Roxas from arrest, he was doing his own part to undermine the Japanese war effort. Laurel assumed accurately that the Japanese would not want open scandals and questions about loyalty that might embarrass them.

The biggest secret, though, was that the Roxas family, the Elizaldes, and other prominent families had a friend on the outside with whom they had once dined, drunk, and played at the Manila Polo Club. That man was now ensconced in Australia and was ready to take the fight to the Japanese: Lieutenant Commander Charles "Chick" Parsons.

Nagahama's War
Manila, October 1943

```
INTELLIGENCE REPORT

KAKI 6551 Force (TN DIV HQ) MILITARY ULTRA SECRET

SUBJECT: PUNITIVE AND PROPAGANDA MEASURES
    AGAINST GUERRILLAS

Southern LUZON Area

Punitive action was carried out against the band
headed by Col. Hugh Straughn in the northern bank
area of LAGUNA Lake and eastern area of MANILA.
Many Home Guards were captured. However, due to
the completeness of their organization, distur-
bance of the peace is expected to increase in Jan.
and Feb.
```

THOUGH NAGAHAMA FAILED to arrest General Roxas, he was making other inroads and used his successes to their maximum propaganda value. The Kempeitai chief knew, however, from reading the intelligence briefings that when one American commander was hit, a replacement emerged.

For public consumption, when a search-and-destroy team, working with military intelligence, seized a prominent American guerrilla leader, Lieutenant Colonel Hugh Straughn, in early August 1943, the Japanese propaganda machine proclaimed the death knell for the insurgents.

Straughn had been evading capture in the ten months since the seizure of his comrade-in-arms Lieutenant Colonel Claude Thorp, forty-five, one of the first Americans who had gone to the hills. In January 1942, still at Corregidor, General MacArthur had authorized a secret mission, led by Thorp, behind enemy lines. Thorp had set up a camp with sixteen men and two women in the mountains above Clark Field to monitor Japanese planes and troop movements.

After the surrender at Bataan in April 1942, the price on Thorp's head was steep. Nagahama's Kempeitai paid off villagers and guides in the hills for information as they hunted for Thorp. They lined up suspected collaborators in village squares, interrogated their friends and neighbors, and were willing to kill the innocent just to terrorize others. The Kempeitai planted informants and sent in double agents posing as guerrillas or young women feigning innocence as they gathered information. Nagahama's men listed their successes in numbers: report after report of search-and-destroy missions. One read:

```
Punitive operation around LAGUNA Lake against
    HUGH STRAUGHN and MARCOS Guerrillas

Surrendered 1
Shot 4
POWS 13
Rifles 1
Hand made pistols 2
Philippine pistol 27
Knapsack 1
Bolos 1
Small Quantities of documents
Camp incinerator 1
Pistol 9
Hunting Rifles 16
Hand Grenades 2
Air rifles 7
Parade swords 3
Hand grenades 3
Shovel 1
Dummy Pistols 3
Rice 4 Bags
```

Thorp survived more than a dozen attacks but was finally surrounded and captured by Japanese counterinsurgency operatives on October 29, 1942. The remnants of his guerrilla unit avoided capture. Japanese intelligence was under no illusions. "Even after the capture of Lieutenant Colonel Thorp, the American Thorp Commando Unit has been succeeding in organizing guerrillas in the Sierra Madre Mountains area."

Japanese intelligence reports said that Thorp's reorganized forces, under new leadership, were still able to gather recruits and organize. "The remaining guerrillas of Lieutenant Colonel Thorp are waiting for the American Army's help or for the time when the Japanese Army's strength decreases. They will then strike."

Military intelligence had now managed to capture Straughn and advertised it as a much greater victory than it was. "The self-appointed American chief of guerrillas in the Philippines . . . predicts collapse of guerrilla warfare" on the islands, crowed a report accompanied by a banner headline in the *Manila Tribune* on August 7. At the same time, a series of staged propaganda photographs suggested Straughn was readily cooperating with the enemy. In one photograph the wiry sixty-four-year-old guerrilla officer posed in a jungle clearing chatting with an interpreter as one soldier listened while seated in a folding chair and another leaned against a tree nearby, none of the three Japanese appearing to be armed. In a second photograph Straughn smoked his pipe and used a pencil to point at features of a map laid out on the ground. It was a fake: No one would believe that capture by the Japanese Army was a civilized affair or that prisoners would be more than willing to help their captors.

The report said Straughn admitted that the guerrillas were deserting their ranks. "Straughn said that his followers had been steadily losing faith in the possibility of the Americans returning to the Philippines. At the same time they were fast being convinced of Japan's generous intentions towards the Philippines."

While the capture of Straughn was significant, none of the claims made about him was true in any sense, and the Japanese military was overinflating his importance. Far from being the leader of all the guerrillas, Straughn was the head of a single guerrilla army south and east of Manila on Luzon. Many more stood in line to replace him. Like Parsons and MacArthur himself, Straughn had been a familiar, long-standing member of the Manila expatriate community. He had fought in the Spanish-American War and was an old colleague and contemporary of MacArthur's. Straughn had retired years earlier and stayed on; after the fall of Manila, MacArthur approved his request in early 1942 to mount a guerrilla force in the Luzon mountains. Straughn moved aggressively and was considered one of the toughest commanders in the early days of the occupation, having launched attacks on Japanese convoys even before the

U.S. surrender. He attracted a large number of volunteers and his operations became a focus of the Kempeitai's antiguerrilla campaign.

At the same time as the capture of Hugh Straughn, Nagahama stepped up his counterinsurgency campaign. He also issued a nationwide proclamation on October 1. Once more he stressed the honorable intentions of the Japanese government and called on the guerrillas to turn themselves in.

"Upon my word of honor I guarantee one hundred percent that your life and the lives of all your followers will be spared and safeguarded if you lay down your arms and present yourselves to the garrison commander in your locality." Apparently, he was speaking to Filipinos and not to the Americans among the guerrillas. "We shall all forget the past differences between us and shall welcome you with open arms as brothers, which you are and always shall be. Must you continue fighting for America at the expense of your own native country now that continuing to fight means obstructing Philippine progress?"

Nagahama was not interested in amnesty or the humane treatment of prisoners, nor was he required by Tokyo to observe the Geneva conventions, which laid out specific requirements for the treatment and protection of prisoners of war. Nagahama wanted to eliminate opposition while maintaining the false image of Japanese-Filipino friendship. He was operating under regulations that said clearly that "the bad elements amongst those who surrender will be unhesitatingly, but unostentatiously executed, and will be counted amongst those killed in battle."

It was not a question of whether Straughn and Thorp would be killed—just a matter of when. Japanese orders said such prisoners "should be detained for a period, and the reactions of the people observed. When the latter have forgotten the incident, these bad elements will be secretly and quietly '00ed' [double zeroed, that is, executed] or under the pretense of taking them off to some distant place, they will be unostentatiously '00ed.'"

Thorp, who had been held since his capture ten months earlier, and Straughn, interrogated for six weeks, had not surrendered, but they were to be treated in the fashion that the command document described. They were summoned before a Japanese military court-martial on September 30, 1943, along with twenty-two other men, including Guillermo Nakar, the Philippine Army lieutenant colonel who had exchanged radio messages with General MacArthur in 1942. The proceedings lasted fifteen minutes.

The men received an English translation of the trial but no chance for defense. The judges then sentenced them to death.

Several days later Straughn, Thorp, Nakar, and six other men were driven to the Chinese Cemetery, while the fifteen other men were taken to the La Loma Cemetery. One witness, Lieutenant Richard C. Sakakida, was a Japanese American double agent who was working as a translator with the Japanese Army, secretly loyal to the United States. He and another witness reported that Straughn refused the offer of a hood to cover his head. A firing squad shot all of them and their bodies toppled into a common grave.

The idea that Straughn's capture led to desertions "in ever-increasing numbers" was pure fantasy. After the deaths of Straughn and Thorp, American officers and their Filipino allies rose to reorganize and extend operations in anticipation of MacArthur's return. With encouragement from Australia and Parsons's imposition of a chain of command as ordered by MacArthur, the guerrillas were well established and operated in a sea of goodwill. The only problem was impatience—both Filipino guerrillas and civilians could hardly wait for the inevitable. "They have ceased wondering who is going to win the war, or whether the war will ever end," Parsons reported to MacArthur. "The people want us to return—they are disappointed that we have not done so sooner."

Holding On
Tsubaki Club, Manila, November 1943

ON NOVEMBER 14, the day Claire returned home after about six weeks in the hospital, a massive typhoon slammed into Luzon, provoking a week of torrential rains. The resulting flood caused problems in the city, forced a standstill of military search operations against the guerrillas, and increased misery at Santo Tomas for the detainees and even more suffering for the POWs at Cabanatuan.

It was the most violent storm to hit Manila in forty years. Water several feet deep inundated the streets and threatened to wash people away. Electricity was out, the telephones were not working, and transportation was a mess. Fortunately, Lichauco had carried as much furniture as he could to his second-floor bedroom. Four days later it was still raining "and when a friendly neighbor came to visit us in his *banca* [dugout canoe] to see how we were getting along he paddled straight into our living room."

Claire, still recovering, was in no danger in her second-floor room at Tsubaki Club. The club was only a mile or so from Lichauco's house and probably suffered the same conditions. She had not yet resumed writing in her little date-book diary to say anything different. There was a gap in entries from the day of her collapse—September 29—until the end of November.

Conditions at Santo Tomas already were precarious when the typhoon hit. Food rationing had made it more difficult and expensive to provide enough to eat. The housing situation was miserable, the smells pungent, but the rain made everything worse. Winds toppled the open-walled shanties under which many people lived. "Three days of bucketing rain poured masses of bedraggled shanty people into the corridors and hallways of the buildings, where they camped as best they could. The air there became thick from the crowds of people, damp clothing, and the smoke of kerosene lamps; electricity went off for . . . three days. Out in the shanties, some overnight sleepers were marooned for a day until reached by rescuers on bamboo rafts. The water came in over some of the buildings' ground floors too." Only the children of the camp had fun—everything was an adventure, even though the water destroyed some stores of food. While the rain continued, the children were even able to swim for a while before the water turned to brown slime. Claire found out only afterward that Louise was still at Santo Tomas during the typhoon. Louise was moved several weeks later to the new Los Baños camp, where her fiancé, Bob Humphries, had been sent to build housing.

The situation was at least as bad for the POWs at Cabanatuan. The storm knocked down many of the flimsy barracks. "At one time it looked as if the rain was not falling but going parallel to the ground. Everyone and everything gets wet and stays that way, bedding, blankets, shoes, clothes, all develop green mold."

The guerrillas also hunkered down in miserable, drenched jungle hideouts, but at least Japanese patrols had to curtail their search-and-destroy missions during the week of rain and floods.

■ ■ ■

After a month Claire was back at work. She contacted Boone to report she was now ready to resume operations. She had almost died, but her message was almost an apology for being out of operation. In the interim Fely had been running the food and supply operations, and Claire would once again focus on intelligence gathering.

Claire threw a Christmas party for her employees and friends at the club on December 22, 1943. The staff gave speeches belatedly commemorating her thirty-sixth birthday but also to mark her return and remarkable recovery. She resumed singing her torch songs as she gained a bit of strength and weight. Fely's allure brought new Japanese officer friends, and the hostesses resumed gathering information with their cooing questions. Meanwhile Claire said Ichikawa, the composer still enamored of Fely, had invited Fely to sing at a party that he was throwing at the ballroom of the Bay View Hotel, a few blocks away. Fely asked Claire to come along with her, probably as a chaperone so she would not be alone. She argued that it would be a good chance to meet Japanese officers. Claire agreed to go. "Nip big-wigs would be present and we might pick up some important news." At the party Ichikawa introduced her to a captain named Kobayashi, who asked her some pointed questions—he understood she was Italian, but had she ever been to the United States?

Claire stuck to her cover story that her parents were Italian but added that she had been born in the Philippines and had visited neither Italy nor the United States. Kobayashi teased her that once Japan took over, he would be in charge of the Pacific Northwest and could give her whatever province she wanted.

"I have seen pictures of Portland, in Oregon," she replied. "I have heard it is called the City of Roses, and they are my favorite."

"Portland shall be yours," Kobayashi said.

In her next report to Boone on Japanese contacts, she told him that a Japanese captain had bragged and joked with her about the future occupation of the United States. She had one other piece of more serious business. Her old friend at the Park Avenue School, William Bruce, had sent through information about troop movements. Along with a request for money, Bruce had sent a message through a trusted Filipino with a list of every man in the camp. Meanwhile, he reported: "We are loading ships for the Japs and whenever anything looks fishy I will tell you. One thing right now is that these Red (double) Cross ships of theirs are bringing in troops, not wounded soldiers. We are now loading one of these ships and I would swear the cargo is guns and ammo. Send this info on if you can."

Mellie, Boone's wife, was now pregnant and pulled back from making the supply and message runs. Claire came up with a new runner, whom they called Zigzag. He shared duties with Pacio. Zigzag's reputation preceded him and he was easy to identify. He had six fingers on one hand—two thumbs. One of the most recent shipments was sizable, more than either Zigzag or Pacio could handle alone, so they worked with additional trusted helpers, men and women. The prices were high, but food and supplies were far easier to find in Manila than in Dinalupihan. Claire sent food and cooking oil, gin and cigarettes, spices and shoelaces, books and newspapers, and the latest radio transcriptions from the San Francisco radio broadcasts. Boone was more than grateful: "Thanks a million for the food supply," he wrote, thanking Claire more than once. "You have no idea how those things help the situation."

On the political side, Claire happily had missed the main event of the season while in the hospital. José Laurel, recovered after the June assassination attempt, had been inaugurated on October 14 as president of the new, supposedly independent Second Philippine Republic. Neighborhood block captains had warned attendance was mandatory, with the obvious possibility that the Kempeitai might otherwise pay a visit to inquire about the loyalties of those not attending. Most Filipinos seemed to scoff at or to be disinterested in the declaration of Philippine independence. Laurel gave a lengthy inaugural address that, if not written by the Japanese, fit fully with their pan-Asian ideal. Laurel repeated the call for an end to guerrilla operations: Stop fighting, he said, or "I shall have no other alternative than to consider them public enemies of our government and deal with them accordingly."

General Shigenori Kuroda, now the top Japanese commander in the Philippines, also delivered an address, greeted almost entirely without cheers or applause—a protest of silence that showed the depth of opposition to the occupation. After the speeches Japanese planes flew overhead and a parade accompanied newly named President Laurel to the official residence, Malacañang Palace. German and Japanese residents were prominent in the ceremony. The Germans raised their arms in the Nazi salute and the Japanese wore white caps and short uniforms, marching in unison.

Despite restrictions, most Manila residents still had access to news from the outside world via shortwave radio and illegal newsletters. They soon heard President Roosevelt's reaction to the inauguration. He called Laurel "the latest puppet whom the Japanese have set up in Manila to head the government which they have established there. . . . The only accredited Filipino officials are temporarily here in Washington."

Parsons's Second Return

**Aboard the USS *Narwhal*, Mindanao Sea,
Philippines, November 11, 1943**

"GIVE A GANDER, Chick, isn't that a pretty sight?"

Frank Latta, the commander of one of the submarines assigned to Philippines operations, the USS *Narwhal*, invited Chick Parsons to the bridge after spotting his prey—a fully laden Japanese oil tanker lumbering through the Mindanao Sea. The Japanese vessel lay within sight of land, near an inlet between Negros and Siquijor islands.

Latta and Parsons were two weeks out from Brisbane, one of a series of dozens of supply runs planned between Australia and the Philippines to provide food, personnel, radio and spotting equipment, and other supplies, as well as to withdraw important refugees and provide transport in both directions for intelligence operatives. However, a radio message two days earlier from Brisbane had reminded Latta and the crew that enemy operations took precedence. He had detoured from his assigned route to the island of Mindoro and was lying in wait. The *Narwhal* was appropriately named because it was a whale of a submarine, double the size of more nimble attack submarines in the U.S. fleet. It had been stripped of unnecessary gear to fit a full load of supplies, though of course it was still fitted for war.

Latta had seen no sign of a destroyer escort—the tanker appeared to be an open target.

"When are you going to make an approach?" Parsons asked.

"Right now!" Latta said, and gave the order to clear the bridge and dive. Seconds after he fired off four torpedoes, he took a look at periscope depth. The torpedoes had skipped past the target but trouble was closing in. The ship's full accompaniment had been hidden by land. "A hornet's nest of destroyers, destroyer escorts, and heavily escorted transports and tankers" had been waiting.

Within minutes the crew felt a concussion, a telltale bump from an exploding depth charge still far off. Then another glanced by closer, and several more. Latta decided to make a break for it in the dark—the *Narwhal* could run at only 9 knots underwater but double that on the surface.

Thankfully, Chick knew the lay of the land. "We surfaced to get away and were chased into what looked like a blind alley," recalled Robert Griffiths, an officer on the *Narwhal*. "When we asked Chick Parsons if he recognized the surrounding mountain peaks, he said, 'Yes, keep going straight ahead.'"

Latta ordered all-ahead emergency speed to outrun artillery from the ships and smaller fire from the patrol boats pursuing in the narrow passage. The *Narwhal* hit 17 knots and more. Plummer, the engineering officer, started sweating out the readings of the engine RPMs. He was not sure how much pressure the diesels could take above the red line. "Is it necessary to keep the engines going at this pace?" Plummer asked.

"Keep it there or you won't need engines," Latta said.

They escaped with a bit of help: Chick's knowledge of the channel saved them. Clouds, rain, and fog from the approaching typhoon also helped make it a lucky escape. If the sky had been clear, the submarine would have been visible in the light of a full moon just after midnight.

The *Narwhal* was one of a fleet of submarine transports designated for a special mission: to run supplies, gear, insurgents, and spies into the Philippines for the duration, part of MacArthur's plan to support the guerrillas and pave the way for retaking the archipelago whatever the cost.

While on duty with Parsons's guerrilla mission, the *Narwhal* was quite ready and able to pursue Japanese ships and undertake other missions that came its way. In this case, operating solo in the Pacific, escape was the best possible course. By the time they had evaded their Japanese pursuers, Parsons was minimizing the encounter. The first stop was on the northwest coast of Mindoro, about ninety miles south of Manila. It was completed "without difficulty," he said, "delayed one day due to unexpected enemy interference." Parsons and a contingent of commandos landed at Paluan Bay on November 13, 1943, carrying forty-five tons of supplies. Along with supplies, the delivery also included counterfeit Japanese occupation currency, which would buy supplies for the guerrilla operations, counteract inflated prices for food and supplies, and undermine attempts to regulate the economy.

Nine commandos also came ashore with the assignment of setting up close-in radio communications with Manila and the rest of Luzon. For the first time communications from Claire and the others would be carried by boat overnight across the Verde Island passage between Mindoro and Luzon. Parsons made arrangements for transit to and from Manila for supplies and agents. The fulfillment of the hope of providing real-time intelligence to General MacArthur's headquarters was at hand, though still probably months away. Parsons reminded the guerrilla leaders that MacArthur was adamant that they avoid direct offensive action against the Japanese. They were to continue their focus on intelligence gathering in preparation for a U.S. invasion.

Parsons then organized a smuggling operation with a fleet of commercial ferries in Mindoro that were licensed by the Japanese to carry lumber but whose crews were deeply loyal to the United States and had been secretly prepared all along to fight the war in whatever way possible. He found that the logistics at Paluan Bay were ideal. Soon the ferries were carrying "shipments of propaganda, bundles of money, vitamin tablets for the POWs and internees, radio sets and spares and any other article desired to be gotten into Manila. This is a situation hard to believe, and could not be better had it not been planned ahead of time." Parsons also set up a forgery unit that produced fake IDs for him and other insurgents. He said that the infrastructure for operations was so good that he was concerned that he himself might have been the victim of a sophisticated counterintelligence ruse by the Japanese. He decided to double-check on the people he was now working with; his knowledge of the country and his network of friends paid off as usual. "I found the family of an old trusted employee of my company—as well as a number of people known to me in Manila—all of whom I consider to be reliable." Meetings with them "convince me that all in the town were okay."

Before leaving Mindoro, Parsons sent word to his friends in Manila about the streamlined route. Intelligence documents that Claire had been forwarding to Boone and to Ed Ramsey could follow the same route. Maintaining operational security, Claire had expanded her guerrilla contacts to include Ramsey, Colonels Loyd and Wright, among others. Boone had told his colleagues about Claire and they were getting in touch. Within less than a year of opening the club and beginning her operations, Claire's supply and intelligence line had proven valuable to most of the top guerrilla leaders in central Luzon.

Parsons continued on his mission from Mindoro to Mindanao, where he delivered another forty-five tons of supplies to guerrillas led by Colonel Wendell Fertig. He held meetings with Fertig and other guerrilla commanders and gathered information about the mood of the Filipinos. He told MacArthur that support for the Allies was as dominant as ever and Filipinos mocked the country's independence under Japanese control; they were ready to fight. The *Narwhal* picked up Parsons and evacuees at Mindanao and Negros before turning back for Australia on December 5. That same day Captain Latta had a second chance. At around dawn he spotted a Japanese cargo ship, the *Hinteno Maru*, and blasted it to an ocean grave in a hail of gunfire.

A Spy Breaks Through
Manila, January 1944

FRANCO VERA REYES, a flamboyant Filipino novelist and sometime convict before the war, showed up at the door of Blanche Jurika, saying he had just been with Chick Parsons, her son-in-law. Blanche had stayed behind in Manila when the rest of the family fled in June 1942. Like many people in Manila, she was collecting food and clothing for POWs. No one in the underground could figure out with certainty what Vera Reyes had said that day or what message he carried; all that was known was that he had convinced Blanche that he had real information and that he was working with the guerrillas.

Vera Reyes apparently told Blanche Jurika that he had just come from guerrilla territory and delivered on behalf of Chick a letter from Katsy, Chick's wife, along with photographs of their children—Blanche's grandchildren. Vera Reyes said that he had returned to the Philippines with

Chick on the *Narwhal* and carried along a recent copy of *Life* magazine. Chick probably had visited his mother-in-law during his secret visit to Manila in June 1943. The family was intensely concerned for her well-being, knowing that she would be in danger if either her activities or Chick's activities were discovered. It was likely she would be under surveillance, and Chick's friends in Manila questioned whether he would have risked sending incriminating material to her. Vera Reyes might have gotten the letter from a courier captured by the Japanese. It also was possible that the message Vera Reyes brought along was a forgery, but Blanche told friends and associates that the letter delivered by Vera Reyes was genuine.

Whichever was the case, one thing eventually became certain: Vera Reyes was a spy working for Colonel Akira Nagahama, the chief of the Kempeitai.

Vera Reyes was an unusual fellow. Before the war, in the thirties, he had written two novels—*Bagong Kristo* (*New Christ*) and *Makata at Paraluman* (*Poet and Parallels*). Yet he was also a businessman, and some of his dealings had landed him in jail for larceny and embezzlement. When war broke out, it was said, he had earned parole from Bilibid Prison by convincing military authorities that he could help them identify American operatives and guerrillas. Vera Reyes was already suspect among guerrillas in Bataan as possibly having helped in the capture of Hugh Straughn months earlier. However, no one in Manila had received that information. So he was relatively safe to be making the rounds in Manila, describing himself as a liaison officer for the guerrillas.

Nevertheless, some of Blanche Jurika's allies were suspicious. Boone's guerrilla commander, Lieutenant Colonel Ed Ramsey, got word through underground-message channels that Vera Reyes wanted to meet him. Ramsey was on a dangerous temporary assignment inside Manila, under deep cover, accompanied by his comrade-in-arms and lover, Ramona Snyder. Ramsey wavered on how to proceed. "I was routinely suspicious of unannounced contacts, but this one seemed genuine enough," Ramsey said. As a test, though, he decided to plant some information with Vera Reyes to see what happened. He sent along a friendly response to Vera Reyes that he had to leave town for a few days: He said that Huk Maoist guerrillas had just murdered a number of rival guerrillas during a clandestine meeting in the town of Malabon, outside Manila. As a result,

Ramsey said, he had to investigate the killings and would meet with Vera Reyes when he returned.

Ramsey then alerted Ramona Snyder to check with her sources at Japanese military headquarters. Part of the story was true—the Huks had killed the guerrillas, but Ramsey's plan to travel to Malabon was not true and was his own invention. Within days Ramona confirmed that Japanese forces were mobilizing to look for Ramsey at Malabon. Clearly, Vera Reyes was the only possible source.

Separately, another check on Vera Reyes was just as damning. Colonel Narciso Manzano had done his own due diligence. An engineer and former operative with the American military in Bataan, Manzano had been held by the Japanese for a while but released under a Japanese general amnesty. He feigned loyalty to the Japanese but claimed illness as a result of his detention and was judged exempt from joining the pro-occupation Philippine Constabulary.

To test his own suspicions, Manzano proposed a luncheon meeting with Vera Reyes at Tom's Dixie Kitchen, a popular downtown restaurant. Tom's was one of the few popular hangouts still open, though the menu was limited, the quality uncertain, and the prices exorbitant. Two fried eggs with rice and a tiny bit of bacon could cost as much as ten pesos, many times the prewar price and the equivalent of five dollars at the time and more than sixty dollars in 2017.

After setting the lunch, Manzano called in two former police detectives familiar with the underworld and agile in dealing with the military occupation. He told them to go to the restaurant on the same schedule and then follow Vera Reyes after lunch. Manzano was cordial during the lunch but avoided making any anti-Japanese declarations. After lunch, the agents followed Vera Reyes. They spied him coming and going several times at Nagahama's Kempeitai headquarters. Now convinced that Vera Reyes was a Japanese agent, Manzano told his wife that he had to leave town on a special mission. He provided no details and set off for Mindanao.

On February 19 the Kempeitai raided Manzano's house in the dark, terrorizing his wife, Rosario, and their children. When they realized the colonel had bolted, they hauled Rosario away to Fort Santiago instead. It probably became obvious that she knew nothing, only that her husband had left town a few days earlier, and that she did not know when he was coming back. The arrest was tantamount to holding a hostage. Japanese authorities announced that only if Manzano "returns to Manila and gives a satisfactory account of his absence will Mrs. Manzano be released and allowed to rejoin her children." Manzano did not return and the Kempeitai finally gave up. By the time she was released, Rosario Manzano was so weak and starved that family members had to carry her from Fort Santiago. Blanche Jurika had been arrested shortly after the raid on the Manzano house. She shared a cell for a time with Rosario Manzano, but Blanche was never released.

Manila Dragnet
Manila, February 1944

NAGAHAMA'S MAJOR BLOW against the Manila intelligence net came on February 5, just a few days after Vera Reyes had come to town. A group of Juan Elizalde's friends had stopped by his house to help celebrate his birthday. The friends stayed late, a soiree seasoned with drinks and friends sitting around chatting; just after midnight, Kempeitai agents swooped in and arrested them all. Next the police went to the house of Manuel Elizalde, Juan's brother, arrested him as well, and took them all to Fort Santiago.

Once at the prison, guards took their money and possessions and made fingerprints. Manuel and Juan were led to a cell block in sight of the Pasig River. Jailers roused the men from their cells the next morning; each was questioned separately. The interrogators seemed to be interested in the Elizalde family origins and businesses. Japan still considered Spain and Spanish citizens to be friends of the Axis, but who were these men—Spaniards or Filipinos? The Elizaldes's grandfather had come to the Philippines in the early 1800s from the Basque region of northern Spain. Over generations the clan had become one of the best known and wealthiest in Manila.

What business were they in?

Manuel answered that question: "Practically everything, shipping, broker, paint, distillery." The Elizaldes had covered their anti-Japanese sentiments by carrying on with business as usual aboveboard during the Japanese occupation.

Despite the threat of torture and the fear generated when the interrogators invoked the name of Colonel Nagahama, Manuel was surprised that both of them were returned to their cells without mistreatment. A new round of questioning came the following day. The brothers could only look at each other from a distance; they were not allowed to speak to each other. Manuel could only guess what was happening and had no information to provide even if he had been willing to. Juan had kept much about his guerrilla activities secret; while Manuel helped raise money to support the POWs, he said he had no information to offer.

The brothers were beaten without mercy for seventeen consecutive days. If the Japanese really intended to extract information, the method was illogical and useless. They sometimes asked foolish, unimportant questions, then stood up and beat the men for inconsequential answers, using a two-by-four piece of wood, a baseball bat, or a pool cue, hitting them with blows on the back and right in the face. Other times the inquisitors asked compromising questions; when the brothers lied or avoided giving direct answers, the questioners didn't seem to notice. Manuel began to wonder whether the interpreters could even understand the questions or the answers.

"I was punched right and left every day. It was a matter of routine the way you got hit, and it was an impossibility to defend yourself," Manuel said. "You were completely at the mercy of the investigator. He might translate your answer in such a way that you do not know whether it was translated or he might translate it completely detrimental to your case. That was the way it appeared to me anyway."

Manuel could see that his brother was receiving the same treatment. He saw Juan several times a week when they were released to the prison yard to take showers. The questioning and the beatings went on intermittently for at least two more months. On Friday, May 12, Manuel and Juan were allowed to walk near each other in the yard. Manuel wrote down the date; he did not see Juan again after that. "He was taken away with several others . . . and I never saw him again alive."

The Kempeitai released many of the people who had been attending Elizalde's birthday party, including the women, concluding they were of no intelligence value. The extent of Nagahama's penetration into underground activities was not yet clear, but Juan Elizalde and his friend Enrico Pirovano, also arrested that night, offered a potential opening to incriminate General Roxas. If the torture led to an admission of Roxas's work with the guerrillas, he would be arrested, and cascading arrests could reach the Amusateguis, Claire, Peggy, and everyone who worked with them.

The question was whether the captured men would be broken, confess, or mention the general's name. Marcial Lichauco figured that even if Roxas was fingered in the interrogations, his standing with the Philippine people was so high that Nagahama would still need to tread carefully. On February 15, ten days after the arrest of the Elizaldes, Lichauco went to check on General Roxas and to express his concern. Roxas warned him to avoid contact. "I found him very much worried over the fate of his friend and seriously concerned about this own position."

"Better stay away from my house until this thing blows over," General Roxas said, "for I don't want to see you implicated in it."

"If Anything Happens . . ."
Tsubaki Club, Manila, February 1944

ONE MORNING Claire was still in her bedroom when she answered the phone at Tsubaki Club. Lorenza Amusategui was calling. "The cookies are about ready," Lorenza said, the code meaning they were preparing to send Evangeline Neibert up to Cabanatuan with messages and supplies. Claire heard a strange scratching on the line and in the background the distinct sound of someone clearing his throat.

"Do you still have that bad cold, dear?" Claire said, signaling to Lorenza that she had heard the strange sounds and they were not coming from her.

"No," Lorenza replied. "I'm feeling fine again."

The women tried to behave as though they were having an innocuous conversation about food and recipes and spoke a few moments more before hanging up. It was obvious that someone had been listening in. "I knew that my good luck had been stretched like a rubber band, and did not know at what moment it would snap."

Whenever she used the phone after that, she thought she heard clicking sounds or breathing. What was worse, one day a Filipino boy stopped at the back door of the club and delivered a message from someone named "Captain Bagley," supposedly one of the guerrillas, seeking help in the hills of Luzon. Claire looked at the book and looked at the note, poorly written and without any code words. It was an open request for help from someone she had not heard of and delivered by someone she did not know.

She threw the boy out, saying that she did not care about what was happening with the Americans. "At a sign from me, Mamerto followed the messenger who crossed the Luneta Park and was met by four waiting Nip military police."

Mamerto rushed back and warned Claire that the operation had become too dangerous—they should quit and get out of town. Claire refused. "If anything happens to me, Fely and you are to get [Dian] out of this house as fast as you can and up in the hills to Boone."

Peggy came to see Claire at the club. Claire owed her own health—probably her life—to Peggy's quick action in September. If there had not been transportation on the day of Claire's ulcer attack and if Peggy had not supervised, Claire might not have survived long enough to get to the hospital. Despite their rivalry, there was still a kinship between them. Peggy was recovering now from her own hospitalization after uterine surgery. Claire could see she was more nervous than ever before. Claire knew that her other friends had a problem with Peggy's behavior, but she did not remark about it openly. Claire did know that procedures had changed and that Ramón was taking more responsibility. Ramón was now using the Malate Church as a clearinghouse and storage site for supplies destined to be taken north to the POWs at Cabanatuan. After multiple raids it was too dangerous to use Peggy's apartment as the main storage and meeting place. Peggy was off-limits.

She surprised Claire by saying that she wanted to leave Manila and return to Bataan to join the guerrillas. Until this point there had been no indication that Peggy had had direct contact with Boone. All of Boone's communications had been through Mellie or Pacio and the other messengers and carriers who reported to Claire. Peggy's reaction reflected the paranoia on the street these days; people were more nervous and frightened than ever. The course of the war was barreling downhill toward both victory and chaos. The daily routines—fakery and survival—were unchanged, but life itself was more stressful than ever. It took more time than ever before to search out supplies of food staples, and the costs were increasing daily. The Japanese also seemed more edgy and suspicious.

Ramón had a convenient excuse for not working with Peggy those final days of 1943. Peggy's apartment, not Peggy herself, was the problem—the Japanese had now come to search there at least twice, once when the Kempeitai came looking for Naomi and the American stragglers and again when they came to arrest Peggy herself. Ramón and Lorenza handled the Christmas shipment to the boys at Cabanatuan on their own. All of them had written letters to their friends and pen pals in the camp. Each letter was carefully censored and screened to eliminate anything that could incriminate the organization or anyone in the camp. No real names, no real places. After that, they packed food and supplies as always with money hidden in the woven bags. They made lists of contributions, one for Lieutenant Colonel Mack to distribute to the POWs, another for Naomi. When Horacio Manaloto showed up, he headed north by truck; Evangeline usually took the train to Capas and from there met up with Naomi on the outskirts of Cabanatuan. From the Manila side everything seemed fine. They had completed one of their final supply missions of the year, completing a full year of sending survival packages to the men of Cabanatuan. A few days later, though, Manaloto came back with a warning from the POW officers they worked with. The packages had gotten through but the Japanese overseers at the camp were acting strangely suspicious. Ramón ordered a halt to all deliveries until further notice. The letters were too suspicious. For the time being they should avoid communicating directly with the camp.

That decision led to a supply backup that created separate problems. The Manila team was storing large amounts of food and supplies at the Malate Church and had to move the goods somehow along the line. Ramón and the others did not know what the specific problem was, and neither did Naomi. They had to assume that the military police were investigating and developing information about the underground supply operation.

Ramón sent word that they should avoid congregating; instead he went to each home individually with this message: "If any of you are arrested before me, or after me, just blame everything on me—just tell them I am the leader of your group, and I am to blame, and that is all you must answer, nothing else."

Claire was now convinced that she was being targeted. She had been careful all along about whom she spoke to and whom she worked with. Only a few people in town even knew her as Claire—even Fely knew her as Dot—short for Dorothy. In addition, hardly anyone could tie the name "Dot" or "Claire" to a message writer who signed her messages as "High Pockets." She disclosed nothing, even when American stragglers stopped by and especially when unknown people came to the club or when she received unexpected, unexplained messages that claimed to be delivering information.

The rising sense of danger, though, brought caution and some additional safeguards. She was convinced that her diary would never be found, but she had a lot of other incriminating evidence stored around the club. She sorted out material to destroy and material to hide. She had several ledger books with earnings from the club, disbursements. It was logical for a business to keep those on hand. However, addresses of black-market contacts had to be burned. She had other personal papers—her passport, the lists of prisoners, and messages from Boone and some of the prisoners in Cabanatuan and other POW camps. She gave these to Fely, whose father, Vicente Corcuera, came in from Quezon City to pick them up. They stuffed the material in several jars and drove back to Quezon City. Corcuera buried the jars in the yard behind his house and wiped out any trace of where he had done the digging.

April 1, 1944, felt truly like April Fool's Day. The Japanese were still claiming glorious victories in the Pacific, but no one believed them. They ordered a practice air-raid blackout throughout Manila. Claire and other businesses were expected to turn off their signs and lights, but she managed to keep the place open. The front lights were off, but she moved tables to a back storage area so patrons could come in anyway. Any business she could do helped the supply line.

Despite the tense activity those days, Claire received a piece of pleasant news. Mellie, John Boone's wife, gave birth to a baby boy on March 13,

1944, in Dinalupihan. She showed up one day in Manila with the new-born baby for christening by Father Lalor at the Malate Church. Claire and Peggy went to the ceremony, at which the child was named Phillip, in honor of the man Claire told Boone she had married, John V. Phillips.

Losing the War
Manila, March 1944

JAPANESE MILITARY LEADERS were as adamant about holding on to the Philippines at all costs as was General MacArthur about blasting his way back as soon as possible. "With the loss of these islands, not only would Japanese communications with the southern regions be severely threatened," said Lieutenant General Shuichi Miyazaki, chief of the Operations Section at Imperial General Headquarters. "The loss of the Philippines would greatly affect civilian morale in Japan. The islands were also essential and appropriate strategic bases for the enemy advance on Japan."

Nevertheless, with all the Japanese setbacks in the Pacific in 1943 and early 1944, it was obvious that MacArthur would eventually attempt an invasion. Occupation authorities began building air-raid shelters around Manila, a mute but not subtle acknowledgment that the war was not going well. Everyone knew. The worse things looked on the war front, the worse Japanese behavior got. The petty insults gave way to greater outrages. A Japanese sergeant slammed Foke Kihlstedt, a Swedish friend of Marcial Lichauco, in the face with a stick for failing to remove a cigar from his mouth when he bowed before a sentry. It was one incident of many. A Japanese guard savagely beat Elena Moreno, a pretty girl in her twenties, when she dared to wave at American POWs riding by on a Manila street. The prisoners had to restrain themselves; if they tried to save the bleeding girl, they knew they would be killed on the spot.

Filipinos knew what the Japanese knew. The Americans were on the move. The daily war report was on the street: they had reached Bougainville in the Solomon Islands and New Britain, off New Guinea, by late 1943 and into 1944. By March, a two-pronged campaign by General MacArthur and Admiral William "Bull" Halsey had isolated Japanese forces in the Pacific. Next were the Admiralty Islands, farther north, stepping-stones toward the Philippines. There had been victories in the Gilbert Islands, and MacArthur had outflanked the Japanese on New Guinea in a series of strategic jumps from south to north. MacArthur was racing back. The Filipinos knew it, the prisoners kept themselves informed, and the Japanese occupiers knew as well.

Backing the promising news, the Philippine president in exile, Manuel Quezon, spoke directly to his compatriots via a KGEI shortwave broadcast from San Francisco. "We are well on the road to victory," Quezon said. "The United Allies are triumphantly marching together. People of the Philippines, we shall soon be with you." It was one of Quezon's last major addresses. Quezon, sixty-five, had been suffering from tuberculosis and died on August 1, 1944, at Saranac Lake, New York. He was succeeded by his vice president, Sergio Osmeña, also exiled in the United States.

Hunger diminished hope in Manila. Food was sparse and prices were astronomically high. The Japanese took advantage. They needed workers to build new airfields as they dispersed their airplanes, preparing for the unspoken, inevitable moment when the United States eventually would invade to retake the city. "Evidently they intend to scatter their planes around as many fields as possible, a strategy which the Americans should have followed during the first days of the war. To recruit the thousands of laborers needed for these jobs, the Military Authorities have made a most tempting offer to Manila's half-starved population. Every able bodied man willing to work for them will not only be paid good wages in cash but will also be given 300 grams of rice to take home at the close of each day's labor."

Food shelves were bare. A bag of rice on the black market could cost more than a month's salary. Claire just listed the prices as if the numbers alone told the story—a small sack of rice was 250 pesos; four weeks later the price had tripled. People who had enough money ate in restaurants when there was food, and then were accosted by children left to beg for scraps of food on the street.

If those who were free to beg on the streets were hungry, the situation was worse for prisoners and detainees. At Santo Tomas food supplies had been waning since the end of 1943, when the last Red Cross ship brought in supplies. Then the Japanese camp administrators had blocked off all access to Santo Tomas by outsiders. As of February, no one could send in food or medicine for any of the thousands of detainees who were held under deteriorating conditions and the increasing threat of disease.

"Breakfast was several ladles of 'mush' (boiled rice flour) in coconut milk with a spoonful of sugar, plus tea or coffee and a banana," said Rupert Wilkinson, eight years old at the time, recalling the suffering decades later. "Lunch was usually a ladle of boiled corn or rice, plus a slice of corn bread and sometimes a bit of coarse greens from the camp gardens. Dinner might be *dilis* (a very salty and skinny small fish) or a little *carabao* meat boiled with corn, followed by tea and a banana or calamansi (lemon). Any milk or eggs that the Internee Committee could get went to the camp hospitals or the Annex kitchen for young children."

Protests and appeals to the humanity of the Japanese authorities were of little use. The only exception was on April 29, when, to commemorate the emperor's birthday, the Japanese allowed some people to visit their family members. The outsiders were shocked. The detainees were gaunt and weak. "The principal sufferers," said Marcial Lichauco, "of course, are the children who are being deprived of the milk, the eggs, the vegetables and other kinds of nourishment that all fast growing youths need."

Hunger had turned Manila into a city of beggars and thieves. Desperate people had taken to exhuming bodies in the local cemeteries, hoping to find rings and bracelets that could be sold. Still they survived. Parents stockpiled food for their children and endured the hunger, managing to survive a step ahead of starvation. It was much the same throughout Manila. The floods that swept the islands at the end of 1943 destroyed rice fields and drowned livestock. When rice or oatmeal was available, it was rationed almost by the grain, then devoured. When Marcial Lichauco, one of the wealthier people in town, finished off a high-priced meal with rice and a bit of condiments at a restaurant, a street urchin slipped in and swept the few remaining grains off the plate into his mouth. On Christmas Day 1943 there was no rice available in the city at all. People survived on a bit of cornmeal for a few days, the kind usually fed to pigs, but there were no more pigs—they had mostly been devoured long ago.

"Evil Days Are Upon Us"

Cabanatuan, May 3, 1944

NAOMI WALKED FROM her rented room at Miss Bell's house into the morning sun to signal to Fred Threatt, her POW contact, as she had done so many times before, although not recently. Mr. Threatt and the other oxcart drivers were parked along the Cabanatuan bridge, across from the rice fields. Recent days had been tense and the Japanese guards were in foul moods. Undoubtedly the gossip was getting through that they were losing the war. The day before, guards for no apparent reason had beaten one of the POW officers, Captain William Blackledge, while he was out on the farm detail. His fellow officers thought he might have tried to say something in Japanese but had been misunderstood. Blackledge's head was bleeding, but the guards blocked anyone from coming to his aid.

There were new warnings from Manila in the days after Juan and Manuel Elizalde were arrested. After the admonition in December from Mack and other officers inside Cabanatuan, Evangeline was not making the trip north and Naomi was only rarely delivering messages to the camp. Mr. Threatt was now even more worried than before; he felt something was up.

Naomi brushed her long black hair in one long stroke and Threatt understood.

Even though Captain Tiffany, the chaplain, also had sent out a message to put the deliveries on hold, they now had an urgent request from the POW hospital for a drug shipment in hopes they could save the life of a dying patient. Naomi had gotten word to Manila, and Ramón had sent the needed medicine, along with some money.

Mr. Threatt waited a good while and then went over to the bridge as if to rest and drink from his canteen, which had a false bottom for hiding money and notes. He bent over by the designated tree and dug out and pocketed Naomi's little package wrapped in paper. Something caught a guard's attention; perhaps the white wrapper glinted and reflected the sun. Possibly the guard had been clued in to expect something unusual. He walked over to Threatt and took the package. He held on to the money and the bottle of medicine, wrapped with a note scribbled on the inside.

The guard glanced at the note and, fortunately, told Threatt to tear up the paper and throw it away. That was lucky, Naomi said afterward. If others had seen the note, "he would have been shot when he got inside because the guards in the prison camp are more strict than the ones that used to go with the cart detail."

When the workday was over, Threatt and his fellow carabao cart drivers carried the men of the work detail back to Cabanatuan. "As he approached the unloading platform inside the fence [Threatt] managed, though closely watched, to whisper to [one of the POW officers], 'The fat is in the fire.'"

Moments later, guards seized Threatt and the other oxcart drivers, S. J. Bish, Virgil Burns, Reed Phillips, along with two men identified only as Tysinger and Rose. They were held in isolation. Within days the Japanese had picked up a paper trail of money transactions and deliveries, lists and messages and invoices that went far beyond the commissary, where Mr. Threatt and Manaloto were supposed to be doing a cash business. News about what had happened spread quickly in the camp—along with deep concern about what the Japanese might be doing to Threatt and the others. One of the officers, Major Tom Maury, had a good enough relationship with a Japanese lieutenant named Itoh to ask for information. Itoh had been friendly with the POWs and sometimes bought black-market cigarettes from them. Itoh said that the Kempeitai had been called in to investigate. Nothing good would come of it.

A week later Kempeitai investigators drove into the camp and went right for Lieutenant Colonel Mack, took him into custody, and questioned him nonstop for a day. They seized a dozen men in all. On May 11 the men "were all loaded on a truck and taken out of camp, destination and fate . . . unknown. The truck stopped at the gate, where more Filipinos were loaded, and then proceeded west." Colonel Arthur Lee Shreve watched as the truck pulled away. Shreve was in charge of handling accounts at the commissary and the camp hospital. He made his way to the hospital as quickly and inconspicuously as possible. "I checked the Group and Hospital Commissaries to assure myself that their books would stand inspection. I also disposed of Main Commissary surplus funds and papers. During disposition the Japs went into the building next door. Close—but we made it." The next day they brought in Captain Tiffany for questioning as well.

The Kempeitai tortured and interrogated the men, then dumped them back in Cabanatuan on May 16. The prison guards separated Mr. Threatt and Colonel Jack Schwartz, one of the doctors at the camp hospital, and forced them into "sweat boxes"—solitary-confinement cages—open to the elements in the hot sun in the middle of camp. For weeks they received minimum rations: little to drink and one scant meal a day.

For the first time in eighteen months, the Bataan survivors had been cut off from the lifesaving operation that began in late 1942 when Peggy and her boss, Dr. Ramón Atienza, had started the shipments into Camp O'Donnell and then to Cabanatuan. POW officers at the camp estimated that the Manila-based relief operation had spent more than one million pesos on food and supplies to feed and keep thousands of men alive.

Within minutes of Threatt's capture, Naomi knew she was in grave danger. By the afternoon, Japanese military police had begun searching the neighborhood around Miss Bell's house, which was a few miles from the center of Cabanatuan. She jumped out a window at the back of the house, hid in the jungle underbrush at a corner of the bridge, and waited for nightfall. Then she moved in the shadows toward the center of town, hoping to warn Horacio Manaloto that they had to escape. However, Japanese police patrol cars were cruising the streets and she couldn't make it out of town. People told her that the military police had seemingly stopped everyone to ask about "the girl who sent the notes inside the camp." They were also looking for her friend Joffie Maglaya, who sometimes helped her at the fruit stand. Police said that both women were suspects.

Naomi was especially worried about Joffie, who was young and might be vulnerable under interrogation. She did manage to reach Joffie's house. Her family lived in a barrio where everyone knew about the supply operation—and everyone was willing to help. Friends took in Naomi and Joffie; neighbors managed to hide and protect both young women. They kept out of sight for a month, but the Japanese police remained on the lookout. One day Naomi chanced to peer over a windowsill and saw military policemen congregated close by. One of them was Captain Tossino, the officer who had interrogated her more than a year earlier when she had gone voluntarily to Fort Santiago. She had to figure that Tossino now knew her identity, and she could not risk another session at Fort Santiago. It took weeks more to get away, until August, three months after the roundup, around the time Japanese were redeploying for MacArthur's expected attempt to retake the Philippines. Naomi made it safely to the hills and caught up with Major Bernard Anderson's guerrillas northwest of Cabanatuan. She rode out the rest of the war in the mountains.

On May 18, 1944, German (pronounced "Hair-MANN") Eroles worried as he waited at the Marfusa Restaurant in Ermita, the district bordering the bay close to Tsubaki Club and Luneta Park. He sensed danger; he needed to run. Helen Petkoff was never late for their scheduled meetings. Eroles and Helen worked with Ramón; one of Eroles's jobs was to type up the newsletters compiled from their clandestine radio monitoring. Helen helped distribute the newsletter around the city and was reliable. She worked with them often and had a U.S. Navy boyfriend who was imprisoned at Cabanatuan. When she didn't appear, Eroles knew there was trouble. He was ready to run for the mountains, a notion that Claire, Peggy, and all of the others had also considered. Before he could move from the café, a Japanese man in civilian clothes and two soldiers walked up to him. Too late. They took him away to a waiting car, blindfolded him, and drove away.

Ramón and the rest of the Manila crew, in turn, were waiting anxiously to hear from Manaloto and Evangeline after the special medicine delivery to Cabanatuan. Instead, a Filipino runner who worked with Naomi and Evangeline sneaked into the city to report that Manaloto and Naomi were on the run, Evangeline was missing, and their contacts inside Cabanatuan had been arrested.

Next they got word that both Eroles and Helen had been taken in. The pieces fell into place. Helen sometimes sent letters through their message pipeline to her boyfriend at the POW camp. It was obvious that when the Kempeitai investigators detained Threatt and the others, they had found one of Helen's letters. Claire figured that the letter might be traceable, that it might not have been properly censored to cut out real names. "Helen was a nice girl," Claire said. However, she doubted Helen would withstand interrogation under threat of torture. "The Nips will make her talk."

Two days later Helen was suddenly released. That was the worst news of all—the Kempeitai likely had gotten all the information they needed and then let her go. Interrupting distribution of the underground newsletter was a side victory for Nagahama and his intelligence officers. Agents had long been searching for the source of anti-Japanese propaganda. Several months earlier, Nagahama had received a report on the disruption of one group that "has been publishing anti-Japanese articles, and has been distributing this material among important Filipinos in the government. The American missionary Mary B. Sutago and 21 others who have been spreading propaganda were all arrested on the 28th [January 1944]." Catching Helen and Manaloto would further compromise the distribution of independent news reports.

There was nothing left to be done. Claire counted off the code names one by one in her little diary—in her bittersweet phrasing of what had happened, she wrote they all "were going to school." She believed that she had hidden all dangerous material, had given instructions to all of her employees—had done everything she could possibly do, save one thing. She was not going to run away. On May 22, as she waited for the inevitable, Claire knew that she and the others had done their part in sabotaging the Japanese occupiers in every possible way. No matter what was to come, she also knew it was a matter of time—not if but when—General MacArthur would lead American troops back to Manila. The exact timing would affect whether she would live to see that day.

She was calm as she wrote one last note in the small diary that she had used to blow off steam and to perform her ritual of self-confession. Claire knew what was coming. She wrote: "Waiting for my call to school." She then hid the little date-book diary somewhere that only Fely would know to retrieve it.

Ramón's Turn
Manila, May 23, 1944

FIRST THEY TOOK RAMÓN. On the morning of Tuesday, May 23, five Kempeitai agents arrested him at his office and brought him home to search the place but found nothing incriminating. After German Eroles had been arrested, Ramón and Lorenza had swept their house to gather and protect any and all documents. The incriminating material would have contained more than a year of message traffic with the POW officers at Cabanatuan, including a series of confidential reports written by Lieutenant Colonel Mack. Mack had written details about general conditions and mistreatment and the names of culpable Japanese officials at the POW camp. He wanted the reports to survive the war in the event he was killed. Ramón put it all in four large glass jars and then summoned Angustias de Mencarini, one of the key donors to the POW relief operation. She took it all away for hiding in a safe location. Among other papers, Ramón was holding many dozens of checks written by POWs in return for cash, assuming the checks would be honored when standard banking functions resumed after the occupation. He gave the checks to another trusted friend.

The Kempeitai officers threatened to arrest Lorenza, but she and Ramón held to the script. Lorenza said she was innocent and knew nothing about underground activities. She said all she had done was write personal letters to people she knew at Cabanatuan. The officers harangued the two of them and spewed threats as they searched for clues; Ramón continued to protest. Husband and wife were forced to stand there for about an hour and were not allowed to speak to each other.

Lorenza recalled: "All we could do was to look at each other, my eyes, I imagine, devouring his features, as his eyes were mine, looking at me with a mixture of devotion and inexpressible sadness, as if he knew it was the last time he was looking at his wife."

With a final warning, the police officers told Lorenza she could stay. Ramón looked back at her once more as he was led away.

"He was not even allowed to say goodbye to his children, the small one, three years old at the time, crying because he wanted to kiss his daddy. That such cruelty should exist is inconceivable to the human mind, but we who suffered under the yoke of the Japanese, not only can express this, but also vouch for it."

Sometime after they left, Lorenza dared to visit Claire to report the mournful news. There was nothing more to say. Claire responded the same way that Ramón and Lorenza had. Fely helped her burn more papers in the kitchen sink and they gathered other documents—"a list of names and amount of supplies sent to the different prison camps and guerrillas in the hills." Mamerto, the bartender, also helped scour the place for incriminating evidence one last time. They had already sent some material up to Fely's father, Vicente Corcuera. Now they sent more. They did not take away the club financial books: accounts, expenses, payroll, and the ledgers Fely maintained. Any good accountant would have such paperwork at a legitimate business—it would be suspicious not to have it.

Claire could have decided to do what Peggy was considering—head up to the hills with Boone. Either she did not have enough time, or she figured that she was already being watched or that she might be able to use her persuasive power with the Japanese officers she knew to remain safe. It is equally possible that she just didn't want to submit herself and Dian once more to a life in the jungle. She was taking a chance—she was resigned to being arrested and hoped she would survive.

Claire Goes to School
Tsubaki Club, Manila, Wednesday, May 24, 1944

THEY CAME FOR her the next morning. She was having breakfast with Dian when four military policemen trooped up the stairs to her living quarters. "Hands up!" one of them said. They searched her for weapons and started a full hunt for evidence. "High Pockets," they said, "take us to your office." She was shocked to hear them use her code name.

They "ordered me to open my desk and trunks. They had a suitcase with them, and tumbled my club accounts, treasured makeup and canned goods into it." Before they led her away for questioning, she awakened Flora, Dian's nurse, so she could care for the child.

"I managed to smile at her and said 'be a good girl and Mummy will be home soon.'"

She walked downstairs with the guards and got into a car. Fely and the others had not come in yet. Dian and her nurse were left alone; the car door slammed and Claire was gone.

At midday the workers started showing up. Flora told everyone what had happened. Damian was early among them; he had worked with Claire since the early days of the occupation in the hills of Bataan, when Claire lived with Carlos Sobreviñas and his family. They had traveled together, evaded patrols and ambushes, and survived. Damian was sobbing when Fely got there. She took command and ordered another sweep of the building for anything that could cause problems. When Mamerto arrived for his shift, he looked around, saw the faces, and did not need to be told. Why did it have to happen? Claire could have escaped to Bataan with the guerrillas, he had said. "I told her to go away, but she is so stubborn."

Next Fely walked with Flora and Dian, now four years old, over to Remedios Hospital, where Peggy was working a nursing shift. Peggy was not surprised.

"Well, leave Dian with me," she said. Peggy had spoken with Claire about what they would do if either of them was arrested. Peggy had always promised Claire that Dian would be her priority. She had reassured Claire even when she was in the hospital. "Don't worry about Dian; I will take care of her until you come out."

"Supposing I don't come out?"

"Then I'll still take care of her."

Fely returned to the club. A military police squad showed up and issued the expected order: Tsubaki Club was hereby closed. They searched the place while Fely and Mamerto protested; they said they could not believe the news; they were shocked to hear that Claire had been involved in anti-Japanese activities.

The military policemen left, and hostesses and musicians started gathering for the evening shift. The mood was somber. Fely told them she planned to ask for permission to reopen a scaled-down version of the club on the ground floor of the building, smaller but still needing waiters and hostesses and some music. The Japanese officials would approve—as long as they stayed far from anyone associated with High Pockets. Most of the staff was worried, though, that they might be implicated.

Fely thought she would be able to keep running the nightclub, which had still been making three or four thousand pesos a week, not as much as before, but enough to continue funding supply operations after the Japanese dragnet subsided. That amount of money could also support Fely, Mamerto, and the workers at the club. There were no better options.

Peggy came to the shuttered club through the back entrance that night and gathered Dian's clothes. Fely was sitting there alone in the dark. Peggy was faithful to her word about Dian. She did not leave the child with a nursemaid at home. She took Dian with her all the time. "I kept her right there at the hospital with me, and each day I went to the hospital I took Dian with me and brought her home again at night."

Within days, Fely was running the smaller club, and Mamerto Geronimo stayed on as the bartender. His sister went off to the hills to fight with the guerrillas. Fely hired a piano player to accompany her on the Japanese songs that catered to lonesome soldiers. Fely disregarded the warnings of the Japanese—she was going to send whatever she could up to the guerrillas. The messengers made several more trips and delivered some supplies, perhaps along with an intelligence report or two gathered on the street. Tsubaki Club was no longer a prime destination for Japanese officers, and sources of information had mostly dried up. Claire's intelligence operation was finished.

Ramón Amusategui's brother, José Maria, told Judge Roxas about the arrests. The judge had continued meeting with Ramón almost daily, even after the arrest of Juan Elizalde. José Maria reported that "a Filipina girl, Helen, had given names and code names under torture." The underground organization had been deactivated.

Judge Roxas had no further way to contact Claire or Ramón or German Eroles or any of the other detainees. Torture was to be expected. He knew from the scant testimony of those who had returned from Fort Santiago that they would be kept isolated, caged in with little food and water. Some of them would be broken; others would not. He likely knew what Ramón had told everyone else: "Blame everything on me."

If there was any saving grace in the mass arrests, it was that Claire and many of her comrades had a chance before they were arrested to read the final news summary prepared by Ramón, which probably also circulated around the city, although German Eroles and Helen Petkoff could not do their normal rounds of delivery. If there could be any comfort, the United States was now roaring back toward the Philippines. Shortwave radio broadcasts confirmed on May 9 that American-led bombing raids had blasted Hollandia in New Guinea. Most uplifting was word that the offensive in New Guinea "gave the Allies three strategic airfields within striking distance of the Philippines." That exciting war dispatch was followed by a progression of victories: a report on May 19 that General

MacArthur was "leap-frogging" beyond Hollandia and even farther west toward the Wakde Islands off Indonesia (not to be confused with Wake Island, thousands of miles to the northeast). It had to have been some balm to their deprivations and sufferings—even the men and women who were beaten and tortured and lay ill in their fetid prisons. General MacArthur was en route and they had survived. One other dispatch hinted at that: The Japanese Domei News Agency admitted on May 7, 1944, what had long been evident on the ground: All of the Japanese efforts to subjugate the Filipino people had been a failure. The Domei dispatch said that "Filipinos have been so 'bewitched' for years by American 'motion pictures and dancing' that efforts of Japanese propagandists to 'banish America' from the Philippines has [sic] not been 'an easy matter.'"

A Letter from Boone

Bataan, May 1944

IN THE JUNGLE, in the heat, on the run, never knowing whether he would survive the day, John Boone took solace in the books Claire sent up-country through her informal lending library. The most recent was *Death in Venice and Other Stories*, a collection by the German writer in exile Thomas Mann. The writing was poignant and Boone wanted to read it more than once. "Wrapped in his cloak, a book in his lap, our traveler rested; the hours slipped by unawares."

Something in Mann's writing struck Boone, perhaps the contemplative, somber tone, introspection, and the sense of being lost in time. He was tempted, he said, to hold on to the book of Mann's short stories. "He is a favorite of mine . . . but my conscience got me." He was sending the book back to Manila along with a chatty note and a request for more supplies.

Boone had no idea that Claire might never read this message, completed on June 4, two weeks after the Kempeitai had taken her. He was still waiting for Zigzag, their six-fingered courier, to arrive for the next pickup.

The message mixed gossip with a report on ramped-up preparations for an invasion. Boone told Claire he could sense that the Japanese military was becoming skilled and had sent more men dedicated to apprehending the guerrillas and their underground operatives in Manila. His spies at Kempeitai headquarters reported that Nagahama had sent an additional fifteen agents to Bataan and forty-seven more to Pampanga, to the northeast. "God knows how many in Manila—so watch your step."

The Japanese occupying army was slowly mounting new defenses in Manila for an anticipated American attack. More and more Japanese soldiers were arriving in Manila on troop transports, some disguised as hospital ships. Residents could see the influx of men as well as the result—Japanese authorities were forcing many families to abandon their apartments and houses and confiscating them to house the newly arrived soldiers. The war was not going well for Japan or for its Nazi allies, but the response was to dig in and work harder. Hideki Tojo, who served as both prime minister and minister of war in the imperial government, faced increased criticism as the Allies captured more and more territory in the central and southern Pacific. Instead of backing off, he consolidated his own power in February by ousting the army chief of staff and taking that third position for himself. However, in July Tojo was ousted from the government after U.S. forces captured Saipan in the Mariana Islands—a perfect staging point for MacArthur's pledged return to the Philippines.

Tojo's departure was a sign of Japan's plight, evident to both sides in the Philippines. Japanese commanders in Manila doubled down, working harder than ever. Nagahama and military intelligence were still tracking the guerrillas, and Boone was now on their radar.

"A guerrilla group of about 20, led by an American, Capt Boone, calls itself the 'Bataan Sector Guerrilla Unit,'" read one intelligence report. "They have infiltrated into the mountains of Santa Rita in northern Bataan to maintain liaison with other guerrilla units and to raise funds for weapons and materials. The garrison unit attacked them."

The report far underestimated the strength of Boone's forces, who were dispersed and hidden among the civilian populace. But the report did include a list of Boone's officers, Benton Rigara, Antonio Trinidad, Kait Bachagu, and Juan Naparo.

Boone knew he was a target of Japanese military intelligence, because he had spies right inside Kempeitai headquarters. However, he had to follow his own advice to Claire: "Watch your step." His message to Claire had two related underlying characteristics—one was the focus on security concerns and the other was his unreserved confidence that his communication link was secure and that Claire was his loyal ally. Boone trusted Claire fully and implicitly, and the trust was well founded. Once Claire was seized and tortured, she could have exposed the link with Boone, with disastrous results. But Claire was a steadfast combatant, and so was everyone working with her at the club.

When Boone turned to sensitive information about Ramsey's recent operations, he began with a warning: "Please be careful of this information. Destroy when read." Boone told Claire that a number of Ed Ramsey's intelligence operatives had been captured inside the city. He then issued a third warning to Claire—far too late. "I don't think these boys will talk, but you must be very careful these days." Boone said that fatigue was setting in beyond the hunger and deprivation, although news about the war was encouraging.

Ramsey, he said, had gone to meet up with the commando team that had come ashore at Mindoro with Chick Parsons from the *Narwhal*. The mission of the commandos, led by Major Lawrence Phillips (no relation to John Phillips) was to establish a series of radio surveillance stations along the coast. Japanese spotters and spies had found the commandos and launched an attack, killing Major Phillips and several of the men with him. The attack delayed Parsons's plan for island-wide radio communications in Luzon, but Boone was confident they would soon be in direct contact with General MacArthur.

Ramsey replaced Major Phillips on the rendezvous with Parsons and other guerrilla leaders. Despite setbacks, Parsons offered Ramsey and the others an uplifting report. Many of the Filipinos and Americans traveling with Parsons on the *Narwhal* had just been stateside. "They told Ramsey that everything is well in hand at home," Boone wrote. "We must just take it easy." When the meeting with Parsons and the others was over, Ramsey received the offer to hop on board. "Ramsey turned down a chance to go to Australia. What do you think of that?"

As tempting as it was, Ramsey said he did not consider the offer for more than an instant. "I was no longer merely *with* the Filipino people; I was *of* them. I was not simply organizing among them; I had grown organically to be a part of them. Their struggle had become my struggle, and their liberation, inevitably, would be mine as well." Ramsey was proud to have made and announced his decision to remain in the Philippines before one of the other guerrilla leaders handed a message to him. "It was a radio signal from Australia addressed to me. . . . Request that you return to Luzon and command of your resistance forces." It was signed by General MacArthur himself.

The guerrilla confab at Mindoro and the steadily improving radio communications from MacArthur's Pacific Command were a sign that the organized resistance was maturing to prepare for an eventual invasion. Boone's forces on Luzon had now grown to seven thousand troops. In addition, he reported that there were thirty thousand new guerrilla recruits on Mindanao alone. Yet Boone and the others were facing potential attacks from all around them. As he wrote in his message to Claire, there was more pressure than ever from Japanese military intelligence. Meanwhile, the Japanese-created Philippine Constabulary had been circulating in Bataan. The constabulary was now fighting with tenant farmers and had even had a skirmish with Boone's units.

Boone's men and other guerrilla bands sometimes ambushed trucks, stole weapons, and sabotaged utilities serving Japanese installations. While earlier orders from MacArthur had been to hold back from direct contact with Japanese troops, encounters were becoming more frequent. Still, the first order of business was to prepare for the U.S. invasion, which seemed to be coming in a matter of months. Reports of American victories were coming through almost daily. Boone had one dangerous distraction: He had not been able to normalize relations with the Huks, the Filipino Maoist communist fighters who fought the Japanese and at the same time challenged other anti-Japanese guerrillas for territory and food supplies. Boone and the other guerrilla commanders cheered when the Huks launched fierce attacks on Japanese troops. "We must give credit where credit is due," Boone said. He had almost given up hope of coordinating with the Maoist units. Though he had a temporary agreement running those spring months, he thought they would end up fighting, the equivalent of a civil war between two groups that should be allies. "We must prepare to put Huk in their place. I think we can whip them in short order because they are just about out of ammunition."

After finishing his report on the latest war news and gossip, Boone asked Claire for some new supplies. He needed cooking oil and clothing, especially underwear and shirts. He was even looking for mentholatum rub, recommended by the doctor who was checking up on his and Mellie's baby son, Phil. The child had a persistent cold, although in general the baby was "fat and healthy and growing like wildfire every day." Along with the book of short stories and the message, Boone attached a receipt from May 15, Claire's final shipment.

In retrospect, Boone's message to Claire was bittersweet; it demonstrated how beholden he was to her for her support and friendship while warning that the danger level for all of them was high. Boone kept a copy in his files, but it is not known whether the original ever reached Manila. Fely did send a new supply run, whether or not she received it. If the original message had not been sent, Boone would have kept the lending-library copy of Thomas Mann's short stories—a sad reminder of his friend Claire, who had disappeared into the Japanese prison system.

Zigzag did make it into Manila eventually, either with this message or with a new one for Fely directly. Fely gathered the supplies she could and sent them up to Boone's hideout in the hills. It was one of the final shipments from Manila. After the crackdown and increased patrols, the danger had grown immensely. Even if Pacio and Zigzag could make it through, prices were soaring and the new, downsized Tsubaki Club was making less money. Although Fely still sang her Japanese and Filipino folk songs to charmed Japanese soldiers, the men noticed that the long-legged proprietress was missing in action.

PART THREE

. . .

Survival

You Are High Pockets

Japanese Administration Building, Manila, May 24, 1944

CLAIRE WAS SURPRISED when the destination for her captivity was not Fort Santiago. Her captors drove instead a few blocks from the club to the Japanese Administration Building on San Luis Avenue and led her to a cell. It was a barren room with a cement floor and no furniture, just a hole in the floor for use as a toilet with a pipe trickling water into it. The door slammed shut.

She paced back and forth, then sat on the floor and waited for several hours without knowing what to expect. She was about to bang on the door of the cell and ask for water when she heard an automobile stopping. Shortly a guard came in and blindfolded her. She could hear people bringing in chairs and a desk as she stood against one wall.

A man then spoke and addressed her by her code name: "High Pockets," he said, "answer our questions truthfully, and you may soon be out."

At least some of her inquisitors spoke English, and she thought she recognized one or more of the voices. She wondered whether that was the reason that she was wearing a blindfold. The men let her know what they already knew: "We know you are not an Italian."

"It is true," she replied. "I am an American by birth [but] my status is that of a Philippine national . . ."

"Do you deny that you have written and received letters from Cabanatuan?" one inquisitor asked. Claire thought quickly about how much she should say and how much she should not say. She figured they already had this information because Ramón, Horacio Manaloto, and Helen Petkoff had been arrested before her. Even if they had not spoken, the Japanese probably had the evidence already.

"Yes," Claire answered, "I did write a few letters to Cabanatuan and received some answers."

Luckily, she had confirmed what the interrogators already knew. The questioner then said:

"I shall read your last letter and then you can explain. . . . Dear Everlasting . . . Now, who is Everlasting?" "Everlasting" was the code name for Captain Frank Tiffany, the Cabanatuan camp chaplain.

"I don't know," she answered.

Someone immediately punched her in the side of the head.

"You don't expect us to believe that statement, do you?"

"I have spoken the truth so far. Why can't you believe me now?"

The questioner asked more: "Then tell us how these letters got back and forth from Cabanatuan to you."

"There's a Filipino boy who came to my house every few months. I don't know his name."

Someone punched her again and then kicked her shins with his boots.

They beat her repeatedly in this first session, for trying to disguise her handwriting and for foolish things.

She said they read to her from a message she had written. "Dear Everlasting: I was glad to hear that you received cal and feel so much better. Will you please sent out demijohn."

The questions kept coming back to the same thing—*Who is Cal? Who is John? Who are Cal and John Demi?*

She could have laughed: They thought the references to calamansi (lemon) and demijohn (a narrow-necked bottle) were references to people named Cal and John. She said they beat and slapped her for the answer until she fell to the floor.

"Look in a *Webster's Dictionary*, if you have one," she said. "You will find the word 'demijohn' there. Ask any native if they do not call their lemons 'calamansi.'" Claire answered truthfully when she calculated it was safe, and she knew not to speak when it was dangerous for the others.

She answered, for example, that she knew who Spark Plug and Fancy-Pants were—Ramón Amusategui and German Eroles, who had already been arrested. However, the Japanese said Ramón and German had already confessed everything they knew about her. She did not believe it.

"I don't know what they could say about me . . . except to say that I have sent money, letters, and medicine to Cabanatuan."

"They say you are also doing guerrilla work. What do you say to that?"

"It's not true, so I am sure that they would not say that."

"We know you were doing guerrilla work and so were they. Speak now and we will let you off easy. If you persist in being stubborn, I will see that you get the limit. We can bring your child here and make her suffer too. Maybe that would make you talk!"

Threatening little Dian was certain to terrify her. They left her back in her cell for three days to think about that, with no more contact with her inquisitors.

Mizu, kudasai, Claire called out, some of the few words she knew in Japanese. "Water, please." A guard came to the cell and spit at her. *Baka,* he said. "Idiot." For two more nights, there was little water and occasionally a small bowl of rice. When thirst overwhelmed her, she drank from the dripping pipe spattering into the cement hole in the floor.

Claire struck up a conversation with a Filipino child in the cell across from her. She judged him to be nine years old. He said he had been arrested for stealing food and clothes.

A new guard came along in the evening and gave Claire and the boy each a cup of water. She spent three days in the dungeon before the guards brought a ball of rice and some tea. As the days passed, she began to search for some way to break out of the temporary cell. She kicked and clawed at boards on the wall, but it looked impossible. They held her in the cell for two weeks, every day providing just a small ration of rice, water, and tea. The boy was her only companion. She comforted him when he cried and figured he might be released long before her. They would not keep a child. If he was released, she told him, he should go to see two people: Judge Roxas who lived on Batanga Street and Fely Corcuera at Tsubaki Club on Mabini. Tell them she was alive. Somehow she had scrounged paper, and she gave him notes—she wanted to make sure that Dian would be taken to safety.

After two weeks of the same routine, Claire finally was taken to Fort Santiago. This meant that she was likely in for more torture. She did not know whether the boy would get word to her friends or whether the Japanese would follow up on the threat of grabbing Dian.

All the while, Judge Roxas had been fretting about the arrests: first Blanche Jurika, then the Elizalde brothers in February, then Ramón—these were his friends. Now the Japanese had taken Claire, a member of the family. He had been powerless to do anything. Then one day, a little Filipino boy was standing before him with a note. Claire had managed to do what the others could not do—she had smuggled out word from within the Japanese prison system.

▪ ▪ ▪

Claire asked Roxas to locate Peggy and to make sure that Dian was safe.
The judge tracked her down at the Remedios Hospital, where Peggy was
still working nursing shifts. "She told me that she was [Claire's] intimate
friend . . . and that Dian had become very close to her and that she had
decided to take care of the girl as long as necessary." In fact, Peggy had
hardly let Dian out of her sight since Claire was taken. The judge went
home, satisfied that the child was well, that Peggy was a close, caring
friend to Claire, and that there was a bond between the woman and the
four-year-old.

For her part, Dian was Peggy's joy, "the best baby I ever saw," more
than twenty years since her son Charles was born. Within weeks, Peggy
decided that Manila was now too unsafe for them and that they had to
leave for the hills. With help from the runners, she joined Boone as a field
nurse, taking Dian with her. She stayed in his camp for a while but also
operated with Frank Loyd, Ed Ramsey, and Colonel Victor Abad, a Filipino guerrilla leader, wherever it was safe and wherever she was needed.
She had precious little medicine to combat tetanus or malaria or any
other disease. She dealt with gunshot wounds and barbed-wire cuts and
worse. When there were tools to be sterilized, someone started a small
campfire to make do.

"Guerrilla nursing would have been greatly simplified if we could
ever have remained in one spot [but] we struck camp twenty times. We'd
move on a little way, put up some more huts for our patients and carry on
the best we could." "No authority on childcare would ever recommend
the kind of life Dian had to live, without shelter or sanitation or anything
like sufficient food, and constantly in danger of her life, yet she never cried
and never complained. Lessons no baby should have to learn had been
drilled into her" by experience. Peggy was commissioned as a guerrilla
lieutenant, a full member of the fighting forces.

Claire languished in a series of miserable cells at Fort Santiago for several
more weeks. Her face was bruised and beaten, and she and the women
with her all were underfed—rice gruel and wormy potatoes were their
standard fare. Claire described her cell at Fort Santiago in similar fashion

to the cage Roy C. Bennett had been held in—a barred door facing an open courtyard and walls of stone. Once more the toilet was a cement hole with dripping water. Here her cell mates included two American nuns, a young woman named Carmen whose husband was also imprisoned, and three German Jewish women. Like all prisoners, they were to remain quiet, although they could whisper. The guards could watch and leer at the women when they took off their clothes or used the cement hole or very occasionally were allowed to take a quick shower in a cubicle nearby. The women could not protest and knew it would be fatal to do so. Others suffered more than she did—men appeared to be treated even worse. Male prisoners nearby were beaten every day. "Ours was the only cell containing women. When I arrived there were probably two hundred men in the fifteen other cells, and the moans of those poor devils came constantly to our ears."

All military prisoners received a version of the standard practices meted out two years earlier, at the start of the war, to Roy C. Bennett—beatings, deprivation, and as Bennett had warned, "be prepared, they may come for you in two minutes, two hours, two weeks, or never."

Finally they came for her again. Two officers repeated many of the same questions she had faced two months earlier. When her blindfold came off, she saw that one of them was Kobayashi, the captain who had joked with her at the club at the beginning of the year about making her the provincial head of Portland under Japanese occupation. Kobayashi played the good cop. He promised she would be released if she told the truth. This time they had a chart with code names of each of her contacts and asked for their real identities. She still told them only the names of people who already had been arrested. She said she did not know any more names. There were plenty of bad cops to go around. The other Japanese officer beat her and kicked her. The torture increased.

"They beat me in an attempt to make me divulge the names of the others. I was tied to a bench so that I couldn't move and a garden hose was put over my mouth and the water turned on until I thought I'd drown. Then to bring me back, they would put lighted cigarettes on my legs. I still have the scars."

Water-boarding was routine torture for many—the prisoners called it "the water cure." Some were forced to sit or kneel in uncomfortable positions. The prisoners wore hoods at times and could not see their inquisitors. There were Japanese speakers and English speakers among the interrogators. The interpreters' skills were sometimes weak and that was potentially deadly. Prisoners suspected they sometimes were tortured because the interpreters had not understood and misinterpreted their answers.

When that bout of torture ended, Claire returned to her cell. After a while, a new Japanese guard recognized her as he walked by and agreed to contact Fely and ask her to send toiletries. He returned a few days later with soap, laundry detergent, a small towel, toothpaste, and a toothbrush. She said she shared the items with the other prisoners. She also said that she saw her fellow member of the underground, Ramón Amusategui, led in for a few days and held temporarily in a cell close by. They managed to speak quickly in whispers. He told her that he had in fact done what he intended—he had taken full responsibility for everything they had done. The others of their group were apparently safe—Lorenza had not been arrested, and German Eroles, though weakened and sick, had been released. Claire realized that she had been implicated only as being among a group of smugglers and that there was no information to suggest that she was connected to Boone, Mellie, Pacio, Zigzag, Juan Elizalde, or anyone else with the guerrillas. If they asked more questions, she would stick with the same line she had followed: She would tell them only that she knew the people who were already under arrest. She did make one mistake, however, when they tricked her into giving hints that might have led to Maria Martinez's arrest. Claire and Maria had a special relationship. Maria was the only other member of their group who was working directly with the guerrillas. Maria had been gathering donations and sending supplies to Boone's camp. Worn down one day, and measuring how much information to give, Claire gave an answer she regretted when an interrogator said they knew that Claire was working with a friend code-named Papaya and asked, "Who is he?"

"Papaya is not a man, but a woman," Claire answered. She then went on to say that Papaya was a short woman with dark brown eyes. She realized that she might have given too much information, even though the interrogators said they already knew this. This was the balancing act: pretending to be willing to provide information but saying she did not know that much. In this case she might have inadvertently helped the police capture Maria, although almost any young Filipina could fit that general description.

▪ ▪ ▪

Eventually Claire was able to send out notes again with another Filipino boy who brought the gruel they ate every day. Fely messaged back that Dian was safe with Peggy and Boone, who had sent a message that the Americans were working their way back to the Philippines. Boone expected real fighting before long. Claire said the message ended: "Hold on and pray." After more than two months of imprisonment, things got worse: Claire was moved to a different cell, about fifteen feet by twelve feet, with twenty-two women crammed in with her. "There was room here for all of us to sleep at night, lying spoon-fashion. When one turned, the rest of us had to follow suit." Food rations decreased to two cups of rice gruel per day, and the women became increasingly weak.

One morning at 2:00 a.m. she was dragged out of her cell and blindfolded, and interrogators started again. Who were her contacts in the underground? What were the names of the men they worked with at Cabanatuan? She continued to say she did not have the names of men who received aid there or in any other camp.

"Are you still going to continue telling us lies?" one said.

"I tell you the truth, but you won't believe me."

The men dragged her out of the interrogation room, along a corridor, and then outside onto the grass, close to the Pasig River. They pushed her to the ground.

"We don't like to do this, but you must die unless you speak the truth. You have two minutes to decide."

Claire said she felt a blade cold on her shoulder; it was then released quickly and suddenly as if someone were preparing to bring it down hard on her neck. She fainted.

When she awoke, she was back inside. When the other women in her cell asked what had happened, like many before her, she was afraid to say anything for fear of retaliation and more torture.

A Chase Across the Pacific

Philippine Sea, Summer and Fall, 1944

INVASION PLANS WERE coming together. By mid-1944, Parsons was able to report huge progress to MacArthur. After more than a year of clandestine missions from Australia to the Philippines, they had done well in their goal of uniting, organizing, and supplying guerrillas in the Philippines. "Some of the islands were swinging beautifully into line under strong individual leaders," Parsons said. Some problems were to be expected, but tens of thousands of American and Filipino guerrillas were prepared to rise up, greet and support the general's return to the Philippines. Parsons was frank in his assessment. "Because of jealousy and strife between the aspirants," some guerrillas were still disorganized and "could not be recognized as unified districts until just before invasion." It would not be a problem.

In July 1944 that invasion was coming hard upon them. The United States had already launched a major offensive in the waters east of the Philippines. The Battle of the Philippine Sea on June 19 and 20 was an overwhelming victory for the Allies. In head-to-head battles the United States knocked out three Japanese aircraft carriers and more than 500 Japanese planes. On June 19 U.S. carrier-based planes launched attacks on Japanese forces in the Mariana Islands, a 1,065-mile stretch of stepping-stone islands from Guam toward Japan. The American victory became known as the Turkey Shoot; more than 200 Japanese planes were destroyed, ten times more than American losses. Overall in the sea battle, U.S. losses were minimal in weaponry and manpower, with one ship damaged and an estimated 123 planes shot down. Controlling the sea meant the Americans had bisected the supply lines from Japan and severely damaged the empire's sea and air operations. After that, in more than two weeks of fighting from July 21 to August 10, the United States wrenched away control of Guam, decimating Japanese forces there. Only 1,500 miles of open water separated Guam from the closest Philippine landfall to the west. More victories followed Guam: U.S. ground troops landed at Morotai on September 15, less than 500 miles from southernmost

Mindanao, and soon at the Palau archipelago, about the same distance away.

MacArthur, aiming all the time for the quickest possible return to the Philippines, welcomed the analysis of Admiral William Bull Halsey, who suggested that the first attack on the Japanese-controlled islands should be at Leyte, a central island 350 miles southeast of Manila. President Roosevelt cabled his support for the idea. MacArthur's return was marked for mid-October 1944.

The United States command began to assemble an attack force of three hundred ships and 1,500 airplanes for what became known as the Battle of Leyte Gulf and was considered by many historians to be the largest naval battle in world history.

The submarine missions between the Philippines and Australia were occurring on a regular schedule—forty-one missions by nineteen submarines from late 1942 until the end of the war. The operation was known as Spyron. The missions delivered more than one thousand tons of food and other supplies, equipment, and propaganda material. Despite the danger of discovery and the possibility of attacks at sea, the return trips carried more than four hundred American civilians and Allied foreign nationals to safety, including women and children.

> About 120 radio sets were furnished to coast watchers and others. . . .
> Aside from arms and ammunition, the Spyron cargoes consisted of
> medicines, sewing kits, cigarettes (with the box bearing the promise, "I
> shall return"), shoes and hundreds of thousands of counterfeit Japanese
> yen. Submarines made landings in practically all parts of the Islands
> and even occasionally came alongside a dock in Mindanao to the music
> of "Anchors Aweigh," by a bamboo band.

General MacArthur's command was now producing daily radio programming directed at the Philippines and a monthly magazine with news of the war both in the Pacific and in Europe. Parsons was successful enough on his distribution lines that Japanese military intelligence often saw copies themselves, with the irritating (to them) refrain on every copy "I shall return."

While Boone and the other commanders on Luzon listened to the rundown of U.S. victories on the sweep toward the Philippines, more requests than ever were coming in for intelligence. Claire's ground-level reports on Japanese military officials and their comings and goings were replaced now with new information compiled by intelligence drops throughout the city. Ramona Snyder, Ed Ramsey's longtime lover and intermediary with General Roxas, managed to elude detection, even though the Japanese were certain that Roxas was conniving against them.

The Japanese were digging in for a fight throughout the Philippines and particularly in Manila. Leyte was the natural point for Japanese occupation forces to mount a defense against an expected American attack. However, General Tomoyuki Yamashita, now commander of the Japanese Fourteenth Army, focused on a defense line in Luzon itself. Ramsey's intelligence operation was close enough to military intelligence, even inside headquarters, to report the strategy. Yamashita "was resisting the pressure to shift his forces southward," Ramsey's informants told him. "We relayed this information to MacArthur: Luzon, and not Leyte, remained the main enemy stronghold."

Welcome Bombs
Manila, September 21, 1944

ON THURSDAY, September 21, around noon, people across Manila heard a sound, first buzzing, then roaring—airplanes, then the telltale sound of planes diving in the air—followed by explosions. Antiaircraft fire, more planes diving, more cannon fire. They saw billows of smoke in the direction of Japanese installations and on the horizon.

Thirteen-year-old Juergen Goldhagen and his parents were huddled in a makeshift shelter in their living room. The Goldhagens had managed exit visas and left Germany in 1937 for the Philippines, escaping the Nazis before the start of the war. Martin Goldhagen, Juergen's father, was Jewish. Charlotte, his mother, was Christian, but being Jewish, or being married to a Jew, or being the son of a Jew meant the same thing in the Third Reich. Here in Japanese-occupied Manila, though, they were free as German nationals. "We sat on a mattress with a cork on a string around our necks. We would put the cork in our mouths as the explosions drew near because somewhere Mom or Dad had read that a large explosion could cause you to bite your tongue off. I also had an aluminum pot over my head and wished I was a soldier, because they had strong helmets."

The prisoners of war, the once vanquished, the victims of the cruel occupation, could only describe the strange sensation of welcoming an attack in which they themselves might die. They cheered whenever and wherever Japanese soldiers could not hear them. In Manila people ventured outside to peer at the airplanes, then retreated quickly when they spotted shrapnel falling from the sky. They saw that American attacks were focused close to Manila Bay, hundreds of planes diving and dodging Japanese fighters and ground fire. The Americans had returned.

Claire first heard the distant sound the following day, Friday, September 22. She and her cell mates were returning from their weekly shower. The distant hum grew toward a crescendo. They were not sure what was happening, but then they were herded quickly back to their cells. The woman who came in last was able to report details to the rest of them. "Planes! About five hundred or more, I guess," she reported, "They are so very high that they look like specks." If there had been any doubt about the origin of the planes, it was put to rest: The Filipino guards were nervous as they locked Claire in her cell, and they told the women to lie close to the ground on their stomachs. The explosions had to be an attack by American planes coming to retake the city.

The women celebrated, quietly, they thought, but then were punished by not receiving any food that night and reduced rations of only one meal a day after that.

Guards brought Maria Martinez to Claire's cell that night; she had been arrested about a week earlier. Maria was code-named Papaya, and she was the other member of the underground who was in touch with John Boone and other guerrillas in Bataan.

This was potentially dangerous. The Kempeitai had interrogated Claire only about her work as a member of the Cabanatuan supply organization—there still was no sign that they knew about her connections to Boone and the guerrillas. If Maria could be broken, both of them would be in far greater danger. Both women were taken out several times for interrogations. Claire said the interrogators went back over old material and slapped her repeatedly. Maria was also beaten and appeared to be getting the worst of it. Still, neither woman gave any sign that either of them was connected to the guerrillas.

Meanwhile, Claire told Maria that she felt guilty because she perhaps had accidentally given the Japanese interrogators information that led to her arrest. "I don't want you to think that I have squealed on you," Claire said. Maria had just been slapped around during an interrogation session. She was wiping away tears. She told Claire: "I have never asked you whether you did or whether you didn't. I have never even thought that you had squealed on me."

Claire had not seen or heard from Ramón for months and was worried. One day she asked one of the Filipino food carriers if he could find anything out about him. An answer came four days later: Ramón was in the dungeons and had been severely tortured, the young man said. He was paralyzed in one leg and unable to walk.

The Japanese military authorities eventually told Claire and Maria that the investigative cases against them were complete; they were taken to Bilibid Prison to await court-martial. On November 20 the women were led into a room. Seated before them were three Japanese military judges; a photograph of Emperor Hirohito, draped with a Japanese flag, was displayed behind them.

Then Ramón was brought in. Claire said that Ramón had been so badly beaten that, when a Japanese interpreter told them to bow before the tribunal judges, he could hardly follow orders. "Ramón was shaking from weakness and pain, and toward the end I doubt if he knew what was being read. When asked if he was guilty, he replied 'Yes' in a barely audible voice, and then collapsed in a chair."

Marie and Claire were tried next; charges were read in English and Japanese, and they answered as ordered when asked about their pleas. "Guilty," both of them said. They were led away, one cell for women, another for men. Claire never saw Ramón again.

Parsons Sets the Table

Leyte Gulf, October 1944

AT 4:30 P.M. on the afternoon of Thursday, October 12, 1944, a Catalina "Black Cat" flying boat skimmed the ocean off Leyte, about forty miles south of Tacloban, the southern Philippine island's capital. As the aircraft slowed to a moderate taxi speed, crew members tossed an inflatable raft out the blister port and dumped in some supplies. Next, Chick Parsons and his partner, Lieutenant Colonel Frank Rawolle of Sixth Army Special Intelligence, dove out headfirst. By the time they had righted themselves and were ready to paddle to shore, the airplane was picking up speed and headed back toward its base in New Guinea. (MacArthur had relocated to New Guinea from Brisbane in April 1944.) Parsons now had four days to survey Leyte before U.S. bombers began to soften up Japanese defenses in advance of the long-awaited invasion of the Philippines.

Lieutenant General Walter Krueger, commander of the Sixth Army, had summoned Parsons a few days earlier and told him that the invasion was confirmed for October 20. Parsons's mission was to notify guerrilla leaders in person and ask them for information on enemy positions and their hour-to-hour movements. The guerrillas were expected to deploy and attack Japanese troops when they began to retreat under the frontal U.S. attack. Parsons was also supposed to create an administrative structure on land once the invasion was successful.

General MacArthur intended the invasion, vast as it was, to be surgically precise in avoiding collateral damage. That meant the guerrillas also had to know that they needed to protect themselves and civilians from the American onslaught. Parsons needed to provide enough information but maintain operational secrecy. That was the conundrum presented by General Krueger: "How to remove loyal Filipinos out of the various areas to be attacked without giving advance information to the enemy is something else again."

"Likewise how to coordinate Colonel [Ruperto] Kangleon's troops with our own, without revealing exact invasion plans." (Kangleon was commander of guerrilla forces on Leyte.)

One final thing, Krueger said. "Be sure that the enemy doesn't get information about our plans, this is one time you definitely must not be captured."

"I won't be," Parsons said.

Parsons and Rawolle made it to shore as planned, then sent a coded message to the Pacific Command: "Party Arrived Safely." They hid their raft and set to work. They first made contact with Kangleon and passed along the orders without providing details of the overall invasion. A mass bombing attack would begin in seventy-two hours, they told him. His fighters were to "seek safety in the hills" and "remain under cover . . . round up every possible guerrilla and surround all [Japanese] retreat routes."

That mission accomplished, Parsons remained onshore with the guerrillas. After four days of bombings, a U.S. invasion force of seven hundred ships and 174,000 men converged on Leyte.

On October 20 General Douglas MacArthur surveyed the initial attack from the bridge of the USS *Nashville*. "High overhead, swarms of airplanes darted into the maelstrom. And across what would ordinarily have been a glinting, untroubled blue sea, the black dots of the landing craft churned toward the beaches."

The American contingent sailed steadily under cover of darkness. Within the convoy, tank landing ships (LSTs) were always the most exposed to enemy attack as they tried to beach themselves to open their giant hinged forward doors and disgorge tanks, trucks, and soldiers onshore. Many years later, speaking with his son Peter, Ensign Bernard Eisner was to recall that distant morning when he stood watch before dawn on LST 463 as it steamed northnorthwest in the convoy at about 8 knots. He rang general quarters, calling all hands to battle stations when they approached within several miles of Red Beach, their objective on Leyte Island. At the same time, he saw a twin-engine Japanese plane, possibly a reconnaissance flight, high overhead. Latimer, the navigation officer, took the watch at 8:00 a.m. Eisner took his battle station, scanning the sky for Japanese planes. At 11:00 a.m. the ship approached land among a dozen LSTs heading toward Red Beach. They encountered heavy mortar and artillery fire and beached so that a battalion of engineers could take smaller craft to shore. Other LSTs were damaged; LST 463 pulled off and took on the first wave of casualties.

MacArthur decided to go ashore himself on a third assault wave. A landing craft carried him within fifty yards of the beach and he then waded to shore. He was accompanied by aides, other officers, and a committee of Filipinos led by Sergio Osmeña, who had acceded to the Philippine presidency in exile when Manuel Quezon died in August. A mobile microphone had been set up on the beach for the general, who declared as the battle raged on: "People of the Philippines: I have returned."

Deadly Passage
Cabanatuan, November 1944

WHEN THE POWs at Cabanatuan saw the American planes that first day, September 21, 1944, the starving, sickly men restrained themselves to avoid reprisals from the guards. "No cheers, just grins," Colonel Arthur Shreve said.

More flyovers followed, and then there were direct attacks nearby. Shreve saw "our Navy aviators . . . flying high over the mountains in formation. They strafed and bombed the field near here. Sometimes I have felt a little ashamed of the way we took cover in the early days of the war, but my heart glows with pride at our conduct as compared with these Japs."

The three thousand men were consumed with keeping up on the latest war news. Enterprising tinkerers among them had jury-rigged radios that they hid under floorboards or in holes in the ground. Months earlier, they had heard about D-Day and the invasion of Europe; Belgium was free; Holland and France were being retaken. In the Pacific the United States was on the march, taking stepping-stone islands and then finally invading the Philippines at Leyte. MacArthur and men were working their way back toward victory.

Weeks into the American campaign, word began spreading in the camp that the Japanese were planning to start shipping able-bodied prisoners to labor camps outside the Philippines. The Americans hoped the Japanese would not have enough time to organize before the U.S. onslaught that could rescue them. However, in December the order came to start shipping out. Shreve was among a wave of thousands—all but the most sickly and infirm—who were transported from Cabanatuan to Manila itself—and to Bilibid Prison, where Claire and Ramón had been held just a few weeks earlier. Also among this group of POWs were Mr. Threa* and Colonel Mack, both having recovered sufficiently to be considered able-bodied laborers despite having survived almost six months in solitary confinement. As they waited at Bilibid, they received miserable rations, the worst they had suffered in weeks, and now without supplements from the outside—rice, fetid water, and a bit of corn.

Then, on December 13, Shreve and the others received the order to ship out. He was among 1,619 men who had been in Cabanatuan who now marched under guard out the front gate of Bilibid about a mile to the port. There they boarded the *Oryoku Maru*, a Japanese transport converted during the war from a passenger and cargo vessel. The men came to call it a hell ship for good reason. The POWs were packed tightly belowdecks in holds so small that no one could lie down; at best they could barely sit with knees hunched up. The air was foul and the food was no better.

At the same time, the ship carried about nineteen hundred Japanese civilian and military passengers in berths higher up and certainly under better conditions. The *Oryoku Maru* set sail from Manila harbor, headed southwest, and skirted Corregidor before turning northward toward the Asian mainland. The ship bore no markings as a vessel carrying prisoners of war.

They had made it no farther overnight than the vicinity of Subic Bay, just west around the Bataan peninsula from Manila, when American warplanes launched their first attack. Waves of attacks followed. A bomb hit the deck and blew a gun over the side. Passengers and crew died in the first blast and many were injured. Strafing machine-gun fire also wounded prisoners in the hold below. The POWs were held on board despite the destruction and mayhem but finally were allowed to abandon ship as the burning vessel began sinking on December 15. Prisoners who could swim helped others who could not. Colonel Shreve was among the survivors. He used a floating piece of a hatch cover to ferry men to the shore. "The Japanese had placed machine guns along the shore and anyone who didn't come directly from the ship to the shore was immediately taken under fire."

Those who made it ashore alive remained at a temporary camp for more than a week; Japanese soldiers marched fifteen of those who were sick or had been wounded by the ordeal to a cemetery, where they bayoneted and decapitated them and then dumped them in a common grave. Colonel Shreve and the other survivors eventually boarded another hell ship bound for labor camps in Taiwan, Korea, and Japan itself. This time they survived the journey. An estimated 21,000 Allied POWs died at sea as they were being transported on 156 Japanese hell-ship voyages around the Pacific, victims of U.S. submarine and air attacks.

By the end of 1944, the population of Cabanatuan had dropped sharply. In December there were fewer than 900 men at Cabanatuan; then 346 of the remaining prisoners were sent to Puerto Princesa, about five hundred miles south of Bataan on the southern island of Palawan; about 500 men remained at Cabanatuan. The new year brought promise of an American victory, but none of the remaining prisoners or detainees in the Philippines could know what might be in store for them.

Power of the Spirit
Manila, January 1945

AS JAPANESE FORCES prepared for a decisive moment, buoyant rhetoric from their commanders encouraged and reminded them that the Japanese Army could still prevail. Tsuyuo Yamagata, the commander of the Japanese Twenty-sixth Division, counseled wisdom. "This is a real battleground," he told his assembled officers. Be wise, he said, and recognize your strengths. "You cannot regard the enemy as on a par with you. You must realize that material power usually overcomes spiritual power in the present war. The enemy is clearly our superior in machines. Do not depend on your spirits overcoming this enemy. . . . Devise combat methods based on mathematic precision. Then think about displaying your spiritual power."

MacArthur's forces were advancing on Luzon from the north and the south. Manila residents heard gunfire every day and saw American planes frequently flying overhead. The military profile in Manila was ominous and changing. At first the Japanese had been moving troops out of the city and were destroying military installations. That plan changed with the decimation of the Japanese naval fleet at Leyte. The Japanese flew in aircraft from outside the Philippines; instead of destroying bases, they were using Luzon airfields as bases to strafe American positions.

They also used an airfield at Angeles close to Clark Air Base to introduce a new tactic in the war—they had assembled a corps of suicide pilots—kamikaze—who used their planes as guided missiles to blast American ships. The Luzon-based kamikaze flew their first missions in the waters off Leyte on October 25, 1944. It was a terrifying prospect, and the kamikaze sometimes hit their targets, but American shipboard gunners adapted.

Manila, meanwhile, was being converted into a fortress. Japanese officials wavered and argued about whether to make a stand here or retreat to high ground in Bataan and beyond. Nevertheless, they continued setting up barricades and pillboxes throughout Manila. If the Japanese staged a last stand in Manila, civilians would be caught in the middle of a major battle.

As MacArthur's forces advanced toward the city, Japanese troops mined bridges across the Pasig River and reinforced gun emplacements. Civilians were being pressed into work crews. "The Japanese are obtaining this forced labor in a most haphazard manner. Many sentries are stationed in various parts of the town and every able-bodied Filipino pedestrian who is unfortunate enough to pass before them is seized and placed in a waiting truck. When enough men have thus been corralled, the Japanese take them to the places where they are most needed and there they are put to work."

It was not clear whether the Japanese military command intended to distinguish at all between civilian detainees and military prisoners of war. The Tokyo High Command had issued a secret kill order in August 1944 that detailed plans for dealing with prisoners.

At such time as the situation became urgent and it be extremely important, the POWs will be concentrated and confined in their present location and under heavy guard; the preparation for the final disposition will be made.

The time and method of the disposition are as follows:

(1) The Time. Although the basic aim is to act under superior orders, individual disposition may be made in the following circumstances:

(a) when an uprising of large numbers cannot be suppressed without the use of firearms; (b) when escapees from the camp may turn into a hostile fighting force.

(2) The Methods. (a) Whether they are destroyed individually or in groups, or however it is done, with mass bombing, poisonous smoke, poisons, drowning, decapitation ... dispose of them as the situation dictates; (b) in any case it is the aim not to allow the escape of a single one, to amilhilate [sic] them all, and not to leave any traces.

Officials at the Palawan POW camp were among the first to follow through on the secret order. About 150 POWs, some of them from Cabanatuan, were left at Palawan; others had been shipped to labor camps. The men who remained were at work seven days a week completing a 1,500-foot airfield. They drove trucks, crushed coral for a base layer, and then poured concrete for the tarmac. It was slave labor under starvation food allowances, with no medical treatment and particularly harsh, vengeful behavior by Japanese soldiers. The POWs at Palawan also saw the formations of U.S. planes flying overhead and celebrated in silence. However, when B-24 bombers attacked the base twice in October and destroyed Japanese planes, the American reaction, though muted, was duly noted by the guards. The Japanese responded by cutting rations and treating the prisoners with more brutality than ever.

The American laborers were at work on the tarmac as usual on the morning of Thursday, December 14, 1944. Guards called them back to camp at noon and ordered them to take shelter because U.S. planes were reported en route for another attack. The men sought shelter in the log-covered trenches they had been allowed to build for themselves. By 2:00 p.m. the POWs were crowded into the trenches, awaiting word on the attack. Suddenly guards dumped gallons of gasoline into the air-raid trenches, which had only small entry holes at both ends. The commander, Lieutenant Yoshikazu Sato, then issued the order to torch the gasoline-soaked logs and the prisoners inside. A fireball engulfed them. A few of the men managed to crawl out, but they were bayoneted and shot. Several fought the Japanese on the spot and a few of the 150 POWs were able to evade their tormentors and dive into the ocean to swim for safety. One of those survivors was Private First Class Eugene Nielsen of the 59th Coast Artillery, who swam for nine hours, though wounded.

> One shot hit me in the armpit and grazed my ribs. Another hit me in the left thigh, then another one hit me right along the right side of my head, grazing my temple. I think it knocked me out temporarily. For a short period, I was numb in the water; and I nearly drowned. Then I found a large coconut husk, bobbing around in the bay and I used it to shield my head as I swam. . . .
>
> I came down to a place along the shore where there were a lot of trees and bushes in the water. I knew they were following me, so I went toward shore and splashed to make a little noise. I wanted them to think I was finally coming in. Then I abruptly turned around and went out just as quiet as possible and started swimming across the bay. They never shot at me again. Probably it was too dark for them to see me. I swam most of the night.

Filipino guerrillas plucked Nielsen from the surf and brought him to army intelligence officers on the island of Morotai. MacArthur received an immediate report on the Palawan massacre: He and all other officials reacted with revulsion and anger; the reality of what they faced became starkly present. The Pacific Command had not seen the Japanese directive to annihilate all POWs, but they had no reason to believe that Palawan was an isolated case. General MacArthur resolved to make the rescue of prisoners a high priority.

By now, U.S. Army Air Forces reconnaissance planes were taking photographs of the buildings at Cabanatuan. Naomi, Peggy, and Claire's contacts had smuggled out messages earlier in the war that could produce a good map of the prison compound—they could point to which buildings housed the POWs, the prison hospital, guard quarters, weapons, and equipment stores. The same was the case with the other camps and detention sites. Old Bilibid Prison was in the form of a wheel hub and spokes; they knew where the prisoners were. Chick Parsons himself could describe Bilibid, Fort Santiago, and Santo Tomas. The latest intelligence gave an approximate count of the thousands of Americans held in Manila and its environs. The report on Palawan from Nielsen gave MacArthur a sense of urgency. "With every step that our soldiers took toward Santo Tomás University, Bilibid, Cabanatuan and Los Baños, where these prisoners were held, the Japanese soldiers guarding them had become more and more sadistic. I knew that many of these half-starved and ill-treated people would die unless we rescued them promptly."

In from the Hills
Bataan, January 1945

BOONE'S GUERRILLAS had been champing at the bit to take the fight directly to the Japanese instead of staging hit-and-run sabotage operations. His Filipino commanders even countermanded standing orders in October to celebrate MacArthur's return with a direct attack on a Japanese garrison. Though Boone was on Japanese intelligence radar, he remained elusive. With the return of U.S. troops, Boone was ready to launch attacks on long-identified targets. After MacArthur landed on January 9 at Lingayen Gulf about eighty miles north of his camp, Boone sent a team of engineers on a mission to destroy a major Japanese ammunition dump. The men moved in on some huts along the road close to the ammunition stores and encouraged a local farmer to use gasoline to set them on fire. The poor man was overenthusiastic and used too much fuel. The resulting fire killed the farmer and set off a chain reaction that blew up tons of bombs and ammunition with a thundering roar that echoed miles away back at Boone's mountain hideout. His troops staged a series of operations throughout January and into February to support arriving U.S. troops.

On February 5, 1945, almost exactly three years after he lost contact with the regular army, John Boone, now with a field commission as a guerrilla major, walked into a U.S. Army command post and reported for duty. He immediately provided intelligence information on Japanese installations at the so-called Zig Zag Pass, a highway crossing in dense jungle through the Zambales Mountains where Japanese forces were making a last stand in Bataan. American troops were pinned down at Zig Zag, unable to break through a warren of Japanese defenses in the thick undergrowth, woven with tunnels, trenches, and pillboxes where they could pick off the invaders at will.

Boone used his knowledge of the area to avert disaster and provided intelligence that brought an important victory at Zig Zag. On the first day of fighting, without his help, U.S. commanders had been lured into the Japanese trap and four hundred Americans had been killed, as Boone put it, the result of "very poor judgment on somebody's part." The U.S. general in charge was stripped of his command as a result; Boone met with the new commander, Brigadier General William C. Chase, and provided detailed information about Japanese installations at the pass. "Overnight the division took on a new spirit and morale and fought that campaign very well." Still, the fighting lasted for two more weeks. American troops killed an estimated 2,400 of the estimated 2,800 Japanese soldiers there and took only about twenty-five prisoners; the remaining Japanese escaped into the jungle. From there Boone's forces continued south to fight remaining Japanese stragglers in Bataan and then moved into Manila for mop-up operations.

Meanwhile Boone had an irritating command problem back in the hills. His commanders said they would have preferred dealing with five-year-old Dian rather than with Peggy. She had also proved to be difficult under fire. Boone had assigned her to run a medical operation at the camp of Colonel Victor Abad, second regiment commander in Bataan. Peggy was horrified one day when Abad asked her to administer a lethal dose of strychnine to a Filipina woman who he said had been found guilty of spying for the Japanese. Peggy refused on the reasonable grounds that she was a healer, not a killer. Abad just shrugged; his troops forced the woman into a grave-sized hole and an aide shot and killed her and her child with a single bullet.

Peggy immediately demanded that she and Dian be allowed to leave. It was a dangerous trip, but Abad agreed to send her to Frank Loyd's camp, accompanied by an Aeta guide. They made it to Loyd's camp with a letter of introduction after a rough trek through the jungle. Frank Loyd complained that Peggy never stopped talking and complaining. Besides talking incessantly, she griped about the lack of equipment and adequate nursing facilities and tended to berate the rough-hewn guerrillas she was working with.

Boone sent Peggy an irony-tinged note. "I am very sorry to hear of the inconvenience and unnecessary hardship caused you recently during the Jap general raids. This trip to the camp of Colonel Loyd must have been hectic." He assigned her to a civilian aid station away from his troops. "I can arrange for you to take charge of one of these Aid Stations in an area where the better class Filipino will evacuate and I am sure your supply line and other such problems would cease to exist."

Boone had one final bit of news for Peggy. They all knew that Claire had been held for several months at Fort Santiago, along with Ramón, but no word had gotten out about what the Japanese planned to do. When the sentencing period was over, the possibility had existed that they all would be killed. Claire, at least, had survived. He added a note in capital letters: "I AM SURE YOU WILL BE ELATED TO HEAR THAT MRS. PHILLIPS IS REPORTED ALIVE IN WELFAREVILLE [the women's prison at Mandaluyong]. This report came from Father Lalor but no details." At the same time, it had become nearly impossible to obtain food and medicine shipments from Manila. Claire had not been the only supplier, but she had been the first contact point. Messengers had attempted to find a source of supplies but were "unable to procure either money or medicine."

A Race Against Time
Lingayen Gulf, Luzon, January 1945

ON JANUARY 26, 1945, Major Robert Lapham, a guerrilla leader operating in the hills alongside John Boone, Frank Loyd, and Ed Ramsey, made an urgent trip to the new U.S. Sixth Army command field headquarters near Lingayen Gulf. General Krueger's Sixth Army—which in October had landed at Leyte with the help and advance work of Chick Parsons— now had redeployed at Lingayen Gulf. Krueger's forces were the northern portion of the vise that was squeezing Japanese resistance, with the Eighth Army, led by Lieutenant General Robert L. Eichelberger, moving up from the south.

Lapham, long supported by Parsons's supply and intelligence operation, covered the region around Cabanatuan. He sought out Colonel Horton White, the Sixth Army's chief intelligence officer, to provide emergency information. He warned that the remaining POWs at Cabanatuan were in grave danger and faced possible execution as American forces advanced. White reported this immediately to General Krueger and noted Lapham's long service in central Luzon and his ability to monitor the POWs. Krueger agreed that they had to move quickly to rescue the prisoners. U.S. forces were expected to fight their way to the vicinity of the camp within days. Eugene Nielsen's chilling story of escape from the mass murder at Palawan had produced more than anger and revulsion—the military knew the consequences of waiting.

They decided to organize a rapid rescue operation and designated Lieutenant Colonel Henry Mucci as the leader. Mucci was the commander of an elite special forces team, the Sixth Ranger Battalion, a highly trained unit that was aching to engage and employ its skills to the best possible use. Mucci and his subordinate officers Captain Robert W. Prince and First Lieutenant John F. Murphy were accompanied by the Sixth Army's intelligence unit, a total of 121 U.S. Rangers. Joining them were several Alamo Scouts and Filipino guerrilla units. The final strike force of 370 men launched its mission on January 27, fearing all the while that any security leak or delay could lead to the killing of the remaining Cabanatuan prisoners. The team included a doctor and medical staff, combat photographers, and support personnel. The Alamo Scouts left first as an advance team and moved onward to the village of Platero, along the Pampanga River about three miles from the POW camp.

Mucci's men—traveling without identification or insignias—faced not only chance discovery by Japanese patrol but also the possibility that the Huk guerrillas, their reluctant allies against the Japanese, would be hostile. The Rangers moved first to the town of Guimba, where they met up with a guerrilla leader, Eduardo Joson, who had worked with Lapham's guerrillas. Before dawn on January 29, they forded the Talavera River and reached a staging point on the outskirts of Cabanatuan City. There, another guerrilla officer, Juan Pajota, reported that a Japanese division of eight thousand men or more was within five miles of the POW camp. Despite pressure to move quickly, Mucci decided to hold off the rescue mission for twenty-four hours.

The delay allowed further development of a complex rescue-and-retrieval operation that depended also on the support of civilians. Guerrillas took every conceivable precaution, down to the detail of telling civilians in the vicinity to muzzle all dogs and to pen their chicken flocks far from the road to avoid alerting the Japanese to unusual movements. Meanwhile the one-day postponement allowed for new surveillance of the POW camp—guerrillas monitored troop movements inside and nearby, and Mucci's Rangers reviewed maps, including the location of prisoner quarters, and chose attack and firing positions on the perimeter of the camp. The final plan was to establish guerrilla roadblocks on the main Cabanatuan road—including one at the bridge near where Naomi had often brushed her hair to signal to Mr. Threatt when she had delivered messages and supplies for the camp.

The Rangers and the guerrilla units left Platero at 5:00 p.m. with the attack on the camp planned for 7:30 p.m. The guerrillas planted a bomb charge at the bridge that would be detonated fifteen to twenty minutes after the attack; that would block reinforcements from the Japanese division up the road. Guerrillas dug in on the periphery to shoot individual Japanese troops who might try to ford the river or come in from the opposite direction on the highway.

One additional detail had been called in ahead of time and worked perfectly. About forty minutes before the rescue assault, a futuristic P-61 Black Widow fighter plane buzzed the camp in two passes at two hundred feet to distract Japanese soldiers while the Rangers slithered into place on their bellies over an open field on the other side of the highway. Neither the prisoners nor the Japanese had seen a plane like that before—seeing the modern double-tail three-man fighter was about as strange as seeing a flying saucer. Murphy's unit took extra time to cross under the highway and circle around to the back of the camp while Prince's unit waited in place. Murphy gave the signal to open the attack at 7:45 p.m. The Rangers pulverized guard towers, shacks, and pillboxes and then charged through the gates in less than a minute; using their detailed maps, they moved toward the POW quarters.

They encountered 513 startled, disbelieving POWs. Many of these hollow-eyed men had been the original defenders at Bataan and Corregidor and had survived the death march more than two and a half years earlier. No longer among them were Mr. Threatt, Captain Tiffany, and Colonel Mack—all had died on hell ships or in camps in Japan. Long gone were Jack Utinsky, John Phillips, and the thousands of men who died at Cabanatuan or Camp O'Donnell. Colonel Arthur Shreve, who had survived the attack on one hell ship, was now en route to a labor camp. Major

Dwight Gard, the Portland man who had been corresponding with Claire, had also survived a hell ship and was at a labor camp in Fukuoka, Japan. These remaining prisoners were left behind because they were for the most part too sick or weak to work.

Mucci's Rangers led the men out the front gate and loaded them onto waiting oxcarts. All were skeleton thin; most were barefoot and wearing only G-strings. The Rangers managed to get them clear of the camp and to the banks of the Pampanga River within forty-five minutes.

The surprise attack was a devastating victory. In the process, about 220 Japanese Army prison guards were killed; Pajota's guerrillas destroyed four tanks and blocked and killed hundreds of enemy troops who tried to cross the blown-up bridge on his side of the roadblock. Joson's contingent faced little problem on their side—the guerrillas provided rear support as the Rangers led the sickly POWs north to safety in a train of fifty-one water buffalo carts. The POWs arrived at an American field hospital at Guimba the following day, January 31, at midday. None of the prisoners was hurt during the rescue—one died of a heart attack, another of a lingering illness along the road to safety. Two American soldiers died, and four were wounded; no guerrillas were killed, but twenty of Pajota's guerrillas were injured.

The rescue was a prototype for lightning operations beyond Japanese lines to rescue prisoners and detainees. General MacArthur ordered Major General Verne D. Mudge, division commander in the 1st Cavalry Division, to race ahead to Manila. A series of "flying columns" would cross Japanese lines to liberate Santo Tomas, Los Baños, Bilibid, and, not least, the women's prison at Mandaluyong that housed Claire and her cell mates.

Liberation
University of Santo Tomas, Manila, February 3, 1945

CARL MYDANS, the *Life* magazine photographer, had seen the war from many sides in the two and a half years since he had left Santo Tomas for the Asian mainland. After Manila he had been held as a prisoner of the Japanese outside Shanghai until the fall of 1943. He and his wife, Shelley, got back to the United States in December 1943 via the SS *Gripsholm*, about sixteen months after the Swedish ship had participated in the first prisoner exchange from the Philippines, when Chick Parsons and his family had taken the same route from Manila to China and onward around the Horn of Africa to New York. Only weeks after his return to the United States, *Life* magazine sent Mydans to the European theater. He went along on the Allied march northward from Sicily to retake Italy, then to Marseille in August 1944, two months after the D-Day invasion. However, when his editors in New York heard in September about the imminent return of General MacArthur to the Philippines, they told Mydans to make his way back to Asia.

Mydans caught airplanes westward to Pearl Harbor, from Kwajalein to Saipan, and then to Tacloban, the capital of Leyte, arriving days after MacArthur waded ashore. After experiencing the first tentative scent of victory along with the men of Krueger's Sixth Army, he knew the road north to Manila was for the taking. "As the year closed, our forces drove up the steaming valleys of Leyte and converged on the last strongholds of the enemy," he wrote. "The Japanese had thrown one-fifth of their total Philippines forces and the last of their great fleet into the fight for Leyte—and they had lost."

He went north to Lingayen for the Sixth Army landing there, then doubled back with other correspondents in a jeep past Camp O'Donnell and Cabanatuan just days after Lieutenant Colonel Mucci and his men rescued the remaining prisoners. From there he signed on with the mission that meant most to him—the liberation of Santo Tomas.

Mydans rolled with the 8th Cavalry as they raced in from Cabanatuan, skirting past Bataan on the route that Peggy and her helpers had taken, along the path Claire had followed from the hills in the early days of the Japanese occupation. Guided by Filipino guerrillas, the American troops drove through enemy territory and reached Santo Tomas on the evening of February 3. About four dozen Japanese guards had barricaded themselves in the education building with about two hundred internees. After an overnight stalemate, U.S. officers negotiated a deal in which the hostages would be released in return for safe passage for the still-armed Japanese guards away from the university in the direction of their own lines. As agreed, the prisoners were released and the Japanese soldiers marched out the front gate while American soldiers stood by. The Americans met their part of the bargain, but Filipino guerrillas lay in wait several blocks away; they blasted and wiped out the Japanese contingent when it turned the corner.

Mydans had an emotional reunion with his old cell mates and called together many of the prisoners before the university administration building for a group photograph. When the photograph was published in *Life* magazine, a ten-year-old girl saw her own picture. She recalled that a white flag had been raised on the flagpole to replace the Rising Sun. By now the prisoners were standing beneath the Stars and Stripes. The ten-year-old was Joan Bennett. Her father, Roy C. Bennett, her mother, and her sister were nearby.

The detainees were overjoyed and the soldiers were delighted, but they were horrified to see the skeletal figures who had been starving to death inside the Santo Tomas gates. In three years of detention an estimated 10 percent of the four thousand internees at Santo Tomas had died.

The Battle of Manila raged for another month, though life at Santo Tomas had changed. The U.S. troops set up a row of howitzers and machine-gun emplacements looking outward, ready to protect the former detainees against Japanese attack. The university kitchen was still turning out food, but the fare was quite different. Army rations became gourmet dining: The detainees gorged on reconstituted potatoes, canned beef, tasty bread baked fresh by army cooks, cans of fruit, and real coffee. Medics and nurses were warning people to adapt slowly to normal quantities of food, but people made themselves sick by overeating. Others still died from malnutrition and diseases contracted over the months of imprisonment.

General MacArthur delighted in the success of the flying squads. He stopped at Guimba as he moved with his forces south from Lingayen Gulf and met up with the survivors of Cabanatuan, who were now resting and slowly recovering. Days later he entered Manila and showed up at Santo Tomas on Wednesday, February 7, accompanied by top commanders. He moved so quickly that Carl Mydans was himself photographed in the early arrival picture before he could grab his own cameras. MacArthur was inspired by the outpouring from the former internees as soon as he walked through the gate. "In their ragged, filthy clothes, with tears streaming down their faces they seemed to be using their last strength to fight their way close enough to grasp my hand." People alternately wept and laughed and reached toward the center of the circle to touch his jacket, shake his hand, kiss his cheek, and embrace him. "It was a wonderful and never-to-be-forgotten moment—to be a life-saver, not a life-taker."

In typical fashion, MacArthur had led his aides into an active conflict zone with shells exploding and rifle fire heard not far away. Within hours of his visit, Japanese guns lobbed in shells and mortars at the start of four days of battle, damaging the administration and education buildings and the gymnasium. At least seventeen internees died and nine Filipino workers contracted by the army also were killed. Dozens of people were hurt, some gravely. "Dorm rooms became a mass of debris and severed limbs before army squads swiftly came in to rescue and clean up," recalled Rupert Wilkinson, the eight-year-old internee who wrote about his experiences years afterward. Hours after being bold enough to crawl through the crowd and touch MacArthur's sleeve, he witnessed horrifying scenes, people with mortal wounds and gashes lying on bloody stretchers.

A Few More Hours

Mandaluyong Prison, Manila, February 10, 1945

HUDDLED AND STARVED those first days of February, Claire and the other women at the women's prison realized that the Americans were advancing toward them and feared they might end up in the middle of a firefight. They were isolated: They did not see any Japanese soldiers in those final days of imprisonment and could sometimes hear explosions but heard rumors rather than news.

In November 1944 Claire and Maria Martinez had been sentenced to death and had assumed that they would be executed immediately. Instead, Japanese guards had driven them here—the Correctional Institution for Women at Mandaluyong, where they were ordered before a Japanese officer, who said:

> Because of the mercy of His Imperial Highness, the emperor of Japan, your sentence has been commuted to twelve years confinement at hard labor. If you try to escape, your time will be doubled and you will be taken to Japan to finish your sentence. If at any time you wish to retract

your lies, send for a Japanese official. In such event, you may have a new trial, and if the court sees fit, you may be released or pardoned. You are to have no outside contacts. No mail. No visitors. No food sent to you.

Treatment improved immediately—the prison was under the jurisdiction of the Philippine civilian government, although Mrs. Garcia, the warden, said she had no leeway in dealing with Japanese regulations. "I am sorry that you are here, but I'm compelled by the Japanese to treat you military prisoners exactly as they say. You will be treated the same as the rest of the other prisoners. You will receive no special privileges, so don't ask for any." They were assigned to a cell with ten other women, but neither Claire nor Maria complained about physical abuse after that. The sentence of forced labor consisted of clearing stones and weeds in the prison courtyard, and the grounds were subject to inspection by Japanese officials to make sure the women were doing their work. The main problem was food—they were hungry. At first they received the kind of gruel they were accustomed to—"three tablespoonfuls of boiled, dried corn for breakfast. Lunch consisted of thin, soupy rice and half a tin of boiled weeds and then at five p.m. a cup of thin boiled rice."

Then, despite the Japanese prohibition, the women were able to receive food from the outside—Maria, apparently with the help of bribes, had been able to get messages to her mother and sister. Claire contacted Fely and Judge Roxas, who used contacts inside the prison and were able to smuggle in food as well. However, both Maria and Claire sniped, each claiming that the other was hoarding food and not giving it to anyone else. The women were arguing and grating on each other. Everything seemed to center on food supplies. Claire called one of the women in her cell a kleptomaniac who stole food from her neighbor's plate if she wasn't watching.

Maria said she herself did share with Claire but that Claire would not share. "Many times we would find food under her bed," Maria complained. For her part, Claire claimed that she received little of the food that the judge and her other friends were trying to send in. Maria agreed with her on that. "The guards practically stole two thirds of what was supposed to be brought in."

Once, when Claire was able to get a little package from Fely, she opened it to find one thousand pesos, which were not worth very much because of rampant inflation, and cigarettes, but no food. Fely wrote that the people of Manila were also starving. "We are subsisting on coconuts and boiled talinum [a green leafy tropical vegetable] ourselves."

Claire, Maria, and the others at the women's prison were hungry too, but they also were relieved that the worst of their imprisonment seemed to be over. The Filipino prison guards were kindly and no Japanese had shown up for some time. The prisoners at Mandaluyong could feel that liberation was near. Once they realized they had survived, Maria complained that Claire was starting to brag as if she were a big shot. "She had convinced a number of the other prisoners that she was going to do great things for them in the future and they fawned on her."

Those petty rivalries were pushed aside in anticipation of freedom. Japanese troops had withdrawn from some parts of the city, but others fought on. Japanese artillery units were firing from the southwest bank of the Pasig River in the Santa Ana district, less than a mile from the women's prison. Explosions and gunfire reverberated almost nonstop. The U.S. Army was fighting its way north toward Mandaluyong; the prison was not far from where Claire had once shared a house with her husband Manuel L. Fuentes. Other American units were encountering heavy fighting in the direction of Los Baños, where remaining detainees had been sent from Santo Tomas more than a year earlier.

On Saturday, February 10, a unit of the 1st Cavalry, nicknamed the Texas Rangers and led by Lieutenant Colonel Charles Young, made it to the prison gates without enemy resistance. The priest who ministered to the inmates ran into the courtyard, shouting: "I have seen the *americanos* with my own eyes. . . . They are here!" Claire and Maria and the others decided to wait in their cells rather than risk gun battles. Claire said she hid under the bed for a while and tore her prison dress in the process. Within minutes, American soldiers were standing in the courtyard. She wrapped herself in a blanket and ran outside. "There stood ten of the tallest Yanks I had ever seen! I rushed up to the nearest soldier and timidly touched his arm." When the soldier smiled, she planted a kiss right on his lips.

"Yes, I'm real," he said.

Colonel Young and his men carried Claire and the others to their jeeps and drove to Santo Tomas, which was still in a battle zone, but now guarded and safer than it had been in the first days after liberation. "We drove along the smoke-clouded, traffic-infested highways threading our way through a maze of tanks, trucks, and military vehicles on their way to the rapidly changing front. It was not a tranquil ride for the ping of sniper bullets, the staccato chatter of machine guns, and the burping of mortars came from all directions."

American units encountered an outpouring of spontaneous celebration as they headed across the Pasig River. Residents in the Santa Ana neighborhood across the river ran out to the street, cheering. A priest at the Santa Ana parish church climbed the church tower and rang the church bells for the first time in seven months. "People on the streets cheered when they heard the familiar chimes once more," said Marcial Lichauco, who lived in the neighborhood. "Those who went inside . . . to say a prayer of thanksgiving wept copiously as they knelt before the high altar."

"Manila Is Finished, Completely Demolished"
Manila, February 12, 1945

PRAYERS OF THANKSGIVING became entreaties for survival. Fires roared across the bay front along the Port of Manila, and mortars blasted the battlements of old Intramuros. After the brief, teasing notion that Manila had survived, the city collapsed into suicidal chaos. The Japanese Fourteenth Army commander, General Tomoyuki Yamashita, had ordered withdrawal from the city, but he could not control other commands, notably the Japanese Navy, which decided to defend the city with more than sixteen thousand ill-trained fighters.

U.S. troops could not force the surrender of several thousand of the Japanese troops, who were holed up at Intramuros. U.S. commanders set up loudspeakers and blasted demands that the enemy soldiers give up. When that failed, the U.S. commanders ordered a massive artillery attack on the old city. Japanese units had also set up positions behind the Philippine General Hospital and lobbed shells from behind the hospital toward American positions. "For five days seven thousand civilians and several hundred patients were thus isolated within the walls." Survivors testified that some Japanese soldiers executed civilians, raped women, and burned people alive.

In the two weeks after the liberation of Santo Tomas, the Americans fought the Japanese street by street, building by building. They drove the Japanese out of Malacañang Palace, fought them at the Manila Hotel and in downtown business districts. Sometimes the fighting was floor to floor. For a time U.S. troops held the main floor of the Manila Hotel but the Japanese launched sniper fire from the upper floors. Japanese and U.S. troops fought back and forth to retake city hall four separate times.

Remaining Japanese troops huddled in Intramuros and other pockets of hopeless resistance. Desperate and unyielding, they began demolition of military facilities that devolved into wider destruction. They committed reprisals and random executions of civilians in Intramuros and elsewhere downtown. There were deaths even among the former detainees at Santo Tomas in the days after the cavalry ousted their Japanese guards. The Japanese standoff against 35,000 well-equipped U.S. soldiers and 3,000 guerrillas devolved into a month of unimaginable carnage. When it was over, most of the Japanese troops had died and more than 1,000 U.S. troops had been killed. An estimated 100,000 Filipinos were dead. Manila, the Pearl of the Orient, had steadily been stripped of its remaining glory—three years of occupation, hunger, dehumanization, decay, and the underlying horror of the conflagration to come. By March 3, 1945, the city had been flattened and the Pearl was gone.

The business district was dust and cinders, and the smell of rotting flesh permeated the streets. The Malate and Ermita districts, where the Japanese had set up barriers, were hard hit—they torched buildings as they retreated. Father John Lalor, who had worked with Claire, Peggy, and Ramón, had been killed during a shelling on February 13. As they destroyed local infrastructure, Japanese troops left whole neighborhoods without water, food, or housing. The two-story Tsubaki Club building on Mabini Street was gone; all that remained was rubble behind a rough-hewn fence.

On February 22, 1945, even as fighting raged elsewhere, General Douglas MacArthur raised the American flag over the U.S. embassy on Manila Bay, recovered after a two-day battle with the Japanese. Fires smoldered, battles still raged, and the U.S. forces faced no alternative but to answer the Japanese gunfire with howitzers.

In one of the final entries of his war diary, Marcial Lichauco described the drive from his home in Santa Ana to survey the damage. "As far as they could see every direction nothing was visible except the remains of what had once been thousands of residential houses. Here and there were reinforced concrete buildings which had not collapsed but their interiors were so gutted by fire that they were no longer habitable. Most of the time I had to hold a handkerchief to my nose for the stench of the dead, soldier and civilian, was unbearable. Driving along Tennessee Street our chauffeur had to maneuver his way around to avoid running over dismembered pieces of a human body which lay scattered in the middle of the street."

MacArthur called it all a waste of humanity with no purpose: "a desperate element of the enemy entrapped by our encirclement [that] fought to the death." The scale of urban destruction in the capital of the Philippines was a singular horror, rivaling the lethal battle for Warsaw, comparable to the firebombings of Dresden and Tokyo. Buildings that had not been bombed in the U.S. assault to retake the islands were destroyed by the Japanese as they often fought to the death. The Sixth U.S. Army continued sweep-up operations on Japanese holdouts throughout February. The port area was secured by the end of the month. Finally the bloody siege of Manila was declared over on March 3.

Chick Parsons stood silent sentinel in the remains of the city. Parsons, suffering from the effects of malaria and from general exhaustion, had been rotated out of the Philippines after conducting his ground operation in advance of the October 20 landing at Leyte Gulf. After two months with his family in the United States, he was back in the Philippines by January, conducting raids with guerrilla groups to root out remaining Japanese strongholds. In February he returned to Manila and set out in search of clues to the whereabouts of his mother-in-law, Blanche Jurika. It was hard to find clues or even gather information amid the devastation.

"Manila is finished, completely demolished," he wrote in a letter from those days.

I have seen sights that I shall remember a long time. I arrived on the heels of the Yanks as they pushed the enemy down the Boulevard toward the Luneta, and visited the house of a good friend, Don Carlos

Perez Rubio, a wealthy Spanish-Filipino. In the garden of the house, I counted twenty-two bodies—the entire family including women and children, three people who were visiting at the time, and servants— liquidated in a most brutal fashion. Bayonets mostly. A number of my other friends have suffered a like fate. Such sights give me a feeling of satisfaction at having been in a small part connected with the elimination of a few Nips here and there. I could never feel conscience-stricken after viewing some of the results of Jap atrocities in Manila.

He kept searching for Blanche. The last word about her had come months earlier: She had been detained at Fort Santiago. He then got a tip that she might have been taken to Mandaluyong. One report said that she had been taken from the prison just before the invasion of Manila. It would be months before Chick found out that was not true. For now, however, he feared the worst. "I am afraid she has paid heavily for being my mother-in-law." He found out much later that he was right: She had been executed and decapitated in late August 1944 by the Kempeitai at the Chinese Cemetery in Manila.

The Wounds of War
Manila, March 3, 1945

CLAIRE WAS ADMITTED to a hospital soon after she arrived at Santo Tomas. She said doctors treated her for anemia, scurvy, and skin infections. She said she weighed ninety-five pounds, less than she had after her ulcer surgery and bout with tetanus a year and a half earlier. An Associated Press report on the liberation of the women's prison had singled her out as an underground operative freed by U.S. Army cavalrymen. She was identifying herself as Claire Mabel Phillips, the widowed wife of John V. Phillips of the 31st Infantry. She was no longer Dorothy or Dot Fuentes or Claire De La Taste, nor was she Madame Tsubaki or any of her previous aliases. The army offered to airlift her to Tacloban and from there directly to the United States by plane. She declined because she had not yet heard from Peggy and Dian. She did, however, ask help from the Red Cross to send letters to her mother and to John Phillips's mother, Vada Phillips.

The army also delivered a surprise—a letter from Manuel Fuentes. He was very much alive, having been with the navy throughout the war, and was now hoping to reunite.

Once the fighting in Manila was over, the army gave Peggy and Dian a ride down to Manila from Bataan. Peggy sought out Claire with mixed emotions—she loved Dian, now five years old, but the foster child deserved to be with her mother. Peggy found Claire in the hospital at Santo Tomas, waiting with the other Americans there for word about when they could return to the States. The reunion of the three of them was difficult—they had not been together since Claire had been arrested ten months earlier. Claire was upset that Dian once again did not recognize her. It took a day before the little girl tentatively held Claire's hand and said, "Are you my Mummy?" The reunion, Peggy said, "proved to be harder for all of us than I had anticipated. You cannot take care of a child for so long a time without coming to love it, and I hated to let Dian go."

Sometime days after that, Claire asked Peggy to drive with Fely up to Quezon City to retrieve papers and valuables they had hidden with Fely's father, Vicente Corcuera. The papers included receipts both from the club and from Claire's guerrilla activities, money, letters from prisoners, and—almost definitely—Claire's diary. The documents were in several narrow-necked jars buried in Vicente Corcuera's yard. Fely said there were dozens of receipts from Boone and lists of men who had received supplies at Cabanatuan, Park Avenue School, and Bilibid Prison. Peggy looked over the paperwork; she delivered papers and documents to Claire back at Santo Tomas, along with several thousand dollars in old pesos still negotiable at the bank.

It was now safer to travel around Manila, but Peggy said she carried a sidearm and wore a drab blouse and skirt given to her by the Red Cross, just in case. One day Claire asked her to check out Tsubaki Club to see what she could find. Peggy went to the site with Dale Risdon, an Army Signal Corps photographer, who took a picture. The two-story building was blown to rubble. Some of the fence was still intact and the Tsubaki Club sign was still there. Peggy stood on the crumbled sidewalk just in front of the double wooden fence. Above the gated entrance was a semicircular iron framework with the remains of a lantern. Fastened between the top of the wooden portion of the gate and the metal frame was a five-foot sign with white lettering on a dark background, reading TSUBAKI CLUB.

Peggy turned her head to the left over her shoulder, looking directly at the camera. She wore sturdy shoes and a calf-length skirt. She carried a bag in her left hand that might have covered her sidearm. Her hair was straight and long; wire-rimmed sunglasses obscured her eyes. It was the last picture ever taken of Tsubaki Club—a bittersweet memory for them all. Claire had been too weak to go there herself.

PART FOUR

. . .

Fame

Claire's Recovery

University of Santo Tomas, Manila, March 1945

EVEN IN THE HOSPITAL, suffering from malnutrition, injuries from torture, and most likely the disease that would one day become known as post-traumatic stress disorder, Claire began to tell the story that would make her famous. Frederick C. Painton, a veteran freelance war correspondent, came to visit her. Painton had covered the North African campaign, the Allied landing at Anzio, and the invasion of France. He arrived in the Pacific for MacArthur's landing and followed U.S. forces into Manila, where he hoped to develop a first-person story about prisoners and internees of the Japanese. Claire was a perfect subject for an account of surviving the occupation.

Claire described how Judge Roxas had warned her against guerrilla activities but she opened Tsubaki Club anyway and began spying on Japanese officers. She related the story of the Sally Rand dance and how she, Fely, and the other hostesses fought sexual abuse by their Japanese customers. She played down the idea that she or the others were sleeping with Japanese soldiers. The Japanese "first wanted to make me and the hostesses their concubines or mistresses. I would insist this was not *that* [italics in original] kind of a place. Some girls were beaten and I was slapped for our refusal. Gradually, however, as I built up a clientele of high-ranking Japanese, this trouble ceased." She proclaimed that John Phillips was her husband, described the supply operation to Cabanatuan, and told about torture at the hands of Japanese interrogators after her arrest on May 24, 1944. "I was stretched out, bound hand and foot, head tied rigidly. Suddenly a garden hose was held to my mouth and nostrils. This was the water treatment and it is just like drowning, only more horrifying."

Painton wrote up his piece and sent it off to his editors. Claire, meanwhile, had to realize that her story was about to be published nationwide, declaring to the world for the first time that she was the widow of John Phillips. She wrote a second letter on March 10, 1945, to Phillips's mother, telling her this time that she had left something out. "I didn't tell you in my first letter that I was his wife. I thought it best to let you get over the first shock; first . . . we were married in Bataan at the outbreak of the war here."

Painton's story was published in the May 1945 issue of *American Mercury*, a magazine founded by H. L. Mencken and now owned and edited by Lawrence Spivak, later well known in his own right as the founding producer and moderator of the television program *Meet the Press*. Neither Spivak, one of the great journalists of his time, nor Painton, respected among his peers as a fearless, diligent correspondent, had the ability to fact-check or any reason to doubt this portrait of an American war heroine. The first-person account, "I Was an American Spy," was one of Painton's last dispatches. Six weeks after he sent in the story, Painton collapsed and died of a heart attack at an airstrip in Guam as he covered the predawn departure of a B-29 bombing mission bound for Japan.

Aboard the SS <u>John Lykes</u>
Manila Harbor, April 2, 1945

IT WAS SEVERAL weeks before the U.S. command could declare that the Port of Manila and Manila Bay were safe enough for ships to come in and collect passengers to carry them back home. Claire, Dian, and Peggy were among five hundred civilians—most of them survivors of Santo Tomas—and five hundred soldiers who left port on Monday, April 2, aboard the SS *John Lykes*, a medium-sized merchant cargo ship that had been leased during the war as a troop transport. Roy C. Bennett's wife and two daughters were also on the ship. Bennett remained in a hospital in Manila for several months more. The destination was Honolulu and onward to Los Angeles, but the route home was complicated. Allied forces had just invaded Okinawa, about 925 miles to the north, the start of what would be a two-and-a-half-month siege. So the *Lykes* was escorted far south to New Guinea, then cut a wide circle before heading north beyond the range of any possible remaining Japanese warships or submarines. The month-long journey was not always peaceful—drills and alarm bells sounded from time to time and reminded passengers that the war was still on.

Simmering hostility between Claire and Peggy boiled over during the voyage, though the exact source was never clear. There were elements of old jealousy—it might have been about the quick notoriety Claire had received within days of rescue; or the fact that Claire had always been favored by men and Peggy, forty-four and only seven years older than Claire, was nicknamed "the old lady"; or that Peggy was angry that she had to give up Dian, whom she dearly loved. Claire, on the other hand, could have been angry that Peggy had been recognized as a guerrilla officer, was allowed to parade around in a uniform, and was entitled to salary and benefits.

Many people on the ship noticed that the women were bickering and arguing. Then the sniping went public. Claire marched up to the captain of the *John Lykes* one day and told him someone had entered her cabin, rifled through papers in her room, and stolen some receipts and paperwork, while not taking money or other valuables.

The captain was dubious but reported the charge to two FBI agents who were on board checking out the passengers as part of wartime surveillance operations. The FBI agents, Royal L. Stauffer and S. Charles Straus, learned that the U.S. immigration agent also on the ship already had questions for Claire. While many of the passengers did not have ready proof of citizenship, Claire did have a passport. However, the document was mutilated and the photograph had been defaced. Claire explained that the passport had been buried for a year and that her daughter, Dian, had torn up the passport photo while she was playing with it. Whatever name had originally been on the passport, it could not have been Phillips, which was Claire's current stage name. She had not adopted the name until she met John Phillips, and no one was issuing U.S. passports in Manila during the war.

The FBI agents saw Claire not as a heroine but as a stumbling, devious subject and had suspicions about the confusing versions of her life. Others on the ship, meanwhile, told them she had been going around bragging about her wartime exploits and implied that she herself was working with the FBI. The agents wondered why someone would rob papers and receipts without stealing money that was also right there.

"The subject related a fantastic story which had many discrepancies," the agents said in a report for their investigation. "She also had considerable money in her possession which she could not satisfactorily explain as to how she came into possession of it."

On repeated questioning, Claire acknowledged that she had never formally married John Phillips but claimed she had planned to do so after the war. She may also have implicated Peggy in the theft. They also interviewed

Peggy, who apparently came across as serious and believable. Peggy dismissed Claire as a minor participant in the POW smuggling operation. She said Claire had told her that she had never intended to marry Phillips but was now thinking about claiming widow's compensation from the army. She also charged that Claire had been arrested not because of her underground activities but on civil morals charges. Everyone in town knew, Peggy said, that Claire had been sleeping with a married bar owner down the street from Tsubaki Club, Ramón Infante, and that Ramón's wife had informed on her to the Japanese.

That charge was dubious—Claire had been held originally as a military prisoner and had been sentenced to hard labor for crimes against the state. Claire acknowledged that she was friends with Ramón Infante, but only because he was contributing to the guerrilla supply operations. But Infante's wife, Emma, Claire said, was sleeping with a Japanese colonel. When Emma intercepted a message from Claire to Infante, she interpreted it as a secret love letter. Claire said it was a coded underground message. Emma handed information to her Japanese officer lover about Claire, which added to the case against her. Claire's claims could later be proved, at least in part. Emma Infante was arrested by U.S. Army counterintelligence agents on April 10, 1945, on a charge of "active collaboration with the Japanese." The agents spoke to Yay Panlilio, who had been a guerrilla in the Luzon hills alongside Hugh Straughn and Ed Ramsey. Panlilio, en route to Washington on assignment for the newly restored Philippine government, also said Claire had been boasting about her exploits, but she had tried to avoid speaking with her.

Claire told agents Stauffer and Straus she had returned home in 1941 to obtain a Nevada divorce from Manuel Fuentes and had managed to do so. She waffled, though, on whether she was really married to John Phillips. The agents noted, meanwhile, that Claire was carrying a life insurance policy in the name of Mabel C. Enette, which gave an indication that she possibly had never divorced Joe Enette back in Seattle.

The final report by the FBI agents itself had mistakes, spelling errors of proper names, and wrong dates. It was understandable that the agents chose to believe what Peggy said, rather than Claire's version, although they had no factual basis while on the ship to know whether either woman had ever worked for the Manila underground. The two Los Angeles–based FBI agents concluded in their report that Claire was weaving "a fantastic story of her activities while in the Philippines which had many discrepancies." However, they disposed of the matter upon arriving in port. "No further investigation is being conducted in this office," they wrote, "and this matter is being referred to the Office of Origin [Portland]." Based on their report, though, FBI director J. Edgar Hoover authorized an investigation of whether Claire had collaborated with Japanese occupation officials in the Philippines and whether she had committed fraud and lied during interviews with immigration officials.

Public Affairs
Wilmington Harbor, Los Angeles, May 2, 1945

CLAIRE, PEGGY, and the other passengers of the SS *John Lykes* returned to the United States on May 2, 1945, in an atmosphere of war-weary triumph. Adolf Hitler had committed suicide on April 30, Nazi Germany was in its death throes, and Americans were looking for heroes. The latest edition of the *American Mercury* was on the street and an Army Public Affairs officer was on hand looking for Claire when the ship docked at Wilmington south of Los Angeles. Peggy was already irritated with Claire when they arrived, but the star treatment Claire received must have rankled. The army officer said news outlets were clamoring to speak with her about her experiences. Her story appeared on network radio and in national gossip columns. After playing bit parts in road shows around the Pacific Northwest before the war, Claire had never made it in show business. FBI doubts notwithstanding, she was now returning to the United States as a celebrity.

Red Cross relief personnel met the civilian passengers. The refugees each received vouchers for hotel rooms, money to buy food and clothing, and free phone calls to contact home. "I believe it was seventy-five dollars we could buy in clothing for an adult, like myself, for instance, and a fifty dollars' requisition for a child," Claire recalled. "That was so we would have decent clothing to go home in and meet our families."

A day or two after arrival, Claire visited a downtown Los Angeles airline office to see if she could book a flight to Portland. "Just as I was getting into the limousine in front of the airplane office, I saw him"—it was

Manuel Fuentes, who had gotten word that she was on the ship's manifest and had come to persuade her to take another shot at their marriage. Somewhat surprisingly, Claire said yes. "I tried to make a go of it, I thought maybe I could." After the Portland visit, the Fuentes family—Claire, Manuel, and Dian—moved into a house they bought at 448 Madrid Street in San Francisco's Excelsior District. The other passengers, meanwhile, dispersed to their hometowns or built new lives. Peggy was bound for Washington, DC. She and Claire did not remain in contact.

Claire was soon meeting with film executives and potential ghostwriters to tell the fuller version of her story. On June 17, 1945, she appeared on the popular CBS radio program *I Was There*, which dramatized and retold her first-person account. At the end of the dramatization, Claire was interviewed by Chet Huntley, live in a studio in San Francisco.

Huntley: Mrs. Phillips, what happened after you were sentenced to be shot as a spy?

Mrs. P: I was taken to Bilibid Prison and thrown on the floor. There I lay for day after day, waiting to be shot, but still the Japs didn't come after me. Then, to my amazement, I was taken out for a new trial. The charge this time was not espionage but "acts harmful to the Imperial Japanese Government."

Huntley: How do you account for the new trial?

Mrs. P: I don't know for certain—except that the Japs apparently had no idea I was sending information to the guerrillas. They just thought I was smuggling food and medicine into the Cabanatuan prison. Anyway, I was sentenced to twenty years' hard labor.

Huntley: And you were put back in prison?

Mrs. P: Yes. Then came the blessed day, February 10, 1945. The helmeted American boys came in. I went forth barefooted and ragged but happy in my liberation and in the hope of seeing my Dian and my native land again. That's my story, Mr. Huntley—I was there.

The war in the Pacific was over before the end of the summer, with a series of events more shocking than the attack on Pearl Harbor less than four years earlier. The United States dropped atomic bombs on Hiroshima and Nagasaki in August, and the Japanese war machine was halted. Even before Japan's formal surrender on September 2, 1945, before General MacArthur on the USS *Missouri* in Tokyo Bay, American publishers and filmmakers craved stories of heroism during the war.

Claire was already shopping her tale—the memoir of an American spy: how she fought for love and country against the Japanese occupation of Manila. She soon landed a book contract with a small publisher in Portland. All the while, FBI officials were monitoring Claire's activities and continuing to reject anything Claire said and to accept Peggy's version at face value.

By the end of 1945, Claire was at work on her memoir, collaborating first with a woman named Cunningham, who helped mold the story and conduct background research. That version did not make the grade. The publishers in Portland, Binfords & Mort, wanted more flash. Myron B. Goldsmith, based in San Francisco, was hired as the new ghostwriter. He "dressed up" the story, promising to make it sellable. In other words, Claire admitted, he exaggerated some parts and twisted the truth for the sake of a good story. "He elaborated on some of the scenes [and] made it more dramatic," she said. "I can say that it is actually true, the facts are, but he, as I say, dramatized on some of them." Claire received a small advance and was looking forward to making more money from a movie. With few prospects in the working world, it was by far the best deal Claire could imagine.

The publisher approved this second draft and the book, *Manila Espionage*, was distributed nationwide by William Morrow and Company in the first half of 1947. Peggy certainly would have noticed that she was hardly mentioned, and even then not by name—she was referred to as "auntie," likely the name by which little Dian knew her during the war. As the central character, Claire was the ringleader, and Tsubaki Club was the site of clandestine meetings that might not have actually taken place. In the book version, Claire controlled Naomi's shipments to Cabanatuan. Ramón and Lorenza Amusategui and all the others were bit players. None of the survivors was going to be very happy with her version of events. John Boone was an exception. He was on convalescent leave in California in 1945 after leaving Bataan and would soon revert from major in the U.S. Army guerrilla forces to sergeant in the regular U.S. Army. He provided a foreword to *Manila Espionage* in which he wrote: "I wish to state that all the facts in it of which I have any personal knowledge are, to the best of my belief, true and properly expressed."

Claire's growing celebrity started to gnaw at the other surviving members of their underground operation in Manila. Lorenza, for one, was disgusted. She also was considering writing a book that would tell the story of the underground and would not be a memoir. She was talking about the possibility of collaboration with a cousin by marriage, Oliver La Farge, the prolific author whose book *Laughing Boy* had won the Pulitzer Prize in 1930. La Farge had also been a major in the Army Air Forces during the war and had worked with military intelligence. "Oh boy, what a bunch of lies," she told La Farge. "So-called Claire Phillips has written a book through some ghostwriter of course (she can hardly write a letter, much less a book). . . . I would very much like to see the old woman's [Peggy's] face when she reads it."

Mention of Peggy's face was more to the point than Lorenza realized. In Claire's book, opposite page 27, the publisher had printed the photograph of Peggy standing in front of Tsubaki Club. However, in the print they used, Peggy's face had been sliced off and replaced with an outsized photograph of Claire's face pasted on top of Peggy's body. "From the neck down, it is me," Peggy said. "And from the neck up, it is Dorothy [Claire]. . . . You can tell by her height and by my height that if that were she, her head would be up to the top of the fence." Not my fault, Claire said later, although she did not block publication of the fake photograph. She explained that when she was ill and in the hospital after her February 10, 1945, rescue from prison, she had asked the army photographer, Dale Risdon, to send her a picture of Peggy in Manila as a remembrance. "When I asked her and Dale to get the picture, I didn't ask her to stand in front of the club." Now that she had the photograph and the publisher was asking for one, it ended up being useful. "He wanted a picture of the club with me standing in front of it, and the only picture I had was of Mrs. Utinsky standing in front of it, and he said, 'we can put your head over her head,' and he said, 'it will look as if it were you standing there.'" For years the altered picture, wrongly attributed to the National Archives, was republished in partly unsubstantiated accounts of Claire's life.

Claire's book became the basis for most of what was known about her and her life before, during, and after the war. Her ghostwriter made his own voice and dramatic intentions immediately obvious in the text. Why was Claire involved in the resistance? "Bill Shakespeare said that 'all the world's a stage' and maybe I was not fond of sitting in the wings, so for some unexplainable reason the States soon lost their lure for me." It was unlikely that Claire herself was going to be quoting good ol' Bill Shakespeare in that way.

Some details in the book contradicted other accounts and facts and others were simply implausible. Claire claimed that she was able to observe part of the Bataan death march, which began on April 9, 1942. Her diary made no mention of that, and the march took place along the eastern coast of Bataan from Mariveles northward, many miles from the Sobreviñas family camp in the hills beyond Dinalupihan. Claire also claimed that she was in touch with Colonel Hugh Straughn and sent supplies to him. She said he wrote a note to her calling himself "just a tired old man." It is possible, but not provable based on John Boone's testimony at the Court of Claims and his letters to Claire during the war. Boone did say in his letter to her in June 1944 that he had put her in touch with other guerrilla commanders besides him. Claire also claimed that Colonel Akira Nagahama stopped in at the club the same day that Straughn was executed at the Chinese Cemetery in Manila and claimed to have fired the coup de grâce. There is no evidence that Nagahama ever went to Tsubaki Club or that he would admit the execution of Straughn by his own hand. In any case, Claire would not have been at the club to see him even if he had been there that night. In the book, Nagahama is quoted in stereotypic racially tinged language: "'See dis hand,' he boasted, 'Dis is hand dat used gun on him in Chinese cemetery.'" This is unlikely on several counts. First, Straughn was executed alongside Colonel Thorp on or about October 5, while Claire was in the hospital in and out of consciousness after contracting tetanus following ulcer surgery. There are eyewitness accounts from the cemetery, none of which mentions the presence of Nagahama or an officer having fired a coup de grâce after the prisoners were executed by firing squad. Meanwhile, Nagahama was on trial for war crimes in Manila in 1946 as Goldsmith was ghostwriting Claire's story. Reports of the trial were in the newspaper, and it would have been easy to pile more charges on the accusations against Nagahama. The Straughn case did not come up in the war crimes testimony against Nagahama, who was characterized as a reticent person who let others carry out his orders, though he was not always in control of their actions. It does not appear in character for him to have gotten drunk in public nor to have confessed to murder at Tsubaki Club.

Safe at Home
Los Angeles, 1947

THE FBI TOOK more than a year to complete its investigation of Claire's activities. While finding her statements questionable, the Bureau was convinced that she had not been a collaborator, as implied by Peggy's statements. Claire was indeed a loyal American citizen and had worked for the underground, and there was no evidence she had provided information to the Japanese. The original charge was probably based on gossip: Peggy and the other women had seen Claire consorting with Japanese officers in Manila. While the women knew nothing themselves about Claire's spying mission and the means to which they resorted to gather intelligence, her actions were endorsed by John Boone during and after the war. Boone trusted her, even though he criticized some of what she said. If she had been a double agent, the entire operation could have been swallowed up quite early and easily by the Kempeitai—Boone and his lieutenants included. J. Edgar Hoover did not pursue such unfounded charges, but he did send a letter to Claire telling her never again to claim to be working for the Federal Bureau of Investigation.

In the months after the war, both Claire and Peggy made formal requests to the government for restitution of funds they spent during the Japanese occupation of Manila. A private bill passed Congress in 1946 to award Peggy $9,280 ($87,000 in 2017 dollars) and she received the Presidential Medal of Freedom on October 17, 1946. The awarding of restitution was based on an uncontested list Peggy provided of household items and goods she said she had sold in Manila to finance her supply operation to POWs from 1942 to 1944.

Lorenza Amusategui and her husband, Ramón (posthumously), Naomi Flores, Maria Martinez, and many of their colleagues in the Manila underground also received the Medal of Freedom, an honor created by President Harry S Truman in 1945 to recognize civilian contributions to the war effort. Claire had not yet received the honor.

Claire actually had more backup expense details than Peggy did. She applied on February 6, 1946, seeking $15,000 restitution from the War Department for providing support to Boone and the Bataan guerrillas, also providing a list of expenses. The department denied her claim on December 6, 1946, on a technicality—that Boone's guerrillas were not officially recognized as part of the Philippine Army until 1945. That technicality was grossly unfair—Boone and tens of thousands of Americans and Filipinos were operating in the hills, sanctioned by MacArthur and supported by Chick Parsons as his surrogate.

Problems like this increased as the government began to limit its liability after the war. President Truman had signed the so-called Rescission Act of 1946, which retroactively took away millions of dollars in payments due the estimated 250,000 Filipinos who fought on the U.S. side against the Japanese, both in the regular army throughout the Pacific and as guerrillas in their own country. As claims for war restitution poured into the Truman administration, members of Congress were concerned that not all claims were legitimate. Senate and House bills on Claire's behalf to award her $6,000 in compensation for support to the guerrillas were introduced in Congress on May 15, 1947, and August 2, 1948, but both failed passage. Claire's chance of receiving any payment worsened more on July 3, 1948, when President Truman created the War Claims Commission. While Truman said he hoped that the government would now sort out legitimate payments "at the earliest opportunity," the measure froze all payments for a year as the new commission analyzed existing claims. The sheer number of requests for restitution was so great that the army and the War Claims Commission began to follow stringent guidelines for issuing payment and for doing anything that might establish a precedent for future claims. As a result, the atmosphere for approving claims and private congressional bills was much worse than it had been when Peggy's private bill breezed through congressional passage. Claire by then had hired attorneys in Portland, and Senator Wayne Morse of Oregon filed a resolution on her behalf in the Senate, and Claire was now asking for additional reimbursement for money spent in supporting both the guerrillas and POWs. The purpose of the resolution was to ask the

U.S. Court of Claims to conduct a hearing into the facts surrounding Claire's claim. Claire appeared at a brief hearing in Washington on October 2, 1951. Her attorneys had now increased the restitution amount to $50,000. "I do not ask that I be paid for the work I did," she told the Senate Judiciary Committee, "just for the money I spent, my own money."

Privately she knew she might not get the entire $50,000—equivalent in 2017 to almost $500,000—but she asked for backup from her old friends in the Philippines. "I might not get all I am asking for," she wrote to Evangeline Neibert, "in fact they usually cut a bill like that in half or less. But whatever I get, I will share. We used to share, and I believe people should always share. Why should some be rich and some poor?"

Morse promoted Claire's claim and was likely confounded by Congress's failure to pass the bill. He appealed to the patriotism of his fellow members of Congress but now only asked for a hearing resolution, rather than outright issuance of funding. "We are asking only for the right for Mrs. Clavier [Claire] to bring action in federal court and prove her loss," Morse said. "She can tell her own story . . . there is no question but that the story of Mrs. Clavier's life has great impact." Morse's request was approved, setting the stage for a hearing before the U.S. Court of Claims.

About a year after publication of Claire's own book, Peggy told her own story in *Collier's* magazine in 1946. She followed that with a book, *Miss U*, published by the Naylor Company, a regional publishing house based in San Antonio, Texas. Her book did not take off; she did give occasional talks about the book and her experiences, but she had none of Claire's notoriety—nor was a film produced. In the book she got back at Claire by hardly mentioning her, and when she did, awkwardly so. Claire appears a third of the way into the story—as one of the people who contributed to the relief organization that she ran for Cabanatuan, the last in a long list of collaborators and their code names. "Dorothy Claire Fuentes," she wrote, "mother of little Dian—of whom a great deal more later—was called High Pockets." Peggy wrote lovingly of Dian. However, it was the only time Peggy mentioned Claire by name in the book, referring to her once more as an unnamed hospital patient in the fall of 1943 and again as Dian's unnamed mother, who reunited with her after the war. Peggy's book also often ranged into fiction. She glorified her time in the hills in late 1944 and 1945 as if she were a pistol-packing fighter when actually, others said, she had quarreled with the guerrilla leaders around her, and Boone had tried to bust her back to civilian nursing duty. She also implied that she had been the leader of the supply line long after Ramón and Lorenza Amusategui had taken over, fearful that her drunkenness and threatening behavior were dangers to all of them. In addition, she claimed she had been tortured and severely injured. Lorenza said that was not true, that she and Ramón had ransomed Peggy out of jail quickly and that they had seen Peggy hours after her release, none the worse for wear. "She had lost 15 pounds in the 15 days of incarceration, but neither her arms nor her legs bore any marks of the Jap mistreatment," Lorenza reported to U.S. intelligence. "I remember distinctly how on the day of her release, my father, Ramón, my sisters and I commented on her flawless white skin, how that skin would have bruised had the Japs maltreated her." Peggy claimed further in the book that she went to the hospital because of the torture, but Lorenza had direct information that this was also not true. Lorenza's father was the doctor who examined her. The medical treatment was a uterine operation for a preexisting condition unrelated to torture.

Claire's book and popularity overcame FBI questions and criticisms, though several agents saw that a film deal was brewing in Hollywood and wrote complaints in the official investigative file. "She's a prostitute. Got a lot of publicity and is a phony," read one complaint. Nevertheless, on January 23, 1948, less than a year after the book appeared, Claire received word that General MacArthur had awarded her the Presidential Medal of Freedom, the same honor Peggy and her other allies had received in 1946. However, recognition of Claire carried special significance—it specifically mentioned that the commander in chief, Far East, that is, MacArthur, had authorized the award.

Claire had become a media star, whether or not the coverage was flattering. An odd, questionable report about Claire appeared in the national media just before her memoir was turned into a film. She was famous enough that the story went out on the newswires. On January 19, 1949, Claire told the sheriff's office in Vancouver, Washington, that Dian had been kidnapped after school. She said that a man stopped by and told her he was holding Dian for ransom: He demanded Claire's 1947 gray Frazer automobile. Claire, "sobbing and terror-stricken," gave the keys to the man, who then told her, "Your little girl is waiting for you down at the corner." Just as police took evidence and set up a manhunt across the Northwest, nine-year-old Dian ambled home and into the house and said she had come directly from school and "knew nothing of the tall stranger."

Claire's fame crested on March 15, 1950, with the national broadcast of *This Is Your Life*, a popular radio program produced and hosted by Ralph Edwards. The show included a telephone hookup from New York with Carlos Romulo, the Philippine ambassador to the United States. Claire, he said, "at the risk of her life, gave valuable assistance to my countrymen, many of whom were fighting as guerrilla warriors, and to others who were made prisoners by the ruthless Japanese invaders." Fely, who had come to the United States, re-created one of the Japanese folk songs she had sung at Tsubaki Club. Louise DeMartini was there as well. So was Colonel Charles Young, who had rescued Claire from prison. Major General Mark Clark participated via a telephone hookup and praised Claire for heroism, and a former POW rescued from Cabanatuan, Lawrence Courtney, confirmed that Claire had provided aid to the camp. Using Claire's book as a guideline, Edwards went along with Claire's unfounded claim about helping sink "a flotilla" of seventeen Japanese submarines. Anyone familiar with the Pacific campaign knew that Claire had not been able to provide immediate information on submarine movements because the guerrillas did not have direct radio communication from Luzon until late in the war. In any case, there was no record of the United States having destroyed seventeen Japanese submarines traveling in a single convoy.

In a final segment Edwards arranged for impressive gifts. A local developer awarded Claire, Robert Clavier (her new husband), and Dian a new house in a new subdivision outside Portland; the local Jewish Community Center provided furnishings for the house. Herbert Templeton, the chairman of the board at Lewis & Clark College in Portland, awarded Dian, now ten years old, the right to eventually claim a four-year paid scholarship to the school.

PART FIVE

. . .

Telling the Story

I Was an American Spy

Hollywood, 1951

You're about to witness a motion picture story of a woman who performed a magnificent service to her country under hazardous wartime conditions. In time of crisis, she recognized a call to duty and reacted as we hope all Americans will if confronted with similar circumstances. As an underground agent and civilian patriot, she acquitted herself with great courage and made an important contribution to the war effort. Her actions were exemplary and reassuring. To preserve world freedom will require sacrifices and devotion to our cause on the part of every citizen. As we face the task that lies ahead, we may all derive great inspiration from the story of the deeds of this fine American woman.

—MAJOR GENERAL MARK CLARK

WITH THOUGHTS OF WORLD WAR II still fresh, the United States was now fighting a new war in Asia—this time on the Korean peninsula. Veterans who had come home just six years earlier had returned to active duty. Among them was John Boone, who had retired in 1945 and lived for a while back in the Philippines with Mellie and their growing family.

Claire had become the personification of American heroism in the last war. She had finally sold the film rights to *Manila Espionage* and received $1,500 ($13,000 in 2017 dollars) from Allied Artists Pictures. The film went into production quickly, directed by Lesley Selander, a B-movie studio specialist who breezed through the production along with eight other six-week wonders that year, including one science-fiction piece called *Flight to Mars*. Ann Dvorak was cast to play Claire. The film also featured Douglas Kennedy as John Phillips, Gene Evans as Boone, and Richard Loo as a menacing Japanese officer. A precocious six-year-old, golden-curled child actress, Nadine Ashdown, played the part of Dian, erasing the fact that the real Dian was an Asian foster child.

Most unusual was the prologue by Major General Mark Clark, who testified to Claire's valor and served to introduce the drama itself. Clark declared that General MacArthur himself had nominated Claire for the Medal of Freedom. The final scene of the film switched from Ann Dvorak to the "real" Claire Phillips, who stood at attention, back to the camera, wearing a subdued woman's suit of the period, calf-length skirt, high heels, and pocketbook in hand as General Clark faced her and reenacted the ceremony of awarding of the Medal of Freedom. (He had given her the award at a ceremony at Fort Lewis, Washington, on August 19, 1948.) "Yours is a heroism of which all your fellow Americans may well be proud," Clark said. "Your award bearing this citation was recommended by General MacArthur and approved by the President of the United States." It is not clear why Clark would have been chosen to issue the award or appear in the film in the first place. The controversial commander of Allied ground forces in Italy was not accustomed to speaking with the news media, let alone appearing in Hollywood films. He had nothing to do with MacArthur or with the Pacific campaign during the war, though he was appointed in May 1952 (after the film was released) commander in chief, Far East, a post created for MacArthur in 1947 as he supervised the occupation of Japan.

The jingoistic tone, Clark's appearance, and his grave delivery could not be separated from the moment. The United States had entered the battle in Korea in mid-1950, led by General MacArthur, returning as head of the United Nations Command; Senator Joseph P. McCarthy had begun his communist witch hunt. Just six years after World War II, several hundred thousand Americans were now fighting and facing fierce battles with Chinese and Korean communist troops over the 38th parallel that separated North and South Korea. On April 11, 1951, President Harry Truman had dismissed General MacArthur as supreme commander in Korea, an earth-shaking political development. The dismissal was on his disagreement with Truman on Korea policy—MacArthur had publicly criticized Truman, who sought to contain the Korea fighting as a "limited war," rather than risking a much greater world crisis. MacArthur returned home as a hero and on April 19, 1951, gave his valedictory speech before Congress: "Old soldiers never die, they just fade away."

I Was an American Spy opened three weeks after MacArthur's appearance before Congress. The film was based on the fictional persona Claire had created in her book and took off from there. The portrayals were stereotypical and just plain wrong. Claire had become a loving, demure wife and mother; John Phillips was described as a sergeant, not the private he actually had been, with impossible freedom of movement under war conditions. Among other details, Claire's rescue in the film involved a shoot-out between Japanese guards and U.S. soldiers that never took place. Claire traveled with the film to Washington, DC, for its world premiere on May 16, 1951, and then to New York for a showing on July 4. The *New York Times* called the film a "little drama, while occasionally tense, [that] isn't especially stimulating either as a narrative or as a tribute to personal courage." The story was "pat" and the direction was "sluggish," the reviewer said. "It is sad though to see a gallant lady on display in such a threadbare little showcase." The most memorable feature of the film was the song "Because of You," written by Arthur Hammerstein and Dudley Wilkinson. It was the first number one hit on the charts in the long career of a then twenty-four-year-old crooner, Tony Bennett.

As Claire traveled and made personal appearances around the country during the film's showing, her Portland-based attorneys, Frank S. Sever and Frederic W. Young, were working on a lawsuit against the government to demand restitution that had now twice been refused by Congress.

The lawyers had now upped the ante on Claire's claim, from $50,000 to $146,850, the equivalent of more than $1 million in 2017.

On Trial

U.S. Federal Courthouse, Portland, Oregon, November 10, 1953

CLAIRE'S CLAIM for restitution before the U.S. Court of Claims brought together survivors of the Manila underground for a final, sometimes bitter reunion. Many of the former allies testified against her, and Claire insisted until the last minute that her ghostwritten memoir was all true.

The federal hearing provided unprecedented evidence to bolster her claim to a role in supporting and providing information to the guerrillas. The court transcript and exhibits provided rare testimony from Claire, Peggy Utinsky, Lorenza Amusategui, Maria Martinez, and, notably, John Boone's only first-person account of his activities as a guerrilla commander in Bataan. The picture he painted supported Claire's story. According to him, Claire not only helped Boone but also brought him into contact with others in the Manila underground. Boone, in turn, put Claire in touch with guerrilla leaders in the mountains. Together they comprised a circle of people who fought valiantly against the Japanese occupation from beginning to end; the circle ultimately connected with Chick Parsons, spymaster extraordinaire, who was the pipeline to General MacArthur. Claire, for her part, connected important Philippine contacts. She was a relative by marriage of General Manuel Roxas, who sought to subvert Japanese rule and became president of the Philippines in 1946; he served as president until his death in 1948. During the war Claire was faithfully passing along intelligence gleaned by the hostesses at Tsubaki Club as they sweet-talked their Japanese military consorts. Boone said more than once that Claire had provided excellent intelligence, even though he had not had the means to use it as real-time information that might launch attacks on Japanese planes, ships, and submarines.

The Court of Claims case convened at the imposing Renaissance revival federal courthouse on a typically drizzly November morning in downtown Portland. The Portland session was dedicated to Claire's testimony and supporting appearances by her old friends Louise DeMartini and Bob Humphries, now married and living in Canada. Claire's attorneys, Frederic Young and Frank Sever, presented their case with confidence, as if they expected they were headed toward a quick victory. However, Warren E. Burger, a future chief justice of the United States, then a little-known assistant attorney general, asked the FBI to investigate Claire's case for restitution. FBI Director J. Edgar Hoover, who already had been involved in tracking Claire's activities after returning to the United States, enthusiastically took up the case. Hoover ordered "that this matter be given prompt attention by all offices and that the investigation be completed at the earliest possible date." The FBI investigation outflanked and overwhelmed Claire's attorneys and their ability to respond. Testimony began before federal claims commissioner George H. Foster without a jury. Louise and Bob Humphries and five former POWs at Cabanatuan spoke first and confirmed that Claire had in fact provided the food, medicines, and support she said she had. Most important among the POW testimony was that of Dwight Gard, the president of Multnomah Bank and a prominent figure in Portland. As a former prisoner at Cabanatuan, Gard said that Claire had regularly sent food and medicine into the camp and written letters that gave hope to the prisoners. Claire's lawyers also introduced depositions that supported her claim. Claire's protector and guardian, Judge Roxas, who remained an eminent and highly respected jurist after the war, confirmed in a written statement that he had monitored Claire's activities all along. "I do not in the least doubt that Mrs. Claire Phillips had been helping the American prisoners during the war, as all that information which she had been giving me had been confirmed by Ramón Amusategui, in whose office at the Calvo Building, at Escolta, I used to assemble with a few friends almost every day to talk and comment on the war." Fely's father, Vicente Corcuera, submitted an affidavit that confirmed that Claire had hidden documents with him; and Carlos Sobreviñas wrote as well, saying that he had worked with Claire, sheltered her, and guided her to Manila from the mountains in mid-1942.

With all of the character references and depositions supporting her case, Claire took the stand confidently, assuming that everyone would see that she was simply asking for what she deserved. She related her story along the lines she had told for over eight years, in *American Mercury*, in her memoir, *Manila Espionage*, and finally in the film about her life, *I Was an American Spy*. She said it was all true, but her confidence evaporated under cross-examination. The attorney for the government, Thomas C. Fleming, began to challenge Claire's reliability and truthfulness. Had she really married John Phillips? Wasn't she already married to someone else? Hadn't she planned to seek widow's compensation from the U.S. government as Phillips's wife? How could she substantiate the claims she was making? Fleming then introduced an early bombshell in miniature.

"Did you have a little book in which you used to write in, issued by the Insular Life Assurance Company?" he asked.

"Yes."

"A sort of running diary, was it not?"

"Well, if you call that a diary, I guess it is."

The government attorney then entered the diary into evidence.

"I now show you a bound volume . . . and ask you if you recognize the book?"

"I do."

"What is it, please?"

"Part of it is notes on different activities. There are probably phone numbers and addresses in there. It's been so many years."

Claire said that she had kept the diary well hidden at Tsubaki Club; she had not seen it since the war. Over the course of three days of testimony, the attorneys and the federal commissioner examined many of the scrawled entries (hard to read and coded enough so that even Claire sometimes could not decipher what she had written) and transcribed them. The government used the diary to build a case that Claire's real story varied from the Hollywood version and, central to undermining her claim, that she had not been making as much money at the club as she said she had and therefore could not have been providing very much money to the POWs.

Claire's diary was a window into her experience of the war, a contemporaneous, unadorned account of her life before a better-educated, profit-minded scriptwriter could grab hold of the story. There was no indication, however, of how the government could have found it. Claire said she was surprised when she recognized her little lost diary. "I wondered how they could find it when I couldn't find it," Claire said in redirect questioning by her attorney, "and the Japanese couldn't find it." A writer for a Portland newspaper made a glancing mention of the diary and its introduction in court, reporting that it had been found in a bar. Not likely. The answer likely will never be known, but there were only a few possibilities—since Claire didn't have it when she was arrested, her friend Fely must have rescued it between May 24, 1944 (the day of Claire's arrest), and February 1945, when the Tsubaki Club building at the corner of Mabini and San Juan was destroyed. However, Fely didn't have it—the U.S. government had it. The only other person who had access to the diary was Peggy Utinsky. Court proceedings were recessed without explanation after Claire's testimony and sessions did not resume for nine months.

The next hearing opened at the U.S. Court of Claims in Washington, DC, on August 23, 1954. Fely Corcuera had come to Washington from her home in Hawaii, where she was now married to a physician. She testified about accounting at the club and confirmed Claire's role in sending supplies and intelligence to Boone and food and medicine to POWs at Cabanatuan and prisons in Manila. She withstood questioning from the government about the financial standing of Tsubaki Club and confirmed that Claire had provided material support on a regular basis to the guerrillas and to POWs in Manila and at Cabanatuan. She was unable to confirm the amount of money Claire had spent on these items. She and Claire had burned some documents when they realized the Kempeitai might raid them at any time. She agreed with Claire that other documents and receipts were missing or stolen.

After another hiatus of more than a year, the Court of Claims held another hearing, again in Washington, on September 14, 1955. Now, however, the government was ready to present its case. Two of Claire's former colleagues were there to testify against her. One of them was immediately recognizable as he stood there in an army sergeant's uniform. Government attorney Walter Kiechel Jr. presented him to the court. It was John Boone. The expressions on the faces of old friends and the glances across hearing tables can only be imagined.

Claire had not seen Boone since just after the end of the war. His name would have been listed in advance, so Claire would have known he was coming and the anticipation of the encounter with her old friend would have been nerve-racking. Would he truly testify against her?

It was thirteen years after Boone and Claire had met in the hills of Bataan. Boone had reverted to enlisted status in the regular army. Claire was back in Portland, newly divorced from Robert Clavier, her fifth husband (not counting John Phillips), and was living with Dian, now a teenager. Boone was now forty-two years old and balding a bit, but he was trim in his uniform and still had that thin-lipped, world-weary look that almost betrayed a smile. He told the court he was now stationed at Fort Ord, California. For some reason the government had elected to fly him in cross-country instead of presenting his testimony two years earlier when the proceedings had convened on the West Coast. Boone's testimony was not wholly negative, but he betrayed disappointment in and frustration with Claire.

Boone had seen Claire at least once since their time in the Philippines. He had surprised her a decade earlier in Santa Barbara, California, in late 1945 while she was appearing at an event to talk about her wartime experiences. Afterward Claire and Boone drove together by car back to San Francisco, at least an eight-hour trip if one were to take it nonstop on Highway 1, which winds along the Pacific Coast. During their 325-mile trip, the subject of compensation came up and they calculated the amount Claire was owed for helping his guerrilla operation. When they got to San Francisco, Boone was shocked to learn that she was married to Manuel Fuentes, a man he had never heard of before. Boone had thought Claire was a war widow. Boone was still married to Mellie, but he was upset and felt deceived. "I remember when I went to her apartment, to Fuentes's apartment in San Francisco, the fact that she was living with this guy amazed me. But she never made any effort to tell me anything about it, and of course, I didn't want to stick my nose into it. It has always been a great mystery to me."

Despite the unexpected news, Boone signed an affidavit later that year, on October 12, 1945, saying that Claire had sent supplies to his guerrilla operation "in a value exceeding 30,000 pesos or Fifteen Thousand Dollars ($15,000)." Neither of them ever spoke publicly about other details of their time together, and the court case did not delve further into the subject.

Boone testified before the Court of Claims that Claire had provided excellent intelligence information in addition to the material support she gave to the guerrillas. He recognized the current climate, in which the government had been inundated with requests for money from civilians and veterans. He said those requests sometimes exceeded people's actual service and what they should have claimed. But he described his strong feeling that Claire merited compensation for her role during the war. If all the others had been paid, he said, Claire definitely deserved to be paid as well.

"I felt that in view of what the American government had done in the Philippine Islands, after the liberation, I felt that if every other little so-called resistance movement operator there had been compensated, I felt this woman was entitled to some sort of U.S. government compensation. And I feel right now, when I look at this—I feel that I leaned over backwards to sign" the affidavit for a $15,000 claim. Now he said, however, that amount probably was an exaggeration. "It is true if I can stretch my imagination to the maximum," he told the court hearing. "I did it out of the goodness of my heart."

Boone said that his memory was dim about details and that he had not kept financial records. However, unpublished and unseen in the court record was evidence that showed that Boone's estimate could have been closer to an accurate figure than he thought after all. In fact, Boone had compiled a list of supplies and money obtained from all sources from September 1943 to September 1944, including fifteen thousand pesos in cash, clothing, food, and medicine from Claire. That did not include the support Claire provided in the eleven months between when she opened Tsubaki Club in October 1942 and September 1943. Nor did that include Claire's costs to supply the POWs.

The second witness against Claire that day was Lorenza Amusategui, who had remarried and was living in Maryland at the time. She wept more than once during testimony when she recalled the events surrounding her husband Ramón's capture and death. She also said that Claire had overstated her position in the supply operation they had run to Cabanatuan and other prisons. She said Ramón, not Claire, had assumed leadership of the group when Peggy was pushed aside.

Another four months went by. The final hearings in the case opened at the U.S. District Court in San Francisco on January 9, 1956. The first witness was Naomi Flores. Perhaps more damaging than Naomi's testimony were exhibits presented by the government: copies of letters that Claire had written to Evangeline Neibert, Lorenza, and Naomi, asking them to confirm that the government owed her money. The government attorneys said that Claire's letters implied that she would even pay a kickback to the women once the case was settled. Claire, even without a high school degree, should have known the implication. If she didn't, her lawyers should have warned her.

The government attorneys held their star witness for last, more than two years after the case opened. Peggy had been quietly working on behalf of the U.S. government defense team all along. She now stepped forward to offer her testimony, telling the court she had not traveled too far. She was living in Long Beach, California, for the winter. Claire and Peggy were in the same room together for the first time since their passage on the SS *Lykes* in 1945, and it was probably the last time they would meet; it is impossible to know whether Peggy and Claire looked directly at each other or spoke on the sidelines. Matronly Peggy—"auntie," as Claire had called her, or "the old lady," as Lorenza had called her—said that Claire was just a minor player in an operation that she claimed to have run.

In the course of several hours of testimony, Peggy told the court that she had gone with Fely after liberation in February 1945 to pick up Claire's papers and documents in Quezon City at the home of Fely's parents. She said that she had gone over the documents before giving them to Claire and that there were no receipts for payments to the guerrillas there.

Claire's lawyer, Frederic Young, seemed unprepared; he did not ask one obvious question: Did Peggy know anything about the mysterious reappearance of Claire's diary? Peggy was the only antagonist with the ability to have produced it. Peggy was the one who had traveled to Fely's parents' house after liberation and had private access to everything that had been hidden away. Young never pursued in open court where the diary had come from.

Peggy went to the extreme in unfairly and wrongly denying that Claire had ever been a "real" member of her supply operation. She said that Claire had hardly ever helped support the organization. She said that she herself had never gone to Tsubaki Club, though both Claire and Fely said she had come and that she had always been welcome to free beer and other alcohol, which was hard to come by elsewhere. Peggy was playing the role of the respectable old lady and was successful in sabotaging Claire's reputation. All the while, government lawyers and the FBI knew that Peggy was a questionable source of information. They received word from Lorenza Amusategui that Peggy had been displaced as leader of the group and had threatened to turn all of them over to Japanese authorities.

She even went to the point of challenging the origin of Claire's nickname, "High Pockets." Peggy said it wasn't because she stuffed secret messages down the front of her dress. "I gave her the name," she said. She and Claire were walking along together on the street one day when Peggy turned to her friend. Peggy was five feet tall and Claire was at least half a foot taller, even taller with heels on. When Peggy turned, she found herself looking straight at Claire's breasts. "She had on a little jacket with some pockets on it, and I am so short when I have no high heels on, and I was looking directly into her pocket, and I said, 'How high your pockets are.' I said, 'That's a good name for you,' and that was it." It seemed a bit of a payback for Claire having pasted her face onto Peggy's body.

The case was closed by Commissioner Foster, at 4:30 p.m. on January 11, 1957. Foster, who had been based in the Philippines during the war, was familiar with Manila nightlife, at least by observation at a distance. He implied that he understood Tsubaki Club to have been a disreputable nightspot. By his conduct of the hearings, Foster left the impression that he thought that Claire's uneducated, unsophisticated demeanor was as disreputable as the club.

Claire's credibility had been shattered. Even she admitted finally that her book blended fact and fiction. "The basic facts are true . . . but my co-author did dress the book up," she finally said. "The way I had written it was like a diary, and he said, 'That is no good.' . . . He insisted it made better reading." The only saving grace for her reputation was that the

American POWs hiked to safety with the help of U.S. Rangers and Filipino guerrillas on January 31, 1945, in Luzon. A day earlier, the Rangers, led by Lieutenant Colonel Henry Mucci, rescued the 513 POWs remaining at the Cabanatuan prison camp.

Claire Phillips wrote diary entries in a small agenda book from the day the war began in 1941 until her arrest in May 1944. The diary was unseen for almost sixty years until it was discovered in a file at the National Archives in Washington, DC.

A U.S. tank blasted through the front gate of Fort Santiago in February 1945. Japanese Imperial Army soldiers tortured thousands of U.S., Allied, and Filipino prisoners at the fort, and hundreds died.

U.S. forces battled fiercely with Japanese troops once they reached the Pasig River when the month-long Battle of Manila began on February 2, 1945. More than 100,000 civilians, 15,000 Japanese soldiers, and 1,000 GIs died, and the city was devastated.

Detainees at the University of Santo Tomas in Manila after liberation in February 1945. More than three thousand people, mostly Americans, were detained in Manila from February 1942 to 1945. They suffered from malnutrition and lack of adequate health care. About 10 percent of the internees died.

Japanese soldiers barricaded themselves in the walled city of Intramuros in February 1945. The sixteenth-century district was destroyed after a month of fighting.

Lieutenant Commander Chick Parsons (in uniform) with released American prisoners at Manila in 1945. Parsons was a long-time U.S. expatriate and remained in the Philippines after the war.

General MacArthur greets liberated U.S. prisoners of war at Bilibid Prison in Manila in February 1945. After the U.S. troops landed, MacArthur ordered them to race quickly to the city to rescue U.S. prisoners and detainees.

Former detainees at the University of Santo Tomas after liberation in February 1945. Among them are Roy C. Bennett, editor of the *Manila Daily Bulletin*, and his wife, Margaret, far right, background, behind an unidentified soldier. Joan Bennett, one of their daughters, is in the foreground, right, wearing a dark skirt and striped shirt.

Seven U.S. guerrilla leaders with Brigadier General Manuel Roxas at Manila City Hall on June 13, 1945, after receiving medals from MacArthur. Left to right: Major Harry McKenzie, Major Robert B. Lapham, Major Edwin P. Ramsey, Roxas, Lieutenant Colonel Bernard L. Anderson, Captain Ray C. Hunt Jr., Major John P. Boone, and Captain Kevin J. Farretta.

Peggy Utinsky, Claire Phillips's colleague in the underground, posed at the gates of the Tsubaki Club in downtown Manila. The building was destroyed in February 1945 during the Battle of Manila.

Claire had no picture of her own at Tsubaki Club; she said that the publisher of her memoir, *Manila Espionage*, decided to superimpose her face on the portrait Peggy posed for after the war. Claire admitted the deception during testimony at the U.S. Court of Claims.

Peggy Utinsky, left, and Claire Phillips, center, sailed home from Manila with other Americans in June 1945. When the SS *John Lykes* reached California, an article about Claire had already appeared in *American Mercury* magazine; she quickly became a celebrity and heroine.

Claire Phillips and actress Ann Dvorak posed in a publicity photo for the release in 1951 of *I Was an American Spy*. Dvorak portrayed Claire in the film based on her memoir, written for Claire by a ghostwriter. Claire later acknowledged that the memoir, *Manila Espionage*, often misrepresented events.

Claire Phillips toured the United States to promote the release of the film *I Was an American Spy*.

The U.S. embassy in Manila named a meeting room for Claire Phillips, displaying a portrait of Claire as a young woman, a copy of her memoir, *Manila Espionage*, a description of her life, and advertisements for the Tsubaki Club.

Before Philippines independence, the U.S. embassy on Manila Bay was headquarters of the U.S. High Commission to the Philippines. During World War II, it was occupied as the Japanese commander's residence and the Japanese embassy.

proceedings were little followed in the press, and the transcripts remained unseen and lost in a dusty file box for more than half a century.

The government had done so well in challenging Claire that it asked that the Court of Claims drop all claims by Claire and that she be cited for perjury. A four-member panel of the U.S. Court of Claims received the court record and findings by Commissioner Foster. It recommended on July 12, 1957, that Claire be paid exactly the amount that the testimony indicated could be verified, the dollar equivalent of about 8,500 Japanese-era pesos, calculated not at the rate of two pesos to the dollar, as Peggy had been paid, but on a sliding scale in which the peso became decreasingly valuable during the war. The amount authorized for Claire, $1,349.21, was equivalent to about $11,000 in 2017. If the amount was a slap at a woman who had indeed served and had indeed provided intelligence information, the judges of the U.S. Court of Claims said essentially they were grateful at least that she had been on the Allied side. "Much of her story was greatly exaggerated, and at times almost fanciful," the court said. But she deserved payment, because "when the rubbish is cleared away it is rather well established by outside testimony that she furnished [money and supplies] to prisoners of war and to organized guerrillas."

Her Own Life
Portland, Oregon, 1957

AFTER THE 1957 COURT DECISION, Claire disappeared from sight. She took odd jobs and sometimes spoke to veterans' groups. At one time she worked in a department store. Her mother listed her last job as a waitress in Portland. The U.S. government decision to pay her a pittance for her wartime service may have pushed her toward bitterness and a new bout with alcoholism.

Claire and Manuel Fuentes had lived together from July 1945 until the beginning of January 1946. Fuentes returned to the Philippines to work for the U.S. Army on an interisland ship. He paid Claire $1,200 in support payments in 1946. Claire took Dian with her back to Portland, where she filed for divorce from Fuentes in 1947. In a court hearing she said Fuentes was not violent but had been cruel and humiliated her. "He drank quite a bit and of course his temper was worse then," she said in court. "He would bawl me out and accuse me of picking on him. He would humiliate me in public and call me vile names." The uncontested divorce was granted in Multnomah County Court in Portland on April 25, 1947. She returned to the court on August 7 and won legal custody of Dian. In the filing, Claire was named Maybelle C. De La Taste and Dian was listed as Dian C. Fuentes.

After John Boone's visit in 1945, she tried to keep up a correspondence with him and with Mellie. Something seemed amiss in that relationship. "He went back to Manila . . . and wrote to me for a few months. But I have been writing and writing him and he don't [sic] answer me." Mellie "wrote me once and I answered but she never wrote again. I don't know why."

Claire met with veterans and paid a Christmas 1947 visit to the veterans' hospital, where she met Robert Clavier, an army private who had been among the POWs at Cabanatuan and was later moved to the Old Bilibid Prison hospital, where he was liberated in 1945. Although Clavier was still being treated in Portland for tuberculosis and other ailments, he left the hospital and married Claire three weeks later, on January 18, 1948. "I, at last, found the right man," she said in a letter to Evangeline Neibert and Naomi Flores. "He is six feet three inches tall (just the way I love 'em). Weighs about 170 . . . has bluish-green eyes, medium brown hair and a nice nose. In fact he reminds me a lot of my Phil. . . . I loved Phil so very much and lost him and I thought I'd never love again." They divorced in 1953 in the course of Claire's attempt to obtain restitution from the government. She apparently did not marry again after that. Claire's talks to veterans' and women's groups tailed off in the late 1950s. Dian, meanwhile, was born in 1940 and could still be among us. She would have turned eighteen in 1958. She did not take advantage of the full scholarship pledged by Lewis & Clark College as a result of Claire's *This Is Your Life* appearance. She could not be located for this book.

There is no indication that Claire had any further contact with her former underground colleagues after the Court of Claims case was settled. Her days in the limelight had come to an end.

Claire Phillips died on May 22, 1960, almost exactly sixteen years after she was dragged to a dungeon by the Kempeitai. An obituary the following day recalled her glory days for a moment. "Private funeral services have been arranged . . . for Claire Phillips, Portlander who was a wartime spy in the Philippines," the story said. "She opened a night club for Japanese officers, using the profits to aid Americans in prisoner of war camps. She was imprisoned, tortured and sentenced to die by Japanese military police, but her term was finally reduced to 12 years at hard labor. She was later rescued by American troops."

A separate death notice listed survivors: Dian, identified as Mrs. Dianne Claire Selness; her mother, Mrs. Mable Snyder; and her sisters, Mrs. Eva Jose and Mrs. Jeanne Childwood. Claire's remains were cremated.

The death certificate filed by her mother declared that she had contracted pneumococcal meningitis two days before her death at the Portland Sanitarium. The disease is caused by the streptococcus bacteria and is more virulent and fatal than the more common viral meningitis. Little more is known about her final years and final days, and neither Dian nor Claire's mother nor her two sisters came forward to discuss the life and death of Claire Phillips.

Good spies and heroes are not necessarily Boy Scouts or Girl Scouts. Claire Phillips was deceptive and foolish at times, but she also fought on behalf of the United States to defeat Japan in occupied Manila. For the eighteen months she was running her nightclub, Claire and the women who worked for her risked their lives nightly to gather intelligence faster than it could be assimilated and used by MacArthur's intelligence headquarters in Australia. If John Boone had managed to have a functioning radio transmitter early on, Claire would actually have done what she dreamed. First she sweet-talked men who, hopelessly drunk with love, provided the names of their crews, their travel dates, and their itineraries. And then, after a final kiss, they would have been blown out of the water by U.S. ships and airplanes.

Claire did not fit the easy mold of a noble hero, a patriot who marches off to war, triumphs, and is acclaimed. She was not alone among the heroes who fell into their roles by accident and circumstance. In the end she was a hero and a survivor. Her diary made the difference for me to be able to tell her story right; for the first time in the seventy years since Claire began telling and adjusting her story, we hear her unadorned daily efforts to live, love, and survive; to avoid disease, vermin, informers, and Japanese officers crowding her door. Her diary shows her toughness of spirit, her fears, heart, and humanity.

Claire's story is a significant, if still slightly mysterious, part of the larger story of the saga of American and Filipino guerrillas in the hills who refused to surrender to the Japanese after the invasion of the Philippines. These fighters successfully harassed and evaded the Japanese occupiers of the Philippines throughout the war, forced Japan to maintain a large force in the islands, and laid the groundwork for the U.S. return. There were thousands of Filipinos who resisted and fought the occupation of their country. They all stood up, people of all types, wealthy and poor, beggars, thieves, and chiefs. To this moment most of the Filipino guerrillas who fought for freedom in their own country have not received the recognition nor the compensation they deserved as soldiers in the U.S. Army. That failure should be and can still be corrected while the dwindling corps of survivors of the war are still alive. With their help and with assistance from Claire and her comrades, Japan's war machine failed in the Philippines. That part of the story is no mystery at all.

After the War

Peggy Utinsky

After living for a while in Washington, DC, Peggy Utinsky moved to Texas and later to California after her book, *Miss U*, was published. Like Claire, she gave occasional speeches about her wartime experiences. During the Court of Claims hearing, she gave indications she often was not well and was on government disability, but she lived ten years longer than Claire. Peggy, seventy, died in Los Angeles on August 30, 1970. A gravestone at Roosevelt Memorial Park in Los Angeles County reads: "Margaret Utinsky 'Miss U' Valiantly served her country by working with the Filipino resistance movement to provide medicine, food, aid and hope to Allied POWs in the Philippines during WWII."

John P. Boone

After the war, John Boone returned to the United States and stayed in the military. He received the Distinguished Service Cross for his wartime service in the Philippines. He retired from the army but reenlisted during the Korean War and served as an intelligence officer with the X Corps in Korea. He was stationed at Fort Ord in northern California for a time and rose to the rank of major. As a civilian in retirement, he was a news photographer and pursued photography enthusiastically on his own. Boone was at Fort Gordon, Georgia, when he died in 1980 at the age of sixty-seven. He and Mellie had six children, three boys and three girls. They had always planned to write a book about their wartime experiences and had made an audio recording to start the process when Mellie died in 1965, forty-two years old. "We couldn't find the tape and my father just couldn't write the book without my mother," said their daughter Jeanne. "He needed her to do it." Mellie and John are buried at Arlington National Cemetery.

Chick Parsons

Navy commander Chick Parsons and his family remained in the Philippines after the war. Parsons resumed his business career. He had received multiple awards for his service during the war, including the Distinguished Service Cross, two Navy Crosses, and the Bronze Star from the United States and the Medal for Valor from the Philippines. Parsons came closest to telling his own story in the 1946 book *Rendezvous by Submarine*, written by Travis Ingham with Chick's assistance. He took an aw-shucks attitude toward his service, telling Ingham, "I am not a colorful figure and I wish to be kept out of the story of the guerrilla movement as much as possible." After the war, he reconstituted his import business and traveled frequently to Japan, where he made friends and business contacts, leaving the war far behind him. He died in March 1988 at the age of eighty-eight. Chick Parsons's son, Peter—the five-year-old who helped his father smuggle intelligence documents by sitting on them on a pier in Manila—returned to the Philippines and has produced half a dozen films about the war in Manila, the guerrillas, and his father's exploits. Prior to moving to the Philippines, Peter Parsons lived and worked for forty years in California.

Fely Corcuera

Fely Corcuera spent time with Claire in Portland after the war and gave occasional talks about her wartime experiences. She married a physician, Manuel Santos, and settled in Hawaii outside Honolulu. She died in 1984 at the age of sixty-four. Her children live in Hawaii.

Lorenza Amusategui

Lorenza Amusategui married Edward P. O'Malley and moved with him to Maryland after the war. She became a naturalized U.S. citizen in 1949. She and her late husband, Ramón, were awarded the Presidential Medal of Freedom in 1946. On August 11, 1955, Congress passed a private bill that awarded $20,000 to Lorenza and $5,000 each to her sons, Ramón and José Maria, "in full settlement of all claims against the United States for money and supplies furnished and distributed by Mrs. O'Malley and her former husband, Ramón de Amusategui (now deceased), to American prisoners of war in the Philippines during World War II." U.S. Court of Claims commissioner George H. Foster, who heard testimony in Claire's case, used a different standard for Lorenza's claim of restitution. He noted that no documentation was available to back up Lorenza's claim, because the material had been burned to avoid detection by the Japanese. Lorenza died in Monterey, California, on May 25, 1967, at the age of fifty-one. She was buried at Golden Gate National Cemetery in San Bruno, California, where she was listed as a lieutenant colonel in the U.S. Army.

Naomi Flores

Naomi Flores had long-term connections with the United States. She had been raised in the Philippines in the family of a retired American Army officer, Colonel William E. Dosser, a longtime expatriate who had been governor of Mountain Province in northern Luzon. After the war she married an American, John F. Jackson, became an American citizen, and moved to San Francisco. She received the Presidential Medal of Freedom, as did many of her underground colleagues.

President Manuel Roxas and Judge Mamerto Roxas

Judge Roxas, related to Claire through Manuel Fuentes, remained an influential jurist for the rest of his life. He died in the Philippines in 1954. His younger brother, General Manuel Roxas, became the first president of the Philippines after the United States granted independence on July 4, 1946. As president, Roxas granted amnesty to Filipinos who had collaborated with the Japanese during the war, unless those people had committed violent crimes. President Roxas suffered a fatal heart attack on April 15, 1948, after delivering a speech at Clark Air Base, north of Manila. He was fifty-six years old.

Roy C. Bennett

It took a long time for Roy C. Bennett to recover from nearly four hundred days of "unadulterated mistreatment in a Japanese prison cell." At Santo Tomas "American forces won the race to rescue us and still unbelieving we tested our minds and hearts as human beings again. We lost weight, but we never lost hope." He eventually joined his family in Los Angeles and became an editor at a local newspaper. His daughter, Joan Bennett Chapman, who had a long career as an attorney in Los Angeles, said her father never told the full story of his captivity. "He couldn't do it; he couldn't bear to do it. He was urged to write a book after the war and he cracked up trying to write it." Roy C. Bennett died in Los Angeles in 1967; he was seventy-eight.

Douglas MacArthur

After General MacArthur was relieved of his command because of his position on expanding the Korean War, he was so popular that he was considered as a possible candidate for president in 1952. His onetime aide in the Philippines, Dwight David Eisenhower, was elected. MacArthur was an adviser to President Eisenhower and to President Kennedy in his final years. His memoir, *Reminiscences*, was published in 1964, the year he died at the age of eighty-four. "The shadows are lengthening for me. The twilight is here," he wrote at the end of that book. "Today marks my final roll call with you. . . . I bid you farewell." MacArthur is buried at the MacArthur Memorial museum and library in Norfolk, Virginia.

Masaharu Homma

The United States convened a special army war crimes tribunal in Manila, separate from international proceedings conducted in Tokyo and Nuremberg. About two dozen cases were heard at the recovered headquarters of the U.S. high commissioner, which had served as the Japanese embassy during the war. Among the defendants was General Masaharu Homma, commander of Japanese forces in the Philippines from occupation until his dismissal and forced retirement in August 1943. His trial opened on January 3, 1946, lasted one month, and focused mostly on his role in and responsibility for the Bataan death march. His defense lawyers argued that Homma had not been personally involved and had not ordered the atrocities surrounding the march. Despite pleas for mercy that went directly to General MacArthur, Homma was found guilty and sentenced to death on forty-eight counts of violating international law and was executed by a firing squad on April 3, 1946.

Akira Nagahama

The Tokyo High Command had also ordered Colonel Akira Nagahama out of the Philippines before the end of the war on charges within the army that he had been too brutal in his treatment of prisoners in the Philippines. He was arrested in Japan after the war and was brought back to Manila, where he also faced a war crimes trial. Many of the charges against Nagahama involved testimony about torture and executions of civilians and military personnel at Fort Santiago. Manuel Elizalde was among the witnesses, describing his treatment and the torture of his brother at Fort Santiago when he and his brother were arrested in February 1944. He said that after the war he had found the decapitated bodies of his brother and of Blanche Jurika, Chick Parsons's mother-in-law, both of whom were executed after being tortured at Fort Santiago. Nagahama was convicted and sentenced to death by hanging on March 11, 1946. Nagahama did not testify on his own behalf but after the proceedings wrote a letter to the court requesting a new trial on grounds of false testimony. "Witnesses for the prosecution have presented false statements and . . . I was not given the opportunity to say my part against such false statements through my defense counsel," Nagahama told the court. After appeals and review, General MacArthur confirmed the sentence in a terse statement, and Nagahama was among eleven Japanese officers executed by hanging on July 17, 1947.

AUTHOR'S NOTE

The search for the "mysterious woman known to the prisoners only as 'High Pockets,'" took me 8,500 miles from the National Archives in Washington, DC, to the corner of Mabini Street and Kalaw Avenue (formerly San Juan Avenue) in front of Luneta Park in Manila. Urban sprawl made it difficult to imagine the little two-story wooden building once enclosed by a fence that housed Tsubaki Club on the second floor, where Claire and Fely once sang and entertained Japanese officers. Now there are nondescript buildings, a gas station, and a jumble of cars, motorbikes, and people clicking along in their flip-flops as they dodge the jeepneys—the distinctively painted minibuses that career around the city. Mabini is a narrow urban street that runs one way toward the park, a few blocks away from what was once Dewey Boulevard—now renamed Roxas Boulevard in honor of President Manuel Roxas.

Only at the Luneta can one imagine Claire holding Dian's hand as they strolled along to get close to the POWs on maintenance detail. The monument and grave of José Rizal stand apart at one end of the park, where army soldiers guard his burial site. Families picnic, friends play games, and a mini trolley guides tourists around the circumference of the 140-acre (58-hectare) park. A Japanese garden was built to one side of the park, intended to promote friendship between Japan and the Philippines. Beyond it are the outer walls of Intramuros, the old Spanish city, which never fully recovered from the destruction of the war. Across Roxas Boulevard is the still-imposing Manila Hotel, severely damaged but restored after the war. General MacArthur's penthouse suite and offices overlooking the port have been rebuilt and redesigned in his honor.

A few blocks away the U.S. embassy also commands a privileged view of the Pacific Ocean. It was ground zero in one of the cruelest battles of World War II. A scorched, bullet-pocked flagpole stands as it did in 1945, marking the entrance of the three-story bayside building that was rebuilt after having been taken over by the Japanese in 1942 and wrecked under repeated bombings during the recapture of Manila. Even as the battle raged, General MacArthur raised the American flag here on February 22, 1945, completing his pledge—"I have returned."

Before the war the embassy had been the headquarters of the U.S. high commissioner to the Philippines. During the occupation it became the residence of the Japanese occupation commander and the Japanese embassy. Going past the flag and into the restored embassy building, one approaches the main embassy meeting room, which is named for Claire Phillips. A copy of her ghostwritten memoir, *Manila Espionage*, is part of a display there. Two other portraits of World War II heroes flank a painting of Claire. One is General Douglas MacArthur; the other is navy commander Charles "Chick" Parsons.

The tribute, touching though it is, is replete with errors, propagated by using *Manila Espionage* as the source. Perhaps the strangest aspect of the display is the fact that in death Claire has managed to disguise even how she looked. The portrait shows a confident, smiling young woman, arms folded, looking out at the world. It is based on a popular photograph identified as her when she was quite young, possibly even in high school. A physiognomist would need to confirm without a doubt that this early photograph and the painting are the same woman known to be Claire Phillips in photographs after the war. I was left with the impression that Claire was victorious finally in disguising her true self. With all her aliases and altered photographs, who was to say that Claire Phillips was Claire Phillips?

Claire is rightly honored on the U.S. embassy wall, and she is mentioned in some anthologies as one of the great women war heroes. She was among those who risked their lives during the war; others have received more recognition and more compensation for doing less. I would not take her name down, though I might add a few others to the list.

Claire died decades before this tribute was arranged. Other than the commemoration, she has been recalled in books and in occasional broadcasts of the old film *I Was an American Spy*. A local historian in her hometown, Portland, Oregon, spoke of raising money for that purpose. Until now, little has been known about Claire's wartime record, and she still defies full disclosure.

From the U.S. embassy I drove to the Manila American Cemetery and Memorial in Taguig, a southeastern suburb, the former site of the World

War II U.S. base Fort William McKinley. John L. Silva, executive director of the Ortigas Foundation in Manila, provided a comprehensive historian's view of the creation of the memorial during our tour. By coincidence, we were linked by friends in common, the Aboitiz family and Maitena Aboitiz, who has helped me so much on this book and my other work in understanding both the history of the Philippines and its relation to the Basque country, where she and my wife's family are from.

I took a moment at the cemetery to peruse the names of the dead—in addition to the 17,206 people buried there, the largest number of World War II U.S. military war dead in any foreign burial place. Many of them were killed in the battles of New Guinea and the Philippines; more than 36,000 MIAs are also memorialized. Searching through the alphabetic list, I found the name "Jacques R. Eisner," a U.S. Navy officer buried at sea on November 13, 1942. Though apparently not a relative, he was born in 1919 in New Jersey, as was my father. I was reminded of the randomness of lives lost and lives saved.

This was a story of superlatives. The U.S. retreat in the Philippines after Pearl Harbor, punctuated by General MacArthur's pledge to return, was part of the largest American military defeat in history and the largest surrender. When MacArthur made good on his promise three years later, he mounted a huge naval task force. The Battle of Leyte Gulf from October 23 to October 26, 1944, was by many accounts the largest naval battle of World War II and perhaps in world history, larger than, though obscured by, the D-Day attack on Normandy about four months earlier. Repeating the shocking statistic: 100,000 people died in one month in the Battle of Manila from February 3 to March 3, 1945. Most of them were Filipino civilians.

While in Manila, I attended events that marked the seventieth anniversary of the liberation of Manila. Americans and Filipinos now well into their eighties and nineties spoke of those days. Among them was Emmanuel de Ocampo, ninety-one, a retired banking executive, then a teenager among three hundred Filipino students armed with World War I Enfield rifles, if that, who joined the fight with the guerrillas.

I was there on February 3, 2015, for ceremonies at the University of Santo Tomas to mark the seventieth anniversary of freedom for the Santo

Tomas internees. There I stood with Joan Bennett Chapman and other survivors of the detention camp. Some were old and bowed, but were determined to tell future generations about their memories of those days. Joan provided vivid stories and I am grateful for her friendship. She was born in Manila and detained at the university with her father, Roy C. Bennett, her mother, and her sister. "My goal in coming back here was to put physical reality into the memory of the experience," she said. Joan had not been in the Philippines since she left in 1945 on the SS *Lykes*, the same ship that took Claire and Peggy back to America. In Manila Joan went off in search of her childhood home. The house was no longer there. Next she went unannounced to the offices of the *Manila Bulletin* in Intramuros, where her father had been the editor until the Japanese invasion. She was welcomed and the newspaper published a story about her visit the following day. She told a reporter that her visit gave her a sense of closure, as if she were bringing her father home. "His goal was to help develop a free, good, Filipino press. . . . As long as I'm alive and I've got my kids, the *Manila Bulletin* will always be a part of who we are."

The destruction of Manila during the recapture of the city from the Japanese was nightmarish. "Looking at it in terms of the whole picture of World War II, Manila should be on the map," said Dr. Ricardo T. Jose, a professor of history at the University of the Philippines. "And yet few people know that. It was one of the worst battlefields of the war."

Much of the credit for my ability to tell the story of *MacArthur's Spies* goes to those Philippine historians, veterans, survivors, and relatives of those who lived through World War II. The often-mentioned warmth and friendliness of the Philippines descended upon me within moments of my arrival in Manila in February 2015. My thanks to John Silva, his sister, Marie Vallejo, and her husband, Agustin Vallejo, who were instant friends and companions on the Manila trip. We took a tour north of Manila one fine Sunday, surrounded by memories of the war wherever we went. Marie spent months at the National Archives in College Park, Maryland, leading a team of researchers copying and cataloging World War II files. It is part of her campaign to document and justify Philippine guerrillas' claims for wartime compensation. She is also engaged in recovering history. She told me: "Out of the 270 boxes and almost 300,000 records scanned, the numerous stories can rewrite history." The documents reveal many stories of heroism long hidden in dusty folders on back shelves. "Now here we were, almost seventy years [after World War II ended], scanning these same hidden and crumbling records and bringing them out into the world." Marie and I essentially are looking to tell the same stories.

My thanks to many other people in Manila: to Soledad Vanzi, a journalist who is tireless in her efforts to make connections and smooth the way; to Dr. Ricardo T. Jose, eminent historian at the University of the Philippines, who was so generous with his time whenever I sought help and advice; thanks also to the family of Marcial Lichauco, including Sunshine Lichauco de Leon, his granddaughter. My greetings to Jesse Lichauco, a Filipina American and Marcial's wife. At the age of 104, she continues to hold court. The Lichaucos opened their home during the occupation to the sick and wounded and provided aid to war refugees. Thanks to Ambassador Harry K. Thomas Jr., who served as U.S. envoy to the Philippines from 2010 to 2013. Ambassador Thomas provided contacts and helpful advice and put me in touch with the Lichauco family. Thanks also to Tina Malone, counselor for Public Affairs at the U.S. embassy, for a tour and providing photographs of the embassy. The staff of Ateneo de Manila University was very helpful in providing access to their archives. Many thanks to the management and staff of the Luneta Hotel; the historic little hotel was two blocks from Tsubaki Club and across the street from Luneta Park and Intramuros, around the corner from the U.S. embassy. The beautifully remodeled building maintained the air of the Manila that once was.

It was great to get to know Peter Parsons during and after my Philippines stay; Peter appears as a child in the narrative. He has spent decades researching the activities of his remarkable father, Chick Parsons. Peter provided commentary, advice, and corrections on the first draft of this book; he is a font of information about the occupation of the Philippines and continues his research. Peter and his colleague, Lucky Guillermo, produced an excellent and highly recommended set of documentaries about Chick Parsons, the occupation, and the Battle of Manila.

I was fortunate to have the chance to travel and chat in Manila with James Zobel, archivist at the MacArthur Memorial and Library in Norfolk, Virginia. Jim also read and provided corrections for the first draft and I am grateful. He is a generous, eminently knowledgeable, and indefatigable source of information about the Pacific war, General Douglas MacArthur and his life and times.

The staff at the National Archives in Washington, DC, is well known for its expertise and generosity. Archivist Robert Ellis at the old building in downtown Washington was the point man in locating the lost files of *Clavier v. US*, hidden away in a location only he was able to find. My thanks to everyone who helped me at the archives, more names than I can recall, but especially Richard W. Peuser, William H. Davis, Rebecca L. Collier, Megan B. Dwyre, Christina Violeta Jones, and Eric Van Slander. My apologies to those inadvertently not mentioned.

Thanks also to the staff of the UCLA Film and Television Archive; Karen Clay and Katie Townsend at Pierce Library, Eastern Oregon University; and Ariel Evans at the Harry Ransom Center, the University of Texas at Austin.

Chris Schaefer's fine history of the guerrillas on Bataan was an excellent resource, and Chris kindly helped me with book suggestions, documentation, and other advice; John and Mellie Boone's daughter Jeanne Boone was kind and generous in providing information from her files; thanks to Louis Jurika, Peter Parsons's cousin, for his information and advice; Elliott Waksman for his ground game; to Stuart Levy for the introduction; and to Federico Baldassarre. Thanks also to Malcolm Decker, his information and his books.

I am indebted as always to my agent, Flip Brophy, for her friendship and constant attention; and to my editor, Wendy Wolf—it is a pleasure and honor to be working with her again. I am grateful for the diligent, precise editing of Tess Espinoza and for the line work of Georgia Bodnar. Thanks to my friend and colleague Jim Mulvaney for the idea. A number of people helped with moral support and in many cases read early edits of the manuscript. Miguel Pagliere helped research, prepare, and edit photos and documents. My readers were Michael Birkner, Steven Christensen, Henry Heilbrunn, Lynne Heilbrunn, Karl Horwitz, Kenton Keith, Peter Perl, Knut Royce, and Daun Van Ee. My aunt, Maria Teresa Leturia, inspires and always catches errors no one else has. Thanks also to John Burgess, Robert Burruss, Jerry Gropper, Neal Levy, Ian Portnoy, and Jeff Stein for their support.

My wife, Musha Salinas Eisner, is my ever-meticulous and insightful frontline editor and adviser; she helped design and structure this book. My wonderful daughters, Isabel and Marina, always humor me in the process of writing, as does my sister, Wendy. We all share the regret that my late parents, Bernard Eisner and Lorraine Eisner, did not hang around long enough to share the book with us. My dad, especially, who retired from the navy after the war as a lieutenant (junior grade) and remained proudly in the U.S. Navy Reserve for years, would have been thrilled and might have told an extra story or two. *Así es la vida.*

SOURCES

The principal narrative of this book depends on documents contained in the files of Claire Phillips's suit for restitution of funds, *Clavier v. US*. I use *Manila Espionage* as a source when a claim in that ghostwritten book is backed up elsewhere (such as in Claire's unpublished diary), when another source confirms her account, or when *Manila Espionage* provides atmospherics and description of circumstances and events that are confirmed to have taken place. When quoting or relating Claire's description of unconfirmed events in the memoir, I include a qualifier or a textual note. Claire's wartime diary is at the core of this story. The U.S. government used the diary against Claire in defending her three-year federal lawsuit. Claire analyzed the diary in the court proceedings, sometimes forced to compare it line by line with her version of events in *Manila Espionage*. It provides a baseline of truth against distortions she and some of her comrades-in-arms told after the war. The sudden reappearance of the diary is one key to the story of Claire Phillips.

NOTES

Abbreviations

CC: *Clavier v. United States*, U.S. Court of Claims, Record Group 123/16E3/10/27/5, Mixed Claims, 195101960, Entry 1003, Boxes 2 and 3, National Archives and Records Administration.

Diary: Claire Phillips's diary, exhibit in *Clavier v. United States*.

MacArthur Archives: MacArthur Memorial, Library and Archives, Norfolk, VA.

ME: Claire Phillips and Myron B. Goldsmith, *Manila Espionage* (Portland, OR: Binfords & Mort, 1947).

NARA: National Archives and Records Administration, Washington, DC.

Preface

ix **Though many more Americans:** According to the National Park Service, which administers the World War II Valor in the Pacific National Monument in Hawaii, 2,403 Americans died at Pearl Harbor and 1,178 were wounded. See www.nps.gov /nr/twhp/wwwlps/lessons/18arizona/18charts1.htm. About 80 Americans died and 150 were wounded in the first day of attacks in the Philippines.

ix **Japanese leaders, said General:** MacArthur, *Reminiscences*, 112.

ix **At the outbreak of war:** See, for example, Ephraim, *Escape to Manila*.

xi **"The most fascinating of all:** Sides, *Ghost Soldiers*, 184.

xiii **This federal court, originally:** A new, differently organized U.S. Court of Claims was created in 1982 and renamed the U.S. Court of Federal Claims in 1992. The files of the original U.S. Court of Claims are held separately at the National Archives.

World on Fire

4 **Beautiful Filipina hostesses circulated:** Transcript of the Testimony of Felicidad P. Corcuera Santo, Washington, DC, August 23, 1954, CC, 513. Fely Corcuera's testimony provides detailed information about finances at Tsubaki Club and the alcohol and snacks that were served.

4 **The puppet Philippine leader:** Vargas's formal title was Chairman of the Executive Commission. His declaration is Proclamation No. 5, December 28, 1942, held at the Republic of the Philippines Presidential Museum and Library, Manila, and available at http://malacanang.gov.ph/7149-proclamation-no-5-s-1942/.

Life Before the War

7 **"That's newspaper talk,":** ME, 1.

7 **"Call it restlessness, fate:** Ibid.

7 **She had been born:** Records of the 1910 U.S. Census, Racine, WI, Ward 10, District 0082, sheet 15, available by searching at www.ancestry.com.

8 **A loose rail tore:** "Two Immigrants Killed," *Austin* (MN) *Daily Herald*, December 13, 1909, p. 8.

8 **Mabel De La Taste moved:** Records of the 1910 U.S. Census; Records of the 1920 U.S. Census, State of Oregon, Multnomah County, City of Portland, precinct 123,

sheet 4; FBI File 105-377, Record Group 153/270/2/3, Entry A1 143, Box 1191, NARA.

8 **Clara Snyder was:** Edna May Root, "Franklin Clubs Choose Their Officers," *Portland Oregonian,* September 17, 1922, p. 6.

8 **She was still sixteen:** Certificate of Marriage, no. A3762, September 4, 1924, Records of Clark County, State of Washington.

8 **Claire was still a teenager:** Marriage of Edwin George Flinn and Clara Delataste, August 31, 1927, Name index of marriage records, Reference ID 52821, Salt Lake City, County of Salt Lake, State of Utah, available by searching at www.ancestry.com (Utah, County Marriages, 1887–1937).

9 **Claire's third known husband:** Marriage Certificate of Joseph V. Enette and Clara M. De La Taste, December 12, 1929, Series A12526, Seattle, Marriage Records, County of King, State of Washington.

9 **Joe and Clara Enette:** Records of the 1930 U.S. Census, Seattle, Washington. A 1945 FBI file lists one of her names as Mabel C. Evette, one of several misspellings in that FBI document, the cursive *n* changed to a cursive *v*.

9 **The census form had:** Joe Enette (1891–1975) is categorized as of "Ethiopian" ancestry on his World War I draft registration card.

9 **Clara and Joe were:** R.L. Polk & Co.'s *Snohomish, County P.O. Rural Routes* (1933), 728, available by searching at www.ancestry.com (U.S. City Directories, 1822–1995, Everett, Washington, City Directory, 1933).

9 **However, Claire appeared on:** Federal Bureau of Investigation Records: Freedom of Information/Privacy Act request, FBI report on Claire Phillips, File Number 105-77, Report made at Portland, Oregon, August 29, 1945. "According to the FBI files, FBI No. 4363088, this subject as DOROTHY SMITH was arrested by the Sheriff's Office in Seattle, Washington, on March 2, 1933, on a charge of vagrancy. The disposition is not shown."

10 **She was a passenger:** List of Outward-Bound Passengers (Aliens and Citizens) for Immigration Officials at Port of Departure. SS *President Pierce,* Passengers Sailing from Honolulu, T.H. [Territory of Hawaii], April 26th, 1939. Tourist Class Disembarking at Manila, May 13th, 1939, available by searching at ancestry.com (Honolulu, HI, Passenger and Crew Lists, 1900–1959). The manifest lists Claire as "Maybelle Enette, 31."

10 **Once in the Philippines:** CC, *Fuentes v. Fuentes,* Defendant's Exhibit 4, divorce deposition of Claire Fuentes, April 25, 1947, Circuit Court of the State of Oregon for the County of Multnomah, Portland, Oregon.

10 **Many years later Claire:** Transcript of the Testimony of Claire Phillips Clavier, January 11, 1956, San Francisco, California, CC, 1209–11. Claire said Dian was born on February 7, 1940, and Dian's mother died in childbirth. She was then asked by a government attorney: "Have you ever given birth to a child at any time?" She answered: "No, I never did and I never could."

10 **He sailed to the United States:** Manuel L. Fuentes, forty-three, is listed on a ship's manifest as a Philippine-national crew member of the freighter *Cavalcade,* which arrived at San Francisco on October 2, 1941. (The manifest can be found by searching at www.ancestry.com.) His family tree at www.ancestry.com identifies him as the person listed on the *Cavalcade* manifest.

11 **"We're birds of a feather":** ME, 2.

12 **He was John Vincent Phillips:** The service record of John V. Phillips, 31st Infantry, number 6576013, lists him as a private. Claire and others over time have written that he was a sergeant.

12 "The quiet type, I: ME, 1

13 Phillips wrote home: Mrs. Vada M. Phillips, letter to O. D. Boorom, January 31, 1946, CC.

Infamy Across the Pacific

13 When the news bulletin: In 1941 Hawaii Standard Time was five and a half hours earlier than Eastern Standard Time. U.S. radio announced the attack just before 2:30 p.m. EST, 3:30 a.m. Manila time.

15 "*Señora*, excuse me, please: ME, 8.

15 One Manila resident went: Lichauco, *Dear Mother Putnam*, 25.

16 "When we reached the bank: ME, 10.

16 Phillips gave Claire the keys: Claire's diary entry for December 8 says, "bid A farewell, got car, packed." "A" is her code for Phillips or for American soldiers, depending on the context. She writes on December 10, "7 . A arrives-go Pilar-100 stops—no car lights—arrive." Reviewing the diary during the Court of Claims case, Claire wasn't sure what the annotation meant. At first she said that it meant "7 a.m." In further testimony she said "A" represented "American" or "Americans." In *Manila Espionage* she says they drove together to Pilar that afternoon. It is questionable that Phillips could have left his unit a day after the Japanese attack or that he would drive more than half a day with her and only then reach his unit's new camp.

16 "Oh, I don't think: ME, 10.

17 "Bombing far away: Diary, December 10, 1942.

18 Claire waited for Phillips: In *Manila Espionage* Claire says Phillips visited often; that is not clear in her diary.

Invasion

18 MacArthur's commanders had been: MacArthur, *Reminiscences*, 110.

18 "Our air force in the Philippines: Ibid., 120.

19 "How many were the Americans: Zobel, *MacArthur*, 48–49.

19 The intent was: MacArthur, *Reminiscences*, 126.

19 MacArthur, his wife, Jean: Arthur MacArthur IV, Douglas and Jean Marie Faircloth MacArthur's son, was born on February 21, 1938.

19 The twenty-four-foot-wide: Zobel, *MacArthur*, 51; Ramsey and Rivele, *Lieutenant Ramsey's War*.

20 "the exact time of the arrival: MacArthur, "Message to the Troops," January 15, 1942, quoted in James, *The Years of MacArthur*, vol. 2, 57.

20 MacArthur found out long: MacArthur, *Reminiscences*, 129.

20 "You are well aware: Ibid.

21 "The outcome of the present: Ibid., 129–30.

21 "Every foxhole on Bataan: Ibid., 129.

21 For weeks now: Ibid.

Learning About War

22 "I was hit in the toe: Transcript of the Testimony of Claire Phillips Clavier, Portland, Oregon, November 13, 1953, CC, 234.

22 "Every time they would: Ibid., 235.

22 According to her diary: Diary, December 24, 1941: "Infected toe; call Dr. removes toe nail, very painful. Must stay in bed. No co. for dinner Xmas."

23 Phillips was able to come down: Ibid.

23 **Phillips had arranged a room:** Binkowski, *Code Name: High Pockets*, 15; and Diary, December 30, 1941.

Unprepared for War

25 **The mix also included:** The Portuguese explorer Ferdinand Magellan reached the Philippine island of Homonhon on March 17, 1521, during his attempt to circumnavigate the globe and claimed the archipelago for the Spanish crown. Magellan died in a battle with Mactan islanders near Cebu on April 27, 1521. His rival commander, Juan Sebastián Elcano, a Basque, completed the circumnavigation to Spain with the surviving expedition.

25 **A 1940 government census:** "16,000,000 in Philippines," *New York Times*, May 30, 1940, p. 21.

26 **A colonial existence was safe:** Joan Bennett Chapman, interview with the author, February 5, 2015.

26 **"There seems to be:** "Japan's Supermilitarism," *Manila Daily Bulletin*, October 18, 1941.

27 **"My parents and MacArthur:** Joan Bennett Chapman, interview with the author, February 5, 2015.

27 **"Japan is heading full:** "Japan's Supermilitarism."

27 **"Certainly we do not:** "A Philippine Slant," *Manila Daily Bulletin*, October 21, 1941.

27 **"had begun an eleventh-hour:** MacArthur, *Reminiscences*, 109.

28 **Cars burned and smoke:** John W. Whitman, "Manila: How Open Was This Open City?" *HistoryNet*, August 19, 1998, www.historynet.com/manila-how-open-was -this-open-city-january-98-world-war-ii-feature.htm.

28 **"gambling with stakes:** "For the Big Gamble," *Manila Daily Bulletin*, December 29, 1941.

28 **"At the proper time:** "Bombings Called Senseless, Savage," *Manila Daily Bulletin*, December 30, 1941.

28 **"Be calm," Bennett wrote:** "Be Calm," *Manila Daily Bulletin*, January 2, 1942.

The Conversion of Santo Tomas

31 **"The Japs were very:** Caroline Bailey Pratt, *Only a Matter of Days: The World War II Prison Camp Diary of Fay Cook Bailey* (Seattle: CreateSpace Independent, 2012), 20.

31 **Tomayasu ordered that internee:** Rupert Wilkinson, *Surviving a Japanese Internment Camp* (Jefferson, NC: McFarland, 2014), 35–36.

31 **More than two months:** Mydans, *More Than Meets the Eye*, 71–90; and Bob Hackett, "Ija Maya Maru: Tabular Record of Movement," undated, www.combinedfleet .com/MayaM_t.htm. The *Maya Maru* left Manila for Shanghai on September 1, 1942. An earlier exchange voyage had sailed from Manila in June 1942.

Diplomatic Immunity

32 **"It still runs before:** Peter Parsons, "Commander Chick Parsons and the Japanese," undated, via e-mail to the author, July 11, 2015.

33 **Fortunately, the Japanese sentries:** Ingham, *Rendezvous by Submarine*, 35. Spanish was still widely spoken in the Philippines and remained, along with English and Tagalog, an official language for decades after the Spanish-American War.

33 **Parsons, forty-one:** Many biographies of Parsons say he was born in 1902 and that he attended the universities of Tennessee and the Philippines. His son Peter Parsons corrects the birth year to 1900 and says there is no record of his father

attending the University of Tennessee and that his tuition for the University of the Philippines was returned to him when he didn't attend. Biographical details are based on the author's e-mail exchange and correspondence with Peter Parsons in April 2016, and Peter C. Parsons, "The Battle of Manila: Myth and Fact," undated, http://battleofmanila.org/Parsons/htm/parsons_01.htm.

33 **Soon after returning, he was:** Wood served as governor-general of the Philippines from 1921 until his death in 1927.

33 **"To watch the sun-bronzed:** Ingham, *Rendezvous by Submarine*, 5.

34 **Along the way:** Connaughton, Pimlott, and Anderson, *The Battle for Manila*, 35.

34 **Parsons had decided not:** Correspondence with Peter Parsons, April 2016. Peter Parsons said: "Actually, a PT Boat had been sent specifically to pick up Parsons. But he was delayed by not being able to find some senior officer. By the time he arrived at the pier, the boat had left. I had tried to stow away on that PT boat, but my mom had other ideas."

34 **Within an hour, consular:** Ingham, *Rendezvous by Submarine*, 35.

Nurse and Midwife

35 *haciendero* **who was willing:** A variation in the Philippines of the Spanish word "hacendero," the owner of a ranch.

36 **"a tall, wavy-haired:** ME, 48.

36 **"A Japanese flag:** Diary, February 13, 1942.

Boone's Guerrillas

37 **In the process of establishing:** Transcript of the Testimony of John Boone, Washington, DC, September 14, 1955, CC, 657.

38 **"It was pretty obvious:** Ibid., 658.

38 **Claire set out for Maite:** Diary, February 20, 1942. Boone said in his Court of Claims testimony that he thought their first meeting was much later.

38 **It was a five-mile:** ME, 53; Binkowski, *Code Name: High Pockets*, 28–29.

39 **Boone emerged from the tree:** ME, 55.

39 **"a buck-ass private:** Transcript of the Testimony of John Boone, Washington, DC, September 14, 1955, CC, 660.

39 **Boone had been a:** E-mail, Jeanne Boone to the author, April 4, 2016.

40 **"It seems to me:** Transcript of the Testimony of John Boone, Washington, DC, September 14, 1955, CC, 645.

40 **"The first battalion moved:** Ibid., 646.

40 **"We had to go:** Ibid.

41 **"They thought they had:** Transcript of the Testimony of Claire Phillips Clavier, Portland, Oregon, November 13, 1953, CC, 241–42.

42 **"We could make a deal:** Transcript of the Testimony of John Boone, Washington, DC, September 14, 1955, CC, 661.

The Chances of Survival

43 **Emilio V. Reyes:** His given name has been previously misreported. However, see www.mayorgilagarcia.com/index.php/news/the-municipal-government/former-mayors.

44 **"We all have head:** Diary, February 27, 1942.

44 **"She told me that the:** Judge Mamerto Roxas, affidavit, August 23, 1949, CC.

45 **"I agreed with the:** Ibid.

45 **One American soldier hiding:** Richard Sassaman, "The Battling Bastards of Bataan," *America in WWII*, April 2007, www.americainwwii.com/articles/the-battling-bastards-of-bataan/.

45 **On March 31 Claire:** Diary, March 31, 1942.

More Than a Dozen Tremors

46 **"Was God going to rescue:** Felipe Buencamino III, "Diary of Felipe Buencamino III," April 8, 1942, https://philippinediaryproject.wordpress.com/category/diary-of-felipe-buencamino-iii/.

46 **"Five more deaths by malaria:** Diary, February 28, 1942.

46 **She counted thirty deaths:** Ibid.

47 **Of twenty huts in their:** Ibid.

47 **"In the three huts:** Diary, April 13, 1942.

47 **A few days after the earthquake:** Diary, April 14, 1942.

47 **"We're in a tight:** Ibid.

The Death March

47 *I don't think his:* William E. Dyess and Leavelle Charles, *Bataan Death March: A Survivor's Account* (New York: GP Putnam's Sons, 1944), 50.

47 **After informing his commanders:** Morton, *The Fall of the Philippines*, 458.

48 **"Their spirit is good:** James, *The Years of MacArthur*, 95.

48 **"On the dock I:** MacArthur, *Reminiscences*, 142–43.

49 **"A primary objective":** Ibid., 145.

49 **"to make the fight:** Ibid., 152.

50 **"Your worries are over:** Quoted in Shively, *Profiles in Survival*, 55.

50 **"It would have been an ordeal:** Dyess and Charles, *Bataan Death March*, 62. Dyess, a pilot, escaped a Japanese prison camp in April 1943. Chick Parsons was able to transport Dyess from Mindanao to Australia in 1943 via submarine. Dyess met with MacArthur to give his first-person account of the death march. Dyess returned to the United States, where he died in 1944 in a flight training accident.

50 **The march northward was:** Shively, *Profiles in Survival*, 59.

51 **"I wondered whether the Jap:** Dyess and Charles, *Bataan Death March*, 86.

51 **"When the battle becomes:** Allied Translator and Interpreter Section (ATIS) Files, Record Group 407/270/51/9, Entry 427, Boxes 837–8, NARA. Elizabeth Mullener, *War Stories: Remembering World War II* (Baton Rouge, LA: LSU Press, 2002), 42.

52 **Many of the surviving:** Lichauco, *Dear Mother Putnam*, 82.

Escape and Evasion

52 **"I know where there:** John Boone, quoted in undated and unattributed article, "Sgt. Boone's Secret Army," personal files of John Boone, courtesy of Jeanne Boone.

52 **"We knew we would:** Transcript of the Testimony of John Boone, Washington, DC, September 14, 1955, CC, 656.

53 **"I was very guerrilla:** Ibid., 648.

53 **A few did make:** Captain William L. Osborne and Captain Damon J. Gause may have been the first to make the successful sea voyage, reaching Australia in October 1942. See *Reports of General MacArthur, Prepared by His General Staff*, vol. 1, 1994, 299–300, available at www.history.army.mil/books/wwii/MacArthur%20Reports/MacArthur%20V1/ch10.htm#b2.

53 **A few, such as:** Schaefer, *Bataan Diary*, 61.

54 **He worked with guerrilla:** Ibid., 349.

54 **"Some fled for the jungle:** Ramsey and Rivele, *Lieutenant Ramsey's War*, 80.

Hidden in Plain Sight

56 **When he was arrested:** Peter Parsons, e-mail to the author, December 10, 2015.

56 **Chick Parsons's final evening:** Peter Parsons, interview and correspondence with the author, April 2016.

57 **"I never even let:** Peter Parsons, e-mail to the author, July 12, 2015.

57 **"I still remember the fish:** Parsons, e-mail to the author, December 10, 2015.

58 **for Takao, Formosa:** Takao is the port now known as Kaohsiung, Taiwan, about 550 miles north of Manila.

58 **"He said he was impressed:** Peter Parsons, e-mail to the author, July 12, 2015.

58 **of Lourenço Marques:** Now Maputo, Mozambique.

58 **Newspapers were already reporting:** "Gripsholm at Rio, Evacuees Happy," *New York Times*, August 11, 1942, p. 9.

58 **"Every precaution must be taken:** "U.S. Refugees Due from Orient Today," *New York Times*, August 25, 1942, p. 21.

59 **The FBI suspected him:** Parsons, e-mail to the author, July 12, 2015.

Back from Bataan

59 **If he was still:** Claire said in *Manila Espionage* that she had another meeting with Father Cabanguis in Maite, but that is not reflected in the diary, nor is her claim that the priest had seen John Phillips as a Japanese prisoner in June 1942.

60 **There had been:** Agoncillo, *The Fateful Years*, 348.

60 **"I've tried my best:** ME, 75.

61 **Jostled by the other:** Carlos C. Sobreviñas, affidavit, July 12, 1949, CC. In *Manila Espionage* Claire said she made part of the trip back to Manila by boat east across Manila Bay. Her diary does not reflect that, and she acknowledged in the court case she had traveled by land.

62 **"A clever ruse":** Sobreviñas, affidavit.

63 **"the girl in *Rebecca*":** Diary, June 4, 1942.

63 **If alive, he was:** Claire said in her Court of Claims testimony that the Roxas family thought Fuentes had been killed early in the Japanese invasion. While the court doubted her testimony on that and many other points, there was a reason to think he was dead. His ship, the SS *Corregidor*, had hit a mine in Manila harbor on December 17, 1941. Estimates were that most of the crew and more than nine hundred passengers died. See "The Sinking of the SS Corregidor Dec. 17, 1941. 900–1,200 Lives Were Lost," *Pacific Wars*, December 15, 2014, available at: http://thepacificwars.com/sinking-ss-corregidor-dec-17-1941-900-1200-lives -lost/. Under war conditions, there was no reliable tally of the dead and no way to know that Fuentes was not on the ship and had gone to San Francisco in search of Claire.

A Brave New World

67 **They urged compliance and understanding:** Agoncillo, *The Fateful Years*, 311.

68 **"The last thing we:** Lichauco, *Dear Mother Putnam*, 53–54.

69 **Soon they were requiring:** Ibid., 56.

70 **The judge laid down:** Mamerto Roxas, affidavit, August 23, 1949, CC.

71 **"It must have been:** Ibid.

71 **"We agreed that I:** Ibid.

71 **Roxas sent along one:** Ibid. Roxas said he personally did not accompany Claire to the meeting.

72 **"Her husband Manuel Fuentes:** Ibid.

72 **She promised that everything:** Ibid.

72 **She took up a name:** In a letter to Evangeline Neibert on May 20, 1947, Claire said that her friend and colleague in Manila Peggy Utinsky recommended she use the name "Dorothy Fuentes."

Becoming Madame Tsubaki

73 **"I borrowed their patterns:** ME, 84.

73 **By the end of July:** At the Court of Claims hearing, Claire's colleague Peggy Utinsky, who worked with the Red Cross, said she had never seen Claire at Remedios Hospital.

73 **She told the judge:** Mamerto Roxas, affidavit, August 23, 1949, CC.

74 **Unemployment was high after:** Lichauco, *Dear Mother Putnam*, 49.

74 **"Make no mistake":** Anonymous source, interview with the author, Manila, January 30, 2015.

74 **Part of the reason:** ME, 86.

75 **Claire described Ana Fey:** Ibid.

75 **Claire said that a:** ME, 86–88. Besides noting it in her memoir, Claire described the event to U.S. military interrogators in 1945.

76 **Mamerto was acquainted with:** Binkowski, *Code Name: High Pockets*, 3.

77 **Claire told the judge:** Roxas, affidavit.

77 **"I lined the walls:** ME, 97.

78 **He provided a constant:** Transcript of the Testimony of Claire Phillips Clavier, Portland, Oregon, November 10, 1953, CC, 51.

Opening Night

79 **Also attending was:** Claire gave only his family name. This was probably Toshiharu Ichikawa (1912–98), who already had written orchestral works and film scores.

80 **And they repeated the motions:** ME, 99.

80 **Next a spotlight illuminated:** Ibid.

81 **"Our orchestra accompanied his:** Ibid.

81 **"When midnight arrived there:** Ibid., 100.

82 **"God Bless the Philippines":** "Music: Philippine Flop," *Time*, March 12, 1945; and Benjamin Sears, *The Irving Berlin Reader* (New York: Oxford University Press, 2012), 192. Filipinos sang a slightly altered version of Irving Berlin's song in the 1940s. Berlin heard schoolchildren in Leyte sing it, then wrote and performed a new Philippine version, "Heaven Watch the Philippines," in 1946. He offered to donate the proceeds to the Boy Scouts and Girl Scouts of the Philippines, as he had done with "God Bless America" in the United States.

82 **After the successful performance:** ME, 105.

82 **Damian showed the way:** Binkowski, *Code Name: High Pockets*, 81.

82 **Boone was impressed with:** Transcript of the Testimony of John Boone, Washington, DC, September 14, 1955, CC, 694.

83 **"Mosquitoes are troublesome only:** Lichauco, *Dear Mother Putnam*, 59.

84 **"The food was crucial:** Transcript of the Testimony of Robert M. Humphries, Portland, Oregon, November 10, 1953, CC, 5.

84 **One of Claire's new:** ME, 88. Masamoto is mentioned in *Manila Espionage*; he does not appear elsewhere.

84 **She also had someone:** This might have been George Terada, a Japanese American businessman mentioned earlier in this chapter.

84 **"At least, I'll be:** ME, 91.

Night and Fog

86 **"YOU MUST NOT TALK:** Hartendorp, *The Japanese Occupation of the Philippines*, 575–77.

86 **The caged prisoners were:** Shively, *Profiles in Survival*, 538–45.

86 **"It's alright to whisper":** Ibid.

87 **"He was crippled:** Joan Bennett Chapman, interview with the author, February 5, 2015.

87 **Bennett's wife had determined:** Agoncillo, *The Fateful Years*, 577.

The Kempeitai

88 **One of those who:** War Crimes Trial of Colonel Akira Nagahama, 639–41; Record Group 331/290/12/13/3, Entry 1321, Box 1579, NARA.

88 **The Kempeitai functioned parallel:** Syjuco, *The Kempei Tai in the Philippines*, 6.

89 **Colonel Dionisio Banting Jr.:** He was arrested on March 23, 1943.

89 **He was beaten, starved:** Record Group 331/290/12/34/6, Entry 1321, Box 1579, NARA.

89 **From Nagahama's point of view:** Syjuco, *Kempei Tai in the Philippines*, 14.

90 **"To govern alien nationalities:** Quoted in Friend, *The Blue-eyed Enemy*, 201.

90 **"We endured in the Hope:** Quoted in Lichauco, *Dear Mother Putnam*, 70.

90 **"While the commentator kept:** Ibid., 71.

91 **A few months later the bureau:** Asihei Hino, *The Flowering of Racial Spirit* (Manila: Bureau of Information, Japanese Imperial Army, 1942), 5.

91 **"When we entered into:** Lichauco, *Dear Mother Putnam*, 76.

92 **"Substantial progress is being:** Statement on January 28, 1943. Quoted in Agoncillo, *The Fateful Years*, 368.

92 **Many Filipinos, who might:** Lichauco, *Dear Mother Putnam*, 103.

Killing General Roxas

93 **"This is to order:** The account and subsequent quotes are from Colonel Red Reeder, *The Story of the Second World War* (New York: Duell, Sloan and Pearce, 1967), 216–22.

94 **Roxas was not dead:** Jimbo, eventually transferred to China, was arrested and set for execution in 1946. Roxas, now the new president of the Philippines, wrote to Chiang Kai-shek and urged clemency. Jimbo was spared.

Banzai!

95 **(The Philippine post office:** Late in 1943, Claire and others collected mail from detainees at Santo Tomas and from POWs for transport through the guerrilla network onward to Australia and then home.

95 **"My rendition did not:** ME, 158.

95 **"Had to drink to:** Diary, November 20, 1942.

96 **"employees think I'm crazy:** Diary, March 24, 1943.

96 **"If they were army:** ME, 118. While Claire admitted that portions of her memoir were exaggerated, Boone confirmed in his prologue to the book and later that she described her intelligence contacts with him accurately.

Organized Resistance

99   "Detachments of Fil-American: Whitney, *MacArthur: His Rendezvous with History*, 128.

99   "Short as it was: MacArthur, *Reminiscences*, 202–3.

99   "Intelligence report reveals that: Ibid., 128.

99   "Primary mission," he told: Ibid., 130.

100 The goal would be: MacArthur, *Reminiscences*, 205.

100 "This decisive victory restored: Ibid., 159.

100 General George Marshall, the: George Marshall to Douglas MacArthur, June 24, 1944, Papers of George Catlett Marshall, Volume 4: Aggressive and Determined Leadership, Document 4-279, http://marshallfoundation.org/library/digital-archive/to-general-douglas-macarthur-9/.

101 "I felt that if I: MacArthur, *Reminiscences*, 197.

101 Willoughby, MacArthur's intelligence chief: Whitney, *MacArthur: His Rendezvous with History*, 128.

101 Details about the Bataan: Lichauco, *Dear Mother Putnam*, 65–69. Marcial Lichauco, a friend of the Roxas family, traveled north of Manila within days of the death march in search of relatives who had been captured. He wrote in his entry for April 14, 1942, in part: "Many of those who collapsed on the roadway met death there, for the Japanese guards either bayoneted these unfortunate victims or shot them where they lay."

101 "Quezon was thrilled to learn: Francis Burton Harrison, "Diary of Francis Burton Harrison," August 28, 1942, Philippine Diary Project, philippinediaryproject.com/1942/08/28/august-28-1942/.

102 Parsons had one main: Ingham, *Rendezvous by Submarine*, 48.

102 The goal was: Ibid., 50.

103 "The trip, according to Chick's: Ibid., 54.

103 "I don't intend to run: Ibid., 52.

104 "When our beach patrol: Roberto de Jesus, interviewed in *Secret War in the Pacific*, produced by Peter Parsons and Moon River Productions, 2004.

104 "There are no generals: Jones and Nunan, *U.S. Subs Down Under*, 216.

104 With broad authority from: James, *The Years of MacArthur*, 506–9.

Steve the Greek

105 It was dangerous to talk: Lichauco, *Dear Mother Putnam*, 48–49.

106 "American prisoners who were: Stephen Handras, letter to Colonel Marcus, chief, Recovered Personnel Division, July 31, 1945, Record Group 58, Box VI, envelope 2–27, MacArthur Archives.

107 "There were several civilians: Ibid.

107 No one slapped Steve: Ibid.

107 "I saw a truck with: Ibid.

108 The guards warmed up: Transcript of the Testimony of Claire Phillips Clavier, Portland, Oregon, November 10, 1953, CC, 58.

108 That simple act established: Ibid., 57.

109 Yamada began to bring: Ibid., 61.

109 One new contact was: Irvine, *Surviving the Rising Sun*, 321.

110 "Unlike some of the other: Ibid., 331.

110 The list was also: Transcript of the Testimony of John Boone, Washington, DC, September 14, 1955, CC, 699. Boone said he sent Claire's intelligence dispatches

immediately to his commander, Lieutenant Edwin Ramsey, in central Luzon. He did not provide details on how the information was passed on or used locally after that.

110 **all the while working:** Diary, November 5, 1942.

Peggy's Orders

110 **"Orders were orders":** Transcript of the Testimony of Margaret Utinsky, San Francisco, California, January 10, 1956, CC, 945.

111 **Many top U.S. military:** Wainwright was head of the Philippine Division until November 28, 1941, when General MacArthur reassigned him as head of the Central Luzon Command.

111 **Peggy liked what she saw:** Transcript of the Testimony of Margaret Utinsky, San Francisco, California, January 10, 1956, CC, 946. Other sources said that Peggy had come to the Philippines in 1927.

111 **After vacationing for a few:** Ibid., 946–48.

112 **"Before you know it?":** Utinsky, *Miss U*, 5.

112 **"was the last one:** Transcript of the Testimony of Margaret Utinsky, San Francisco, California, January 10, 1956, CC, 947.

112 **"The boat backed out:** Ibid., 948.

113 **"And then I went:** Ibid., 949.

113 **"I came back here:** Utinsky, *Miss U*, 66.

114 **"After this trip through:** Ibid., 20.

114 **"American! American!":** Ibid., 50.

115 **"That stumped me:** Ibid., 49–50.

The Prisoners of Japan

116 **The Tokyo High Command:** Glusman, *Conduct Under Fire*, 272.

116 **About fifty thousand Filipinos:** Office of the Provost Marshal General, "Report on American Prisoners of War Interned by the Japanese in the Philippines," November 19, 1945, available at www.mansell.com/pow_resources/camplists/philippines /odonnell/provost_rpt.html.

116 **"It is regrettable that:** Quoted in Sides, *Ghost Soldiers*, 106.

116 **"little Hitler," among other:** Olson, *O'Donnell, Andersonville of the Pacific*, 45.

117 **Nursed back to health:** Lichauco, *Dear Mother Putnam*, 57.

117 **At first the Cabanatuan:** Sides, *Ghost Soldiers*, 133–34. This is in sync with the tally given by former POW Dwight Gard, quoted below.

118 **The Japanese authorities did:** Japan had not signed the 1929 Geneva convention on treatment of prisoners of war but had pledged at the start of World War II that it would respect it. Japan had signed the separate 1929 Geneva convention for the Amelioration of the Condition of the Wounded and Sick in Armies in the Field.

118 **Observing the conventions when:** At the start of the war, the peso was worth fifty cents. With inflation Japanese occupation pesos were worth only pennies by the end of the war.

The Underground

119 **"If you are working:** Transcript of the Testimony of Naomi Jackson, Washington, DC, September 14, 1955, CC, 788.

120 **"they didn't bother me:** Transcript of the Testimony of Lorenza O'Malley, Washington, DC, September 14, 1955, CC, 733.

Breaking Through to the POWs

121 **That morning, guards were:** Transcript of the Testimony of Naomi Jackson, Washington, DC, September 14, 1955, CC, 794.

122 **"After that, we got:** Ibid., 797.

122 **The other women at the stands:** Ibid., 798.

Condolences

122 **"I am deeply sorry:** Utinsky, *Miss U*, 64.

123 **"In one way, it was:** Ibid., 65.

123 **"Pray to God I can:** Diary, January 30, 1943.

124 **"There is no need:** ME, 100.

124 **"Phil Darling, Father Buttenbruck:** Diary, April 24, 1943. The earlier diary note about Phillips's death said July 7 rather than July 27, probably a mistake.

124 **Claire suffered Phillips's death:** ME, 104.

125 **"Wish I could join:** Diary, March 25, 1943.

125 **He asked her:** ME, 104.

Peggy's Collapse

126 **"Ramón did his utmost:** Lorenza Amusategui, document, undated, Philippine Archive Collection, POWS/Civilian Internees, Record Group 407/270/49/27/1, Box 143A-B, NARA.

127 **"She did start and do:** Claire Phillips to Evangeline Neibert, May 20, 1947, CC.

127 **"Unfortunately," Lorenza said:** Amusategui document.

128 **Ramón "without her knowledge:** Ibid, 17.

128 **"Their names were Tommy:** Transcript of the Testimony of Naomi Jackson, Washington, DC, September 14, 1955, CC, 786.

129 **"In the meantime":** Utinsky, *Miss U*, 54.

129 **"Go to them":** Ibid.

129 **"I didn't have anything:** Transcript of the Testimony of Naomi Jackson, Washington, DC, September 14, 1955, CC, 825–26.

129 **man in charge, Captain Tossino:** Ibid. Naomi remembered his name and saw him once later, but the spelling is likely wrong.

129 **Finally, in mock frustration:** Ibid., 826.

130 **"This is for Japan:** Utinsky, *Miss U*, 55.

Messages at Dawn

131 **Naomi pretended she had just:** Transcript of the Testimony of Naomi Jackson, Washington, DC, September 14, 1955, CC, 806–7.

131 **Threatt, forty-seven, was:** U.S. Select Military Registers, 1862–1985, Fred G. Threatt, available by searching at www.ancestry.com.

133 **"I don't know of any:** Claire Phillips to Evangeline Neibert, June 17, 1947, CC.

133 **"It was concealed by mongo:** Transcript of the Testimony of Naomi Jackson, Washington, DC, September 14, 1955, CC, 805.

134 **"This work brought us:** Amusategui document, 5.

Fan Dance

134 **One night a Japanese:** Transcript of the Testimony of Claire Phillips Clavier, Portland, Oregon, November 12, 1953, CC, 278.

135 **"The commander and his forty guests:** ME, 156.

137 "That was where I: Ronald D. Klein, "Markova: Wartime Comfort Gay in the Philippines," *Intersections: Gender, History and Culture in the Asian Context*, no. 13 (August 2006), available at http://intersections.anu.edu.au/issue13/klein_interview .html.

Relief for the Greater Need

138 "Those poor men are dying: ME, 124.
138 at Nichols Field: Nichols Field is now part of Manila's Ninoy Aquino International Airport.
138 Claire returned to the club: Binkowski, *Code Name: High Pockets*, 110–11.
138 "The soldiers would be: Transcript of the Testimony of Claire Phillips Clavier, Portland, Oregon, November 10, 1953, CC, 57.
139 Before Claire had come: Transcript of the Testimony of Claire Phillips Clavier, Portland, Oregon, November 12, 1953, CC, 267.
139 "It made me think: ME, 115; and Diary, March 29, 1943.

Love Letters and Lives

140 "The additional food is having: Shreve, *The Colonel's Way*, 103.
140 "The men were faint: Ibid., 131–32.
141 "Between you, me: Claire Phillips to Frederick Yeager, August 27, 1943, CC.
142 "It was all High: Transcript of the Testimony of Dwight E. Gard, Portland, Oregon, November 10, 1953, CC, 182.
142 "My code name is: Ibid.
142 When Claire learned that: CC, 175–76.
142 "The people who were receiving: Ibid., 176.
143 Gard said Tiffany: Ibid., 175.
143 Gard kept a diary: Diary and notebook of Major Dwight E. Gard, 1942–1945, Multnomah Bank records [manuscript], 1948–1969, Oregon Historical Society Research Library, Portland, Oregon.
143 Colonel Shreve, Gard's fellow: Shreve, *The Colonel's Way*, 132.
144 "Cheese Casserole, Layer: Ibid.
144 "I told her that: Transcript of the Testimony of Dwight E. Gard, Portland, Oregon, November 10, 1953, CC, 186.
145 Japan had a total: Tanaka, *Hidden Horrors*, 5.

Life and Death Foretold

145 "I'm a psychic": Ramsey and Rivele, *Lieutenant Ramsey's War*, 152–55.
145 "As I was preparing: Ibid., 152.
146 "He greeted me with: Ibid., 141.
146 "Mellie gathered considerable information: ME, 106. This information from Claire is endorsed by Boone, who wrote in the preface of *Manila Espionage* that "all the facts in it of which I have any personal knowledge are, to the best of my belief, true and properly expressed."
146 "I'm the senior officer: Ramsey and Rivele, *Lieutenant Ramsey's War*, 142–43.
146 There in the jungle: Ramsey's book says it was in November (Ramsey and Rivele, *Lieutenant Ramsey's War*, 154), but Boone says it was February 19 (CC, 691).
146 Williams, going on with: Ramsey and Rivele, *Lieutenant Ramsey's War*, 153.
146 "It wound up that I: Transcript of the Testimony of John Boone, Washington, DC, September 14, 1955, CC, 649.

147 **Boone and the other:** Schaefer, *Bataan Diary*, 142; Ramsey and Boone probably would not have heard MacArthur's edict on fighting until at least July 1943.

147 **"They were guys who:** Transcript of the Testimony of John Boone, Washington, DC, September 14, 1955, CC, 652.

148 **Things were quiet for a few:** Ramsey and Rivele, *Lieutenant Ramsey's War*, 151.

148 **Sometime after midnight they:** Ibid., 153.

148 **"There was a sudden:** Ibid., 154.

148 **Boone said he:** Transcript of the Testimony of John Boone, Washington, DC, September 14, 1955, CC, 687.

149 **After that initial trip:** Schaefer, *Bataan Diary*, 243.

149 **Claire was able to send:** Transcript of the Testimony of John Boone, Washington, DC, September 14, 1955, CC, 700–702.

149 **When Claire came out:** Based on Diary, November 15, 1943. Before the war, four pesos were the equivalent of two U.S. dollars, but under Japanese occupation the currency was devaluing steadily. The average price of cigarettes in the United States at the time was fifteen cents per pack. Michael D. LaFaive, Patrick Fleenor, and Todd Nesbit, "A Key Supplier of Cigarettes to Other States During the 1940's," Mackinac Center for Public Policy, December 3, 2008, www.mackinac.org/10050.

150 **"Pacio told me that:** ME, 106.

150 **Essentially, Boone said:** Transcript of the Testimony of John Boone, Washington, DC, September 14, 1955, CC, 698.

151 **"'By the way George:** Ramsey and Rivele, *Lieutenant Ramsey's War*, 155.

Tojo's Parade

151 **"Police everywhere," she wrote:** Diary, May 5, 1943.

151 **"Substantial progress is being made:** Agoncillo, *The Fateful Years*, 368.

152 **He presented a timetable:** Esmeraldo De Leon, "General Says He Is Convinced of Propriety of Independence," *Manila Tribune*, May 7, 1943, p. 2.

152 **"won the hearts":** Jose P. Bautista, "Nippon Premier Is Very Human Person," *Manila Tribune*, May 7, 1943, p. 8.

152 **"The pro-American sentiment:** Lichauco, *Dear Mother Putnam*, 92.

153 **People "cheered him spontaneously":** Photo caption, *Manila Tribune*, May 7, 1943, p. 1.

153 **The gathering, Tojo said: "**Premier Tozyo's Message," *Manila Tribune*, May 7, 1943, p. 2.

153 **On April 21, two:** Irvine, *Surviving the Rising Sun*, 56.

154 **She followed her father:** Joan Bennett Chapman, interview with the author, February 10, 2015.

154 **"I lived under bestial:** Agoncillo, *The Fateful Years*, 577.

155 **Japanese troops were:** "Tojo Finds Trouble in the Philippines," *New York Times*, May 9, 1943, p. 22.

155 **"I think there is:** Lichauco, *Dear Mother Putnam*, 90.

156 **After Nagahama's appeal:** ADVATIS [Advanced Allied Translation and Interpreter Section, sometimes also coded ATIS], Translation no. 37, January 14, 1945, Manila Branch (ATIS files), Record Group 331/290/12/34, Entry 1340, Box 1908, NARA.

Parsons on the Move

157 **Chick Parsons's wanderings during:** Parsons did not say explicitly when and if he had gone to Manila in 1943 or 1944, but multiple sources reported he had been there. While these sources indicated that they had seen Parsons in Manila in June 1943, Colonel Wendell Fertig, a guerrilla commander on the island of Mindanao, recorded

in his war diary that Parsons was present in Jimenez on the northwestern coast of Mindanao at various times that month: June 1–3, then going to southern Mindanao; on June 15, back to Jimenez. (Diary of Wendell Fertig, MacArthur Archives, Record Group 52, Box VIII, folder 2). Parsons's whereabouts were not certain during the rest of June, though he was known to have been in Mindanao in early July to catch a submarine ride back to Australia. While Jimenez is about 450 miles south of Manila, Peter Parsons said his father was resourceful and capable of moving quickly.

157 **Claire's bartender, Mamerto Geronimo:** Peter Parsons, e-mail to the author, December 10, 2015.

157 **John Rocha, a five-year-old:** Rocha, who served decades later as the Philippine ambassador to Spain, gave this account to Peter Parsons. Peter Parsons, e-mail to the author, May 13, 2016.

158 **"The visitor was attired:** Parsons e-mail, December 10, 2015.

158 **"We all know that Chick:** Parsons e-mail, May 13, 2016.

159 **After the war Peter Parsons:** Parsons e-mail, December 10, 2015. Peter Parsons also said he overheard his father talking about the assassination attempt on José Laurel, with the implication that he had been involved or informed ahead of time. This could not be confirmed.

159 **"He was likely in that:** Peter Parsons, e-mail to the author, December 10, 2015, 13.

159 **"We have no documents:** Ibid., 17.

159 **Now she had begun:** Her annotation in the diary on July 4, 1943, for example, reads in part: "S. weiasil se ason and Cheasik Per son se a sons, a re a sived. Must get Ea sall to theasem." Claire helped translate portions of her diary entries during testimony at the U.S. Court of Claims: "Sam Wilson and Chick Parsons arrived. Must get all to them."

160 **MacArthur had directed that:** Ingham, *MacArthur's Emissary*, 87.

160 **"Filipinos employed to serve:** Record Group 331/290/12/2, Entry 1276, Box 1390, NARA.

161 **"As to whether high-ranking:** Ibid.

161 **"White men are common:** Ibid.

161 Filipinos were **"completely fed up:** Ingham, *MacArthur's Emissary*, 89.

Who Is She?

161 **At his hideout:** Decker, *On a Mountainside*, 135.

162 **A man named Phillips:** Decker, *From Bataan to Safety*, 63–67.

163 **"If you read the paper:** Decker, *On a Mountainside*, 135.

Climbing the Wall

164 **"Have colonel where I:** Diary, February 17, 1943.

164 **"I was told when:** ME, 120.

164 **"Anyone could see that:** Ibid.

165 **Claire remembered him as:** Ibid., 121.

165 **"Fear for my sanity:** Diary, March 6, 1943.

166 **"I don't know how long:** Diary, January 23–30, 1944.

166 **"The Japanese curfew was:** ME, 106.

167 **"Only bare necessities now:** Diary, November 15, 1942.

Paranoia

167 **"I was terribly worried:** "War Time Spy Recalls Peril," *Portland Oregonian*, October 17, 1947, p. 12.

168 "The girls think I'm: Diary, July 19, 1943.
168 "We were not allowed: Transcript of the Testimony of Claire Phillips Clavier, Portland, Oregon, November 12, 1953, CC, 272.
169 The young man "whipped: Lichauco, *Dear Mother Putnam*, 108.
169 She dedicated her time: CC; Diary, July 27–29, 1943.

"We're in the Movies!"
170 "They gave us new: Nornes and Yukio, *The Japan/America Film Wars*, 238.
171 Two Filipino American actors: Although Bert Leroy is listed in the film credits and publicity, Nornes and Yukio (*The Japan/America Film Wars*, 237) say that he was replaced by a Filipino radio personality, Johnny Arville.
171 "They took us into: Ibid.
171 "You know the funny: Ibid.
171 Claire also brought food: ME, 160–61.
171 "We're in the movies: Lichauco, *Dear Mother Putnam*, 113.
172 "We had no idea: Nornes and Yukio, *The Japan/America Film Wars*, 238.
172 When it was all: Ibid.
173 "Even to Madame Tsubaki: ME, 150.

Giving Thanks
174 "Doctor Guerrero called: ME, 151–54.
174 "At the end of the fourth: Utinsky, *Miss U*, 114.
175 "When I started to cough: Ibid., 152.
175 "On the following day: Ibid., 153.
175 As Claire regained consciousness: ME, 153.
175 Ramón got in touch: Mamerto Roxas, affidavit, August 23, 1949, CC.
176 "She told me that she felt: Ibid.
176 "You go to Fely: Transcript of the Testimony of Claire Phillips Clavier, San Francisco, California, January 11, 1956, CC, 1230.
177 "I was able to go: ME, 154.
177 "saw and felt death": Diary, December 2, 1943.

Arrest and Ransom
177 As Peggy was checking: Utinsky, *Miss U*, 91. Peggy said it was Friday, September 28, two days after Claire entered the hospital. Her timing is off. That doesn't match Claire's diary, the only contemporary chronology, nor the account of Lorenza Amusategui, who agreed that Peggy had been with Claire at the beginning. This would have been later, in October.
177 "The Japanese soldiers took: Ibid., 92.
178 "My aunt had taken: Ibid., 97.
178 Terrorized, she begged Vásquez: Lorenza Amusategui document, undated, Philippine Archive Collection, POWS/Civilian Internees, Record Group 407/270/49/27/1, Box 143A-B, NARA, 22–24.
179 Peggy's arrest was a sign: Transcript of the Testimony of Lorenza O'Malley, Washington, DC, September 14, 1955, CC, 724–25.

"You'll Have to Kill Me First"
180 "I demand the arrest: Agoncillo, *The Fateful Years*, 413.
180 "You can go: Friend, *The Blue-eyed Enemy*, 200.
180 "If you insist": Agoncillo, *The Fateful Years*, 415.

180 **If General Roxas could:** Ibid., 407.

181 **Ramsey had fallen in love:** Ramsey and Rivele, *Lieutenant Ramsey's War*, 169–70.

Nagahama's War

182 **INTELLIGENCE REPORT KAKI:** Advantis Translation, no. 22, p. 1, Manila Branch (ATIS files), Record Group 331/290/12/34, Entry 1340, Box 1908, NARA. The English names in the translated text are transliterated, so Hugh Straughn appears in the translation as "HIYUSUTORONGU" and Home Guard is "HOMUGAIDO."

182 **seized a prominent American:** The Japanese-controlled *Manila Tribune* said he was captured on August 5. Separately, Claire said in *Manila Espionage* that she was in touch with Straughn, but there is no confirmation.

183 **Punitive operation around:** Advantis Translation no. 22, p. 1.

183 **Thorp survived more:** Ibid.

183 **"Even after the capture:** Ibid.

184 **"The remaining guerrillas:** Ibid.

184 **"The self-appointed American:** "Straughn Predicts Collapse of Guerrilla Warfare in P.I.," *Manila Tribune*, August 7, 1943, p. 1.

184 **The report said Straughn:** Ibid.

184 **Like Parsons and MacArthur:** Schaefer, *Bataan Diary*, 206.

185 **"Upon my word of honor:** Lichauco, *Dear Mother Putnam*, 126.

185 **"the bad elements:** Manila Branch (ATIS Files), Record Group 331/290/12/34, Entry 1340, Box 1908, NARA.

185 **It was not a question:** Ibid.

185 **They were summoned:** Schaefer, *Bataan Diary*, 208. This account is also based on testimony from eyewitnesses, including Lieutenant Richard C. Sakakida, an American double agent who was working inside the Japanese Army. After the war Sakakida was considered an American hero for his role, though some charged that his claims were false and that he had been working for Japan.

186 **Several days later Straughn:** Schaefer, *Bataan Diary*, 208. There are other accounts of the execution. Claire said in *Manila Espionage* that Nagahama told her at Tsubaki Club the day of the execution that he personally had killed Straughn. But it would have taken place on or around October 5, while Claire was in the hospital, seriously ill after ulcer surgery. Nagahama was tried and convicted of war crimes in Manila after the war. Testimony showed that he was in charge and clearly aware of torture and killings, but no evidence showed that he participated directly in the Straughn execution or any other.

186 **"in ever-increasing numbers":** "Straughn Predicts Collapse of Guerrilla Warfare."

186 **The only problem:** Charles Parsons, report, undated, Record Group 58, Papers of Commander Charles C. Parsons, Box 1, MacArthur Archives.

Holding On

187 **Fortunately, Lichauco had carried:** Lichauco, *Dear Mother Putnam*, 139.

187 **Winds toppled the open-walled:** Wilkinson, *Surviving a Japanese Internment Camp*, 59.

187 **The situation was at least:** Shreve, *The Colonel's Way*, 116.

188 **"Nip big-wigs would:** ME, 154.

189 **"We are loading ships:** Ibid.

189 **"Thanks a million:** John Boone to Claire Phillips, January 1, 1944, Record Group 122, Papers of Sergeant John Boone, Box 1, MacArthur Archives.

189 **Stop fighting, he said:** Inaugural address of Jose P. Laurel, Manila, October 14, 1943, available at https://en.wikisource.org/wiki/Jose_P._Laurel%27s_Inaugural _Address.

190 **He called Laurel:** Lichauco, *Dear Mother Putnam*, 134–35.

Parsons's Second Return

190 **"Give a gander, Chick:** Ingham, *MacArthur's Emissary*, 99.

190 **It had been stripped:** Unlike other fleet submarines, the 371-foot *Narwhal* and its sister sub, the *Nautilus*, were equipped with two-deck six-inch cannons.

190 **Latta had seen no sign:** Charles Parsons, action report, undated, Papers of Commander Charles C. Parsons, Record Group 58, Box 1, MacArthur Archives.

191 **"We surfaced to get:** Jones and Nunan, *U.S. Subs Down Under*, 216.

191 **"Is it necessary to keep:** Ingham, *MacArthur's Emissary*, 101.

191 **The *Narwhal* was one:** Peter Parsons, note to the author, April 2016. The fleet became known as the Spyron submarines, named for Parsons's subsection at MacArthur's general headquarters.

191 **By the time they had evaded:** Parsons, action report, undated, p. 1.

192 **Soon the ferries:** Ibid., 3.

192 **"I found the family:** Ibid.

193 **Boone had told:** John Boone to Claire Phillips, June 1, 1944, Boone papers, Record Group 122, Box 1, MacArthur Archives, p. 2. Boone did not know when he wrote and sent a copy of the letter that Claire had been arrested ten days earlier. He writes in this letter that other guerrilla commanders had been in touch with her, but he didn't know the contact procedures they were using. While guerrillas such as Ramsey and Decker said that Claire was providing intelligence information, no documents attributed to her were found at U.S. Army headquarters. It is probable that her reports were combined with other dispatches.

A Spy Breaks Through

193 **Reyes said that he:** Schaefer, *Bataan Diary*, 217–20.

194 **"I was routinely suspicious:** Ramsey and Rivele, *Lieutenant Ramsey's War*, 199.

195 **Ramsey then alerted Ramona:** Ibid., 199–200.

196 **Japanese authorities announced:** Lichauco, *Dear Mother Putnam*, 154.

196 **Blanche Jurika had been:** Schaefer, *Bataan Diary*, 219.

Manila Dragnet

196 **Once at the prison:** Transcript of the Testimony of Manuel Elizalde, *U.S. v. Akira Nagahama*, 686, Record Group 331/290/12/13, Entry 1321, Box 1579, NARA.

196 **"Practically everything, shipping, broker:** Ibid.

197 **"I was punched right:** Ibid., 689.

197 **He saw Juan several:** Ibid., 692.

197 **On Friday, May 12:** Ibid.

198 **"I found him very:** Lichauco, *Dear Mother Putnam*, 150.

"If Anything Happens . . ."

198 **"The cookies are about ready,":** ME, 162.

199 **"At a sign from me:** Ibid., 133.

199 **"If anything happens to me:** Ibid.

200 **"If any of you:** Transcript of the Testimony of Lorenza O'Malley, Washington, DC, September 14, 1955, CC, 730–31.

201 **She gave these to Fely:** Vicente Corcuera, affidavit, January 8, 1949, Transcript of the Testimony of Felicidad P. Corcuera Santos, Washington, DC, August 23, 1954, CC, 591–93.

Losing the War

202 **"With the loss of:** Lieutenant General Shuichi Miyazaki, chief of the Operations Section, Imperial General Headquarters, quoted in "Reports of General MacArthur," *The Campaigns of MacArthur in the Pacific, Prepared by His General Staff*, 1994, vol. 1, p. 166, cf. 1, available at www.history.army.mil/books/wwii/MacArthur%20Reports/MacArthur%20V1/ch07_notes.htm.

202 **A Japanese sergeant slammed:** Lichauco, *Dear Mother Putnam*, 196–97.

203 **"We are well on the road:** Ibid., 342–43.

203 **"Evidently they intend to scatter:** Ibid., 161.

204 **"Lunch was usually a ladle:** Wilkinson, *Surviving a Japanese Internment Camp*, 116.

204 **"The principal sufferers":** Lichauco, *Dear Mother Putnam*, 163.

204 **Hunger had turned Manila:** Ibid., 110 and 157.

"Evil Days Are Upon Us"

205 **"Evil Days Are:** Shreve, *The Colonel's Way*, 148.

205 **Mr. Threatt waited a good:** Transcript of the Testimony of Naomi Jackson, Washington, DC, September 14, 1955, CC, 821.

206 **If others had seen:** Ibid., 822.

206 **"As he approached the:** Shreve, *The Colonel's Way*, 146–47.

206 **Moments later, guards seized :** Ibid., 148.

206 **On May 11 the:** Shreve, *The Colonel's Way*, 149.

206 **The next day they:** Colonel Eugene C. Jacobs, *Blood Brothers: A Medic's Sketch Book* (New York: Carlton, 1985), chapter 5.

207 **She jumped out a window:** Transcript of the Testimony of Naomi Jackson, Washington, DC, September 14, 1955, CC, 823.

208 **When she didn't appear:** Binkowski, *Code Name: High Pockets*, 156.

208 **"Helen was a nice:** ME, 170.

209 **Nagahama had received a report:** Pacific Theater, ATIS reports, Record Group 470/270/51/9, Entry 427, Box 837, NARA.

Ramón's Turn

210 **She took it all:** The material was never recovered.

210 **"All we could do:** Lorenza Amusategui document, undated, Philippine Archive Collection, POWS/Civilian Internees, Record Group 407/270/49/27/1, Box 143A-B, NARA, 27.

210 **Fely helped her burn:** Transcript of the Testimony of Felicidad P. Corcuera Santos, Washington, DC, August 23, 1954, CC, 496.

Claire Goes to School

211 **They "ordered me to:** ME, 172.

211 **"I managed to smile:** Ibid., 173.

212 **Claire could have escaped:** Binkowski, *Code Name: High Pockets*, 163.

212 **"Well, leave Dian with:** Transcript of the Testimony of Margaret Utinsky, San Francisco, California, January 11, 1956, CC, 1075.

212 **She had reassured Claire:** Ibid., 1076–77.

213 **"I kept her right:** Ibid.

213 **Within days, Fely was:** Binkowski, *Code Name: High Pockets*, 163.
213 **Ramón Amusategui's brother, José:** Mamerto Roxas, affidavit, August 23, 1949, CC, 4.
213 **"gave the Allies three:** "Hollandia Seizure Cost U.S. 27 Lives," *New York Times*, May 9, 1944, p. 10.
213 **General MacArthur was "leap-frogging":** The Wakde Islands were in the Dutch East Indies, part of modern Indonesia.
214 **"Filipinos have been so:** "Tokyo Admits Difficulty in Winning the Filipinos," *New York Times*, May 8, 1944, p. 12.

A Letter from Boone

214 **"Wrapped in his cloak:** Thomas Mann, "Death in Venice," *Death in Venice and Seven Other Stories* (New York: Vintage Books, 1989), 18.
214 **Something in Mann's writing:** John Boone to High Pockets, June 1, 1944, Papers of John Boone, Record Group 122, Box 1, Folder 6, MacArthur Archives.
215 **"God knows how many:** Ibid.
215 **"A guerrilla group of:** Intelligence report, November 9, 1943, Advantis Translation, no. 25, Pacific Theater, ATIS reports, Record Group 470/270/51/9, Entry 427, Box 837, NARA.
216 **"I don't think these boys:** John Boone to High Pockets.
216 **"They told Ramsey that:** Ibid.
216 **"I was no longer:** Ramsey and Rivele, *Lieutenant Ramsey's War*, 223.
216 **"It was a radio:** Ibid., 235.
217 **Boone's forces on Luzon:** Transcript of the Testimony of John Boone, Washington, DC, September 14, 1955, CC, 650.
217 **"We must give credit:** John Boone to High Pockets.
217 **"We must prepare to put:** Ibid.
217 **The child had a persistent:** Ibid.

You Are High Pockets

221 **Claire was surprised when:** ME, 174. Claire's diary ends on May 22, 1944, two days before her arrest, with the words "waiting for my call to school." Her memoir, *Manila Espionage*, written with Myron B. Goldsmith, gives an account of her nine months in prison, parts of which could not be corroborated. There was independent confirmation of her imprisonment at the places and at the times she describes—the Japanese Administration Building, Fort Santiago, Bilibid Prison, and the Women's Correctional Institute at Mandaluyong. Fely and Mamerto and Judge Roxas confirmed that they were in touch with her in jail, and Judge Roxas said she was tortured. Claire also was in contact with other prisoners who survived—prisoners held for long periods of time were on starvation diets and were tortured routinely. The details of torture sessions and whatever else took place can be judged only in context. All prisoners were tortured; beatings and water-boarding were routine—she would not have been immune.
      The atmospherics of Claire's capture and interrogation are consistent with other reports, but any possible Japanese documents about her imprisonment were likely destroyed during the Battle of Manila.
221 **A man then spoke:** ME, 175.
221 **"We know you are not an:** The interrogation scene is described in ME, 176–79.
221 **Luckily, she had confirmed:** ME, 175–80.
224 **Claire asked Roxas to locate:** Mamerto Roxas, affidavit, August 23, 1949, CC, 4.
224 **"She told me that she:** Ibid.

224 **"the best baby I:** Utinsky, *Miss U*, 118.

224 **"Guerrilla nursing would have:** Ibid., 134.

224 **"No authority on childcare:** Ibid., 139.

225 **"Ours was the only:** ME, 182.

225 **"They beat me in an:** Claire Phillips, as told to Frederick C. Painton, "I Was an American Spy," *American Mercury*, May 1945, pp. 592–98; Wartime Case Files, Record Group 153/270/2/4, Entry A1 143, Box 120, NARA. Claire describes extreme torture, including water-boarding, during her time at Fort Santiago in this debrief by army investigators in 1945 and also in her memoir and in her 1945 interview with Frederick C. Painton in *American Mercury*. Two of her comrades, Marie Holland and Maria Martinez, said they saw no sign of such treatment of Claire, nor did Claire mention it while either or both of them were with her from July 31, 1944, to February 10, 1945. There is no way to confirm the degree and forms of torture she suffered.

226 **"Papaya is not a man:** ME, 188; Transcript of the Testimony of Maria Martinez, San Francisco, California, January 10, 1956, CC, 999.

227 **"Hold on and pray":** ME, 198.

227 **"There was room here:** Ibid.

227 **One morning at 2:00:** Ibid., 196–99.

A Chase Across the Pacific

228 **"Some of the islands:** Ingham, *MacArthur's Emissary*, 105.

229 **Despite the danger of discovery:** Ibid., 125–28.

229 **"About 120 radio sets:** Lockwood and Chadde, *Sink 'Em All*, 170–72.

229 **Parsons was successful enough:** Ingham, *MacArthur's Emissary*, 138.

230 **Yamashita "was resisting the pressure:** Ramsey and Rivele, *Lieutenant Ramsey's War*, 285.

Welcome Bombs

230 **Thirteen-year-old Juergen:** Goldhagen, *Manila Memories*, 74–75.

231 **"Planes! About five hundred:** ME, 199.

232 **Meanwhile, Claire told Maria:** Transcript of the Testimony of Maria Martinez, San Francisco, California, January 10, 1956, CC, 999.

232 **Claire had not seen or heard:** ME, 195.

232 **Then Ramón was brought:** Ibid., 200.

Parsons Sets the Table

233 **Parsons now had four:** Ingham, *MacArthur's Emissary*, 148.

233 **"How to remove loyal:** Ibid., 140.

233 **"Likewise how to coordinate:** Ibid.

233 **One final thing, Krueger:** Ibid., 143.

234 **Parsons and Rawolle made:** Ibid., 151–53.

234 **His fighters were to:** Ibid., 153.

234 **"High overhead, swarms of:** MacArthur, *Reminiscences*, 215.

234 **Ensign Bernard Eisner was:** Deck log, LST 463, Record Group 24/470/38/5/7, NARA.

Deadly Passage

235 **When the POWs at Cabanatuan:** Shreve, *The Colonel's Way*, 198.

235 **More flyovers followed:** Ibid.

236 **He used a floating:** Ibid., 228–29.

237 **An estimated 21,000 Allied:** Michno, *Death on the Hellships*, 280.

Power of the Spirit

237 **"This is a real battleground,":** Manila Branch (ATIS files), Record Group 331/290 /12/34, Entry 1340, Box 1908, NARA.

238 **They also used an airfield:** For more on kamikaze effectiveness, see Kindred Winekoff, "Kamikaze Attacks by the Numbers: A Statistical Analysis of Japan's Wartime Strategy," *The Fair Jilt*, November 5, 2014, http://thefairjilt.com/2014/11 /05/kamikaze-attacks-by-the-numbers-a-statistical-analysis-of-japans-wartime -strategy/.

238 **Civilians were being pressed:** Lichauco, *Dear Mother Putnam*, 200.

238 **"At such time as:** Document 2710, Tokyo International Military Tribunal War Crimes Trial, available at http://histclo.com/essay/war/ww2/pow/jap/powj-mo01.html.

239 **Officials at the Palawan:** V. Dennis Wrynn, "American Prisoners of War: Massacre at Palawan," *World War II*, November 1997, available at www.historynet.com /american-prisoners-of-war-massacre-at-palawan.htm.

240 **"One shot hit me:** "Primary Sources: A Survivor of the Palawan Massacre," *American Experience*, PBS.org, no date, www.pbs.org/wgbh/amex/bataan/filmmore/ps _palawan.html.

241 **"With every step that:** MacArthur, *Reminiscences*, 246.

In from the Hills

241 **His Filipino commanders even:** See Schaefer, *Bataan Diary*, 281–336, for details about this increased guerrilla activity.

242 **Boone used his knowledge:** Transcript of the Testimony of John Boone, Washington, DC, September 14, 1955, CC, 708–9. Official estimates said that more than 275 Americans were killed at Zig Zag Pass.

242 **U.S. commanders had been:** Ibid.

242 **"Overnight the division took:** Ibid.

242 **Peggy was horrified one:** Schaefer, *Bataan Diary*, 281–84.

242 **"I am very sorry:** John Boone to "Miss U" (Peggy Utinsky), December 24, 1944, Papers of John Boone, Record Group 122, Box 1, MacArthur Archives.

243 **"I AM SURE YOU:** Ibid.

243 **"unable to procure either:** Ibid.

A Race Against Time

244 **They decided to organize:** For a full description of the Cabanatuan raid, see Sides, *Ghost Soldiers*, and Michael J. King, *Rangers: Selected Combat Operations in World War II* (Honolulu: University Press of the Pacific, 2004).

245 **No longer among them:** Tiffany died on the hell ship *Arisan Maru* on October 24, 1944; Mack died in a Japanese labor camp in 1945.

246 **The surprise attack was:** Sides, *Ghost Soldiers*, 326; Lance Q. Zedric, *Silent Warriors of World War II* (Oxnard, CA: Pathfinder, 1995), 199.

Liberation

247 **Mydans caught airplanes westward:** Mydans, *More Than Meets the Eye*, 182.

248 **"In their ragged, filthy:** MacArthur, *Reminiscences*, 247.

249 **"Dorm rooms became:** Wilkinson, *Surviving a Japanese Internment Camp*, 160–64.

A Few More Hours

249 **In November 1944 Claire:** ME, 207.

250 **"I am sorry that:** Ibid., 209.

250 **The main problem was food:** Ibid., 210.

250 **Maria said she herself:** Transcript of the Testimony of Maria Martinez, San Francisco, California, January 10, 1956, CC, 1001.

251 **"We are subsisting on coconuts:** ME, 215.

251 **"She had convinced a number:** Transcript of the Testimony of Maria Martinez, San Francisco, California, January 10, 1956, CC, 1001–20.

251 **"There stood ten of the:** ME, 220.

251 **"Yes, I'm real":** Ibid.

251 **"We drove along the smoke-clouded:** Ibid., 222.

252 **American units encountered an:** Lichauco, *Dear Mother Putnam*, 209.

"Manila Is Finished, Completely Demolished"

252 **The Japanese Fourteenth Army commander:** Yamashita did leave behind four thousand troops north of the Pasig River but withdrew his main force farther north.

252 **Japanese units had also:** Lichauco, *Dear Mother Putnam*, 214.

253 **In the two weeks:** "Fighting Is Close in Manila," *New York Times*, February 23, 1945.

254 **"As far as they:** Lichauco, *Dear Mother Putnam*, 215.

254 **MacArthur called it all:** MacArthur, *Reminiscences*, 246–47.

254 **"Manila is finished, completely:** Charles Parsons, letter to Travis Ingham dated April 1, 1945, quoted in Ingham, *Rendezvous by Submarine*, 246.

255 **"I am afraid she:** Ingham, *MacArthur's Emissary*, 176.

The Wounds of War

255 **An Associated Press report:** Richard Bergholz, "12 Liberated from Manila Insane Asylum," *Wilkes-Barre Record*, February 12, 1945, p. 1.

256 **"Are you my Mummy?":** ME, 223.

256 **The reunion, Peggy said:** Utinsky, *Miss U*, 161.

256 **The papers included receipts:** Transcript of the Testimony of Felicidad P. Corcuera, Washington, DC, August 23, 1954, CC, 590–94.

Claire's Recovery

261 **The Japanese "first wanted:** Claire Phillips, as told to Frederick C. Painton, "I Was an American Spy," *American Mercury*, May 1945, p. 593.

261 **"I was stretched out:** Ibid., 596–97.

261 **"I didn't tell you:** Claire Phillips to Vada Phillips, March 10, 1945, CC.

Aboard the SS *John Lykes*

262 **Bennett remained in a hospital:** Mary C. Dunn, "Grim Stories Related by Former Prisoners in War," *Valley News* (Van Nuys, CA), February 14, 1965, p. 14.

263 **"The subject related a:** Claire Maybelle Phillips, Security Matter J, FBI File No. 105-377, June 6, 1945, Record Group 153/270/2/3, Entry A1 143, Box 1191, NARA.

264 **Emma Infante was arrested:** *Raquiza v. Bradford*, Supreme Court of the Philippines, September 13, 1945, available in the Philippines Law and Jurisprudence Database, www.lawphil.net/judjuris/juri1945/sep1945/gr_l-44_1945.html.

264 **Mabel C. Enette:** Claire Maybelle Phillips, Security Matter J. The FBI agents wrote the name as "Evette."

264 **The final report by the FBI:** Ibid.

265 **Hoover authorized an investigation:** Federal Bureau of Investigation Records: Freedom of Information/Privacy Act request, FBI report on Claire Phillips, Office Memorandum, FBI Director J. Edgar Hoover to Special Agent in Charge, Los Angeles, CA, November 16, 1945. The FBI initiated an investigation into possible crimes concerning "Foreign Travel Control, National Stolen Property Act, Mail Fraud, Perjury." FBI agents questioned people who knew Claire and monitored her mail. No charges were filed.

Public Affairs

265 **Red Cross relief personnel:** Transcript of the Testimony of Claire Phillips Clavier, San Francisco, CA, January 11, 1956, CC, 1325–26.

265 **"Just as I was:** Ibid., 1324.

266 **"I tried to make:** Ibid., 1325.

266 **After the Portland visit:** They bought the house on August 19, 1945, for $3,780. The bill of sale is an exhibit in the Court of Claims case. Uniform Agreement of Sale and Deposit, San Francisco, CA, August 12, 1945 (sale was completed one week later with actual payment), CC.

266 **"Huntley: Mrs. Phillips:** *I Was There,* script, June 17, 1945, KNX Radio Archives, Thousand Oaks Library, Thousand Oaks, CA.

267 **He "dressed up" the:** Transcript of the Testimony of Claire Phillips Clavier, San Francisco, California, January 11, 1956, CC, 1266.

268 **"I wish to state that:** ME, "Foreword," no page number.

268 **She was talking about:** They went as far as to sign a collaboration agreement, but a book never appeared. Oliver La Farge was a cousin of John LaFarge, the subject of my book *The Pope's Last Crusade.*

268 **"Oh boy, what a:** Lorenza Amusategui, letter to Oliver La Farge, October 12, 1947, Oliver La Farge Collection, Series II, Box 23, Folder 6, Harry Ransom Center, University of Texas at Austin.

268 **"From the neck down:** Transcript of the Testimony of Claire Phillips Clavier, San Francisco, California, January 11, 1956, CC, 1117.

268 **"When I asked her:** Ibid., 1326.

268 **"He wanted a picture:** Ibid. The original photo is in the Fred Hill Photography Collection at the Pierce Library of Eastern Oregon University and is available at http://eou.pastperfect-online.com/36819cgi/mweb.exe?request=keyword ;keyword=tsubaki;dtype=d. Hill and Risdon produced two other photographs of Claire, Dian, and Peggy while they still were in Manila.

269 **She said he wrote:** ME, 137.

269 **"'See dis hand':** Ibid.

Safe at Home

271 **Claire actually had more:** Court Findings, October 22, 1956, CC, 2–3.

271 **Problems like this increased:** In 2009, sixty-four years after the war, President Barack Obama signed a measure that would free up funds for Filipino veterans who were never paid, $15,000 each to Filipinos who were U.S. citizens, $9,000 each to noncitizens. But the issue was still unsettled, because a number of guerrilla fights were not registered as having fought. See Josh Levs, "U.S. to Pay 'Forgotten' Filipino World War II Veterans," CNN.com, February 23, 2009, www.cnn.com /2009/US/02/23/forgotten.veterans/index.html.

271 **Claire's chance of receiving:** "Truman Sanctions War Claims Bill," *New York Times,* July 4, 1948, p. 10.

272 **Her attorneys had now:** Frank Halpin, "Liberator Greets Claire Phillips, Famed U.S. Spy," *Washington Times-Herald*, May 1, 1951, p. 11.

272 **"I do not ask that:** U.S. Senate Judiciary Committee, *Hearings on S911 for the Relief of Claire Phillips Clavier*, 82nd Cong., 1st sess., October 2, 1951, vol. 1, p. 7.

272 **"I might not get:** Claire Phillips to Evangeline Neibert, June 17, 1947, CC.

272 **"We are asking only:** Senator Wayne Morse, U.S. Senate Judiciary Committee, *Hearings on S911 for the Relief of Claire Phillips Clavier*, 82nd Cong., 1st sess., October 2, 1951, vol. 1, CC, 2–3.

272 **"Dorothy Claire Fuentes":** Utinsky, *Miss U*, 75.

273 **"She had lost 15:** Lorenza Amusategui, document, undated, Philippine Archive Collection, POWS/Civilian Internees, Record Group 407/270/49/27/1, Box 143A-B, NARA, 23.

273 **However, recognition of Claire:** In the other cases an army awards panel reviewed nominations for the award, which were then forwarded to Washington for approval. In this case, however, MacArthur intervened. The text of Claire's notification of the award reads, in part: "By direction of the President, under the provisions of Army Regulations 600-45, the Medal of Freedom is awarded to you by the Commander-in-Chief, Far East, for meritorious service which has aided the United States in the prosecution of the war against Japan in the Southwest Pacific Areas, from June 1942 to June 1944." Citation for Medal of Freedom, Plaintiff's exhibit No. 2B, CC.

273 **On January 19, 1949, Claire:** "Child Home Safely After Kidnap Scare," *Spokane Daily Chronicle*, November 19, 1949.

274 **Claire, he said:** *This Is Your Life*, Radio Series, CD 29, Ralph Edwards Collection, UCLA Film & Television Archive.

I Was an American Spy

278 **(He had given her:** Frank S. Sever and Frederic W. Young, Statement of Support, Senate Resolution 2837, undated, CC. As mentioned earlier, Claire had received written notice of the award from the army in January 1948.

279 **The *New York Times* called:** "Spy Story Opens at the Holiday," *New York Times*, July 4, 1951, p. 13.

279 **The lawyers had now:** Petition, July 1, 1952, CC.

On Trial

280 **Hoover ordered "that this:** Federal Bureau of Investigation Records: Freedom of Information/Privacy Act request, FBI report on Claire Phillips, Letter from Hoover to Special Agent in Charge, San Francisco, California, May 26, 1953.

280 **"I do not in:** Mamerto Roxas, affidavit, August 23, 1949, CC, 4.

281 **"Did you have a:** Transcript of the Testimony of Claire Phillips Clavier, Portland, Oregon, November 10, 1953, CC, 113.

282 **"I wondered how they:** Transcript of the Testimony of Claire Phillips Clavier, Portland, Oregon, November 12, 1953, CC, 229–30.

283 **"I remember when I:** Transcript of the Testimony of John Boone, Washington, DC, September 14, 1955, CC, 708–13.

284 **Despite the unexpected news:** John Boone, affidavit, October 12, 1945, CC.

284 **"I felt that in view:** Transcript of the Testimony of John Boone, Washington, DC, September 14, 1955, CC, 680–83.

286 **They received word from:** Federal Bureau of Investigation Records: Freedom of Information/Privacy Act request, FBI report on Claire Phillips, Office Memorandum, written by Agent Matthew J. Lightbody, July 31, 1953.

286 **"I gave her the name,":** Transcript of the Testimony of Margaret Utinsky, San Francisco, California, January 11, 1956, CC, 1097.
286 **"The basic facts are:** Transcript of the Testimony of Claire Phillips Clavier, Portland, Oregon, November 12, 1953, CC, 1309–30.
287 **"Much of her story:** U.S. Court of Claims finding, CC, 14.

Her Own life
287 **Her mother listed her:** Claire Phillips, Standard Certificate of Death, State of Oregon, file no. 6609, June 10, 1960.
287 **"He drank quite a:** CC, *Fuentes v. Fuentes*, Defendant's Exhibit 4, divorce deposition of Claire Fuentes, April 25, 1947, Circuit Court of the State of Oregon for the County of Multnomah, Portland, Oregon.
288 **"He went back to Manila:** Claire Phillips to Evangeline Neibert, August 4, 1947, CC.
288 **"I, at last, found:** Claire Phillips to Evangeline Neibert and Naomi Flores, January 28, 1948, CC.
288 **"Private funeral services have:** Obituary: Claire Phillips, *Portland Oregonian*, May 24, 1960.
289 **The death certificate filed:** Claire Phillips, Standard Certificate of Death, June 10, 1960.

After the War
291 **"We couldn't find:** Jeanne Boone, interview with the author, December 18, 2015.
291 **"I am not a:** Ingham, *Rendezvous by Submarine*, 19.
292 **She died in 1984:** Fely said in an interview in 1947 that she was twenty-seven years old, but Social Security records indicate she may have been five years older.
292 **On August 11, 1955:** Private Law 478, 84th Congress, CC; www.gpo.gov/fdsys/pkg/STATUTE-69/pdf/STATUTE-69-PgA162.pdf.
292 **She had been raised:** CC, 784.
293 **It took a long:** Roy C. Bennett, "Jap Prisoner Describes Horrors of Santo Tomas," *Altoona Tribune*, February 16, 1945, p. 5.
293 **"He couldn't do it:** Joan Bennett Chapman, interview with the author, February 6, 2015.
294 **"The shadows are lengthening:** MacArthur, *Reminiscences*, 426.
295 **"Witnesses for the prosecution:** Akira Nagahama, letter to Lieutenant General Styer, War Crimes Trial of Colonel Akira Nagahama, 639–41; Record Group 331/290/12/13/3, Entry 1321, Box 1579, NARA.

Author's Note
297 **the "mysterious woman known:** Sides, *Ghost Soldiers*, 184.
299 **Among them was Emmanuel:** Ocampo died on December 26, 2015.
300 **"His goal was to help:** Rachel Joyce E. Burce, "Sentimental Homecoming for Daughter of MB's First Editor," *Manila Bulletin*, February 5, 2015, www.mb.com.ph/sentimental-homecoming-for-daughter-of-mbs-first-editor/.
300 **"Looking at it in:** Professor Ricardo Jose, interview with the author, February 2015; Associated Press, "US Survivors Mark 70 Years Since One of WWII's Most Hellish Battles: Vets Remember Horrors of the Battle of Manila in Which 100,000 Civilians Were Killed by the Japanese," *Daily Mail*, February 28, 2015, www.dailymail.co.uk/news/article-2973493/American-survivors-remember-horrors-month-long-Battle-Manila-70-years-paying-tribute-100-000-civilians-killed-Japanese.html.

SELECT BIBLIOGRAPHY

Agoncillo, Teodoro A. *The Fateful Years: Japan's Adventure in the Philippines, 1941–45.* Vol. 1. Manila: University of the Philippines Press, 1965.

Binkowski, Edna Bautista. *Code Name: High Pockets: True Story of Claire Phillips, an American Mata Hari, and the WWII Resistance Movement in the Philippines.* Limay, Philippines: Valour, 2006.

Boyt, Eugene P. *Bataan: A Survivor's Story.* Norman: University of Oklahoma Press, 2004.

Chenoweth, Doral. "54 War Correspondents K.I.A. WWII: A Gripping Account of War Journalism 1940–1945." www.54warcorrespondents-kia-30-ww2.com/home.html.

Connaughton, Richard, John Pimlott, and Duncan Anderson. *The Battle for Manila.* Novato, CA: Presidio, 1995.

Decker, Malcolm. *From Bataan to Safety.* Jefferson, NC: McFarland, 2008.

Decker, Malcolm. *On a Mountainside.* Las Cruces, NM: Yucca Free Press, 2004.

Ephraim, Frank. *Escape to Manila: From Nazi Tyranny to Japanese Terror.* Chicago: University of Illinois Press, 2008.

Frank, Richard B. *MacArthur: A Biography.* New York: Palgrave Macmillan, 2007.

Friend, Theodore. *The Blue-eyed Enemy: Japan Against the West in Java and Luzon, 1942–1945.* Princeton, NJ: Princeton University Press, 2014.

Glusman, John A. *Conduct Under Fire: Four American Doctors and Their Fight for Life as Prisoners of the Japanese, 1941–1945.* New York: Penguin Books, 2006.

Goldhagen, Juergen R., ed. *Manila Memories.* Exeter, UK: Old Guard Press, 2008.

Gordon, John. *Fighting for MacArthur: The Navy and Marine Corps' Desperate Defense of the Philippines.* Annapolis, MD: Naval Institute Press, 2011.

Goto, Ken'ichi. *Tensions of Empire: Japan and Southeast Asia in the Colonial and Postcolonial World.* Edited by Paul H. Kratoska. Singapore: NUS Press, 2003.

Guardia, Mike. *American Guerrilla.* Philadelphia: Casemate, 2010.

Hartendorp, A. V. H. *The Japanese Occupation of the Philippines.* Kansas City, MO: Bookmark, 1967.

Ingham, Travis. *MacArthur's Emissary: Chick Parsons and the Secret War in the Philippines in World War II.* Seattle: CreateSpace Independent, 2014.

Ingham, Travis. *Rendezvous by Submarine: The Story of Charles Parsons and the Guerrilla-Soldiers in the Philippines.* New York: Doubleday, Doran, 1945.

Irvine, Liz. *Surviving the Rising Sun.* Raleigh, NC: Lulu.com, 2010.

James, D. Clayton. *The Years of MacArthur.* Vol. 2, 1941–1945. Boston: Houghton Mifflin, 1975.

Jones, David, and Peter Nunan. *U.S. Subs Down Under.* Annapolis, MD: Naval Institute Press, 2005.

Kaminski, Theresa. *Angels of the Underground.* New York: Oxford University Press, 2015.

Kaminski, Theresa. *Prisoners in Paradise.* Lawrence: University Press of Kansas, 2000.

Lapham, Robert, and Bernard Noring. *Lapham's Raiders: Guerrillas in the Philippines, 1942–1945.* Louisville: University Press of Kentucky, 1996.

Lichauco, Marcial P. *Dear Mother Putnam: A Diary of the War in the Philippines.* Self-published, 1949. Republished as *Dear Mother Putnam: Life and Death in Manila During the Japanese Occupation 1941–1945.* Hong Kong: Cornelia Lichauco Fung, 2005.

Lockwood, Charles A., and Steve Chadde. *Sink 'Em All: Submarine Warfare in the Pacific.* Seattle: CreateSpace Independent, 2014.

MacArthur, Douglas. *Reminiscences.* New York: McGraw-Hill, 1964.

Manchester, William. *American Caesar.* Boston: Little Brown, 1978.

Marquez, Adelia. *Blood on the Rising Sun: The Japanese Occupation of the Philippines.* Seattle: CreateSpace Independent, 2014.

McCoy, Alfred W. *An Anarchy of Families: State and Family in the Philippines.* Madison: University of Wisconsin Press, 2009.

Michno, Gregory F. *Death on the Hellships: Prisoners at Sea in the Pacific War.* Annapolis, MD: Naval Institute Press, 2001.

Milligan, W. Denny. *Lest We Forget: The Brave & Honorable Guerrillas and Philippine Scouts of WWII.* Quezon City, Philippines: Central Book Supply, 2010.

Mojica, Proculo L. *Terry's Hunters: The True Story of the Hunters ROTC Guerrillas.* Manila: Benipayo, 1965.

Morton, Louis. *The Fall of the Philippines.* Washington, DC: Center of Military History, U.S. Army, 1943.

Mydans, Carl. *More Than Meets the Eye.* New York: Harper and Brothers, 1959.

Nornes, Abé Mark, and Fukushima Yukio, eds. *The Japan/America Film Wars: World War II Propaganda and Its Cultural Contexts.* Langhorne, PA: Harwood Academic Publishers, 1994.

Olson, John E. *O'Donnell: Andersonville of the Pacific.* Self-published, 1985.

Phillips, Claire, and Myron B. Goldsmith. *Manila Espionage.* Portland, OR: Binfords & Mort, 1947.

Picornell, Pedro M. (Pedro Marti). *The Remedios Hospital, 1942–1945: A Saga of Malate.* Manila: Office of the President, De La Salle University, 1995.

Ramsey, Edwin Price, and Stephen J. Rivele. *Lieutenant Ramsey's War.* Washington, DC: Potomac, 1996.

Romulo, Colonel Carlos P. *I Saw the Fall of the Philippines.* Garden City, NY: Doubleday and Doran, 1942.

Schaefer, Chris. *Bataan Diary: An American Family in World War II, 1941–1945.* Houston: Riverview, 2004.

Scott, James M. *Target Tokyo: Jimmy Doolittle and the Raid That Avenged Pearl Harbor.* New York: W. W. Norton, 2015.

Shively, John C. *Profiles in Survival: The Experiences of American POWs in the Philippines During World War II.* Indianapolis: Indiana Historical Society Press, 2011.

Shreve, Colonel Arthur Lee, Jr. *The Colonel's Way: The Secret Diaries of a P.O.W.* Seattle: CreateSpace Independent, 2014.

Sides, Hampton. *Ghost Soldiers: The Epic Account of World War II's Greatest Rescue Mission.* New York: Random House, 2001.

Steinberg, David Joel. *Philippine Collaboration in World War II.* Manila: Solidaridad, 1967.

Syjuco, Maria Felisa A. *The Kempei Tai in the Philippines: 1941–1945.* Quezon City, Philippines: New Day, 1988.

Tanaka, Yuki. *Hidden Horrors: Japanese War Crimes in World War II.* Boulder, CO: Westview, 1997.

Utinsky, Margaret. *Miss U.* San Antonio, TX: Naylor, 1948.

Villamor, Jesus A., as told to Gerald S. Snyder. *They Never Surrendered: A True Story of Resistance in World War II.* Quezon City, Philippines: Vera-Reyes, 1982.

Ward, Orlando. *The War in the Pacific: The Fall of the Philippines.* Washington, DC: Office of the Chief of Military History, Department of the Army, 1953.

Whitney, Major General Courtney. *MacArthur: His Rendezvous with History.* New York: Alfred A. Knopf, 1956.

Wilkinson, Rupert. *Surviving a Japanese Internment Camp.* Jefferson, NC: McFarland, 2014.

Young, Donald J. *The Battle of Bataan: A Complete History.* Jefferson, NC: McFarland, 2009.

Zobel, James W. *MacArthur: The Supreme Commander at War in the Pacific.* Mechanicsburg, PA: Stackpole, 2015.

INDEX

PHOTOGRAPH CREDITS